Law and Crisis in the Third World

African Discourse Series

General Editor: Abebe Zegeye

No. 1: *Forced Labour and Migration: Patterns of Movement within Africa* (eds A Zegeye & S Ishemo)

No. 2: *Repression and Resistance: Insider Accounts of Apartheid* (eds R Cohen, Y Muthien & A Zegeye)

No. 3: *Exploitation and Exclusion: Race and Class in Contemporary US Society* (eds A Zegeye, L Harris & J Maxted)

No. 4: *Law and Crisis in the Third World* (eds S Adelman & A Paliwala)

No. 5: *Peace, Politics and Violence in the New South Africa* (ed N Etherington)

Law and Crisis in the Third World

Edited by
Sammy Adelman and Abdul Paliwala
*School of Law
University of Warwick*

*Published for the Centre of Modern African Studies
University of Warwick*

HANS ZELL PUBLISHERS
London • Melbourne • Munich • New Jersey • 1993

All rights reserved. No part of this publication may be reproduced or transmitted in any form or by any means (including photocopying and recording) without the written permission of the copyright holder except in accordance with the provisions of the Copyright Act 1956 (as amended) or under the terms of a licence issued by the Copyright Licensing Agency, 90 Tottenham Court Road, London W1P 9HE. The written permission of the copyright holder must also be obtained before any part of this publication is stored in a retrieval system of any nature. Applications for the copyright holder's written permission to reproduce, transmit or store in a retrieval system any part of this publication should be addressed to the publisher.

Warning: The doing of any unauthorised act in relation to a copyright work may result in both a civil claim for damages and criminal prosecution.

© 1993 Hans Zell Publishers and individual contributors
Hans Zell Publishers
is an imprint of Bowker-Saur, a division of Reed Reference Publishing,
60 Grosvenor Street, London W1X 9DA, United Kingdom.

British Library Cataloguing in Publication Data

   Law and Crisis in the Third World. -
   (African Discourse Series;No. 4)
    I. Adelman, Sammy II. Paliwala, Abdul
   III. Series
   349.1724

   ISBN 0-905450-88-4

Library of Congress Cataloging in Publication Data

  Law and Crisis in the Third World/edited by Sammy Adelman & Abdul Paliwala.
    344p. 220cm. — (African discourse series : no. 4)
    Includes bibliographical references and index
    ISBN 0-905450-88-4 (acid-free paper)
    1. Law-Developing countries. 2. Law--Africa. 3. Sociological jurisprudence
   I. Adelman,Sammy. II. Paliwala, Abdul. III. Series
   K561.L38 1993
   340' . 0917214—dc20   93-16562
                                                                                      CIP

Cover design by Robin Caira

Printed on acid-free paper.

Printed and bound in Great Britain
by Antony Rowe Ltd,
Chippenham, Wiltshire.

Contents

Preface vii

Contributors viii

Abbreviations xi

1 **Sammy Adelman and Abdul Paliwala**
   Law and Development in Crisis   1

2 **Peter Fitzpatrick**
   Law's Infamy   27

3 **Yash Ghai**
   Constitutions and Governance in Africa:
   A Prolegomenon   51

4 **Alan Norrie**
   Criminal Justice, The Rule of Law and Human
   Emancipation: An Historical and Comparative
   Survey   76

5 **Jill Cottrell**
   Third Generation Rights and Social Action
   Litigation   102

6 **Issa Shivji**
   Rights-struggle, Class-struggle and The Law:
   Reflections on Experiences at the University of
   Dar es Salaam   127

7   **Sol Picciotto**
    International Business and Global Development   149

8   **Sammy Adelman with Caesar Espiritu**
    The Debt Crisis, Underdevelopment and the
    Limits of the Law   172

9   **Sammy Adelman**
    The International Labour Code and The Exploitation
    of Female Workers in Export-Processing Zones   195

10 **Ann Stewart**
    The Dilemmas of Law in Women's Development   219

11 **Anne Hellum**
    Gender and Legal Change in Zimbabwe: Childless
    Women and Divorce from a Socio-Cultural and
    Historical Perspective   243

12 **Abdul Paliwala**
    Family Transformation and Family Law: Some
    African Developments in Financial Support on
    Relationship Breakdown   270

References   301

Index   329

Preface

The idea for this book arose from a perceived need to reconsider the major issues in law and development in the context of the remarkable changes that have taken place in the international order in recent years. The thread linking the contributions is the critique of liberal law and development theory and its impact on and relevance to the lives of people in the developing world. The authors, all of whom have strong ties to the Law in Development programme at the University of Warwick, reflect the continuing vitality of critical law and development scholarship in the 'new world order' that has supposedly succeeded that of the Cold War.

A second but no less important goal is to stimulate debate about law and development and co-operation between progressive scholars in the North and the South. To this end, we hope that a volume addressed to students and scholars in the Third World will be of value.

We would like to express our gratitude to the contributors for their support, co-operation and patience: without them this book would obviously not have appeared. Special thanks are due to Margaret Wright, whose wordprocessing skills, eternal good humour and continuous support has been much appreciated. We would also like to express our gratitude to Moyra Butterworth, whose desktop publishing skills are evident on every page. Abebe Zegeye's support and friendship has been instrumental in bringing this project to fruition and we extend our thanks to him. To our publisher, Hans Zell, we extend thanks for his long-suffering patience and his constant support. Mention must also be made of the successive generations of students in the Law in Development programme for their enthusiasm, hard work and intellectual stimulation. Last but not least we would like to express our appreciation to the British Council, which has supported the close and highly productive links between the School of Law at the University of Warwick and the faculties of Law at the universities of Dar es Salaam and Hong Kong: these links greatly facilitated the production of this volume.

Sammy Adelman Coventry
Abdul Paliwala May 1993

Contributors

Sammy Adelman Specialises in Law in Development, Legal Theory, Human Rights and Comparative Labour Law at the University of Warwick. He is a graduate of the University of the Witwatersrand, Harvard Law School and the University of Warwick. Dr Adelman is on the Editorial Committee of the Review of African Political Economy and has acted as a consultant to the Commonwealth Secretariat and the African National Congress. Exiled from South Africa in 1981 he has since returned to teach in Johannesburg. His book on Law as Power: A Jurisprudence of Class, Race and Gender will be published by Pluto Press in 1993.

Jill Cottrell LL M London and Yale. Senior Lecturer, University of Hong Kong. Formerly Lecturer Ahmadu Bello and Ife Universities, Nigeria and Senior Lecturer and Chairperson in the School of Law at the University of Warwick. Her research interests include Indian law, Chinese law, the law of tort, legal services and constitutional law in developing countries.

Caesar Espiritu B A Silliman University, LL B University of the Phillipines, MPA, LL M, Ph D Harvard Law School. Formerly senior visiting fellow, University of Warwick. He has been Professor of Law and Director of Graduate Studies at the University of Phillipines College of Law and has visited the Universities of Aix en Provence, Heidelberg (Max Planck Institute) and Ottawa (Human Rights Centre). He has acted as Phillipines ambassador to West Germany. His main research interests are public enterprises and human rights law.

Peter Fitzpatrick Professor of Law and Social Theory at the University of Kent. He has taught at universities in Europe, North America and Papua New Guinea. He has published numerous works on law and social theory, law and racism, and imperialism amongst the most recent of which are Dangerous Supplements (Pluto Press, 1991) (which he edited) and The Mythology of Modern Law (Routledge, 1992).

Yash Ghai M A Oxon, SJD, Harvard. Sir Y K Pao Professor of Law, University of Hong Kong. Professor Ghai has taught and researched in the University of Dar es Salaam, the Institute for African Studies (Uppsala), Yale University, and the University of Singapore and the University of Warwick. His main interests are constitutional law, the law relating to public enterprises, sociology of law, and law and economy. He has acted as a constitutional adviser to a number of developing countries including Papua New Guinea, the Solomon Islands, Vanuatu and Samoa and has acted as consultant to the East African Community and a number of organisations on economic law. His works include (with Professor McAuslan) Public Law and Political Change in Kenya, (with Luckham and Snyder) The Political Economy of Law: A Third World Reader and Law in the Political Economy of Public Enterprise and Law, Politics and Government in the Pacific Island States. Professor Ghai was responsible for the production of the Commonwealth Human Rights Initiative's report entitled Put Our World to Rights submitted to the meeting of the Commonwealth Heads of Government in Harare, Zimbabwe.

Ann Hellum A lawyer and anthropologist working at the Institute of Women's Law in the Faculty of Law at the University of Oslo, she has been leader of the NORAD Diploma Course in Women's Law for lawyers from southern and eastern Africa. She has published extensively in the fields of women's law, family law, birth law and development law. Along with A Syse and H S Aasen she is Editor of Human Nature and Reproduction Technology (Ad Notam, 1990) and is Editor of the anthology Birth Law (Scandinavian University Press, 1993).

Alan Norrie LL B Edinburgh, M A (Criminology) Sheffield, Ph D Dundee. Senior Lecturer in Law, University of Warwick. Dr. Norrie has researched and written on theories of punishment, legal theory, law and state. His publications include Law, Ideology and Punishment (Kluwer, 1991), Crime, Reason and History (Weidenfeld and Nicolson, 1993) and, as Editor, Closure or Critique: New Directions in Legal Theory (Edinburgh University Press, 1993). He is working on a contextual book on crime, law and development.

Abdul Paliwala LL B, Ph D University of London. Of Gray's Inn, Barrister. Senior Lecturer in Law, University of Warwick; Director of Law in Development Studies, Warwick; Director of the CTI-Law Technology Centre for UK Law Schools and of the Law Courseware Consortium. Formerly Associate Professor and Dean of Faculty of Law, University of Papua New Guinea, Secretary, Law Reform Commission of Papua New Guinea, Lecturer in Law, University of Dar es Salaam and Queen's University of Belfast. Dr Paliwala has published articles on law, development and underdevelopment. His books include (with D Chalmers) An Introduction to law in Papua New Guinea (Law Book Co, Sydney, 1983) and (with D Weisbrot and A Sawyerr) Law and Social Change in Papua New Guinea (Butterworths, Sydney, 1982).

Sol Picciotto B A Oxford, J D Chicago. Professor of Law at the University of Lancaster. He has taught at the University of Dar es Salaam and Warwick University, where he was also Chairperson of the School of Law. Joint Editor of Social and Legal Studies: an International Journal. Formerly lecturer in law at the University of Dar es Salaam. Professor Picciotto has written on Marxist theories of law and state and aspects of international economic law. His latest book is entitled International Business Taxation (Quorum, 1992).

Issa Shivji LL B, Ph D. University of Dar es Salaam. Professor of Law at the University of Dar es Salaam, Visiting Professor at the University of Warwick. Professor Shivji is one of the foremost African legal scholars. He has published widely in the areas of classes state and law, labour law and human rights law. His works include: Class Struggles in Tanzania, Law, State and the Working Class in Tanzania, The Concept of Human Rights in Africa. He has edited books on State and Constitutionalism: An African Debate on Democracy and The Limits of Legal Radicalism.

Ann Stewart LL B, M Jur. Lecturer in Law at the University of Warwick. She teaches courses on feminism and law and has developed a course on Women, Law and Development. She is a founder member of the Graduate School of Women's Studies. She extensive links with universities in Peru, Zimbabwe and India.

Abbreviations

ACP	Africa-Caribbean-Pacific
BCCI	Bank of Credit and Commerce International
BIAC	Business and Industry Advisory Committee of CIIME
BIT	Bilateral Investment Treaty
CCM	Chama Cha Mpinduzi (Tanzania)
CERDS	Charter of Economic Rights and Duties of States
CIDL	Changing International Division of Labour
CIIME	Committee on International Investment and Multinational Enterprise
Daruso	Dar es Salaam Students' Organisation
DUSO	Dar es Salaam University Students' Organisation
EC	European Community
EIWU	Electrical Industry Workers' Union (Malaysia)
EOI	Export-Oriented Industrialisation
EPZ	Export Processing Zone
FIDA	Federal Industrial Development Agency (Malaysia)
GAME	General Agreement on Multinational Enterprise
GATT	General Agreement on Tariffs and Trade
GDP	Gross Domestic Product
ILO	International Labour Organisation
IMF	International Monetary Fund
IPR	Intellectual Property Rights
ISI	Import Substitution Industrialisation
LDC	Less Developed Country
LIBOR	London Interbank Offered Rate
MUWATA	Muungano wa WanafUnzi, Tanzania
NGO	Nongovernmental Organisation
NIC	Newly Industrialising Country
NIDL	New International Division of Labour
NIEO	New International Economic Order
NORAD	Norwegian Agency for Development
OAS	Organisation of American States
OECD	Organisation for Economic Co-operation and Development
OPEC	Organisation of Petroleum Exporting Countries

PIL	Public Interest Litigation
SAP	Structural Adjustment Programme
TNC	Transnational Corporation
TUAC	Trade Union Advisory Committee of CIIME
UDASA	University of Dar es Salaam Academic Staff Assembly
UK	United Kingdom
UN	United Nations
UNCTAD	United Nations Centre for Trade and Development
UNCTC	United Nations Centre on Transnational Corporations
UNGA	United Nations General Assembly
UNICEF	United Nations Childrens' Fund
US	United States
USSR	Union of Soviet Socialist Republics
WHO	World Health Organisation
WILDAF	Women in Law and Development Africa Programme
WLSA	Women and Law in Southern Africa

1

Law and Development in Crisis

Sammy Adelman and Abdul Paliwala

> The Eastern Bloc has collapsed, the cold war has ended, the Soviet Union has disintegrated, there is unity amongst the four Northern permanent members of the UN Security Council, and Iraq has been crushed. I am tempted to add: the Free Market has become religion, and the money speculators have become the leaders of the world. So, we have a 'New World Order'.
> - Julius Nyerere, *The Guardian*, 16 November 1992

According to George Bush, the end of the Cold War ushered in a 'New World Order' which, to Francis Fukuyama (1992), meant the end of history and the inevitabilty of liberal democracy as the only remaining viable option for less developed countries (LDCs). This New World Order appears little different from the 'old': as the superpowers have abandoned their proxies in the South, ethnic and nationalist aspirations suppressed under communism have broken the surface to produce new levels of disorder. Politically unipolar, the New World Order is characterised by US military hegemony and domination of the UN Security Council. Economically tripolar, it reflects the power of Germany/Europe, Japan and the United States. Despite much rhetoric about democracy, the global political economy remains resolutely imperialist. The 1992 Earth Summit in Rio de Janeiro, the Uruguay Round of the General Agreement on Tariffs and Trade (GATT) and Western dominated institutions such as the International Monetary Fund (IMF) and the World Bank epitomise the enduring structural imbalances in the global economy and the undemocratic nature of the international politico-legal order. The ravages of the debt crisis persist even as structural adjustment, its ostensible solution, achieves the status of economic orthodoxy (Adelman & Espiritu, *infra*). As the French are wont to express it, *plus ça change, plus c'est la même chose*. The sound and fury of the Gulf War, the implosion of the Soviet Union and the collapse of Yugoslavia signified little change for the South, where the growth of poverty remained constant. In 1980 approximately 780 million people were living in poverty, 'a condition so characterized by malnutrition, illiteracy and disease as to be beneath any reasonable definition of human decency' (World Bank 1980: 32). At the dawn of the final decade of the twentieth century, humanity's progress was marked by the many more millions who had been condemned to a similar fate. With this as the backdrop to the possibilities of development in the 1990s it is not surprising that development studies are in crisis.

The Crisis in Development Theory

During the 1980s development studies was challenged by a fundamentalist, mono-disciplinary trend in the academic world, and a neo-conservative trend in politics. Both trends reduce the 'development problem' in a highly simplistic way, thus neglecting the insights achieved in the field during three decades of empirical and theoretical exploration into previously unknown territories. (Hettne 1990: 9).

For many LDCs the high hopes which accompanied independence have been submerged under a mélange of debt, corruption, poverty and economic underdevelopment. By the end of the 1980s the discrepancies between development policies and concrete results was so great (Apter 1987: 14) that development studies was beset by a combination of cynicism and despair. In the field of law and development, despair appeared to have supplanted analysis to such a great extent that it seemed as if there was nothing left to theorise.

Explanations of underdevelopment (and, therefore, the policies advocated to overcome it) have fallen broadly into two schools of thought.[1] In one view 'Development was seen in an evolutionary perspective, and the state of underdevelopment defined in terms of observable economic, political, social and cultural differences between rich and poor nations. Development implied the bridging of these gaps by means of an imitative process, in which the less-developed countries gradually assumed the qualities of the industrialized nations' (Hettne 1990: 60). The contrasting view was that the development of 'peripheral' countries is virtually impossible in a global political economy dominated by capitalist relations; indeed, the nature of the world economy facilitates the exploitation of the periphery by the core and leads to the development of underdevelopment, a phrase coined by Andre Gunder Frank.

The Modernisation Paradigm

In Rostow's (1960:4) view, development proceeded on a linear basis from backwardness to the mass consumption of capitalism: 'It is possible to identify all societies, in their economic dimensions, as lying within one of five categories: the traditional society, the preconditions for take-off, the take-off, the drive to maturity, the age of high mass-consumption'. This hypothetical periodisation achieved widespread influence on development scholars, and formed the basis for the emergence of the theory of development as modernisation.

> Modernisation theory...had as its central essence a belief in the inevitable development of the Third World...The well-known metaphor was of course that of developing countries sitting as aeroplanes at the end of a runway, about to take off into a process of self-sustained growth and fuelled by the diffusion of knowledge, capital, and culture from the developed world. The failure of most states to taxi to the runway, let alone get airborne, saw the onset of a bout of pessimism in which the central tenets of the modernisation theory came under challenge (Higgott 1984: 59).

The construction of Western institutions was widely regarded as an essential element of economic development, which would naturally ensue once the appropriate infrastructure had been installed. Multi-party politics, the rule of law, a separation of powers, an efficient bureaucracy and the institutions of the free market were argued to be essential paving stones on the path to development. Development was regarded as a predominantly endogenous and independent process, and was defined almost exclusively in economic terms which demanded political, legal and cultural change involving the abandonment of tradition in order to achieve economic growth. Law and politics, far from being understood as contradictory sites of struggle, were viewed as instruments to be wielded in the resolution of developmental problems. Progress became the god, and was symbolised by Western ideology and institutions. Peter Fitzpatrick's Foucaultian analysis of the culture of law and modernity, aptly entitled *Law's Infamy* (*infra*), demonstrates how Western modernity created savagery as its alterego, the 'other' whose existence legitimised capitalism, Christianity's 'civilising mission' and colonialism. Fitzpatrick demonstrates the process by which Europe defined itself as the centre and the South as the periphery symbolically, ideologically and culturally as well as politically, economically and legally. The imperialism inherent in this process emphasises the important defining and constraining role of the liberal worldview, and of liberal legality and jurisprudence in particular, to development in the South. As several of the contributions to this volume illustrate, the search by LDCs for a mythical modernisation as an escape from backwardness has resulted in an ideology of 'developmentalism' which privileges economic growth and undermines the search for solutions rooted in material social relations.

The wisdom and relevance of establishing liberal institutions which did not fit easily into prevailing social relations was largely ignored by the proponents of modernisation. Lord Curzon believed that the rule of law - achieved in the West by bourgeois classes largely absent in the South - was Britain's greatest gift to its colonies, and modernisation theorists disingenuously assumed that the imposition of modernisation on societies whose legal, cultural and political histories were very different to those of the West was unproblematic. Not surprisingly, there was a discrepancy between theory and reality. Despite its inherent flaws, however, the modernisation paradigm has continued to exercise a significant influence on development praxis, not least as a reflection of Western ability to impose conditions on LDCs. It has proved malleable enough to serve the interests of Keynesians and neo-conservatives and its tenacity is reflected in its reincarnation as structural adjustment. Despite repeated calls for a New (or at least a restructured) International Economic Order there has been no equivalent of a Marshall Plan for LDCs, despite persistent efforts by these countries in the United Nations and elsewhere and calls by the likes of the Brandt Commission for the channelling of resources from North to South.

Dependency Theory

The liberal faith in modernisation was paralleled by the quintessentially modern belief in progress held by Marxists, who argued that the achievement of egalitarian classless societies proceeded via the technological plenitude of capitalism. They viewed development as an inevitable process consisting of successive stages arising from the dialectical resolution of class conflict.

The challenge to the modernisation paradigm came primarily from the proponents of dependency theory, themselves substantially influenced by Marxism. Relations between centre and periphery, the *dependentistas* argued, are dictated by the international division of labour, with the consequence that development and underdevelopment may be conceived as two aspects of the same process.[2] On this basis, they called into question the supposed inevitability of progress from backwardness to modernity and argued that underdevelopment is a consequence of capitalist penetration into the Third World. The logic of this analysis gave rise to economic nationalism in Latin America (where the theory developed), India and South Africa amongst other countries. Import-substitution industrialisation (ISI) involving protectionist measures designed to stimulate industrial growth led to significant levels of economic development, but the failure of countries adopting this strategy to achieve competitive equality constituted both a vindication and an inherent critique of dependency theory. ISI was accompanied by largely futile attempts at regional and South-South collaboration, and calls for a New International Economic Order (NIEO) to address the structural imbalances in the global economy.

Dependency theory criticised the modernisation paradigm for failing to make clear the meaning of development, for being economistic - especially in underemphasising class conflict, for failing to identify the causes of underdevelopment beyond their origin in the metropolitan centre, for the circularity of its reasoning and its limited explanatory value (Hettne 1990:93). In its most extreme form, dependency theory precluded the industrialisation of peripheral economies within the global capitalist economy. Reality, however, provided a critique in the form of the newly developing countries (NICs), most of them in south-east Asia, whose rapid industrial development confounded the theory. The Four Little Dragons, Hong Kong, Singapore, Taiwan and South Korea, are regarded as exemplars of the triumph of market forces. Yet, as Harris (1986) suggests, these four very different cases involve a high degree of control over the national labour market and extensive state intervention to take advantage of international political and economic conditions to promote export-led growth. Far from representing the free sway of international market forces, they represent a new form of mercantilism and call into question the liberal assertion that authoritarianism is incompatible with capital accumulation. The rise of the Dragons popularised export-oriented industrialisation (EOI), and export-processing zones were established in many LDCs (Adelman, *infra*).

Not all dependency theorists were Marxists, but it was the latter who exercised the most profound influence on the debate. Theories based on Marxism avoided the crude instrumentalism of most liberal thought in developing a more sophisticated critique of the contradictions of development, but nevertheless failed to resolve the dilemma posed by the failure of capitalist relations to take hold throughout much of the South. When class formation in the South failed to conform to expectations, and nationalism and ethnicity failed to succumb to theoretical resolution, Marxists too were forced to reconsider their approaches to development.

By the 1980s, the dominant approach to development was based on export-led industrialisation and, in much of the South, took the form of structural adjustment, an approach which combines the mimetic elements of modernisation with an appreciation of the importance of exogenous factors derived from dependency theory. Structural adjustment constitutes a neo-conservative attack on state-centred development, but is contradicted by the success of the NICs, in which a large and often authoritarian form of state intervention has been central to rapid industrialisation. NICs constitute a minority of developing countries, and the corruption, inefficiency and mismanagement which have characterised too many LDC regimes provided soft targets for the neo-conservative onslaught in the 1980s. State-centred development was identified as the central problem, the solution to which must be the freeing of market forces from state intervention. The crisis in development theory was compounded by the widespread neo-liberal assertion that there is nothing specific about development economics. Left to the sway of market forces, business people worldwide would utilise comparative advantage to promote export led growth in less developed countries. This approach has become virtually unchallenged in the World Bank, the IMF and the GATT. Structural Adjustment Programmes (SAPs) impose harsh regimes involving opening up the economy to international market forces, the withdrawal of the State from the economy, and 'good governance' involving a stable legal system within which market forces can operate. Ostensibly designed to promote development, their effects on the poorest inhabitants of the planet have been profoundly negative: social welfare budgets have been slashed, unemployment has soared as privatisation has proceeded apace, and peasants have been forced off their land by foreign capitalist agribusiness. The crisis in development has thus been exacerbated rather than attenuated by this dogma.

The gap between theory and reality in development studies should not occasion great surprise, and more should not be expected of development theory than any other social science. However, the crisis in the field is proportional to the hopes generated - largely by American interventions - in the 1950s and 1960s. Dependency and its offshoots were largely a response to the limitations of modernisation theory, and between them these two paradigms remain the major theoretical frameworks informing development studies. However, neither has been able to adequately identify the causes of underdevelopment, and the nature and role of the state in particular remains unresolved.

The Meaning of Development

Historically, development has been defined almost exclusively in terms of economic growth with the consequence that the rights and freedoms of people have been regularly subordinated to the imperatives of industrialisation. 'Developmentalism' rather than democracy has consistently motivated LDC regimes. Derived from the Western conception of development as progress, such economistic and state-centred conceptions have tended to serve the interests of the dominant North. The limited relevance of these conceptions to people's lives has resulted in a critique which challenges the very notion of development, and the ravages of the debt crisis, structural adjustment, widespread poverty and the ecocrisis have prompted alternative 'people-centred' definitions.[3] It is argued that development should satisfy the direct needs of the people rather than some abstract notion of national wealth. This critique was institutionalised in the early 1970s in the Basic Needs Approach (BNA) adopted by the ILO, the UNDP and, more suspiciously, the World Bank.[4] It was widely agreed that:

> economic growth did not necessarily eliminate poverty. Rather the economic growth that actually took place in most developing countries went togehter with increases in absolute poverty. In response to this the BNA favoured a direct approach, i.e. a straight relationship between development strategy and elimation of poverty rather than waiting for the 'trickling down' effects of growth (Hettne 1990: 167 citing Emmerij 1988).

The early 1970s also witnessed calls, arising from unprecedented concerted co-operation amongst LDCs, for a New International Economic Order. The aim was to cure the structural imbalances in the global economy articulated in dependency theory, and to elucidate the obligations owed by developed countries to the peoples of the South. Demands for a NIEO paradoxically amounted to a radical reformism, with LDCs basically accepting the framework of global capitalism but demanding more balanced treatment. Proponents of a NIEO wrote of a zero-sum process in which the total global potential for development had to be spread more equally. This involved a notion of interdependence that was reflected at the end of the decade in the 1980 Brandt Commission report (and again in 1983), which emphasised the mutuality of interests in a 'one-world system' (Hettne 1990: 115).

More recently, it has been argued that in order to be viable development must be 'sustainable' rather than merely 'growth based', a conception which addresses the ecocrisis facing the planet. Repetto (1986: 15) defines sustainable development as:

> a development strategy that manages all assets, natural resources, and human resources, as well as financial and physical assets, for increasing long term wealth and well being. Sustainable development, as a goal rejects policies and practices that support current living standards by depleting the productive base, including natural resources, and that leaves future generations with poorer prospects and greater risks than our own.

Inevitably, this conception has entered the battlefield of meaning, with the likes of the World Bank seeking to appropriate it to refer to the permanence of development (Redclift 1987, Pearce 1990).

The Peace movement, feminism, the environment movement and the human rights struggles (such as that of indigenous populations in Latin America) bear witness that the definition of development is itself a site of struggle rather than mere academic theorising. In the current world order, for example, the ecological struggle has become a key aspect of this globalisation of resistance in establishing solidarity between the indigenous peoples of the Amazon trying to protect their living environment, and national and international ecological movements such as Greenpeace. The limited achievements of the 1992 Earth Summit in Rio de Janeiro would not have been possible without the international consciousness generated by the worldwide ecological movement.

The amorphous nature of development theory both results from and promotes a tendency towards the colonisation of meaning, in which concepts such as development are not merely areas for debate, but are constructed as myths and countermyths. The myth of modernisation has, for some, assumed the characteristics of a millenial cult. If you prepare a landing strip (modernise) then the mysterious aeroplane will land bringing the goods (development). Postmodern thought has generated a new critique of such mythology sustained by theoretical currents that go beyond the economism of dependency theory and tend to avoid meta-theoretical perspectives. Instead, it draws strength from a close analysis of micro-relationships and the deconstruction of issues from the experience of the colonised and oppressed (Mies 1986, Stewart *infra*). In this respect, the work of the Subaltern Studies group in India is of particular significance, involving as it does a deconstruction of Indian colonial history and its reconstruction from the perspective not of the Raj but of oppressed groups (Guha 1983, 1985, 1987).[5]

Fitzpatrick approaches such deconstruction from a Foucaultian perspective. As he points out in this volume and elsewhere (1992), the myth of modernisation provides cultural contrasts between modern and traditional, rational and irrational, civilised and uncivilised, and progressive and backward which are themselves mythological cultural constructions, words whose meanings have been colonised by the historical dominance of Western capitalism. Concepts such as Basic Needs or sustainable development may arise from popular struggles, but their meanings are frequently distorted in the interests of those who wield power. One response to this colonisation of meaning may be to reject existing concepts altogether. Words such as development and modernisation may have outlived their usefulness and may now even be misleading. Fukuyama's (1992) assertion that we have come to the end of history implies that the notion of 'progress' may be questioned even by adherents of Western liberalism. An alternative approach is to situate each concept within its power context. This should not involve a kneejerk rejection of modernisation in favour of traditionalism, but deconstruction and decolonisation of both concepts in ways which conform to the interests of the people concerned.

After four decades of development theory and practice, the fundamental issues and contradictions are little changed. Instead, the reality of development has stubbornly resisted the nostrums contained in the theories which have thus far informed the activities of development economists, aid agencies, sociologists, political scientists and lawyers. If nothing else, the experiences of the past four decades have demonstrated that the complexities and contradictions of development resist easy classification or incorporation under the rubric of a single theory. We have learned that internal and external factors must equally be taken into consideration, that development policies can never fully account for the vagaries of human behaviour, and that what appears clear on paper is less likely to be so in reality. As Hettne (1990: 11) puts it:

> Development theory may not always have come up with the correct solutions on the policy level, but on the other hand the problems identified and analysed have not disappeared either. Instead, new problems have been added.

The Crisis in Law and Development Theory

The crisis in development studies has been paralleled by the almost self-indulgent pessimism that has characterised the theory and practice of law in development and has led to the widespread paralysis that this volume addresses. Interestingly, however, the crisis in law and development emerged far earlier than that in development studies as a whole. This might be ascribed to the acuity of law and development theorists; more probably it is a reflection of the limits of the law, and particularly of instrumentalist conceptions of its role. The modernisation paradigm was a godsend to lawyers because it enabled them to reduce the complexities of the development process to the mechanics of regulation, adjudication and institution-building. A separation of powers incorporating an independent judiciary trained in the Anglo-American common law tradition, multi-party democracies with regular elections, due process under the rule of law and free-market institutions were regarded as the cornerstones of successful modernisation. There was not an area of social life, from the family to the market, from the criminal justice system to urban administration that was not capable of being developed by and through the law, which thus became the key to development. Law and development emerged as a discipline as the winds of change blew through the South, and especially with the extension of American hegemony in the 1960s. It was conceptualised exclusively in Western terms, characterised by the modernist faith in progress, and reflected the optimism of a period of economic growth in which welfare legislation was widely regarded as a panacea for most social evils. In areas such as abortion, divorce, equal opportunities and racial equality the law was widely and unproblematically regarded as an efficient instrument of social engineering. If the civil rights movement in the US could deliver the Civil Rights Amendment as a final solution to such an intractable problem as the American Civil War, how much more could be done in less developed laboratories in the South. The path trodden by the First World to capitalism and liberal democracy was now open to the Third World. The irony of dispatching from Kennedy's Camelot the Peace Corps to civilize the ignorant of the Third World while counterrevolution was sponsored in the Bay of Pigs was lost in the rush to 'develop' the South. At least the disaster of the latter was shortlived.

The 'civilising mission' of colonialism was transmogrified into the evangelism of modernisation. Whereas the development of underdevelopment under colonialism had been marked by the maintenance of non-capitalist modes of production, under modernisation it would proceed by obliterating the backwardness of traditional societies. The state and its laws were the means to this end. Seidman, for example, stressed the utility of state-made rules (particularly legislation) in fostering development. For him, development (conceived primarily as economic growth) involves the inculcation of new patterns of behaviour, and law was the most useful mechanism for achieving such change (Seidman 1972). Descending pyramidally from a constitution, law provides a range of substantive norms which were the precondition for successful development. LDCs must mix and match from three 'jural postulates', namely Status, Contract and Plan - corresponding roughly to customary law, common law and public regulation.

Dhavan has argued that the major failing of the first wave of law and development scholarship was that it was addressed to the state rather than the people (Dhavan 1992: 10). As a consequence, '[it] has been confined to the management of societies within the national boundaries of the modern state', which is 'assumed to be objective, honest and genuine in its plans'. The state is further assumed to possess the capacity to decree laws which are genuinely pitched towards social change and where there is a 'gap' between state declarations and social acceptance of them this 'can be overcome by evolving bureaucratic, administrative, legal and other techniques in order to secure compliance'. Law and development, being programmatic in nature, is thus argued to be able to secure an 'efficient regulatory system under conditions of the rule of law', and 'is particularly concerned with regulating social behaviour to secure its compliance consistent with the overall plans of society'.

> In this programme of 'law and development', there is very little appreciation of the actual circumstances and constraints within which the political economy functions. There is a very opaque understanding of the compulsions within which the State works; and, still less of how forces in society appropriate law, state and development for their own benefit. (Dhavan 1992: 12-13).

The limitations of the state-centred modernisation paradigm triggered the perception of a crisis in law and development. In 1974, David Trubek and Marc Galanter, significant contributors in the first wave of law and development scholarship, published an article entitled *Scholars in Self-Estrangement: Some Reflection on the Crisis in Law and Development Studies in the United States* which revealed a level of disillusion proportional to the hopes aroused by the evangelism of liberal lawyers during the preceding fifteen years and questioned the direction of the discipline.

> Law and development studies originated largely as by-products of 'development assistance' activities by the United States government, international agencies and private foundations working with legal institutions in the Third World...Legal development assistance was originally justified as a rational and effective method to protect individual freedom, expand citizen participation in decisionmaking,

enhance social equality, and increase the capacity of all citizens rationally to control events and shape social life...[Soon, however,] many scholars began to wonder whether these projects were, in fact, contributing to freedom, equality, participation, and shared rationality. These doubts led the scholars to question the moral worth of some or all legal development assistance activities...[and] have created the malaise we shall call 'self-estrangement', and it is the existence of this malaise which constitutes the present crisis. (Trubek and Galanter 1974:1063-64).

The issues presented themselves very differently to the inhabitants of the South. The history of colonialism, neo-colonialism and imperialism is suffused with resistance against the state, from the Igbo women's protests against British colonial policy in Nigeria to, more recently, the burning of cashew crops by Tanzanian peasants and women's ecodevelopment struggles in India. In the face of states which are oppressive yet too weak to make their oppression stick, populations have acted collectively and individually to defend themselves against the encroachments of those who hold national state and economic power and who, as Yash Ghai points out in this volume, are often the same people.

Unsurprisingly, the capitalism which these lawyers sought to promote in the South proved not quite so liberal, its legal institutions not quite the panacea to all developmental ills. The instrumentalism inherent in this viewpoint derived from the simplistic notion that law could be moulded and manipulated by the developing states to alter human behaviour in a direct and non-contradictory fashion. One rationalisation for the failure of law to facilitate development may be that the full modernisation project was nowhere completely realised. Departing colonial powers bequeathed liberal constitutions, independent judiciaries and legal professions, and other rudiments of the rule of law (Ghai *infra*), but these were soon abandoned in a succession of military coups or were transformed into devices for the patrimonial power of autocratic and corrupt leaders. The result was a paradox in which autocracy grew in proportion to the increasing narrowness and declining legitimacy of the state. The notion that class conflict or socio-cultural relations might affect the functionality of the law seemed alien to most law and development scholars and practitioners. The bizarre logic of this argument is manifested in the reincarnation of modernisation as structural adjustment, which involves *inter alia* the liberalisation of economic activity, the rationalisation of the state, and the imposition of 'good governance' conceived as multi-party constitutionalism, individual human rights and the rule of law.

History remains unlearned as the dominant theories of development in the 1990s take us back to the future; now, however, faith in legal instrumentalism is not confined to bourgeois lawyers. While the goals are noble, the methods remain dubious, especially when the lessons of dependency theory are borne in mind. The success of this spectacular experiment in imposing constitutionalism, the rule of law, freedom and human rights to sustain market mechanisms appears doubtful as evidence from countries as disparate as Algeria and Peru suggests a widening of popular resistance alongside the deepening of the contradiction between oppressive SAPs and the rhetoric of democracy. The compatibility of political repression and economic liberalism revealed in Pinochet's Chile and the Four Little Dragons poses a challenge to development theory as a whole and to law and development in particular. This challenge can only be met by transcending the failure of modernisation theorists and their successors to reconcile the contradictions between (i) the advantages of bourgeois law in a modern state on the one hand and the different cultural and historical traditions of less developed social formations and, (ii) the rhetoric of liberal legality and continuing exploitation and disempowerment of the South. Moreover, the claim that the failure of law in development is due to the incompleteness of the modernisation project means that LDCs have never been in a position to fully embrace the logical consequences of liberal legality under the rule of law. If law arises within social relations even as it shapes them then the grafting of foreign legal, political and economic forms onto less developed social formations was always unlikely to succeed.

Addressing the Crisis

However, even as the law and modernisation scholars descended into despair, the viability and relevance of law and development was reflected in the alternative agenda of progressive academics who exposed the limitations of conventional law and developmment scholarship and demonstrated the possibilities of more appropriate research (Ghai 1987, Snyder 1980, 1981, Fitzpatrick 1980, 1983, Shivji 1986a). Above all they demonstrated the importance of analysing law in a broader context comprising both the nation-state and the global political economy, and the advantages of a multi-disciplinary methodology encompassing other social scientific disciplines as well as law.

The disappointment arising from law's failure to lubricate the wheels of development was a major disappointment for law and modernisation scholars. Few developmental lawyers appeared to be concerned about whether this was either possible or desirable; even fewer appeared to be aware of Marxist critiques of law such as that developed by the Soviet jurist Evgeny Pashukanis. The narrow liberalism of much law and development theory and its consequent confinement within the modernisation paradigm resulted in a failure to take into account the impact of colonialism, imperialism and the development of underdevelopment argument in dependency theory. This was, and remains, inevitable as long as the conception of law informing the discipline is that of bourgeois law with its rhetoric of abstract individualism, formal equality, impartiality and neutrality. In contrast, Marxist critiques offered alternative and more sophisticated responses to the problems of law in development. On the one hand, they revealed the importance of the legal form in facilitating exclusion, exploitation and disempowerment. The historian E. P. Thompson succintly exposed the contradictory nature of the rule of law but argued nonetheless that it is 'an unqualified human good' (Thompson 1987: 68). Many LDCs suffer the worst aspects of modern statehood (like mindless nationalism, deadening bureaucracy, widespread corruption and mindnumbing inefficiency) while accruing few of the supposed benefits of liberal legality such as the protection of human rights and freedoms and a meaningful level of accountability.

The critique of law in development orthodoxy is intimately concerned with the question why bourgeois legality did not take hold in the colonies. An important arena of the analysis is the relationship between traditional legal orders and the new orders imposed by the State (Snyder 1981, 1981a, Fitzpatrick 1980, 1983, Chanock 1985, Merry 1988). It was suggested, for example, that customary law was not a manifestation of the benign tolerance of indirect rule under colonialism but rather a Western creation designed to facilitate exploitation and a reflection of the racism informing the relationship between metropole and colony. Snyder (1981) demonstrated the degree to which capitalist legal relations had penetrated traditional legal orders and Fitzpatrick (1980, 1983) analysed the functionality for colonialism of the relationship between customary and western legal orders arising from the articulation of traditional and capitalist modes of production. Customary law helped to sustain social relations in the traditional rural sector, which subsidised and depressed the costs of reproducing labour power in the urban capitalist sector. This constructed traditionalism also assisted political stability through the ideology of indirect rule. While upto the early Eighties the critique of law and modernisation was rooted in dependency theory, there has been a subsequent process of change which has begun to synthesise some of the insights of dependency theory with new theoretical currents. For example, there was an increasing awareness that the relationship was not simply one of the imposed will of the colonial state, that peoples of different localities responded in their own ways to the challenges, and were, albeit in a situation of unequal power, involved in manipulating what Moore had termed the semi-autonomous social field (Moore 1986, Fitzpatrick 1983, Hellum *infra*). In many respects, the chapters in this book are part of the new synthesis.

Fitzpatrick's essay on *Law's Infamy* reflects the dynamism of the new theoretical explorations in the field. He argues that one of the keys to understanding colonial legal projects and their survival beyond formal decolonisation lies in comprehending the antinomous relationship between modernity and savagery, civilisation and barbarism. The white man's civilising mission was constructed within the ideology of modernity and reflected in the mythology of modern law, which is presented as the epitome of progress in contradistinction to the simple savagery of 'native' law.[6]

Once the myth of inevitable progress was challenged and the creation of 'savagery' revealed as a colonial project, the notion of modernisation through law was opened to deconstruction. The developmental contradiction arising from this realisation is that it is impossible to return to an idyllic pre-capitalist legal order, but the paraphernalia of contemporary legal orders is often incompatible with the social, cultural and legal histories of LDCs.

The failure of constitutionalism is one aspect of this incompatibility as is explored by Yash Ghai in his chapter on *Constitutions and Governance in Africa: A Prolegomenon*. He adopts a Weberian framework in order to suggest that the answer lies in a culture of patrimonialism generated by colonial factors, the manner of development of new elites and the overall weakness of the state apparatus. He incorporates this Weberian analysis within the framework of Marxist political economy to determine the reasons for the failure of constitutionalism. In locating the contradictions of African statehood within liberal and Marxist constitutional theory, he offers the beginnings of a much-needed analysis of the thorny relationship between constitutionalism, legality and the rule of law on the one hand, and development and democracy on the other. Ghai's contribution highlights the significant role of the rule of law, the 'soul of the modern state' as Unger (1976: 192) has termed it, and with it the importance of liberal legality in general.

The contradictory ideology which is embodied in the rule of law lies at the heart of both liberal legality and, consequently, of structural adjustment and provides the point of departure for Alan Norrie's chapter on *Criminal Justice, the Rule of Law and Human Emancipation*. This involves a historical comparison of criminal justice systems in the Western Rechtstaat, under colonial and post-colonial regimes, and under state socialism. He makes the obvious but important point that the nature of the rule of law, positive criminal law and conceptions of justice are mediated by relations of power in specific societies so that the combination of oppression, democracy, popular involvement, authoritarianism and legality which arises will be contingent upon broader social and economic relations. He argues that the workings of criminal justice systems cannot be reduced to stereotypical notions of the Rechsstaat in free market democracies or popular justice regimes under revolutionary socialism. The rule of law is concerned, however, as much with legitimacy as legality, but Norrie does not address its ideological aspects. Since the rule of law implies rule *under* law as well as rule *by* law, it is difficult to envisage its operation in quintessentially non-liberal states under colonialism or state socialism, where resistance to overtly oppressive legal systems would appear to preclude government by consent rather than coercion.

Norrie's description of the limitations of popular justice raises the question of whether the law is fundamentally incapable of meeting the needs and aspirations of people in LDCs. Jill Cottrell's chapter on *Third Generation Rights and Social Action Litigation* illustrates the possibility of moving beyond analyses which crudely presume the transplantation of Western law to LDCs. She looks at public interest litigation in India, perhaps the most influential legal innovation to have emerged in the South, and one with great potential relevance worldwide. The contradictions of law in development are exemplified by the role of courts in the struggle for rights and justice. They have generally proved unwilling to challenge the state in LDCs, not least because they are peopled by members of the ruling elite. Nevertheless, courts are sites of struggle and they have occasionally been induced to act as champions of the oppressed. The Indian Supreme Court under Justice Bhagwati developed a unique public interest litigation doctrine under which the oppressed, whether by themselves or with the support of civil rights activists and NGO's could have easy and ready access to justice to ensure in particular that state agencies behave in ways consistent with the law. Issues that have come before the courts have included the rights of child labourers, prostitutes infected with the HIV virus, prisoners and street dwellers. The court's creative interpretation of the Indian Constitution provides some scope in the struggle to transcend the individualism inherent in liberal legality and thereby promote human rights on a collective basis more appropriate to social relations throughout much of the South. Public interest litigation is unique in its openness and absence of formalities and thus more relevant to the needs of oppressed groups. Such judicial interventions are, inevitably, not without their contradictions, and an interventionist court without sufficient due process safeguards may be in danger of undermining the very freedoms it seeks to protect. These dangers should not however undermine the significance of public interest litigation as a chink in the armour of state power open to exploitation by the oppressed acting in concert with social action movements.

Issa Shivji's chapter on *Rights-struggle, Class struggle and The Law: Reflections on Experiences at the University of Dar es Salaam* focuses on campaigns by students and staff on the campus of the University of Dar es Salaam. The chapter is a fine example of law and development scholarship which assumes that law - and liberal legality in particular - is not an unproblematic instrument but rather a contradictory site of struggle. The issues he examines capture some of the contradictions of the move towards multi-party democracy throughout much of Africa in the New World Order. His analysis of the interconnection of legal education and political struggles on the campus and in the wider society points to the need to continually redefine and conceptualise legal educational issues within the context of the wider struggles. Shivji suggests that whereas struggles in Tanzania during the 1970s overemphasised class conflict and de-emphasised human rights, legal education and politics of the campus in the following decade tilted the balance in the other direction. The danger is that rights struggles are easily reduced to struggles for individual liberal legal rights rather than people's democratic rights.

The following three chapters by Sol Picciotto, Sammy Adelman and Caesar Espiritu, and Adelman alone specifically address the internationalisation of production and the development of the legal institutions that maintain it. They ask whether law is not in fact succeeding admirably in its role of expediting the establishment of neo-colonialist institutions and the incorporation of LDCs into subordinate roles within an increasingly globalised international economy. Picciotto's chapter on *International Business and Global Development* is concerned with the continuing failure at both national and international levels to regulate transnational corporations (TNC's). He argues that the underlying problem is the form of power relations in the global economy. The tendency of development lawyers to focus on a 'miasma of abstract principles such as the right to development and permanent sovereignty over natural resources' results in vague and contradictory generalisations. While international law assigns rights to individuals, the implementation of those rights is within the largesse of states which are unwilling or unbale to reign in exploitative TNCs. The companies themselves prefer to deal with individual states on a 'good citizen' basis, playing off one state against another as they resist international regulation. One important consequence is that the myriad lawyers involved in the day-to-day mechanics of international business on behalf of TNCs or states tend to ignore the rights and interests of the citizens affected. Picciotto therefore suggests that the possibility of international regulation is contingent upon more active popular involvement by social action movements focussing on such issues as the environment, political prisoners and women's rights.

Adelman and Espiritu in their chapter on *The Debt Crisis, Underdevelopment and the Limits of the Law* examine the debt crisis as a major phenomenon of the exploitative relationship between North and South. They argue that the origin of the crisis should be located not in the profligacy of LDCs, but rather in the structural imbalances in the global economy, the two oil price shocks in the 1970s, and the recklessness of Western financial institutions. The West's response to the crisis, based on managing rather than cancelling the debt, was inspired less by a desire to facilitate development than to prevent the collapse of Western banks and to address its own accumulation crisis. The absurd consequence of this policy was that the poorest nations of the world became net exporters of capital to the richest. Adelman and Espiritu examine legal doctrines such as that of odious debts and conclude that the law has, at best, a limited role in resolving the crisis.

Sammy Adelman's chapter on *The International Labour Code and the Exploitation of Female Workers in Export Processing Zones* is part of the growing body of studies on women and development, but its primary focus is on the exploitative nature of export-processing zones in LDCs seeking to emulate the success of the Four Little Dragons. Like Picciotto, he draws attention to the inadequacy of international legal mechanisms in regulating global capitalism and protecting workers. Adelman's chapter also reflects the degree to which contemporary developmental lawyers practice their discipline within the context of development studies as a whole, and the enduring relevance of such research. His study constitutes a legally oriented contribution to what Munck has termed the new international labour studies, a conception 'which has a global perspective, deploys a range of traditional and novel methods of investigation and is committed to a view of labour studies which we can best label as 'critical engagement" (Munck 1988: 22-23). Adelman's analysis of the impact of globalisation on women provides a point of departure for three chapters dealing specifically with women and the family in LDCs, a rapidly developing field which reflects the vitality of contemporary law and development scholarship.

Historically, men have been identified as the main agents and beneficiaries of development, a focus which neglects the profound contribution of women, not only in the sphere of reproduction but also in resistance. The renaissance of feminism has given women's rights in and to development a greater if somewhat contradictory significance as attention has been focussed on the role of women in food production, and the importance of family, health and population policies. The result is a growing tendency for women to be seen as the new agents of socialisation.

Ann Stewart's chapter on *The Dilemmas of Law in Women's Development* examines the complexities involved in the legal position of women in the South in contrast to those of Western feminists. At the same time, it is simplistic to assume a monolithic Third World women's perspective. For example, whose concerns are to be addressed by the 'modernisation' of women's rights in Zimbabwe - the rural elite, farmers or prostitutes? She argues for the need to deconstruct women studies, women and development studies and women, law and development. Following Harding, she is critical of a feminist empiricism which involves analysis of the way women are underprivileged or standpoint analysis propounded by the Norwegian school of *Women's Law* under the leadership of Tove Stang Dahl, which takes womens' needs and experience as its point of departure but treats the state as unproblematic. Instead, Stewart argues that women's perspectives consist of many different subjugated knowledges which conflict with but are seldom reflected in the dominant culture. While much can be achieved through an analysis of the way law disadvantages women, it is more relevant to explore the specific way in which law is involved in the construction of female and gender roles in different societies through an exploration of institutions such as *Muta'a* marriage in Iran or polygamy in Zimbabwe. Such an understanding would lead to a better appreciation of the complex issues involved within a cultural context rather than the rush to 'modernisation' suggested by positivist reformist analyses. While the reliance on the work of Haeri may be considered controversial, this does not diminish the importance of the chapter in suggesting the possibilities of a constructive cross-pollination between the methodologies of Western feminism and the needs of women in the South.

Ann Hellum's chapter on *Gender and Legal Change in Zimbabwe* analyses the role of law in the construction and regulation of reproduction in the case of childless women among the patrilineal Shona and the matrilineal Tonga in Zimbabwe. Hellum's chapter is open to some of the criticisms that Stewart levels against *Women's Law* in that both law and the state are treated in a relatively unproblematic manner. At the same time, however, the chapter demonstrates the significance of detailed analyses of the legal process in the South and the possibility of placing these in a broader context. It covers pre-colonial, colonial and post-colonial periods, and differentiates between different modes of regulation in a variety of courts in a legally pluralist society. She argues that changes in the social and legal regulation of reproduction during the colonial and post-colonial periods have different effects on men and women, depending upon the nature of the society, the rural-urban divide and the class and power positions of those involved.

Abdul Paliwala makes a similar point in his chapter on *Family Transformation and Family Law: Some African Developments in*

Financial Support on Relationship Breakdown. His study complements those of Stewart and Hellum in examining the broader implication of socio-economic and legal changes in different African jurisdictions. Colonial and post-colonial socio-economic changes have affected family relationships in general and support for wives upon marriage breakdown in particular. Several states have responded by enacting post-divorce maintenance laws and facilitating the development of limited but significant welfare services to tackle the social problems raised by relationship breakdown. Paliwala suggests that there is a need to decentre and refocus research on the role of law in the construction of family relationships. Lawyers need to deconstruct the framework within which dependency operates, including the construction of marriage and brideprice, unequal property relationships in the allocation of land and succession rights, and the division of labour within the family. His contribution is valuable in another way, in that it implicitly addresses the postmodern distrust of metatheory characteristic of much feminist legal theory, and suggests that law and development studies could profit from microcosmic analyses which refuse to privilege the state.

These contributions demonstrate both the cross-pollination which is taking place between disciplines in an academic back to the future, and that between women in the North and the South. The structured academic imperialism reflected in the hegemony of Northern intellectuals in this process should not blind us to the importance of the lessons learned by women in developed countries, not least in relation to law. The plethora of anti-discrimination legislation that has come onto the statute books in the West since the 1970s has proved contradictory. The gap between the rhetoric of formal rights and the reality of enduring sexism being addressed by feminists in the North indicates the difficulty of transcending cultural practices, and Stewart's contribution in particular suggests the potential fruitfulness of research in this area by feminist law and development scholars.

An Agenda for the Future

The thread linking the contributions to this volume is the critique of liberal law and development theory and its relevance to the lives of people in the developing world. The authors, who have strong ties to the School of Law at the University of Warwick, reflect the vitality of alternative law and development scholarship during a period dominated by the dogmas of 'good governance', structural adjustment and conditionalities.

Yet the tasks facing such scholarship are not inconsiderable. There is a need to absorb the many insights gained from new theoretical currents - for example in feminism, legal anthropolgy and postmodernism. Once development is defined not in some abstract terms such as economic growth, but in terms of human development, there is a need to orientate research, education and action towards theoretical perspectives which involve (though are not confined to) the consciousness of the people themselves (Dahl 1987, Guha 1983, 1985, 1987, Moore 1986). Nowhere is this question more apparent than in the consideration of gender issues. It is not a question of what legal changes are necessary to enable women to contribute to the abstract goal of national development, but what patriarchal, local, national and international legal, political and economic factors affect the women's right to their own development in terms of their own environment (Stewart *infra*).

Much of this new scholarship points to the need to reconsider the nature and role of state and law. The developmental state can no longer be taken for granted, nor is there any faith in law as its modernising instrument. Yet, there is also a realisation that law is imbricated in social relations- it may not be the key to development, but it cannot be ignored either. It is therefore necessary to decentre and refocus the role of law. Viewed from the actual situation of those with whom state law is involved, what part does it play in structuring relationships? How does its role relate to that of other forms of legal and social control which exist in a social field? These questions are particularly significant for groups which mobilise around issues for social justice and a saner ecology. These groups necessarily have to consider actions within and without the law, in and against the state. The use of law to promote rights against economic powerholders such as landlords or to struggle against patriarchy is constrained by the tendency of the law to operate to the advantage of the powerful. As Cottrell demonstrates in her study of public interest litigation, this may not be universal, and may not be any more so than is the case with other forms of mobilisation. There is, however, a profoundly conservative tendency in law in general and liberal legality in particular that renders change through law contradictory at best - as Shivji demonstrates in his chapter and his work on human rights (1989b). It is also clear that people are not passive in the face of state power but are often involved in struggles of resistance or in active manipulation of power for their own ends. It is therefore necessary to reconceptualise power relations as consisting not merely of a single powerful hegemonic international or national state apparatus, but rather in terms of flows of power of different strengths derived from a variety of sources and providing spaces, often limited, for the advancement of claims and rights.

A process of uncovering (to borrow from Fitzpatrick 1992) the mythologies of modern law is an essential prerequisite to an understanding of these power relationships at both national and international levels. At the national level, the myth of modernity has led to the branding of tradition and custom as backward and in need of a modern cure despite the fact that romanticised customary law and traditions have been revealed to be colonial constructs.

The international legal order is equally beset with unreal assumptions such as sovereignty and progressive internationalism that have too often led Third World lawyers to pursue grand designs such as the New International Economic Order and the right to development at the expense of a thorough understanding of the forms of regulation that have a real influence on the South. If the New World Order is to have any meaning it can only be on the basis that the end of the Cold War presents an opportunity for greater democracy within the global political economy. Pursuit of this aim requires careful research on the real relationships of power affecting international institutions such as the World Bank, IMF, GATT as well as the operation of the commercial banking system, transnational corporations and state regulatory agencies. It requires transcending formalistic distinctions between public and private, national and international law as is indicated in Picciotto's work. It also requires abandoning the assumption that all states in the South, or even all peoples within a state are uniformly affected by international forces.

It has become increasingly apparent that issues of development cannot be confined to matters affecting economic growth. That sustainable development is intimately concerned with environmental and human social issues. As the Bhopal tragedy in India indicated, both underdevelopment and law were intimately involved in the genesis of the disaster and its unsatisfactory resolution. The absence of a chapter in this book on environmental law is an obvious ommission reflecting the relative unimportance attached to it in the Third World to date despite the fact that environmental issues lie at the heart of broader issues of development. Deforestation in the Amazon or southeast Asia, for example, involves a wide range of issues such as poverty and exploitation through the inadequate allocation of land resources, the operation of foreign logging companies in the international timber trade, fuel resources and employment.

The relationship between development and the struggle for internal democracy and human rights continues to be a central question for the peoples of the South. There are three key issues affecting such struggles that require analysis. Whatever the weaknesses of sovereignty against powerful international interests, it has often been used as a cloak hiding internal oppression. Authoritarianism, corruption and opportunism cannot be explained away merely as by-products of colonialism and neocolonialism; rather, we need to address, as indicated by Ghai's analysis, the extent to which the LDCs themselves are culpable. Finally, multi-party based formal democratisation needs to be examined not merely on an institutional basis in terms of the ideology of modernisation/structural adjustment, but in terms of the social and power structures it promotes and their effects on class, ethnicity, nationalism, religion and human rights.

An agenda for research does not, however, imply a sterile constriction within the parameters of academia. Research is a means to an end and must therefore be conducted against the backdrop of the realities of development and underdevelopment. There is thus a need to integrate analysis and education, critique and practical action. Perhaps the greatest task is to rethink our own role in the process. In demonstrating both the continued vitality and importance of law in development the authors, from both the North and the South, have implicitly challenged themselves to overcome the Eurocentrism that has historically characterised development thinking and to seek ways of more meaningful forms of collaboration between progressive intellectuals and activists.

Notes

1   See Brookfield (1975), Hettne (1990), Peet (1991), Roxborough (1979) and Todaro (1989) for extensive surveys of development theory.

2   A major criticism of dependency theory is, however, that it generally gave little credence to internal factors. For a discussion of the

different approaches within the dependency school see Hettne (1990 Ch. 3) and Roxborough (1979 Ch. 5).

3   The UNDP (1990: 10) defined human development as 'a process of enlarging people's choices'and the 1986 UN General Assembly Declaration on the Right to Development (resolution 41/128) states 'that development is a comprehensive economic, social, cultural and political process, which aims at the constant improvement of the well-being of the entire population and of all individuals on the basis of their active, free and meaningful participation in development and in the fair distribution of benefits resulting therefrom'.

4   It was also in the 1970s that the idea of Self-Reliance entered debates on development: '[It] connotes a development strategy deliberately undertaken to promote a special kind of development. This involves the cutting of links (delinking) to the larger system of division of labour in order to avoid imposed self-reliance and find something better than autarchy' (Hettne 1990: 172).

5   See also Mitchell's (1988) study of the 'disciplining' of Egyptian society through devices such as education and Messick's (1992) study of the way in which changes in forms of legal writing introduced by Turkish colonialism influenced the nature of law and judging in a Yemeni village.

6   See Fitzpatrick (1992) for a comprehensive elaboration of his argument.

2

Law's Infamy

Peter Fitzpatrick

> So far as I know, we are the only people who think themselves risen from savages: everyone else believes they descend from gods (Sahlins 1976: 53).

Introduction

In its infamy, Western law has a specular existence. This law is infamous for some because of its oppression of peoples of the Third World. But the history of law's infamy has tended to exist apart from the socio-political advocacy of law as a vehicle for doing better things, for bringing about development or modernisation, even for becoming 'alternative' and taking the side of the oppressed. This is but an instance of the abstract instrumentalism which typifies most thinking about Western law. Against this can be placed the growing concern with the cultural density of law, with the pursuit of law through the images and forms in which it becomes inextricable with everyday life (Goodrich & Hachamovitch 1991). In this light, law is involved with infamy in a more obscure and intractable way. Law could once impose the status of infamy; it could deny people a being in law. Not only has law done this to the peoples of the Third World, but that very denial, I argue, is integral to the constitution of Western law itself. If this is so, it follows that the blithe advocacy of law in the cause of development is flawed in its very foundation.

In 'law and development' and its variants, law is usually seen in instrumental terms (Franck 1972: 787, 789). Law, if used aright, can bring about development or modernisation, or it can secure an order in which other transforming agents can operate. Law is now even held capable of turning against its origins and supporting the very people it once oppressed. In this, it serves the cause of 'alternative approaches to development' such as development from the 'bottom-up' rather than from the 'top-down', development as the satisfaction of 'basic needs' and as the provision of 'access' to state benefits (Dias & Paul 1981: 362-3). The state may have to be particularly obliging in this 'aspirational agenda for law and lawyers in development' since 'government intervention seems clearly necessary if an economic base for these services is to be created' (Dias & Paul 1981: 356, 378). This current orthodoxy is seen by Dias and Paul as a 'growing international interest in studying endogenous, human-needs-centred groups, particularly by working *with* them' (Dias and Paul 1981: 380; their emphasis). What is particularly insidious about all this in its connection with law is that a unitary 'law' is not confined to the law of the state but extends to 'endogenous law and shared ideas about justice which can be employed to articulate grievances persuasively, legitimate claims' and so on (Dias in Soliman 1990: 2). The struggles of the oppressed are thus contained within a project of 'law' by conceptual fiat and by nothing else. Even radical critiques that see law effecting the purposes of imperialism and underdevelopment do not displace the instrumental orientation. They still leave open the prospect of law's virtuous use. How does law retain its innocence? In *Discovering "Social Control"'*, Marilyn Strathern draws a distinction that may yet prove seminal between Western law and the modes of regulation among the people of Hagen in the New Guinea Highlands (Strathern 1985). With these people, one mode of regulation, such as fighting or exchange or 'talk', is deeply influenced by and even transformable into another. In contrast, with Western law we find a 'conceptual split between social action which incorporates the ideal, the normative, and what that action controls/regulates/modifies. Certain types of behaviour thus have the potential for transforming others' without themselves being affected (Strathern 1985: 128). Thus, adjudication is seen 'as not itself participating in the events under scrutiny' (Strathern 1985: 120).

The argument can be furthered through Goodrich's moving account of a recent case involving the Haida Indians who had attempted to prevent a logging company desecrating their ancestral land (Goodrich 1990: 179-84). The company operated under a licence given by the government of British Columbia. It brought an action seeking to uphold the licence and to obtain an injunction preventing further interference with logging by the Haida. The Indians wished to represent themselves and to speak in their own terms. The first response of the Court to this desire was portentous. It consisted of attempts to persuade the Indians to employ legal representatives, to bring themselves within the language and the mastery of the law. To this, the Indian response was that 'the issue of our lands is too important to leave in the hands of lawyers who are unfamiliar with our people' (Goodrich 1990: 180). The Court then adopted a seemingly liberal stance and accepted testimony which 'took the form of symbolic dress, mythologies, masks and totem poles as well as the legends, stories, poems, songs and other forms of interpretation that such art and mythology implied' (Goodrich 1990: 182-3). These told in Haida terms of the mythic origin of the Haida and of their identification with the land. The Haida also extended themselves to the European by including evidence in Western terms about Haida customary law concerning dispute settlement and land claims. The judicial response was brutal in effect if not intent:

> Unreserved judgment was given by the court the day after argument ended. Justice McKay observed that the court would not normally have allowed argument of the political kind heard but that, in view of the fact that the Haida had no other arena available to them, he had been prepared to listen and generously recommend that a record of the evidence present should be kept for posterity. The judgment itself was extremely brief. The evidence presented as the Haida title to and relationship with the islands was not legally relevant to the case being heard, which simply concerned interference with a valid logging licence. (Goodrich 1990: 183).

The argument of the Haida to be preserved for posterity was but 'a curiosity, a relic, a primitive remnant of a more savage past' (Goodrich 1990: 183). The attempt 'to speak for ourselves' was comprehensively negated - the Court treated it as a charade, admitting it because there was 'no other arena available to them':

> The Court would not compare mythologies, *it refused even to countenance the question of the 'other'*, because to do so would raise

questions of its 'self', of the social and mythic construction of its own body, its social role and actions, its own clothes. (Goodrich 1990: 183; his emphasis).

Law as myth is thus held inviolable whilst being able to go forth and order the world. Law also has a part in the mythic narration of how modernity and the West came to be. It is also a particular telling of that myth. I will now pursue law as myth and locate its inviolable elevation, its infamous foundation, and the connection between the two.

Law and Savagery

It is relatively easy to establish links between law and that massive 'second imperialism' of the 19th and early 20th centuries. Law was only somewhat less conspicuously involved in the beginnings of modern colonialism in the late eighteenth century. But the complicity of modern law in all this has not derogated from its true liberal being as exemplified within those very nations which were the predominant colonizers. Indeed, the authoritarian law of the colonies, in a feat of legerdemain typical of myth, could be presented as a sub-type of its antithesis - of liberal legality. The contradiction was mediated through its transformation into a natural or necessary consequence of the inadequacies of the colonized. The contradiction would disappear when or if the inadequacies of the colonized did likewise. In other words, contradiction was ultimately mediated in the pervasive modern myth of progress. When the contradiction was no more, law could resume its full liberal identity without that detraction. If, however, the contradiction is traced further back and as far as the mythic origins of modern law, that law can then be seen as entirely compatible with the authoritarian rule of colonized peoples. Those mythic origins, I now argue, are to be found with the advent of the European Enlightenment and it is that period on which I concentrate.

Despite claims to total originality, the Enlightenment often repatterned old mythic themes, making them its own. In one such theme, law is contrasted fundamentally with the savage state. For example, having left the land of the Lotus-Eaters, with understandably 'downcast hearts', Ulysses and his company

> came to the land of the Cyclops race, arrogant lawless beings who

leave their livelihood to the deathless gods and never use their own hands to sow or plough.... They have no assemblies to debate in, they have no ancestral ordinances; they live in arching caves on the tops of high hills, and the head of each family heeds no other, but makes his own ordinances for wife and children. (Shewring 1980: 101, Book IX).

As we shall see, many elements of law's mythic origins are compressed into this description - the lawless nature of the savage, the emergence of law being associated with agriculture, the equation of law and sociality in contrast to the solitary state of the savage or the savage family. It was indeed common among the Greeks and Romans to identify an uncivilized or wild state with the absence of law (Kelley 1984: 620, Ch. I, White 1978: 165). For the medieval world, exotic peoples were often monsters which did not have the capacity to follow the law because they lacked human form (see Goldberg forthcoming, Ch. 1).

'In the beginning all the World was *America*' (Locke 1960: 343; his emphasis). As a source of savage origins, the Americas remained predominant until well into the period of Enlightenment - until, that is, they were displaced as the main location of European imperial expansion. The 'discovery' of the Americas almost immediately produced a profoundly ambivalent European regard of the Indian which was to become characteristic. The Indians were wild, promiscuous, propertyless and lawless (White 1978: 186-7). Or they inhabited a 'golden worlde without toyle...wherein men lyved symplye and innocentlye without enforcement of lawes, without quarrelying, judges, and libelles' (see Hodgen 1964: 371). Admiration tended to decline with the intensity of aggressive European settlement. Montaigne's essay '*Of Cannibals*' from the late sixteenth century was a greatly influential marker of this change (Montaigne 1978). Although not without admiration for their uncorrupted state, Montaigne saw the Indians in negative contrast with the civilized state. They were typified by lacks - of law, government, husbandry, and much else. Montaigne also saw the Indians as exemplars of a general state of savagery. At about the same time, this state of savagery came to be widely viewed as a general prelude to 'civil society', the main instances continuing to be the savages of the New World 'dispersed like wild beasts, lawlesse and naked' (see Hodgen 1964: 468). Comparisons were increasingly drawn between the once savage state of the Greeks and the Romans and that of the inhabitants of the Americas '...living onely by hunting...without tilled landes, without cattel, without King, Law, God, or Reason' (see Meek 1976: 48-9) or '*ni foi, ni loi, ni roi*', in what appears to have been a catchcry of early French explorers and settlers in North America (Axtell 1985: 12).

These elements and more were wrought into a mythic charter by Hobbes in the mid-seventeenth century (Hobbes 1952, Introduction and chapters 13, 15, 17, 18, 26-7). Through a primal covenant between 'men':

> is created that great LEVIATHAN called a COMMONWEALTH, or STATE (in Latin, CIVITAS), which is but an artificial man, though of greater stature and strength than the natural.... The pacts and covenants, by which the parts of this body politic were at first made, set together, and united, resemble that *fiat*, or the *Let us make man*, pronounced by God in the Creation. (Hobbes 1952: 47; his emphasis).

Although this Leviathan is but a 'mortal god', it is not restrained by mortal attributes. The binding and bonding covenant may no longer issue from the godhead but it is still attended with a mythic transcendence, inviolability and persistence. The resulting Commonwealth and its representative, the sovereign, are coequally imbued with these sacred qualities. The foundational terms in which a person enters into the covenant are taken to be: 'I authorise and give up my right of governing myself to this man, or to this assembly of men, on this condition; that thou give up thy right to him, and authorise all his actions in like manner' (Hobbes 1952: 100).

Hobbes proceeds with formidable rigour to secure this pact and its creations, the Commonwealth and the Sovereign, against any change or possibility of legitimate disturbance. To take just one line of argument:

> They that have already instituted a Commonwealth, being thereby bound by covenant to own the actions and judgements of one, cannot lawfully make a new covenant amongst themselves to be obedient to any other, in anything whatsoever, without his permission. And therefore, they that are subjects to a monarch cannot without his leave cast off monarchy and return to the confusion of a disunited multitude; nor transfer their person from him that beareth it to another man, or other assembly of men: for they are

bound, every man to every man, to own and be reputed author of all that he that already is their sovereign shall do and judge fit to be done. (Hobbes 1952: 101).

The commitment to Leviathan is total and interminable. It is attended with the mystical union of subjects within the Commonwealth. They are taken up into the sacred realm in which they mythically participate. In being 'the author of' the Commonwealth, the subject becomes comprehensively committed to all actions of the sovereign 'as if they were his own'; subjects are thus inextricably bound 'to him that beareth their person' - 'none of his subjects, by any pretence of forfeiture, can be freed from his subjection' (Hobbes 1952: 100-1). Ultimately, this sovereignty is the 'soul' of Leviathan, 'giving life and motion to the whole body' (Hobbes 1952: 47).

Hobbes proceeds to erect law in the same dimension as sovereignty. He is concerned with 'law in general', his 'design being not to show what is law here and there, but what is *law*': 'none can make laws but the Commonwealth, because our subjection is to the Commonwealth only', and since the sovereign is the representative of the Commonwealth 'the sovereign is the sole legislator' (Hobbes 1952: 130; his emphasis). It is the 'authority of the legislator' which gives to laws a mythic persistence, which enables them to 'continue to be laws' (Hobbes 1952: 131). Law takes form as a 'command' of the sovereign 'addressed to one...obliged to obey him' (Hobbes 1952: 130). This command theory was to become the predominant notion in English jurisprudence but it involved an immediate problem in that people have to know of commands in order to obey them. Hence, the command of the Commonwealth is law only to those who have means to take notice of it. 'Over natural fools, children or madmen there is no law, no more than over brute beasts' (Hobbes 1952: 132). But if law were to be dependent on popular knowledge, this could undermine the whole edifice of authority. With uncharacteristic equivocation, Hobbes opts largely, and understandably, for the maxim that ignorance of the law is no excuse (Hobbes 1952: 139).

What could be the impetus or force impelling the absolute and eternal transfer of power to a mortal god? Such impetus or force comes from a negative necessity. 'Our natural passions' are incompatible with political society: they put us in opposition to each other in 'a war as is of every man against every man' (Hobbes

1952: 85). Given this and given the rough equality of physical and mental ability among 'men', it is only through deterrence that relations between humans can emerge and they can only be crude and precarious. For anything more, a superordinate power is needed. There can be no peace 'without subjection': 'men have no pleasure but on the contrary a great deal of grief in keeping company where there is no power able to overawe them' (Hobbes 1952: 85, 99). Such a power has to be sustained - it has to make the covenant 'constant and lasting' - for without its persistence there would be a reversion to a state of war, to a chaotic pre-creation, a 'return to the confusion of a disunited multitude' and 'to the sword' (Hobbes 1952: 100-3).

> It may peradventure be thought there was never such a time nor condition of war as this; and I believe it was never generally so, over all the world: but there are many places of America, except the government of small families, the concord whereof dependeth on natural lust, have no government at all, and live at this day in that brutish manner. (Hobbes 1952:87-8).

The American Indian and a general invocation of savage 'places where men have lived by small families' provide the only (supposedly) tangible basis of this pre-creation (Hobbes 1952: 99). Hobbes intends the American instance to be universalized, even if 'it was never generally so', at least to the extent that 'where there were no common power to fear' some such state would prevail (Hobbes 1952: 86). He affirms the similarity of that brutish state with the absence of a feared 'common power' when peaceful government comes 'to degenerate into a civil war' (Hobbes 1952: 86). He also invokes the antagonistic condition existing between 'kings and persons of sovereign authority' (Hobbes 1952: 86). Neither of these instances is developed, and neither would long stand comparison with the primordial chaos provided by the simple savage, yet Hobbes does clearly intend them to be contemporary equivalents of the savagery that still lies below and that results from an absence of overarching order.

The savage state provides more than the force creating and sustaining political society. It is also a specular repository of the virtues mythically attributed to high civilizations:

> Whatsoever therefore is consequent to a time of war, where every man is enemy to every man, the same is consequent to the time

wherein men live without other security than what their own strength and their own invention shall furnish them withal. In such condition there is no place for industry, because the fruit thereof is uncertain: and consequently no culture of the earth; no navigation, nor use of the commodities that may be imported by sea; no commodious building; no instruments of moving and removing such things as require much force; no knowledge of the face of the earth; no account of time; no arts; no letters; no society; and which is worst of all, continual fear, and danger of violent death; and the life of man, solitary, poor, nasty, brutish, and short. (Hobbes 1952: 87).

To this catalogue of negatives there are two which need to be added more specifically. These assume a close relation in the period of Enlightenment. One is the absence of property, something which Hobbes often adverts to. In the savage state there can be no security of possession and expectation: 'there be no propriety, no dominion, no *mine* and *thine* distinct; but only that to be every man's that he can get, and for so long as he can keep it' (Hobbes 1952: 86; his emphasis). The other negative is the absence of law: 'where there is no common power, there is no law' and a law cannot 'be made till they have agreed upon the person that shall make it' (Hobbes 1952: 88).

Hobbes is the mythmaker of the tradition of overwhelming order, including its equivalent in law, legal positivism. What comes after could be seen as more or less elaborate footnotes to Hobbes' *Leviathan*. Knowledge continued to flow from the Americas of people 'without subordination, law, or form of government' joined increasingly with efforts 'to civilise this barbarism, to render it susceptible of laws' (Axtell 1985: 50). Such knowledge came to be generalized into that of an original, savage state. By the early eighteenth century, says Stein (1980: 1), 'the usual explanation of the origin of the state, or 'civil society', as it was called, began by postulating an original state of nature, in which primitive man lived on his own. He had few social relationships with other men, and was subject to neither government nor law'. The 'securalized' natural law of Enlightenment was in part based on the negative reflection of this state, on what was said to be common to those nations said to be civilized (Stein 1980: 4). The monumental classifications in nature revealed by Linnaeus in 1735, after God had 'suffered him to peep into His own secret cabinet', definitively related types of *homo sapiens* to types of regulation, or lack of it: the American was regulated by custom, the European governed by laws, the Asiatic by opinion and the African by caprice (see Hodgen 1964: 425). No less influentially, Montesquieu attributed governing 'causes' to groups of people in a more sociological way, savages being dominated by nature and climate, the Japanese by laws, and so on (Montesquieu 1949: 293-4, Book 19 Ch. 4).

The minority tradition of seeing the savage vices as virtue persisted. Rousseau on the whole thought it a good, if irretrievably lost thing to have 'no society but that of the family, no laws but those of nature' (see Meek 1976: 86). With a modernist versatility worthy of the creator of Rameau's nephew, Diderot could, on site as it were, extol the Tahitians for following their natural, especially sexual, inclinations and for not being constrained by laws; yet when closer to the Western tradition he declaims - passionately - 'the laws, the laws; there is the sole barrier that one can erect against the passions of men' (Diderot 1950, Bloch & Bloch 1980: 37, Riley 1986: 203). Even Ferguson, who censured an emerging modernity so percipiently in his *Essay on the History of Civil Society* of 1767 and who so admired the savagery it displaced, at least in its Scottish location, saw the 'rude nations' as ultimately restrained and inferior through want of 'subordination' in a 'system of laws' and 'perpetual command' (Ferguson 1966: 121).

For the myth of law, the longest footnote to Hobbes is that provided by John Austin. It is a considerable chronological leap now to 1832 when Austin's *The Province of Jurisprudence Determined* was first published to only modest success. It is an even longer leap to the position of dominance which this work assumed and retained for a long time in English Jurisprudence from the later nineteenth century. But Austin is very close to Hobbes and to the tradition of overwhelming order. The Austin secured in English Jurisprudence is well nigh indistinguishable from Hobbes. This is immediately evident in Austin's initial announcement that law is a command of a political superior to a political inferior (Austin 1861-3: 1, 5 - I). This 'superiority...is styled sovereignty', and it entails 'the relation of sovereignty and subjection': an exclusive and independent sovereignty accorded general and habitual obedience, is necessary for 'political society' and law to exist (Austin 1861-3: 170-3, 179 - I). And 'in every society political and independent, the actual positive law is a creature of the actual sovereign' (Austin 1861-3: 313 - II). Although Austin does not follow Hobbes in the concentrated care devoted to foundations, the sole base evoked for his structure is savagery and it is evoked frequently. Austin draws on both a general and existent state of savagery and the 'imaginary case' of a 'solitary savage' which he takes 'the liberty of borrowing from...Dr. Paley' (Austin 1861-3: 82 - I. The borrowing could be from (Paley 1828 (1785): 4-5). This solitary savage was 'a child abandoned in the wilderness immediately after its birth, and growing to the age of manhood in estrangement from human society' (Austin 1861-3: 82 - I). As such, it could not be a 'social man', would not appreciate the necessity of property, would be in total conflict with 'his' fellows, and hence 'the ends of government and law would be defeated' (Austin 1861-3: 85 - I). The savage 'mind' is 'unfurnished' with certain notions essential for society: 'they involve the notions of political society; of supreme government; of positive law; of legal right; of legal duty; of legal injury' (Austin 1861-3: 85 - I). Austin also discovers and adverts often to a general state of savagery which he calls 'natural society' as opposed to 'political society' and which is illustrated by 'the savage...societies which live by hunting or fishing in the woods or on the coasts of New Holland' and by those 'which range in the forest and plains of the North American continent' (Austin 1861-3: 184 - I).

> A natural society, a society in a state of nature, or a society independent but natural, is composed of persons who are connected by mutual intercourse, but are not members, sovereign or subject, of any society political. None of the persons who compose it lives in the positive state which is styled a state of subjection: or all the persons who compose it live in the negative state which is styled a state of independence. (Austin 1861-3:176 - I).

This negative state has none of the robust virtue of, say, Ferguson's unsubordinated Scottish Highlanders. Being a state of nature, it is lawless (Austin 1861-3: 9 - II), and even if it were not:

> Some, moreover, of the positive laws obtaining in a political community, would probably be useless to a natural society which had not ascended from the savage state. And others which might be useful even to such a society, it probably would not observe; inasmuch as the ignorance and stupidity which had prevented its submission to political government, would probably prevent it from observing every rule of conduct that had not been forced upon it by the coarsest and most imperious necessity. (Austin 1861-3:258 - II).

It is the savage which in 'negative' terms gives content to the 'political' and gives content to law as, for Austin, the command of a political superior. Yet Austin does take most eloquent account of a domestic challenge to order which might seem to provide a foundation in addition to savagery, the challenge posed by 'the poor and the ignorant', especially in their misguided propensity to 'break machinery, or fire barns and corn ricks, to the end of raising wages, or the rate of parish relief' (Austin 1861-3: 62 - I). This affliction is attributed to their ignorance of the imperative good of property and capital and its cure lies in a full appreciation of the principles of a supposedly utilitarian ethics, particularly of the Malthusian variety: 'if they adjusted their numbers to the demand for their labour, they would share abundantly, with their employers, in the blessings' of property (Austin 1861-3: 62 - I). Unlike the 'stupid' savage who can only respond to the imperatives of the inexorable (Austin 1861-3: 258 - II), 'the multitude...can and will' come to 'understand these principles' (Austin 1861-3: 60 - I). This will be merely a boon to the law for 'an enlightened people were a better auxiliary to the judge than an army of policemen' (Austin 1861-3: 63 - I). Law is not eventually affected since such things can be resolved in terms of personal knowledge and morals. It is only the irredeemable savage which provides the ultimate limiting case against which law is constituted. One final point is needed to complete the comparison with Hobbes. As we saw, if law were a command, people needed to know of the command in order to follow it. This requirement introduced a dangerous popular element into Hobbes' scheme of things. Austin agonises less over this and simply adopts the maxim 'ignorance of the law is no excuse': 'if ignorance of law were admitted as a ground of exemption, the Courts would be involved in questions which it were scarcely possible to solve, and which would render the administration of justice next to impracticable' (Austin 1861-3: 171 - II). In all, the enlightening of the people can only be an aid to making existent law more effective. It cannot be intrinsic to law. Unlike the elimination of savagery, it cannot be allowed as a condition of law's existence.

Nothing could more aptly reveal the mythic nature of this law than the effrontery of welding it to order in times of its infliction on massive disorder. In the increasing effort to subordinate the Indians, to 'reduce them to civility', law and order were constantly combined not just in opposition to, but as a means of subduing the 'disordered and riotous' savages in their state of lawless 'anarchy', but often with the realization that they may, after all, remain uncontrollable and unpredictable (Axtell 1985: 136-8). This scenario precisely reverses what was the case. European intervention was freighted with the deathly disordering of an ordered situation. Nonetheless, this association of law with order, security and regularity rapidly became general. The violence associated with the establishment of law and order assumed an insignificance in the immeasurability of the violence and disorder of savagery (see *e.g.* Ferguson 1966: 221-2, Meek 1976: 204). For Austin, 'general security' and a 'general feeling of security' are 'the principal ends of political society and law' and these are the antithesis of that 'negative state which is styled a state of nature or a state of anarchy' (Austin 1861-3: 84, 122 - I). The very mind of the savage, as we saw, is 'unfurnished' with the notions of political society and law' (Austin 1861-3: 85 - I). As with the Cyclops 'his thinking is lawless, unsystematic and rhapsodical' (Horkheimer & Adorno 1979: 65). This contrasts essentially with, 'the uniformity of conduct produced by an imperative law' (Austin 1861-3: 159 - I). The colonial situation provides another monumental instance of law initiating and sustaining pervasive disorder even in the pursuit of its pretence to secure order. An abundance of instances can be found also in the more domestic European settings where modern law explicitly confronted and sought to undermine an existing order which was often, in the process, rendered in the terms created for savagery and barbarian despotisms. As a mode of modernity, law was an instrument of far-reaching change integral to the 'tearing down and building up' (Cassirer 1955: ix). But no matter what its visitations of disorder and no matter what the distance between its practice and the perfection of its order, law remains mythically inviolable in its intrinsic equation with order.

Disorder on law's part cannot, then, be located in law itself. The sources of disorder must exist outside the law - in the eruptions and disruptions of untamed nature or barely contained human passion against which an ordering law is intrinsically set. The savage was the concentration of these dangers and the constant and predominant want of the savage was order. Savages had 'no skill of submission' (see Axtell 1985: 271). Ferguson admired them for their lawless minds, for being unable to 'accept commands' and for being opposed to 'subordination', something which could be taken as an exact counterpoint to Austin's idea of law (Ferguson 1966: 84).

A particular and indicative obsession of colonist and *philosophe* alike was the lack of fixity in savage life. Indians could not begin to be civilized until they were in a 'fixed condition of life': 'Their Nature is so volatile, they can few or none of them be brought to fix to a trade' (see Axtell 1985: 141, 160). Lacking resolution themselves, they could not project it onto a world: they 'have none of the spirit, industry, and perseverance necessary in those who *subdue* a wilderness' (see Axtell 1985: 149; emphasis in the original). The savage was a wanderer or related to land in an indefinite communal way - not sufficiently 'removed from the common state Nature placed in it' (Locke 1960: 329, para. 27). In either capacity, the savage had no sufficiently fixed relation to things to support a legal right to them. In the state of nature, confirmed Austin, 'men ... have no legal rights' (Austin 1981-3 - II). The convenient ignorance of the European thence found a 'void' and 'wilderness' in savage climes, a lack of fixed position and tenure, such as to justify and even require the assertion of an 'exclusive right' and the acquiring of 'sovereignty' over them - borrowing here the sentiments of de Vattel, 'perhaps the most widely read of all eighteenth-century authorities on international law' (Curtin 1971: 42-3). For de Vattel and for this so-called international law, it is not simply a matter of when 'a Nation finds a country inhabited and without an owner, it may lawfully take possession of it' but also a Nation may likewise occupy a territory 'in which are to be found only wandering tribes whose small numbers can not populate the whole country', since 'their uncertain occupancy of these vast regions can not be held as a real and lawful taking of possession' (Curtin 71: 44-5). Inadequate production as well as inadequate peopling justified European appropriation:

> For I ask whether in the wild woods and uncultivated wast of America left to Nature, without any improvement, tillage or husbandry, a thousand acres will yeild the needy and wretched inhabitants as many conveniencies of life as ten acres of equally fertile land doe in Devonshire where they are well cultivated? (Locke 1960: 336, para. 37).

Old myths, it seems, were thereby sustained:

> Settlement in a new, unknown, uncultivated country is equivalent to an act of Creation. When the Scandinavian colonists took possession of Iceland ... and began to cultivate it, they regarded this act neither

as an original undertaking nor as human and profane work. Their enterprise was for them only the repetition of a primordial act: the transformation of chaos into cosmos by the divine act of Creation. By cultivating the desert soil, they in fact repeated the act of the gods, who organized chaos by giving it forms and norms. Better still, a territorial conquest does not become real until after - more precisely, through - the ritual of taking possession, which is only a copy of the primordial act of the Creation of the World. In Vedic India the erection of an altar dedicated to Agni constituted legal taking possession of a territory. (Eliade 1965: 10-11).

Likewise, 'the English navigators took possession of conquered countries in the name of the King of England, new Cosmocrator' (Eliade 1965: 11).

Law becomes generally and integrally associated with the settling of the world. Blackstone provides a most significant account in his *Commentaries on The Laws of England*, first published between 1765 and 1769 (and amended by Blackstone up to the sixteenth edition of 1825 which I use here). Although it is customary to portray Blackstone as the supreme systematizer and popularizer of English law, his originality has been denied more than extolled (*cf.* Lieberman 1989:31-3, Milsom 1981). Unfair as this assessment may be for his work in general, what is important about his account of law and the settlement of the world is that it is, style apart, so unremarkable. It reflects and encapsulates the thought of the age and brings it to bear on the creation of law. It is to be found at the outset of the second volume of the *Commentaries* dealing with property. 'There is', he begins, 'nothing which so generally strikes the imagination, and engages the affections of mankind, as the right of property' (Blackstone 1825: 1 - II). He then sets out 'the original and foundation' of the right of property, proceeding by way of *Genesis* and the pervasive dominion 'the all-bountiful Creator gave to man' to the 'state of primeval simplicity: as may be collected from the manners of many American nations when first discovered by the Europeans; and from the ancient method of living among the first Europeans themselves' (Blackstone 1825: 2-3 - II). Property was then held in common and the only personal element in property was the holding of things for immediate use. 'But when mankind increased in number, craft, and ambition, it became necessary to entertain conceptions of more permanent dominion' (Blackstone 1825: 4 - II). The result was first a transition from the 'wild and uncultivated' nations to a pastoral existence when the 'world by degrees ... grew more populous', whence it 'became necessary' to resort to 'the art of agriculture' and for this private property was found to be essential:

> Had not therefore a separate property in lands, as well as moveables, been vested in some individuals, the world must have continued a forest, and men have been mere animals of prey; which, according to some philosophers, is the genuine state of nature. ... Necessity begat property: and in order to insure that property, recourse was had to civil society, which brought along with it a long train of inseparable concomitants; states, government, laws.... (Blackstone 1825: 7, Vol. II).

This was and remains a common story. Whether or not impelled by an increasing population, the joint arrival of agriculture and property - property not just as things but as the great figure of settlement and order - requires a complex and more intense regulation than the episodic assertions called for in the nomadic or even in the pastoral state; what is required is an explicit, permanently sustained ordering that is law (see Meek 1976: 93, 102-4; Stein 1980: 28, 33-6).

Such an outcome had been refined in advance by Locke. Even if less dire than it was for Hobbes, the state of nature in Locke's view was still savage, uncertain and unstable. These defects were cured by entering into a political or civil society marked by law:

> Those who are united into one Body, and have a common establish'd Law and Judicature to appeal to, with Authority to decide controversies between them, punish Offenders, *are in Civil Society* one with another; but those who have no such common Appeal, I mean on Earth, are still in the state of Nature, each being, where there is no other, Judge for himself, and Executioner; which is, as I have before shew'd it, the perfect *state of Nature* (Locke 1960: 367, para. 87; his emphasis).

The 'Civiliz'd part of Mankind', in contrast, is characterized by 'positive laws' (Locke 1960: 331, para. 30). Then, most famously, Locke ties that entry into political society with the securing of property: 'The great and *chief end* therefore, of Mens uniting into Commonwealths, and putting themselves under Government, *is the Preservation of their Property*' (Locke 1960: 395, para. 124; his emphasis). He immediately proceeds to delineate the rule of law as a response to 'many things wanting...in the state of Nature', as a response, at its most general, to the chaos of merely individual assertions of passion and self-interest.

> *First*, There wants an *establish'd*, settled, known *Law*, received and allowed by common consent to be the Standard of Right and Wrong, and the common measure to decide all Controversies between them. ...*Secondly*, In the State of Nature there wants a *known and indifferent Judge*, with Authority to determine all differences according to the established Law. ...*Thirdly*, In the state of Nature there often wants *Power* to back and support the Sentence when right, and to *give* it due *Execution*. (Locke 1960: 396, paras. 124-6; his emphasis).

This new law is characterised by a unifying strength. For Adam Smith, in his *Lectures on Jurisprudence*, 'barbarous nations' had weak governments unable, for example, to enforce the death penalty for murder, 'the only proper punishment' and the one inflicted in 'strong', 'civilized nations' (Smith 1978: 106, 476). This capacity is elevated in those terms of sovereignty which were earlier traced to Hobbes. To take a famed definition from Austinian jurisprudence:

> If a *determinate* human superior, *not* in a habit of obedience to a like superior, receive *habitual* obedience from the *bulk* of a given society, that determinate superior is sovereign in that society, and the society (including the superior) is a society political and independent. (Austin 1861-3: 170 - I; his emphasis).

Although this position is ultimately sustained in terms of strength, the stronger state does not incorporate the feeble since 'there is neither a *habit* of command on the part of the former, nor a *habit* of obedience on the part of the latter' (Austin 1861-3: 173 - I; his emphasis). Each retains its distinct force, its distinct centre of power and, hence, its own determinacy: 'no indeterminate party can command expressly or tacitly, or can receive obedience or submission: ...no indeterminate body is capable of corporate conduct, or is capable, as a body, of positive or negative deportment.' (Austin 1861-3: 175 - I). 'Every law properly so called flows from a *determinate* source, or emanates from a *determinate* author' (Austin 1861-3: 120 - I; his emphasis).

Austin's consolidation of the idea of sovereignty replicates within modernity the powerful symbolism of the centre. The centre - whether a sacred mountain, the garden of Eden, a city or a temple - was a foundation and a source of creation, the point at which the chaos of pre-creation was ordered or crushed and the point where a transcendentally ordered realm met and conferred 'enduring, effective' reality on the world (Eliade 1965: 18). The centre was thus the very image of the world, the *Imago Mundi*. Law exists by virtue of its 'position' in identification with the sovereign and centre (Austin 1861-3: 2 - I). It takes on the impression of the *Imago Mundi*, affirming the ordered, normal course, often by correcting deviations from that course. The creation and en-forcement of any law is a ritual reassertion of the foundational strength and ordering of the centre (*cf.* Eliade 1965: 2). And what is being affirmed is not just a particular order in opposition to disorder but the very being and force of order itself.

To function in this way, law must sustain a mythic persistence. Savagery is an immediate and obverse support. Without law, there would, for Hobbes and others, be a reversion to the chaos of savagery. For some, however, the disorder of simple savagery was not the only foil. There was also a significantly qualified savagery. Even in 'a territory of considerable extent', wrote Ferguson, where the inhabitants retain their 'warlike and turbulent spirit', they can be ordered by the 'bridle of despotism': and in the later eighteenth century it was becoming a fashion to contrast law with fickle despotisms, particularly of the oriental variety (Ferguson 1966: 103-4). Law was integrally part of and endured as the civilized European order. Outside of this order, there was either the unpredictable arbitrariness of despotism or the inconstancy and mindless hedonism of the simple savage (Ferguson 1966: 93, 95). In law, human projects could be initiated by members of political or civil society and secured in time (see *e.g.* Locke 1960: 344, para. 50). Rousseau combined all elements of the mix: law was needed because 'society must have activities and ends'; law also embodied and sustained what civilization had managed to inculcate so far and it dealt with those continuing assertions of nature inimical to order (Strauss & Cropsey 1972: 542-4). So, returning to Austin, law is not just a peremptory command: it is also 'a command which obliges a person or persons to a *course* of conduct' (Austin 1861-3: 15 - I). 'An imperative law or rule guides the conduct of the obliged, or is a *norma*, model, or pattern, to which their conduct conforms' (Austin 1861-3: 159 - I). Law creates enduring rights and obligations of which the pre-social savage can know nothing (Austin 1861-3: 85 - I). Law's persistence, then, produces a contradiction between law as a command of a sovereign and law as a project, model and obligation, and thus dependent on popular support and adherence. I will outline the mythic resolution of the contradiction towards the end of this essay.

In the meantime, there is another contradiction to be confronted. The process of law's mythic creation in opposition to primaeval chaos does involve that basic identification of law with transcendent order which we have just explored. Yet, modern law also comes into being in a process of change and progression through which it is continually impelled away from the order of origins. It is not tied fixedly to any order and in its constitution it responds to change in 'society'. This part of the myth, which I now explore, is worked out in the narrative of law and progress and the story, as we shall see, is told in such a way as to enable it to be reconciled with the imperative of order. Although the 'progress' invented in this period is different to its later Occidental equivalents, it did provide a vocabulary and general orientation for them.

Law and Progress

There are certain precursors of progress to be sketched in first. Law has to be linked to society, or distinct types of law linked to distinct 'nations', as they were called. The significant ancestor figure here seems to be Montesquieu. The 'laws' whose 'spirit' he sought cannot readily be equated with modern ideas of law but that difficulty has not obstructed his received reputation as the progenitor of the connection between law and society. Montesquieu thought that laws have or ought to have a relation to several shaping factors and 'that it should be a great chance if those of one nation suit another' (Montesquieu 1949:6). He enumerated a considerable number of shaping factors - climate, geography, 'principal occupation of the natives', 'the degree of liberty which the constitution will bear', religion, and so, considerably, on: 'all these together constitute what I call the Spirit of the Laws' (Montesquieu 1949: 6-7).

There were contemporaries and predecessors who made connections between law and society if of a different kind. Both Hobbes and Hume, to take potent instances, equated sociality with a necessary minimum legality (Hobbes 1952, Chs. 14 & 15, Hume 1988, Book III, parts 1-2). Given supposedly obvious circumstances of the human condition - circumstances of moderate equality of power, moderate selfishness and moderate scarcity - the existence and civility of human society must depend 'on the strict observance' of laws securing 'the stability of possession, its transference, and the performance of promises' (Hume 1888: Book III, part 1, para. 6). This equation of a distinct configuration of bourgeois law with universal necessity had no more existent foundation than the assertion that everyone slept between clean sheets but it has nonetheless endured in the mythology of modern law. Neither these contributions nor that of Montesquieu sought to relate different laws to different societies in a scheme or sequence of progression. Montesquieu did, however, outline one influence on law which was to prove momentous in its development by the chroniclers of progression, that is the

> very great relation to the manner in which the several nations procure their subsistence. There should be a code of laws of a much larger extent for a nation attached to trade and navigation than for people who are content with cultivating the earth. There should be a much greater for the latter than for those who subsist by their flocks and herds. The must be a still greater for these than for such as live by hunting. (Montesquieu 1949: 275).

What is more, Montesquieu provided a way of recognizing a diversity of types of law in different settings. Law did not, in this view, simply emerge at some stage and prior to that there was non-law. Even those with the most adverse assessment of savages could attribute some law to them even if it be 'irrational and ridiculous': although 'laws have been justly regarded as the master-piece of human genius...the jurisprudence, the customs and manners of the Negroes, seem perfectly suited to the measure of their narrow intellect', including their inability to create 'regulations dictated by foresight' (Long 1774: 378, Book III). As Long's 'scientific' assessment indicates, the linking of law and society was accompanied by an expansion of the peoples brought into contention, an expansion beyond the previously predominant concern with the American Indian. Indeed, the historical and geographic range of peoples considered by Montesquieu could be seen as a large contribution to the universal sweep which the doctrine of progress inexorably imports.

The mythic notion of movement or progression in society was itself hardly a new one. In the seventeenth century, to take matters no further back, it was usual to associate the variety of people with their dispersal and progressive decline following some original unity. This decline included the gradual loss of law and civilization. Thus, Sir Matthew Hale related such a decline to the effects of environment in *The Primitive Origination of Mankind*, a work whose fame has not matched that of his contribution to law (Hale 1677: 195-7, 200-1). In the first half of the eighteenth century, the direction of movement of societies tended to be reversed with the recognition that the Greeks and Romans as forebears of the European had been savages much like the Indians: so some, at least, could change and progress, and perhaps the savages were not devoid of law and government (see *e.g.* Lafitau 1724: 5 - I).

These various lineaments of a mythic progression coalesced in the second half of the eighteenth century into an explicit relating of law to four sequential stages of the progress of societies conceived in terms of their modes of 'subsistence' - the hunting, the pastoral, the agricultural and the commercial (see Meek 1976). The overall trajectory of these stories remained the same as those idylls of order in which the primordial and savage gives way to the civilized life. There was a rough similarity in the numerous tales of progression but probably the one of most enduring influence was provided by Adam Smith in his *Lectures on Jurisprudence*, a work which even now silently sets the broad terms of the comparative sociology of law. With the progression of societies, law for Smith increased in quantity and complexity and in its distinctness as a social form. As with many of these accounts, the advance of law was tied integrally to the progressive consolidation of property: the 'early age of hunters', as typified by the American Indians, had no property, and hence few laws and an uncivilized legal system (Smith 1978: 16, 102). With the pastoral stage, people are more numerous, there is a greater division of labour, property is more extensive, and 'distinctions of rich and poor' emerge: 'permanent laws' and the expansion of authority are now needed to secure property and the rich (Smith 1978: 202, 208-9). With such 'useful inequality in the fortunes of mankind', the poor could yet be consoled because they lived in a far greater opulence than any savage prince (Smith 1978: 338, 562; see also Locke 1960:339, Chapter V, para. 41). No new foundational impetus is adduced for law's progression into the ages of agriculture and commerce but there are further changes in law. Quantitatively, there is more law and an increasingly stronger central authority. Qualitatively, the simple legal regime of the whole community which characterizes pastoralists gives way to more complex and institutionally separate forms of authority, to legislatures and regular courts (Smith 1978: 204-5). Although the procession of stages, for Smith and its other chroniclers, seems to have been serially supplanting, the progression was still continuously traced back to the state of savagery which remained a constant contrast and point of reference no matter for what stage. I will now look a little more closely at the nature of this progression before bringing matters to a conclusion.

It may seem rash to depart from the admirable work of Stein (1980) and Meek (1976) showing that, for law and for the social sciences, this progression is a type of evolution. Matters seem to be more mixed and, for my purposes, more revealing. For a start, there was hardly that underlying, unitary and unifying dynamic inhabiting the progression which is usually associated with evolution. The impetus for the progression varied greatly with the different accounts of it. In some tales, progress depends on the characteristics of those who progress - 'the more industrious and discerning part of mankind', the more highly educated, or those who increase in 'craft, and ambition' (Blackstone 1825: 4, Riley 1986: 248, Stein 1980: 22). In other versions, or sometimes in the very same version, there was great emphasis on more external factors, such as the increase in population, the greater need resulting from pressure on resources, or conversely, the greater amount of resources available to meet a need. What in one moment were consequences of progress became in another its cause, and *vice versa*. Thus, an increasing sociality results from increasing population or an increasing population results from increasing sociality (see Meek 1976: 163). All of which is mixed with inspiring metaphors of the 'rise' and 'spirit' of society (Meek 1976: 5; Stein 1980: 28).

To labour such incoherence would be little better than facile because there was no coherent evolutionary dynamic involved in the progression. The contrary assertion, to borrow it from Stein, is that the thinkers in France and Scotland who developed the idea of progression 'treated the mode of subsistence as not merely one of several factors affecting the character of a society's laws but as the crucial circumstance which dictated their nature and scope', and on that basis they erected 'a scheme of development' (Stein 1980: 19). Such a notion of 'legal evolution' is presented by Stein in a careful and abundant illustration. There certainly is progression but, as we have just seen, there is no general dynamic giving it identity and effect. Something else is at work. Law is being typologically related to diverse and distinct modes of subsistence. In the 'spirit' of the times, law is identified in simplifying and classifying relation to other things, in 'a coherent pattern', as Stein describes the object of the quest (Stein 1980: 27). Law is thus located and identified in 'the order of things', in an order that springs from within the things ordered (Foucault 1973; 209). Progression becomes a mode of tracing that identify. This can be exemplified in a quotation which Stein provides from Kames' metaphorical journey on the Nile - a Nile whose enormous and inextricable complexities are indicatively reduced to the simple progress of more straightforward domestic streams:

> When we enter upon the municipal law of any country in its present state we resemble a traveller, who crossing the Delta, loses his way among the numberless branches of the Egyptian river. But when we begin at the source and follow the current of law...all its relations and dependencies are traced with no greater difficulty, than are the many steams into which that magnificent river is divided before it is lost in the sea. (see Stein 1980: 26).

This sustained progression emanating from a source in savagery exists within a still foundational order. It is the story of something achieved, not of something still being achieved. What is talked of here is the perfection and completeness of law and what comes before are simply its pale precursors. The chroniclers of law and progression did not see themselves as departing from a foundational equation of law with order. The progression does not supplant the order of things and proceed to identify law as part of a pervasive and encompassing dynamic. The thought was not there to elevate a dynamic of progression into an impelling and cohering evolution. Rather, concern with an actual dynamic of progression was, diverse, inconsistent and almost incidental.

Conclusion

Progression can be an elaboration of order because both are traced to the same constituting source. In 'the order of things', to find the origin of a thing is to locate its being. The opposition between the progression of law and law's order is mediated and the two are united in the origin of a primal and chaotic savagery. Both the progression and the order of law take their being in the negation or denial of this 'state of nature'. There is a double negation involved here. The first step, as Ferguson recognized, is 'to imagine...that a mere negation of all our virtues is a sufficient description of man in his original state' (Ferguson 1966: 75). From this 'negative state which is styled a state of nature or a state of anarchy' is derived, in the negation of it, a 'positive' state of civilized 'subjection', including the determining order of 'positive' law (Austin 1861-3: 222 - I). In the void created by this replete and inviolable double negation, modern law has the capacity to import a mythic order in any civilizing progression. So, as we saw earlier, law's persistence produces a contradiction between law as the command of a sovereign and law as dependent on popular support and adherence - law as project, model and obligation. This contradiction is mediated through law's relation to savagery: since in both these situations law is created as a negation of the savage state, these dimensions are thus created the same and law is unified.

The negative constitution of law denies any affirmative measure against which the effectiveness of law's relation to order can be tested. The element of custom in pre-modern law tied law intrinsically to an effectiveness in its operation. But custom becomes reduced to a peripheral category set in opposition to law through its association with the savage and with those domestic remnants of a recalcitrant past yet to be transformed in modernity. The transcendent and reflective contents of a natural law having the comprehensive consistency of the godhead is eliminated through its union with an old order. And secularized natural law becomes subject to the self-sufficient determination of positive law. Such law, being constituted simply in terms of what it is not, can be self-contained and self-presenced. Change becomes a refinement of legal order and contributes towards its perfection. In its being without restriction, law can now do anything. An infinite capacity for change - law changing itself and effecting change - is associated with order. This enviable instrument of rule is presented in more spectacularly virtuous ways as the rule of law - for law to rule, it must be able to do anything. The incredulous cannot definitively attribute shortcomings to a law constituted in negation.

3
Constitutions and Governance in Africa: A Prolegomenon[1]

Yash Ghai

Introduction: The Constitution That Came in from the Cold

The present crisis in Africa is widely regarded as the crisis of the state, which has always been perceived as the key player in African development. The state achieved this centrality because there has been no realistic alternative to it as the mobiliser, organiser and manager of resources. On a political level, it was regarded as crucial to the task of national integration and the maintenance of law and order. It also performed an important role in mediating between the local and international economies. This pervasive instrumentalist view prompted the building of state institutions and the burgeoning of its bureaucracy. State building, however, focused on technical aspects such as strengthening the reach and capacity of the administration, bureaucratic training, new management styles, and the incorporation of peasants and co-operatives into the structures of the state, etc. This technocratic approach suited both the new ruling groups in Africa, foreign states, and international political and economic organisations.

Relatively little regard was paid to constitutions, the law being viewed instrumentally as an adjunct to economic modernisation. Nonetheless, the politics of constitution-making were not unimportant in the run up to independence. Constitutions were frequently burdened with the settlement of all kinds of social, political, ethnic and economic problems whose settlement became the *sine qua non* for the granting of independence. This sometimes resulted in prolix and complex instruments. There was an air of unreality about this process and the resulting constitutions in that those who initially had the power to impose particular provisions (minority groups, the metropolitan state) would subsequently have little power to enforce them. For the most part constitutions became merely *rites de passage*. The leaders who inherited colonial power set about undermining both their overall legitimacy and specific provisions in the name of national sovereignty, centralisation and modernisation. Post-independence policies further eroded the autonomy of constitutions and their schemes of governance. Foreign economic and political interests acquiesced in this process because they found it convenient to deal with an authoritarian executive untrammelled by the uncertainties of parliamentary supervision or the complexities of federalism. Nor did the academic community show much interest in the constitution or the law. Legal academics who tried to put law on the agenda of development studies were themselves influenced by modernisation or Marxist theories, neither of which had much time for law as process or value.

Independence constitutions were rapidly dismantled or ignored in favour of political systems which emphasised the authority of the president at the expense of parliamentary and judicial institutions. Today, as African economies collapse and states are threatened with fragmentation, the blame for these failures is placed on authoritarian and undemocratic regimes. It is argued that such regimes cannot provide the fair and calculable environment necessary for economic development, and that corruption squanders scarce resources, distorts consumption patterns, and discourages private initiatives and enterprise. The lack of accountability of the government and the public service results in poor policy and inefficient administration. The elimination of these undemocratic, anarchical and inefficient systems is consequently necessary for proper social and economic development. This approach passes under the name of good governance. Its proponents claim that governance is different from government or administration in that it encapsulates political values and processes likes pluralism and accountability missing from earlier conceptions. Central to the securing of good governance is the constitutional order. Thus in the international community there is much talk of human rights, multi-party systems, fair and internationally supervised elections, strong and independent judiciaries, and efficient and responsible administration on the foundations of effective constitutions and laws (for the clearest statement of this position see World Bank 1991). African governments have reluctantly and partially been forced to yield to these demands (which to be fair, also reflect the wishes of most of their own citizens). The Constitution has come in from the cold. The state and its processes are, yet again, to be refashioned from the superstructure of a constitution. Can it be done?

Unfortunately there is no adequate theory of the African constitution which may help us to answer this question. The purpose of this chapter is to provide a framework within which such a theory might be developed. I look first at theories that help explain the role and operation of liberal and communist constitutions in order to explicate factors that govern the influence of constitutions and their functions in different socio-economic systems. This comparative approach is useful because African constitutions have been influenced by both liberal and communist political thought and constitutions. I then proceed to an examination of the constitutional experience within the context of the political economies of African countries. I conclude with some general observations about constitutionalism in Africa.

The Theory of Liberal Democratic Constitutions

Liberal Western constitutional theory has been fully articulated. Basically, it is the theory of the social contract. Fundamental concepts of authority, jurisdiction, rights and obligations, representation, obedience and resistance, accountability, and so on have been developed within a contractual framework.[2] Although the terms of the contract that give body to the constitution may vary between the key ideologies of the modern Western state (reflecting the contingencies of the times), its underlying premise is the separation between state (as the apparatus of government) and civil society (representing social and economic institutions and processes autonomous of the state) (Shils 1991). Captured in the concept of constitutionalism or the rule of law, it is premised on the belief that the primary function of a constitution is to limit the scope of governmental power and to prescribe the method for its exercise, thereby preserving the autonomy of civil society. In its modern form, the constitution performs these functions typically through the separation of powers, the incorporation of democratic principles, and some form of judicial review. The constitution validates certain fundamental values and, subject to their overriding supremacy, establishes a framework for the formation of government and the conduct of administration. These values are essentially liberal and market related, emphasising individual civil, political and property rights underpinned by the concept of the equality of all citizens under the law. The constitution is thus an embodiment of values and an instrument of neutrality, a marketplace of competing ideas and policies. This was not always so. Liberal values preceded democracy and gave birth to it. There has occasionally been a tension between fundamental values and democracy, but in recent times this has generally been moderated due to a broad agreement on these values. In this century this has been supplemented by a general but tacit agreement on the value of social welfare in mitigating the worst consequences of the market. It is this understanding, a kind of class compromise, that has facilitated western constitutionalism (see MacPherson 1962). There is also a broad public acceptance of the role of courts and other judicial bodies as arbiters of social and political disputes. Consequently, it is claimed that the constitutional order is legitimated by its consensual basis and its protection of political pluralism.

Constitutionalism (or the rule of law) with its constituent concepts of the secularisation, nationalisation, separation and limitation of public powers emerged in Europe as part of the bourgeois revolutions (Neumann 1986). Important roots of constitutionalism lie in the need of capitalism for predictability, calculability and security of property rights and transactions. The concept of general rules was particularly well suited to these aims. The generality of rules prevented discrimination and arbitrary action, prevented the subordination of judges to the legislature in specific disputes while curbing judicial adventurism, and precluded retroactive legislation. In part, the movement towards general rules was a reaction to special privileges and monopolies accorded in royal charters and instruments of incorporation. There is considerable tension between the needs of capitalism in general and the desires of individual enterprises or sections of industry, which modern states resolve in different ways.

The rule of law or constitutionalism reached its apogee in the nineteenth century. This came about not only because capitalism was still competitive, but also because the propertied class had achieved political dominance. This class exercised its dominance essentially through an autonomous and decentralised economy, the state merely providing a legal and political framework. It enabled a relatively neat separation of the state and civil society and it may indeed be a precondition for the rule of law that there is a significant congruence of economic and political power. Since the nineteenth century the rule of law has receded from its high water mark for a variety of reasons: the political need to accommodate new economic and social interests (especially the working class); the broadening of the franchise; the internationalisation of capital and the rise of TNCs and other corporate groups (diminishing the importance of state representative institutions as policy makers) (see Picciotto *infra*) and periodic economic crises that invited state intervention in the economy. These led to a co-penetration of the state and the economy and undermined the regime of general rules through discretion, discrimination and a larger role for the state (Poggi 1978). Despite this it is still possible to talk of constitutionalism in the West, of a search where possible for generalised rules, competitive political systems, independent judiciaries, etc.

The continuing imperative of the rule of law is closely connected with its other major function - as ideology. Both Marxist and liberal scholars agree that the dominant ideology of the liberal economic order is the rule of law. There is little doubt that it is a powerful means for the legitimation of Western regimes, and is carefully cultivated by their rulers. It masks the way in which power is exercised in these societies, it gives the impression of pluralism and competitive political systems responsive to new interests and change, and it emphasises the primacy of state representative and judicial institutions thereby mitigating the appeal of radical politics. Following Marx's analysis of the masking functions of legal concepts and relationships, Poulantzas (1973) argued that legal ideology serves the interests of capitalism by procuring the economic isolation of individuals through emphasising their separateness and autonomy while hiding the dominance of one class over another behind notions of equal and free citizens unified in the political universality of the nation state. Bourgeois legal ideology reinforces the notion that human beings are free and equal, and that the processes and application of the law are autonomous and impartial. The appearance of neutral autonomy is possible because the primary form of subordination is not law itself but social and economic forces which rely upon equal and neutral legal concepts and rules to achieve that effect.

Because of the very power of this ideology, overt behaviour inconsistent with it - on the part of the rulers or the ruled - is likely to be called into question. In this way the ideology acts to restrain official excess and to secure to some extent the liberties and freedoms of citizens (Thompson 1975). For though in its origin the rule of law had little to do with democracy, political freedoms or social justice (and was indeed an instrument of class rule), it has been broadened to encompass them, particularly through the extension of the franchise and the recognition of certain social and collective rights. The rule of law in the Weberian sense of rational-legal administration of a system of rules is in itself unlikely to inspire loyalty. At first its appeal lay in its connection to a market system considered both efficient and just, and more recently its connection with the welfare state. An essential basis of contemporary Western constitutionalism is a social compact between capital and labour under which the market system is accepted within the context of the welfare state.

The Theory of Socialist Constitutions

There is also a well recognised socialist theory of constitutions. In part this takes the form of an attack on bourgeois constitutions. A second aspect, which builds on these implications, provides a rationale for the constitutions adopted by communist states. I have already touched upon some of the principal Marxist criticisms of bourgeois legality. Amongst these are a general criticism of laws and constitutions as instruments of class oppression and domination, and more specifically of the bourgeois legal form (see Poulantzas 1973, Miliband 1969). In traditional Marxian analysis, law is part of the superstructure of a society and serves to support and reinforce the underlying economic structure. Since most societies have historically been class societies, the law has been an instrument for oppressing subordinate classes or groups. As we have seen, the specificity of bourgeois legal forms is that they hide the reality of economic and political power behind the illusion of equality, whether in the economic sphere (the freedom of contract) or the political (universal and equal franchise). The constitutional forms of bourgeois democracy are in fact means towards the domination of society by capitalists. They enjoy various advantages which enable them to acquire control of the apparatus of the state (like ownership of the press, superior access to education and the law and greater resources for political organisation). The separation of powers and institutions is negated by class solidarity as all these institutions are under the control of members of the same class and their purpose is to serve their class interests. The narrow scope of state power also enables them to exercise their dominance over civil society through the economy and other private institutions.

The theory of the socialist constitution is inspired by this view of the law and also by Marxian teleology. This has produced some tension in socialist views of the constitution. On the one hand, law and constitution are decried as instruments of class rule, and their abolition regarded as a precondition for a free and equal society. On the other hand, unlike bourgeois constitutions which (denying the dynamics of their history) emphasise order and stability, socialist constitutions (inspired more by Lenin's perspective than Marx's) espouse as their mission the egalitarian transformation of society. In turn, this requires the dictatorship of the proletariat, the most progressive elements in society with the greatest stake in egalitarianism, to break and appropriate the economic, social and political power of the bourgeoisie. Law and constitution are among the means of achieving this. While the bourgeoisie has for long periods used civil society to dominate the state, the proletariat has little alternative to the use of the state to change civil society, for the communist revolution vests it with political power but does not change the underlying economic structure.

Communist constitutions therefore become overtly authoritarian instruments of class power. The relative weakness of the proletariat as a class and the magnitude of the task it faces lead to the denial of various political and economic rights to the members of the erstwhile bourgeoisie and to the strengthening of the state apparatus. The working class must secure domination over and, if necessary, replace civil society so as to transform it. State power must be unified, so the separation of powers is abandoned in favour of the centralisation of power in representative state institutions. This concentrated monopoly of power in the state body is in turn subject to the supervening authority of the Communist Party, which owes its existence and powers to a mandate higher than the constitution: to history itself.

The socialist theory of constitutions cannot, however, be fairly accounted for by this early form of constitution. Its instrumentalism is governed by Marxian theory of history and dialectics and the ultimate goals of communism (of a classless, egalitarian and participatory society). This means that constitutional arrangements must periodically be altered to reflect new socio-economic realities, and that progress must be made towards the ultimate aim of true democracy and equality. The degree of progress towards these goals is determined by the leadership's analysis of the stage of class struggle. Since the justification for the dictatorship of the proletariat is the presence of 'enemy' classes and their resistance to the revolution, the disappearance or acquiescence of such classes provide opportunities to move towards these Marxian goals. The preambles of socialist constitutions therefore have contained detailed analyses of class struggles and the contradictions that flow from them as part of the framework for the new constitutional order.[3]

It is possible to see a pattern in the changing constitutions of communist states (Kuan 1983, Cohen 1978). In the wake of the revolution, the first constitution tends to be strong on aspiration and weak on institutions since the aims of the revolution are clear but the methods are not. Much institution-building occurs outside the framework of the constitution as the economy is brought increasingly under government control and the political power of the Communist Party is established. The next constitution is often directed towards the consolidation of political and economic progress: it is more detailed, provides for a greater degree of institutionalisation, and sets out more clearly than before the general principles of the economy.[4] It mutes class struggles and emphasises the more technical aspects of management. It is also used more consciously than before as an instrument for the legitimation of socialist principles and policies. Subsequent constitutions travel further along the same path, emphasising the importance of legality and the rights of citizens, the extension of full citizenship to the people, and begin to draw a boundary between state and civil society through the recognition of semi-private economic organisations and markets while paradoxically providing for a full blown state machinery. Kuan (1983: 25) points out that this type of constitution is a response to extremes of repression like Stalinism or the Chinese Cultural Revolution. There is also a tentative move towards the supremacy of the constitution (Kuan 1984). However, no communist constitution has moderated the extra-constitutional status of the Communist Party, its leading role, or the absence of its legal accountability, a factor that has constituted an important contradiction in constitutions claiming to be moving towards greater democracy and legality.

Despite the dismantling of communism in the Soviet Union - which used to set the pace for the others - and elsewhere, the story of socialist constitutions is not at an end. Important changes are taking place in China which will doubtless call for a new constitutional dispensation in the future.

A Comparison of Liberal and Communist Constitutions

While liberal constitutions are not immutable, they emphasise permanence. In contrast, communist constitutions are based on notions of change. Despite this, it might be argued that the generations of communist constitutions reflect essentially similar principles, notwithstanding differences of detail or emphasis. It may therefore be useful to draw some contrasts between western liberal constitutions and communist constitutions.

The aim of the liberal constitution is order and stability, that of the communist (at least in the early stages) the uprooting of old values and social structures in order to transform society. Liberal constitutions give primacy to the individual, socialist ones to the state and co-operatives (as representative of the community). The former (at least in its origin) is a response to the needs of the market, the latter to the imperatives of political control justified in the name of a new economic order in which the means of production are collectively owned. The former tends towards the protection of civil society, the latter towards state domination of it.[5] The two forms of constitution reflect different concepts of power: the liberal a distrust of it, the communist an affirmation of its progressive potential. Partly to protect civil society and partly to ensure fairness in governance, liberal constitutions value pluralism, exemplified in the right of citizens to associate and form parties with which to compete for power and challenge government. Communist constitutions acknowledge (but need not provide for) the supremacy, and frequently the monopoly, of the Party. They also facilitate the transformative potential of political power by abandoning the separation of powers and thus the independence of the judiciary.[6]

Another way in which the two forms are contrasted is through a distinction between normativeness (liberal) and instrumentalism (communist), although it will be clear from my account of the liberal constitution that it continues to have a strong instrumental bias. However, because civil society is an important source of power and the bias of the liberal constitution is towards the market, this instrumentalism is disguised. Values essential to the market are presented as universal norms and assume a detached appearance, above the conflicting class interests in civil society. On the other hand, because communist constitutions are intended to facilitate the transformation of society in pursuit of the teleological view of human destiny governed by historical materialism, their instrumentalism is overt. It is thus possible for the liberal constitution to base its legitimacy upon values (such as civil and political rights) and mechanisms (pluralism) internal to itself and thereby to become a major legitimising device for state and society. The communist constitution (at least in the early stages, when coercion is printed on its face) must seek its legitimacy from elsewhere, namely socialist theory. This places the socialist constitution in a deep contradiction. The source of its legitimacy is external because it is dependent upon extolling the superiority of 'scientific socialism' and the adulation of the Party, and therefore on rhetoric rather than reality. The very emphasis on these external sources of legitimacy demonstrates the secondary and functional nature of the constitution, one not particularly appropriate to legitimacy. It is true that recent communist constitutions do seek legitimacy not only for the constitution but also for the wider political system through provisions for democratisation and legality, but they are still inextricably tied to and dependent on those political systems.

At heart, both types of constitution are a response to national socio-economic circumstances and the aspirations of their ruling classes. The liberal one has developed over a long period of time during which society has fashioned the state more than the other way round, and so the constitution has assumed an aura of naturalness. On the other hand, socialist constitutions represent the storming of the ramparts of the pre-revolutionary state and the transformation of state and society in a 'hot house' fashion through the strength of the state apparatus. This provides transparency of the process of transformation and the exercise of state power, and ties the future of the constitution to the fortunes of the state. But even in the liberal order the acceptability of the constitution is not unconnected with the state management of the economy.

Towards a Theory of African Constitutions

We do not yet have a comparably developed theory of African constitutions. Most of them started life as western liberal style constitutions but, like communist constitutions, underwent rapid changes. Unlike communist constitutions, however, they were less inspired by a teleological view of human destiny. Such theory as exists is of recent vintage and is largely a response to the failure of constitutional orders. Many independence constitutions have been interpreted as compacts between the colonial power and selected local elites, as mere instruments of neo-colonialism designed to accommodate the latter in an otherwise largely unchanged political and economic order. Others have viewed them as charters of liberation and the foundations of new democratic orders. A particular concern of recent literature is an explanation of the failure of the constitutional order, whether based on the independence, liberal style constitution or the innovatory ones introduced subsequently (Shivji 1990d). This work has ascribed principal responsibility either to external or internal factors. Limitations of space preclude a discussion of these perspectives, but I want to pursue and advance a line of enquiry which emphasises the personalisation of power as a dominant constitutional theme for post-colonial Africa. In order to do this, I will provide a brief account of the constitutional orders established at independence using Kenya as a case study to illustrate my general points. This section therefore traces the major changes in the legal structure and organisation of the state in Kenya since its independence in 1963. These were provided in considerable detail in the independence constitution, which also prescribed their power and determined the manner of their exercise (see Ghai & McAuslan 1970). The principal feature of the constitution was a Westminster type parliamentary system. A Governor-General with largely formal powers presided over the system. He appointed the member of the legislature most likely in his view to command the support of a majority of parliamentarians as prime minister, and he in turn decided upon the composition of his cabinet, in whom the power of government was nominally vested. The cabinet operated on the principle of collective ministerial responsibility and was answerable to the legislature, which could ensure its removal from office through a vote of no confidence. The legislature was bicameral, with significant powers vested in the upper house (Senate), which was conceived as a counter-balance to the more populist lower house. This (multi-party) parliamentary system was tied to an extensive system of decentralised legislative and executive powers, in particular to the seven (largely ethnically based) provinces which had previously enjoyed no such power or autonomy. Further restrictions on the powers of the central institutions (and of other public bodies) derived from a wide ranging *Bill of Rights* which, if seriously applied, would have rendered much existing law and administrative practices invalid. The independence of the civil service from political interference was secured by the establishment of an independent public service board with wide ranging powers over it. The Attorney-General and the Auditor-General, with responsibilities for legality and financial probity, were likewise protected. The role of the police (particularly its operational aspects) was insulated from politics. Ultimate responsibility for the supervision and enforcement of this scheme for the division, allocation and limitation of powers and the procedures for their exercise was vested in the judiciary, whose appointment was the task of an independent judicial commission on which judges, who had security of tenure, enjoyed a majority. The amendment of the constitution was made extremely difficult, in some instances requiring a nine-tenths majority in the more conservative and minority oriented Senate.

This system has been subjected to so many modifications that it is presently almost unrecognisable. The first and, in one sense, most important change was introduced on the first anniversary of independence when Kenya became a republic and established the office of the Presidency (*The Constitution of Kenya (Amendment) Act*, No. 28 of 1964). Although the presidency was executive, it was tied to parliament in that the head of government would be a parliamentarian and thus accountable to parliament in person for his government's policy and administration. Although the Constitution was tailor-made in many ways for Jomo Kenyatta, he took little interest in parliament and, except on formal occasions when he occupied a seat on the podium next to the Speaker rather than the front benches, he attended rarely. He also acquired the power to appoint to the public service, including the posts of Attorney-General, Auditor-General, Commissioner of Police and permanent secretaries. The thrust of this amendment was continued in subsequent constitutional legislation, in which the President acquired the power to appoint the Chief Justice and dismiss all judges. Kenyatta was also empowered to remove the disqualification (arising from electoral fraud) of a person from standing for parliament, and to appoint up to twelve members of the legislature. A series of amendments increased his 'security' powers, giving him the right to detain a person for long periods without any charges or a trial without parliamentary or judicial review. These became in the nature of personal powers. His own security of office, although subject to parliamentary pleasure, became entrenched in an amendment that abolished private candidacy for the office. Henceforth all presidential candidates had to be a nominee of a political party. Kenya became first a *de facto* and then a *de jure* one party state (the former by the simple expedient of cancelling the registration of the other major party, and the denial of registration for future applications). Access to the presidency was converted into the gift of the Kenya African National Union (KANU), the one legal party. In his capacity as chairman of that party, the President also controlled its policies and personnel, so that his re-appointment became automatic. These provisions placed the presidency above parliament, the courts or the political process.

From Rational-Legal to Patrimonial Rationality

The powers of the president were intensified by the growing centralisation of power so that, for example, provincial administration became an extension of the president's office. The rapid growth of the public sector, mainly through the establishment of state enterprises, provided additional bases of presidential power. At the same time, further constitutional amendments weakened the rights of citizens: mention has already been made of security powers, detention without trial, and the prohibition of political parties other than KANU. Other amendments weakened the safeguards relating to bail, electoral mispractices and the security of tenure of judges (although this was effectively a formalisation of past practice). New political and administrative processes supplemented these formal constitutional changes. The result was a framework for politics and administration in which power was personalised, there was little or no accountability and the courts were prevented from providing redress to citizens.

Using Max Weber's typologies, one can say that the state established at independence had the characteristics of a rational-legal state, with legality as its underlying principle and major source of legitimacy. The system into which it has been transformed places primacy in the person of the president and corresponds to Weber's model of patrimonialism. Although he was reluctant to commit himself to an evolutionary scheme (these categories being merely 'ideal types'), Weber envisaged a progression the other way, from patrimonialism to the rational-legal state, leading to the growing purposiveness and rationality of the law and public institutions. What has happened in Kenya is the rapid emergence of a patrimonial state on the legal foundations of a constitutionalist state.

Although I use Weber's typology of domination to illustrate the changes in the Kenyan state, I rely less upon a Weberian than a Marxist framework of analysis to explain the shift from one mode of domination to another. Nevertheless there are certain functional relationships between the mode of domination (or the organisation of the state) on the one hand and forms of society and economy on the other that are implicit in Weber's analysis and need to be taken into account since a patrimonial state would appear to be incompatible with emerging economic forms in Kenya.

For Weber, there are several sharp distinctions between the patrimonial and the legal-rational state. The principal characteristic of the latter is that authority is impersonal. It derives from a system of rules, arising in the modern state from a constitution. The powers of institutions and officials are defined and bounded by the law, and do not arise from the personal qualities of the office holder. The obedience of citizens is thus not to individuals but to lawful commands. A patrimonial state, on the other hand, is characterised by highly personal rule. The basis of authority is the overarching power and discretion of the ruler. Weber discussed two versions of the patrimonial state: one, normally in a system of estates, in which the ruler ruled through some form of sharing and delegation of powers, in which the forms of delegation needed to be secured against arbitrary infringements, and which thus promoted notions of binding rules in certain relationships. In the other version, which he called patriarchal patrimonialism, the ruler governed more directly, without any legal limitations on his power. (Although the confederal and clientist nature of Kenyan politics at independence may suggest more an estatist than a patriarchal patrimonialism, the trend since then has been in the latter direction). The wishes, fears and anxieties of the ruler are the paramount determinants of policy and action (consistent with not provoking outright rebellion), with consequent unpredictability. Both rational-legal and patrimonial states rely on a bureaucracy. But the nature of the bureaucracy and its organisation are different in the two systems. In the rational-legal state the bureaucracy is based on rules, which define the office, powers and functions of the bureaucrats. Because its powers and functions are bounded by rules, it is possible both to challenge the decisions of the bureaucracy and to compel it to perform its duties. Rules also ensure the relative autonomy of the public servant (within broad, formally approved policies) from political pressure (including a high measure of security of tenure), and recruitment and promotion are decided on competence and merit. The public servant operates *sine ira ac studio* (without bias or favour), and her decisions have to be fair and reasonable. Public office is a kind of trust, separate from the private concerns of its holder, who is recompensed by a fixed salary, and is not in the nature of private property or a concession. In the patrimonial state, on the contrary, the bureaucracy is an extension of the household of the ruler. There is no sharp distinction between the private and the public (or between the finances of the ruler and those of the administration). The appointment and tenure of officials depend upon the grace and favour of the ruler. His trust and confidence are the key to power and influence and promote the development of court politics, with its intrigues and uncertainty. The powers of the bureaucracy are a matter of delegation from the ruler and their exercise is guided by his (perceived) wishes rather than pre-ordained rules.

The rational-legal state, with its foundations in law, establishes a particularly important functional and symbolic role for the courts, whose responsibility it is to demonstrate the supremacy of the law, maintain the integrity of the system of rules by keeping the administration within its legal powers and give redress to those who have suffered from administrative injustice. Equality before the law is the central value of the rational-legal state. Judges are guaranteed independence through security of their tenure so that they may carry out their responsibilities and functions fairly and impartially. Minimum formal qualifications and professional experience are usually prescribed for holding the office of a judge since the interpretation and application of the law are considered to require both skill and integrity. The autonomy of the judges is enhanced by the presence of an independent body of legal professionals, similarly trained, who provide access for the citizen to the legal system and the courts. The values of the system, especially fidelity to the law and its procedures, are also upheld by lawyers in public service. A formal legal and judicial structure of this kind is incompatible with patrimonialism, since the patriarch claims to be the fount of justice. Judges hold office under the ruler and enjoy no formal independence. The ruler dispenses justice directly or on appeal from his judges. Petitions to him for clemency and generosity substitute for legal writs. He himself is above the law. He is also above any form of criticism. Indeed, criticism of him is equated with sedition or treason.

These modes of domination have, not surprisingly, spawned differing ideologies. The rational-legal state has given rise to the rule of law, a belief in impersonal, impartial and predictable rule that protects the rights of citizens. The ideology of patrimonialism is the greatness and wisdom of the ruler, his goodness, generosity and concern for his people. He is the 'father of the nation', a 'father to his people'. In modern parlance, it is the cult of the personality of the ruler.

Weber used the dichotomy of rational-legal/patrimonialism to illustrate two extremes or pure types of domination rather than to describe real societies.[7] He was well aware of the layers and remnants of tradition left behind by history and the consequent intermingling of modes of domination and ideologies. Nevertheless, he also attributed the rise of particular modes of domination to the needs of the economy, so that the major characteristics of a system are not random but determined and display a degree of consistency. In the present study, I use a similar heuristic device to argue that the trend in Kenya has been away from the rational-legal state as premised in the independence constitution towards the patrimonial, but that the rational-legal has not been completely superseded. Many formal aspects of the rational-legal state still exist and its accompanying ideologies are, to a considerable degree, still persuasive. Nor is it dysfunctional, for without it much of the Kenyan social and economic structure would collapse. It is the dynamics of the interaction between the rational-legal and the patrimonial, the way in which the latter is grafted onto the former, that provides a key to the understanding of the Kenyan system. This study is partly concerned with the way the rational-legal system is manipulated or by-passed to achieve the purposes of patrimonialism. It is also important to realise that many aspects of the Kenyan system like wide scale corruption, tribalism, the plunder of the state and political and economic oppression exist in other systems which are not patrimonial. In Kenya, however, these features are coloured by patrimonialism.

Weber's model does not, however, help us to understand why the Kenyan system has tended to shift from the rational-legal to the patrimonial. The influence of economic forces might provide a clue, but Weber discussed these in the movement from patrimonial to the legal-rational rather than the other way around. The explanation I provide looks to the nature of the state and the purposes to which it has been put. In particular it examines the private accumulation that is facilitated by such a state and the type of politics to which it gives rise. This kind of explanation is not excluded by a Weberian mode of analysis, but belongs more congenially to theories of the state associated with Marxian scholarship.

One reason for the failure of constitutions in Africa is simply that they were expected to carry a much heavier burden than those in the West for example. They were required to foster a new nationalism, create national unity out of diverse ethnic and religious communities, prevent oppression, promote equitable development, inculcate habits of tolerance and democracy and ensure a capacity for administration. These tasks are sometimes contradictory. Nationalism can easily be fostered on the basis of myths and symbols, but in a multi-ethnic society these are often divisive. Traditional sources of legitimacy may be inconsistent with modern values of equality. Economic development, closely checked and regulated during colonialism, also threatens order and ethnic harmony by producing mobility and the inter-mingling of communities in contexts where there is severe competition for jobs amidst scarce resources. Democracy itself can sometimes evoke hostilities as unscrupulous leaders play upon parochialism, religion and other similar distinctions.

This burden was compounded by the nature of Third World polities. Although not unattended by violence, the state in the West had a more organic growth than in the Third World, where it was an imposition, dominated the economy and was instrumental in shaping it. Political factors were consequently relatively more important. In the South political power is harder to control because civil society is weak and fragmented as a result of colonial practices (which have proved congenial to new governments). The Western state also enjoyed relative autonomy from international forces, which facilitated indigenous control over society and enabled power to be diffused and institutionalised to a greater degree. The Third World state owes not only its genesis to imperialism, but even now its very nature and existence are conditioned by contemporary international economics and politics. Hardly in control of its destiny, such a state finds it hard to institutionalise power on the basis of general rule, or to resist encroachments upon rights and democracy engineered by more powerful states and corporations. When Third World states moved to independence the tools of coercion were readily available and made their rulers careless of cultivating the consent of the ruled.

The State and Accumulation

There has been considerable debate on the nature of the state in the Third World. There appears to be general agreement that its role is important in the process of accumulation and reproduction, though disputes rage over who controls the state, the protection of which class is its primary responsibility, and its precise strength *vis a vis* civil society (O'Donnell 1980, Ghai *et al.* 1987). Without going into this controversy, I will refer to the main characteristics of the state necessary to my argument.

(i) Those who accede to state power have at best an insecure base in the economy, which is dominated by foreigners or immigrants. Political leaders cannot therefore allow the market to become the primary agency for integration or allocation, at least not until they have secured dominance over it. In the initial period of independence, state resources are used to establish this dominance (i.e., it becomes in, Habermasian terms, 'the steering mechanism'). This makes evident the interest of political elites to strengthen state institutions while minimising their accountability.

(ii) The use of state resources essentially involves what one may call primitive accumulation. This primarily takes the form of the exploitation of the peasantry, but also of the workers. Compulsory state marketing channels and other forms of state enterprise are frequently used for the former (see Bates 1981), while serious restrictions on trade union rights are imposed against the latter. Most developing countries, whether capitalist or socialist in orientation, are essentially administered economies, where licence is the king and discretion the norm. The role of the state in extracting resources from the countryside and foreign institutions for domestic distribution is crucial. Capitalists seek the embrace of the government, and co-penetration of state and capital is extensive and complex. Markets are the creation of governments whose leaders, not having a secure base in the production or distribution process, are fearful of the free play of economic forces. Multinationals accept that bargains have to be struck with the government and concessions negotiated. Key prices are regulated and controlled. An administered economy is incompatible with generalised norms operating autonomously.

(iii) As the state is the primary instrument of accumulation, corruption is no mere pathology but becomes endemic, woven into the very fabric of the state apparatus. The pressures towards corruption arise not only from economic greed but from the imperatives of political survival, since the primary basis of a politician's support is generally not party or another political platform but clientilism (sustained by regular favours to one's followers). Public control and accountability over that apparatus cannot therefore be permitted. Resistance on the part of the exploited is met principally by coercion, and the state becomes authoritarian as well as unaccountable. The typical political form is a one party system, both because of the fear of opposition and the instability of the system.

(iv) The authoritarian character of the state is its dominant feature. Constant threats to the political hegemony of the ruling group lead to the intolerance of independent centres of authority or power. The state seeks the total subjugation of civil society and permits autonomy only where it is functional to its own purposes. The greater the role of the state in accumulation the less the scope for social autonomy. The right of association is a first casualty, and with it the weakening of the will and capacity of groups in civil society to resist the encroachments of the state. The autonomy of trade unions, churches, co-operatives and professions is seriously undermined, either through incorporation into the state or party structures, or directly. Civil society is fragmented and dispersed and it is in this sense that it is possible to talk of the over-developed state. Unlike in Europe, the state did not grow out of civil society but was imposed from above as a bureaucratic device and was therefore not organically linked to it. In one sense the weakness of civil society may give the appearance of strength to the state, but in the West at least the capacity of civil institutions to exercise various forms of disciplinary control over their members lightens the task and increases the capacity of the state. Indeed, the form of delegation implicit in institutional disciplinary control itself makes possible the rule of law.

(v) While the state is strong in its subjugation of civil society, it is at the same time weak in its capacity to direct the movement of society, whose submission is sullen and resentful. Frequently the only resistance it can offer is through evasion of state diktats and withdrawal from its domain. Because this submission is not through the mobilisation of consent but through coercion (which becomes easier with new technologies of weapons and torture), it is precarious. It thus becomes possible for political adventurers to overthrow a regime without resistance from the people. Indeed it may be the only way to change governments, for the insecurity that governments feel leads them to repress legitimate opposition. Because many political leaders are involved in primitive accumulation and there is not yet a strong or organised peasant or worker opposition to them, class identification is weak and politicians in power tend to rule directly and to share power with as few others as is compatible with maintaining their hold on government. In these circumstances coups, which are merely transfers of power among political elites, are common.

(vi) The fluidity of class relations and the lack of cohesion amongst the dominant classes (compounded by ethnic divisions) lead to and almost require a dictatorial head of government. In one sense he represents the extension of the charismatic leader of the national struggle and inherits the constitutional powers designed for him. Appearing to symbolise the new nation by standing above ethnic and other factions, he seeks legitimacy for the government. He may have the potential to co-ordinate and harmonise the interests of the leaders of ethnic and class factions, but few leaders have filled this role. Fears of his own economic vulnerability and ethnic consciousness fostered by the politics of clientilism prevent him from guiding by example or rising above factionalism. Unable or unwilling thus to assert moral authority, the president seeks wide and untrammelled powers and vast patronage so that ultimately all favours flow, directly or indirectly from him. The consequence is a type of court or patrimonial politics, characterised by sycophancy, intrigues and factions. It is in the interests of those who are in his favour, or seek it, to glorify and pay homage to him in public. Criticism of the president is treated as treason. Access to him becomes more important than rules, the more so because he himself claims and is generally acknowledged to be above the law, which is what he says it is (he is also not wanting in intellectuals who would rationalise these claims for him). Both repression and bounty become selective. But because there is a limit to the favours he metes out (which are not out of his own patrimony but that of the state) and he has to rely heavily on repression or threats of it, his position remains precarious, the political system unstable. The single party, the other characteristic of the African polity, becomes an instrument of control at his disposal, shorn of all the features that are its formal justification.

(vii) The instability of government is aggravated by external factors and it is in its international dimensions that the weakness of the African state is most manifest. It enjoys limited autonomy from the international economic and political system because it is heavily dependent on the outside world for economic and military aid, trade and technology. It is frequently the vassal of a big power and can be held to ransom by international capital. The political fortunes of the country and its prospects for democracy in particular are not always within the control of its people or the government. The rise of authoritarianism in Latin America has been ascribed to collusion among its bureaucrats, propertied classes and foreign capital, whose interests converged on the maintenance of public order, repression of labour and the encouragement of foreign investments and technology. For Africa too it is possible to point to the difficulties of establishing democratic regimes due to the impact of foreign intervention, whether it be the destabilisation policies of South Africa and the United States in Mozambique and Angola, or the support provided for authoritarian regimes (frequently by supplying the means of armed coercion) in Zaire, Malawi and Ethiopia. Foreign powers (and capital) have no principled attitude towards democracy. They are guided by their own interests which, notwithstanding the present vogue for 'good governance', rarely lie in support for democracy since it is easier for them to deal with governments which can disregard popular or worker pressures. In the present conjuncture it suits them to support democratisation, and thus place good governance on the agenda. However, there is no reason to believe that this self-interest will prevail for ever. The contingency of constitutional reform - indeed of the African state - is thus exposed.

(viii) The ideology of constitutionalism has only the most slender of appeals to either the rulers or the ruled. Legitimacy, such as it is, comes from other sources, some of which are antithetical to the rule of law. Closely associated with independence was the ideology of modernisation and development (see Adelman & Paliwala *infra*), in whose names state structures were strengthened and their writ expanded. People appear to regard the promotion of development as the primary task of government which, for their part, justify the aggregation and concentration of power to the detriment of human rights on the imperatives of development. Closely connected ideologies proclaim the supremacy of the party. We have noted the personalisation of power in the president (increasingly the equivalent of the European monarch in the seventeenth and eighteenth centuries, the starting point there for the search for the rule of law). Constitutions and laws are tailored to the hegemony of the Leader out of whose overriding legal powers grows a kind of charisma (even if fear is a major constituent of it) in a neat reversal of the Weberian transition of legitimacy from charisma to law.

(ix) The role of constitutions and laws in these situations becomes totally instrumental, unmediated by processes and procedures. Law itself becomes a commodity that only the state may mobilise and manipulate. Governments regard it as dangerous to allow dominated groups any purchase on the law except as part of careful stage management. Limitations on the powers of the government itself become inconceivable, as on the whole do attempts to enforce human rights. The law is a tool of the government, which inherits much of the colonial legal system, much of which was essentially repressive and vested the administration with wide discretionary powers. These powers are inconsistent with the constitutional norms that are established at independence (and may even formally survive into a one party or military regime). The reality of the legal system is not these constitutional and formally supreme provisions, but the extensive and strengthened legislation carried over from the colonial period. The judiciary is suborned or threatened, the autonomy of the legal profession is curtailed. Sometimes it is convenient to use the processes of the law, suitably tempered, but often it is simpler to proceed without or against the law. Having broken the ability of the legal system to protect the rights and expectations of the people, what method the government uses seems of little consequence. The ethos and ambience of the president and his key advisers produce a predilection for the political or administrative rather than legal approaches. Guilty pleas are so frequently secured that it makes little difference under what provisions of the law a charge is brought, the key factor being the sentence that the government wants. The law continues to be an instrument of control and oppression, used to silence or imprison those disaffected by the regime. Good governance thus requires the rehabilitation of the very concept of law itself.

Conclusion

The liberal constitution in place at independence in many African countries faced challenges from both the political and economic systems over which it was imposed and the underlying legal and bureaucratic systems that were the legacy of colonialism. In the absence of an intellectually strong and politically independent judiciary and a legal profession familiar with the concept of fundamental rights proclaimed in the constitution, the repressive and authoritarian laws that had underpinned colonial authority continued to be deployed. This was central to the establishment and operations of the patrimonial system that developed after independence. The failure to respect the right of courts to review executive actions facilitated the totally arbitrary exercise of lawful authority. Given the dominance of the president over the political system, this resulted in the patrimonialisation of the law. Other aspects of the patrimonialisation of law consisted in the subjugation of the judiciary to the executive and the partisan abuse of prosecutorial powers. More fundamentally, patrimonialism was achieved through the doctrine that the president himself was above the law and could carry out his directives without its assistance.

This reduced the status of law in the eyes of politicians, the bureaucracy and the public. This careless attitude towards the law has undermined the technical basis of constitutionalism, which requires reliance on and obedience to the law. The specificity of law as an instrument of rule has not developed in all societies, even those committed to political liberty and fair administration. The problem in Kenya was not only technical (for example not a single attorney-general had any real understanding of the substance or the process of the law), but also the inconsistency of the rule of law with the imperatives of the political system. The legal system suffered the general corruption of public life. The technical means to its efficient functioning (the reporting of judicial decisions, a reliable system of filing documents and proceedings, a rigourous system of appeal, etc.) were undermined.

As with liberal and communist constitutions, the nature of the African constitution has been determined by the political economy. The liberal constitution of independence thus performed a role subservient to the political and economic imperatives of the post-colonial period. If the colonial period had produced a stronger market system, the steady attrition of the law or the arbitrary exercise of discretionary power might have been checked. Nor have the new leaders shown any predilection for the market. In contrast to the West, the African state has not been dependent on a successful market economy or thus captive to the social forces that control the market. The resources that the state has needed have not come primarily from taxes but through administrative transfers of resources, principally from the rural areas, and from foreign aid. This is why falling agricultural productivity and the withholding of foreign aid have constituted the principal factors in the crisis of the state and of its leaders.

The centralisation of power and the prohibition of political activity outside the sole legal party resemble the approach of the communist constitution. In both cases the aggregation of power has taken place outside the constitutional framework (although perhaps less so in Africa) and the constitutional means of accountability have not materialised. But the African constitution has not resulted in the institutionalisation of power in state bodies or in a well organised political party. A important basis of centralisation in the communist system was the organisation of the economy through collectivisation and central planning. The absence of either this or a powerful collectivist ideology in Africa has facilitated the rise of patrimonialism.

Despite this it is possible to overdo the patrimonialism of the African state, which is clearly of a different kind from that described by Weber, driven by different impulses and rationality, and more a means than an end. The superstructure of the kind of political economy I have been describing can take other forms. Nor is there an inevitability about superstructures. I am sceptical about the possibility of trying to change society from the top down, and the metaphor of the superstructure itself is flawed. The state in Africa enjoys considerable power over civil society. Its economy has little organisational or other resilience. The project of constitutional reform is therefore not necessarily condemned to failure. But it will need to be accompanied by a careful review of the underlying laws and practices that negate the purpose and values of constitutionalism. It will require the institution of wide scale accountability, broader practices of democracy and more transparency. It will need to be sustained by foreign pressures, which often generate major contradictions. And it will have to be buttressed by genuine economic reform since history has shown that a simple reliance on the market will not do. The project must be conceived in more ambitious terms than has so far been the the case or we shall merely repeat the post-colonial experience.

Notes

1 I am grateful to the Ford Foundation (Nairobi Office) for a grant which has enabled me to pursue research on Kenya's constitution, on which this study is based.

2 See Held (1983). The continuing popularity and influence of the social contract concept (as well as its interpretation in contemporary context) is evidenced by Rawls' magisterial study, *A Theory of Justice* (1973).

3 The Preamble to the 1982 Chinese Constitution, for example, states that 'The socialist transformation of the private ownership of the means of production has been completed, the system of exploitation of man by man abolished and the socialist system established... The exploiting classes have been abolished in our country'. On this basis the major priority in the next phase of the revolution is determined to be 'socialist modernisation'.

4 Stalin said of the draft 1936 Soviet Constitution that it 'sums up the distance we have travelled, summarising the achievements already made...and success actually won'.

5 As Kuan (1983) points out, liberal constitutions prevent state interference with private property, while communist constitutions prevent private interference with state property.

6 The ultimate custodian and the final interpreters of the constitution is the equivalent of the National People's Congress. For China, see arts. 62 (2) and 67 (1) of the Chinese Constitution.

7 A few words of caution are necessary about Weber's typologies. It is obvious that his picture of the rational-legal state is overdrawn. There is a considerable degree of myth about the autonomy of the legal system which is fairly central to his model. There is a wide measure of discretion in officials which mitigate the impact of rules and the courts have considerably more room for manoeuvre in decision-making than is allowed in the model.

4

Criminal Justice, The Rule of Law and Human Emancipation: An Historical and Comparative Survey

Alan W. Norrie[1]

Six black men advanced in a file, toiling up the path...; each had an iron collar on his neck, and all were connected together with a chain whose bights swung between them, rhythmically clinking....They were called criminals, and the outraged law...had come to them, an insoluble mystery from the sea....They passed...without a glance, with that complete deathlike indifference of unhappy savages. Behind this raw matter one of the reclaimed, the product of the new forces at work, strolled despondently, carrying a rifle by its middle. (Conrad 1990: 154).

Right can never be higher than the economic structure of society and its cultural development conditioned thereby. (Marx 1968: 320)

Introduction: Law and Human Emancipation

In this paper, I tackle the question of the rule of law from two different but overlapping standpoints. The first concerns an investigation of the nature of legal rule in a variety of different social and political contexts. I look at the 'rule of law' in Western capitalist society, under colonial rule, under neo-colonialism, in the context of national independence and liberation from colonialism, and under state socialism. My argument is that the rule of law develops historically as a form of mediation of relations of power between groups, classes, elites and genders[2], and that the forms that it takes are fundamentally conditioned by the social relations within which it operates. In his *Heart of Darkness*, Conrad expressed the nature of the law between colonised and colonisers in a way that catches the elements both of brute power and of legal definition as unmeaning. The criminal law had come to do the work of naked oppression, and it took the material form of guns and chains, unconnected with ideological forms of legitimation. The 'outraged law' appeared as no more than an 'insoluble mystery from the sea'. In this and other works, Conrad shows the logic of exploitation that underlay and was expressed through the forms of colonial law. These forms mediated social relations based upon outright theft of land and livelihood, and their dictatorial character reflected the basic aim and thrust of colonial policy. Juridical medium and political-economic message enjoyed substantial harmony.

The aim of the inquiry from this standpoint is to provide an awareness of the juridical possibilities available and the structural limitations upon strategies of legal reform in different social contexts. At present, for example, there is much talk of the need for legal and state reform in both Third World and state socialist societies, and it is suggested that the liberalisation of economic, legal and governmental processes will go hand-in-hand towards the achievement of more free and wealthy societies. Yet if we look more closely at the results of economic liberalisation, which forms the context within which new legal forms are to be generated, the increasing polarisation of wealth which it entails leads to the need for more, not less, authoritarian political and legal regimes. Kagarlitsky (1989) has formulated the term 'market Stalinism' to encapsulate this politico-economic phenomenon in the former state socialist societies of Eastern Europe, and it may well transpire that a parallel, if distinct, development occurs in the Third World as a result of the imposition of structural adjustment packages. At the moment the talk is all of democracy and better government, but the overall context is one of increased economic oppression which is more likely to be met with the violence of Western-installed or backed puppet governments than with increased legal freedoms (Shivji 1990e).

In looking at the law in this way, my aim is not to argue for the inevitability of increased authoritarianism, or for the hopelessness of using law as a mechanism on behalf of the poor. Those who suffer the worst kinds of exploitation find their own ways of fighting back, and law can constitute a medium for the articulation of their demands. Law can constitute a form of mediation of conflicting social relations as well as a means of articulating the unsullied wishes of those with power and wealth. Nonetheless, it is important to understand, as well as to struggle against, the deep-seated structural tendencies inherent in many social contexts today towards the authoritarian and the dictatorial.

On the other hand, there are some areas of the world where the recent past has seen not a closing down of social and juridical freedom, but an opening up, and it is important to understand the dialectic of law and social context in these situations too. Here, one can cite the examples of Eastern Europe and the development of significant political and legal freedoms, although this may represent rather an interlude between two social systems (state socialist and underdeveloped capitalist) with distinct but parallel authoritarian tendencies rather than a long term trend. One can also cite a number of underdeveloped countries such as Cuba, Nicaragua and Mozambique where governments have sought ways of emancipating their peoples with important consequences for the development of legal forms.

This leads me on to the second standpoint from which I wish to understand the rule of law. I have thus far used the term in an open and comparative way to talk about the shape of legal rule in different societies, but there is a more conceptually specific usage of the term which owes its provenance to the Western liberal conception of a *Rechtsstaat*, a 'government of laws, and not persons'. This idea trails important claims of virtue concerning human liberty and liberation, but has been subjected to sustained critique by critical legal scholars in the West over recent years. One significant element of this criticism has involved an attack on legal formalism, and an interest in alternative ways of both resolving disputes and running societies. This approach holds up the 'antithesis' of informal popular justice to the 'thesis' of legal formalism. A second aim of this paper is to consider the way in which we may understand the concept of popular justice as an alternative to legal justice. I return to this point in the conclusion to this chapter, although my argument is presaged in the prefatory quote from Marx. Whatever the ultimate attractions of popular justice in a fully liberated society, I will argue that the forms of socialist societies that have emerged thus far have not had the social and economic basis on which it makes any sense to imagine popular participation and justice occurring unmediated by law. Thus the dynamic of this chapter is provided by the juxtaposition of a descriptive and empirical analysis of the rule of law (understood in the broader sense of legal rule) in a variety of contexts, and the more political and evaluative Western liberal conception embodied in the concept of the *Rechtsstaat*. My argument is, against liberalism, that it only makes sense to consider the latter usage within the context of the former analysis.

Criminal Justice in Historical and Comparative Contexts

In this section, I review the basic character and shape of criminal justice systems in a variety of modern societies. The discussion is inevitably schematic, but the aim is to consider the forms of law developed within a number of different contexts in order to consider the nature of the concept of the rule of law in a transhistorical and conceptual way.

Criminal Justice and Capitalism

Capitalist criminal justice emerged out of the struggle over enclosures and the protection of mercantile property and commerce at the end of the 18th and beginning of the 19th centuries. On both the land and in the merchants' yards, the struggle between the social classes took the form of a struggle over the definition of right. For the emerging bourgeoisie, law had to be defined in terms of an absolute entitlement to property, be it dead timber or the sweepings of tea or sugar in a yard. An 'objective' theory of absolute property right emerged as a result of the commodification of property, to which was appended a subjective theory of individual responsibility. Free individualism and inviolate property right were the key ideological figures of Enlightenment criminal law thinking (Hay 1975a; Thompson 1975; Foucault 1977; Pashukanis 1978; Norrie 1990, 1993).

In Britain, these legal forms were given practical substance as bourgeois power developed under the aegis of the *ancien regime* (Thompson 1975; Corrigan and Sayer 1986) but were more consistently created under the reforming Benthamite practices of lawyers like the English Criminal Law Commissioners in the 1830s and 1840s. The aim of a general codification of a rational, individualistic system of law foundered upon the reactionary opposition of senior judges (Radzinowicz 1948) but became the informing principle behind a series of piecemeal reforms throughout the century and beyond (Cross 1978). An essential element in bourgeois criminal law was its abstraction of the concept of individual responsibility from the social conditions of individual agency. For example motive could be used as a socio-economic claim rather than a legal category in the case of theft occasioned by hunger, or a directly political category in the case of claims of right or 'good motive' (*eg* a claim of ancient entitlement to wild game on enclosed land: Hay 1975b). The fundamental separation of motive from intention (mens rea) and will (actus reus), and the demoralisation of the concept of recklessness (Norrie 1992) secured the formal depoliticisation and 'neutrality' of the legal forms. Henceforth, the legal forms would lay claim to a universality of rightfulness on the basis of a general individualistic social consensus to which the only alternative was 'anarchy'.

Accompanying the creation of these legal forms, and making them possible, there was a process of socio-political pacification of the growing working class through the building of institutions of social control such as the police and the courts (see generally Corrigan and Sayer 1986). These bodies were initially established by force (Silver 1967; Storch 1975; Foster 1974) but the process of economic co-optation made possible by Britain's pre-eminence in manufacture and world trade meant that by the end of the century, social relations were characterised by a significant degree of cross-class consensus,[3] a fact revealed by the marked decline in the occurrence of crime (by now a stable juridical, no longer political, category) in the century's second half (Radzinowicz and Hood 1986). The establishment of relative consensus at home was based upon Britain's economic primacy on the world economic stage, and particularly drew upon the transfers of wealth from abroad made possible through imperialist expansion. This wealth, together with the imperialist project itself melded together the social classes in Britain (Norrie and Adelman 1989; Semmel 1960; Garland 1985) at the same time as it divided and conquered overseas.

It was this social process of relative cross-class consensus on the basis of expanded domestic wealth that permitted the stabilisation of juridical forms and institutions. A stable working class could be individualised and juridicalised according to legal doctrine. However, it has always only been possible to achieve such a consensus to a certain extent, as is revealed by the consistent existence of a 'two tier' system of justice; one for public presentation, the other for routine usage for lower class defendants (McBarnet 1981; McConville and Mirsky 1988). It is also contingent upon the existence of domestic political and economic policies which do not put too much pressure upon it. If a government too openly attacks the poorest sections in the society or even the relatively well off members of the 'labour aristocracy' (in Britain in the 1980s: miners, printworkers), the social consensus comes under threat as, in the ensuing conflict, do the individualistic legal forms predicated upon it. In their place, authoritarian measures are adopted without respect for individual rights . In this process, it is often the consequences of empire, from near (Ackroyd 1977) and afar (Hall 1977), that are brought back home, but the structural cross-class alliances permit one to talk of a strategy of 'consensual authoritarianism' at play within the metropolitan centre (Norrie and Adelman 1989). Ex-colonial populations, relocated in the interests of capital accumulation, become the most oppressed sections of the domestic working class, the most likely to rebel, and the most likely to be subjected to colonial style prejudice and authoritarian policing (Institute of Race Relations 1978; Hall 1978; Sivanandan 1982; Davis and Ruddock 1990), with the agreement of important sections of the domestic labour movement and its political spokespersons.

Whatever the level of conflict within the Western capitalist society, it is clearly the case, particularly when one compares such a society with a 'developing' Third World society (Ghai 1986) that the measure of social consensus available keeps the consensually oriented framework of abstract juridical rights and individual safeguards more or less afloat. These forms ultimately owe their shape and logic to the process of commodity formation and exchange (Pashukanis 1978), but their actual instantiation within the legal system is produced by the combined effects of a number of integrative social class mechanisms operating within the society. It is these rather than any intrinsic 'Western legal spirit' that enables the state to rule through formal juridical mechanisms and thereby to guarantee the existence of *rechtsstaatlich* forms and principles, insofar as these exist within the Western polity.[4]

Criminal Justice Under Colonialism: The Example of India

Imperialism and colonialism affected huge sections of the globe, including entire continents. They were and continue to be practised in varying ways by many different, primarily European powers. It is therefore wrong to imagine that there was one kind of colonialism or one kind of colonial criminal justice system.

However, the colonial and imperial enterprise was structured by a set of common economic and political goals which circumscribed the operative sphere of difference. Economically, the aim was either mercantile wealth through import and export, or the extraction of profit from the colonised people through land rent, farming, mineral extraction and other industries. Both aims were essentially exploitative, with the former corresponding to the dominance of mercantile capital and the infancy of industrial capitalism, and the latter to the late nineteenth century period of the dominance of finance capital, although the earlier forms of exploitation were also taken up in the later period.

Because the economic intention was exploitative, the political thrust of colonialism was oppressive, authoritarian and often dictatorial. Imperialist powers sought to impose economic goals, plans and strategies on native populations that were resisted because of their consequences. In British India, the East India Company-state imposed the import of British cotton products upon the Indian market, wiping out in the process the indigenous manufacturing capability with the severest consequences for the economy of the Bengal region (Pieterse 1990; McLane 1985). At the same time, they sought to transform the system of land tenure in the direction of commodification and monetarisation (Stokes 1959; McLane 1985; Spear 1965). Both strategies generated severe disruption of established social relations and considerable disorder, which was then combatted by authoritarian modes of social control.

In connection with the reform of land tenure, the old style feudal landlords (*zamindari*) were squeezed out and replaced by a new rentier class demanding increased rents. A new emphasis on the productivity of land undermined the village way of life and in particular the class of village watchmen (*chaukidars*) who had held land free of charge in return for social control services (Spear 1965; McLane 1985). The increasing demands for rent in their turn forced the eviction of many tenants, the further marketisation of available land and the development of a class of landless peasants, often in conditions of near or actual starvation. The emergence of this class, combined with the erosion of the old controls, produced a serious 'law and order' problem, most evident in the growth of banditry (*dacoitry*) in the late eighteenth century. Colonialism itself thus created the crises of control which it then sought to resolve, according to the forms and institutions it had imported and imposed (Fisch 1983; McLane 1985; Arnold 1985a; Gordon 1985).

The criminal justice strategy of the British was a curious mixture of Western ideas adapted to the particular problems of ruling a colony of oppressed people. Spear (1965: 101) wrote that the British established two innovations in India: 'One was the rule of law which was outside current Indian experience and related to newfangled courts and therefore not taken seriously....The other was the introduction of English landlordism'. The two were connected, both in the forms the criminal justice system took and the functions it was to perform. In place of the old watchman system, the British established a district based bureaucratic police force run by British senior officers, but with the lower ranks drawn from the natives. This force had no legitimacy with the local people and was largely unsuccessful in combating crimes that required the active participation of the population to suppress. The *dacoits* were often quite brutal in their actions, but they were drawn from the villages, and the police were not. Imposed from without, the police were seen as an oppressive force; which rapidly succumbed to corruption and behaved brutally within the community (McLane 1985; Arnold 1985a, 1985b; Freitag 1985).

In this context, the British approach to the 'rule of law' was more double edged than contemporary ideologues like Curzon and Fitzjames Stephen would have admitted. On the one hand, they extolled it against the existing Islamic law because the latter left a substantial amount of power in the hands of the victims of crime and was filled with loopholes through which the accused could escape (Fisch 1983); on the other hand, they relied heavily upon dubious practices such as the creation of networks of spies and informers (Freitag 1985), whose testimony was then manufactured by the authorities to suit their requirements. There thus emerged the so-called 'approver's testimony' (Amin 1987), an early and particularly brazen forerunner of the 'supergrass' system employed in Britain and Northern Ireland in the 1980s. Equally, the British were not above the imposition of draconian sanctions against entire villages thought to be harbouring *dacoits*. Nor were they necessarily opposed to what they officially labelled brutal Islamic sanctions such as the severing of limbs, or the exemption of certain castes such as the Brahmins from the law if these were thought necessary for social control (Fisch 1983).

Coupled with these deformations, there was an emphasis upon the rule of law that was genuine because the rule of law was itself an effective oppressive mechanism in the colonial context. As in the metropolitan centre, the rule of law meant, at least in theory, certainty of conviction according to systematised rules. The old Islamic system, just like that of the European *ancien regime*, was inefficient and unreliable. The bloodiness of the Islamic sanctions was propagandised by the British as a reason for discarding it, but in place of the severing of a limb for theft, they introduced capital punishment in public into the village for the first time. The introduction of the rule of law meant a more, not less oppressive system, valuing the limbs of its subjects much more dearly than their lives (Fisch 1983).

This early strategy worked on the assumption that a sufficient dose of Benthamite radicalism would transform and Westernise Indian social and economic relations, and lead to the assimilation of Indian to Western ways (Stokes 1959). It reckoned without the problems of enforcing a transition that lacked organic roots or the opposition that the policy's contempt for Indian values engendered. These ultimately gave rise to the Indian Mutiny/Rebellion of 1857, combining popular and aristocratic resentment to British rule. Although ruthlessly put down, the British thereafter lacked confidence in their ability to change India, and instead sought to rule through existing cultural forms such as the caste system (Pieterse 1990). In the process, the solidification and objectification of social groups became the basis for a new phase in criminal justice practices. Whereas prior to 1857, the British had seen hill peoples and others who were regarded as 'problems' such as gypsies as ultimately assimilable (Gordon 1985; Brandstadter 1985), thereafter, they increasingly drew upon the old idea of the 'criminal tribe', a tribe that was biologically or racially irredeemably criminal (Yang 1985; Nigram 1990). Just as an earlier generation of lawyers had drawn upon current European ideas of crime control, so this generation drew upon contemporary ideas in the shape of the determinist theories of criminological positivism. As these ideas led to legislation against the habitual criminal in the West, so it led to the *Criminal Tribes Act* 1874 in India, under which millions of people were criminalised, forced to live in particular settlements, and not allowed to move without passes. Was this the forerunner of the pass laws introduced to regulate labour in twentieth century Africa (Van Onselen 1976; Shivji 1982; Cohen 1986)? One effect of objectifying the problem in this way was to legitimate sometimes brutal violence against the outcast group (Gordon 1985).

Meanwhile, the *dacoit* problem had been more or less suppressed, but the old *Thuggee* and *Dacoity* department of the Indian police had a new role to play in the suppression of popular resistance, this time in the shape of the growing nationalist movement in India. It comfortably transferred its methods of surveillance from the proto- to the self-consciously political, becoming a Criminal Investigation Department with the role of policing protest against foreign rule. Policing India was always primarily a matter of collective rather than individual crime. As resistance to the British became overtly political, so too did the role of the police (Freitag 1985).

I have dwelt upon the example of India because I believe that many similar or parallel developments in the field of criminal law and criminal justice could be seen in other colonial contexts. Literature in this area (Sumner 1982) has rightly stressed the relationship between the political and economic interventions of colonialism and the resulting legal systems. In nineteenth century India there was an attempt to turn the colonised, pre-capitalist social formation into a wealth-generating enterprise according to Western conceptions of the market and market relations in a situation where those relations were actually underdeveloped by the metropolitan centre. This in turn provided colonial criminal law with its particular tasks of controlling land, labour, politics and markets in the face of hostility generated by colonialism itself. In the African colony of Tanganyika in the twentieth century, to take another example, it was the attempt to regulate semi-proletarian labour on white farms (Shivji 1982) and to control the peasants' use of, and access to, the land (Sweet 1982) which gave the law its specific form and content. In both, however, it was a radical, alien, and oppressive economic policy which generated a criminal justice system based on authoritarianism, cruelty, and, where necessary, dictatorship. The rule of law in this context meant the certainty of a severely punished regimen of crimes with scant regard for the rights of the criminal (Freitag 1985): the imposition of an 'outraged' law, as Conrad calls it, according to a 'mysterious' socio-economic logic.

Criminal Justice and Neo-Colonialism

In the neo-colonial context, the Western style concept of the 'rule of law' is either radically deformed or non-existent. The neo-colony often operates at the interface of naked violence and the most rudimentary of legal safeguards. The latter often serve only as a patina of respectability for the assuaging of foreign criticism in order to guarantee foreign support. In Central America, some states shift between outright army rule and right-wing civilian government as the requirements of political power and external symbolic 'persuasion' dictate. The distance from the one to the other is frequently small. In this context, the rule of law is primarily for ideological consumption, and where it has a minimal substance this is indicative more of the security of a political and economic elite than of the slow beginning of legality and democracy. It is one thing for an army and business elite to rule directly through naked repression, but it is a deeper mark of its power if it can distance itself from such repression through legal 'normalisation' and say that 'We have the power not to use the power, in order to leave room for people to participate' (Jones 1990).

From this point of view, the achievement of a 'sphere of criminality', a sphere of legally constituted and processed deviance as opposed to a system of organised and freelance death squads, can be seen as an index of the level of consolidation of elite power. Where an elite's position is seriously threatened by the poor or by their organised groupings, it will licence clandestine killings in order to terrorise the opposition. Where its power is more stable, it can permit a sphere of political and juridical power with a measure of autonomy from its most direct interests. Thus Anderson (1990), writing of Thailand in the 1980's, was able to contrast the experience of military dictatorship with the emergence of a political sphere as evidence of the consolidation of power of by an emergent local bourgeoisie. One indicator of this change was the enthusiasm for political murder among the Thai elite as they struggled amongst themselves for access to the patronage that went with democratic office. Individual elite crime gained its significance in a situation where a measure of political stability had, for the time being, rendered army rule and naked repression redundant.

Similarly, this connection between the consolidation of political power and the juridification of violence can be observed in Calathes' (1990) account of elite politics and criminal law in Jamaica. In the 1970s under the two party system, elite groups struggled for control of the streets in order to win power in increasingly violent elections. Both sides armed their supporters to defend themselves and to attack their opponents. In power, and in order to defend its members, the People's National Party (PNP) then passed draconian legislation to criminalise the use and possession of firearms. The political use of guns thus passed into the realm of the criminal, at the hands of those who had previously instigated their use, and the violent political conflict was redefined as a matter of criminality, of the rule of law and, of course, order. In this process of criminalisation, the most repressive measures were targetted against the lowest classes (which had supported the PNP) while the political gangsters of the 1970s effortlessly transformed themselves into the armed drugs barons of the 1980s. Violence in Jamaican society never went away, it moved from the terrain of the political to that of the criminal as the Jamaican elite threw away the ladder on which it had climbed into power.

These examples reveal the political instability of the labels of law, crime and criminality in the neo-colonial context. Where political power coalesces, violence is sidelined as criminal. It was argued above that in the West, the establishment of a politically neutral, technical law of crimes was itself a political achievement, and that this was possible on the basis of cross-class agreements which generated political stability. The neo-colonial contexts we have examined thus far represent the mirror image of this picture, for the stability of the Western forms is gained by draining the neo-colony of its resources. The underdevelopment of the neo-colony through the servicing of foreign debts keeps the West economically, and therefore politically, afloat. For this reason, the instability of the political-legal divide in the Third World neo-colony is the organically underdeveloped twin of the successful, *rechtsstaatlich* West.

Not every neo-colony is thus stripped of legality and legitimacy. The essential feature of the neo-colonial social order is the transfer of political power to an indigenous social elite within the former colony as a means of preserving the economic interests of the erstwhile colonial rulers while simultaneously permitting the general penetration of capitalist relations of production within the society. Colonialism generally was obliged to train up a small native middle class of administrators and teachers to help run the colony, and this small educated group was then able to articulate the general grievances of the colonised and to lead popular movements for national independence. Schooled in Western ways and separated from the majority in position and life-style, this middle class could then be co-opted as a compradorial class operating on behalf of Western economic interests, under an ideology of nationalism, modernisation or even socialism.

Ghai (1986) has argued that it is the underdeveloped nature of the Third World neo-colony that leads to its adoption of non-

rechtsstaatlich ideologies to legitimate its authoritarian rule. The material and organic bases for consensus, and therefore a measure of 'rule of law', do not exist in the underdeveloped society. The new ruling class cannot tolerate opposition in a situation of heightened volatility brought about by wholesale poverty and initial high expectations of change. At the same time, the market cannot be relied upon as the primary allocator of materials and resources. An overdeveloped state, compensating for an underdeveloped economy, must take an interventionist role in the organisation of social relations from the top down (Alavi 1972; Saul 1974). The one-party state operating under a nationalist or socialist ideology and ruling the law is a paradigmatic consequence of underdevelopment. Thus even in a country such as Tanzania, which developed under an Africanised Fabian socialist ideology, the trajectory of development from independence (the crushing of an independent trade union movement) to the present (the resistance until recently by the state elite to multiparty political activity) has been characterised by an authoritarian populism that has fundamentally shaped the criminal justice system (Shaidi 1989; Williams 1981, 1982) at the same time as it has assisted in the formation of a native bourgeois class operating through the state (Shivji 1986b; Mueller 1981). Thus a *Preventive Detention Act* was introduced in 1962, enabling detention without charge on political grounds. From the late seventies, the use of this Act was extended to deal with a spread of criminal activities including cattle rustling, brewing illicit alcohol and corruption. In the 1980s, as the economic situation worsened, 'traditional' defence groups known as *Sungusungu* began to take the law into their own hands and were responsible for the death and torture of suspected cattle rustlers. The state's response to these unlawful activities was to legitimate *Sungusungu* actions by incorporating them within the People's Militia (*People's Militia Laws (Miscellaneous Amendments) Act* 1989). The situation cannot be characterised as purely authoritarian, however, since it is clear that *Sungusungu* and other defence groups have enjoyed considerable popular support in the country areas, and latterly in the cities as well. The Government's action in legalising them is probably an attempt to control as well as to condone. It is for this reason that one must talk of an authoritarian populism that strives to enlist popular support for the government, the party and the state. The rhetoric of socialism and anti-colonialism which leads the main street in Dar Es Salaam to be named Samora Machel Avenue is an important ideology in this regard, although one that looks increasingly threadbare under the pressures of IMF 'structural adjustment' and liberalisation of the economy. Other authoritarian measures worth pondering in the Tanzanian case include minimum sentences legislation providing for the re-introduction of whipping shortly after independence, bringing praise of the virtues of the old German colonial system of punishment from politicians who a short time earlier were most vociferous in their opposition to such colonial forms of barbarism (Shaidi 1989). Also of significance is the creation of vagrancy and 'human resources deployment' statutes designed to control the dislocation brought about by the marketisation of agriculture and the pauperisation of the peasantry. These laws allowed the compulsory ejection of the unemployed from the cities and resettlement in the *Ujamaa* villages. The unbalanced relationship between the city and the country, which cannot be transcended, requires authoritarian measures to keep people on the land as the city draws them like a magnet. In this regard, the neo-colony inherits the contradiction of the colony: a peasantry which must remain stable if capital is to be accumulated even as capital dislocates it (Shivji 1982; cf on India, Pande 1986).

Criminal Justice and State Socialism

In an earlier essay (Norrie 1990), I have argued that the particular shape of the Soviet criminal justice system emerged from the forced development of the forces of production in the Soviet Union under Stalin. The decisions to collectivise agriculture and rapidly develop an urban, industrial economy were products of an increasingly bureaucratised Bolshevik party in the 1920s, and the effect of violent collectivisation was to consolidate that bureaucratic rule in the 1930s. The overall success of the bureaucratic road to state socialism was underwritten by the erosion and degradation of the revolutionary social forces that achieved power in 1917, while the basic structural dilemma for the revolutionary party was the achievement of proletarian revolution in a society dominated by feudal-peasant relations of production. As in the Third World today, the basic contradiction was between town and country, between an urban political development of great advancement and a rural context of great backwardness (Deutscher 1967).

In criminal justice terms, the upshot was a system of dictatorship under the control of the party and state run by the Ministry of Internal Affairs (Narkomvnudel - NKVD) and the procuracy. Legal safeguards, particularly in the period of the show trials in the 1930s, were empty, sham forms manufactured to attract legitimacy abroad. This dictatorial approach to criminal justice was eased off after the death of Stalin, but the social system remained one in which a military-industrial and party elite (the nomenklatura) maintained control over the society as a whole. I have argued that there existed in the 1920s the germs of another approach to socialist development, and therefore to law and criminal justice, which asserted the need for consensual development and transformation of the forces of production in a socialist direction. Such an approach would have retained a commitment to individual protections for both workers and peasants from 'their' state, recognising the contradictory nature of the role of the state in the process of development. Such an approach would have held fast to the progressive penal policies of the 1920s, and would not have led to the use of the criminal law as a surrogate form of economic policy through the extended use of slave labour camps. However, the combination of economic impoverishment and the decimation of the proletarian population of the cities strengthened the hand of the bureaucracy and provided a material basis for their opposition to the people as a whole. This weighted the likely outcome of political developments in favour of an authoritarian, conflictual approach and against a more consensual and progressive one. The gradual successes of the former fed upon themselves, until, the terror of land collectivisation was turned upon society as a whole through the bureaucratic dictatorship of the 1930s (Deutscher, 1967). The labour camps and the show trials of this period emerged out of the contradictions of what we would now call a Third World revolutionary situation. It was the overlapping contradictions between town and country, peasantry and proletariat, party and people that ultimately structured the Soviet criminal justice system.

There is much in the Soviet experience that is relevant to other state socialist societies not just because they are all societies of the same kind but because they developed in similar circumstances. Thus, to take a representative sample, Poland, Cuba, Mozambique and China were all countries with a very limited capitalist development and a reliance upon peasant production to keep socialist development alive. All these countries were therefore prone to the creation of bureaucracies in substitution for independent bottom-up socialist development. In part, bureaucracy is a necessary function in such a society for the purposes of coordination, but it runs the risk of enhancing the divisions within the society that predicate its existence: divisions between those who direct and those who are directed. In situations of underdevelopment and scarcity, it encourages those in control of the bureaucracy to put their own interests before those of the rest of society (White G 1983, 1988).

There is no hard and fast rule as to how these structural features will manifest themselves in alternative societies, and there is an inbuilt historical dynamic which means that different directions will emerge as earlier solutions appear to fail. In Poland, the fact that socialism was largely imposed at the end of the Second World War in a context of forced underdevelopment by fascism meant that the division between people and bureaucracy was always large, giving rise to a repetitive cycle of state authoritarianism and promises of improvement in living conditions and liberties. The state was unable to fund these by internal industrial development, so they could only be achieved by foreign borrowing, which ultimately led to the imposition of austerity measures (Ascherson 1981). The gap between state and society always remained large, with legitimation being provided by 'external' ideologies such as Catholicism and Polish nationalism.

In Cuba, by contrast, the bureaucratic nature of the party is mediated by the development of grassroots democratic forms and the creation of relatively independent legal institutions from the mid 1970s. In addition, the peculiarly charismatic relationship between the people and Fidel Castro represents a partial check upon bureaucratic ambitions at the same time, ironically, as Castro heads the bureaucracy. Cuban democracy remains 'top down' and as a society, Cuba has tended to reject rather than come to terms with its dissidents by encouraging emigration. Nonetheless, Cuban socialism operates with a fair though incomplete degree of consensus (Azicri 1988; Stubbs 1989; Habel 1991), and this is reflected both in judicial institutions that are separate from the party, and in a continuing progressive penal policy (Salas 1985; Azicri 1980; Van der Plas 1983; National Lawyers Guild 1988). Under threat the system is not above producing the odd dramatic 'show trial' (Preston 1989; Habel 1991), but this is the exception rather than the rule.

In countries that undergo genuine national, popular revolutions with a socialist content, there is always a predisposition to the use of popular forms of self-rule, including forms of justice such as people's courts or tribunals. In the first decade of its revolution, the Cubans instigated such a system consistent with their 'popular voluntarist' approach to the organisation of the economy. However, it was impossible in the long term to develop the economy and society in this way because of the limits of a voluntarist approach, symbolised in the failure of the 'ten million ton' campaign for the expansion of sugar production in 1970. As the economy became more bureaucratised, so the criminal justice system became more institutionalised. Nonetheless, the ideology and practice of popular involvement in the running of a socialist country remains important, even if it is limited and controlled by bureaucratisation and institutionalisation.

In recent years, the Cuban 'rectification' campaign has again evoked the image of the 'new socialist man' originally popularised by Guevara and Castro and associated with the original forms of popular justice developed in the 1960s (Berman 1969; Brady 1982). However this does not appear to be re-opening mass popular involvement in political and legal decision making (Habel 1991). In any case, it has been demonstrated historically in the Cuban context that there are practical limits to such social voluntarism (Brady 1982; cf White G 1983). The essential problem with and paradox of this popular (populist?) socialist ideology is that it seeks to rely upon forms of moral agency which according to Marxist theory ought to be the end product of a process of communist development rather than the means to achieve it. To think otherwise is to engage in idealism. The image of the socialist 'new man' is an abstraction in a society undergoing enforced material deprivation and influenced by the example of the United States. The reality in Cuba since the Revolution is that, while old forms of crime such as gangsterism and widespread violence, vice, and drug-dealing have been almost entirely wiped out, the current Cuban social environment does not, and cannot produce a society of angels. New, less dangerous forms of deviancy such as juvenile delinquency, prostitution and corruption within the bureaucracy have developed or re-emerged (Salas 1979; Marshall 1987; Stubbs 1989). In the first wave of popular enthusiasm, it was thought that the society would achieve a new social order at one fell swoop. The development of institutions and bureaucracy was due to a recognition that the process would be slower, and would require stabilising mechanisms. Part of this was a recognition that the objective circumstances would not allow the people to transform themselves immediately into ideal socialist actors. The return to these ideas is a useful form of moral exhortation, and perhaps necessary within the current economic and political climate, but it would be foolish to think that it could become the basis for a renewed and full system of popular participation and justice.

Criminal Justice and Popular Justice[5]

Consideration of the topic of popular justice, touched on in the last section, confirms the argument of this paper, that the forms of justice adopted within a society reflect prevailing social relations of production, and will be structured according to the nature of the developmental route adopted. It is these overall factors that determine the outcome of systems based initially upon ideas of popular justice. The example of Mozambique confirms this standpoint. Much has been written about the popular justice system adopted by the Mozambicans after their war of liberation in the 1970s (Isaacman and Isaacman 1982; Sachs and Welch 1990). Initially, this system was boosted by the creation of liberated zones in the North of the country run on co-operative socialist lines by Frelimo and the local people. This provided a model for the system as a whole after independence but had to be coupled with a recognition that the new egalitarian democratic forms of the liberated areas had to be transplanted into the other parts of the country that remained dominated by the Portuguese until independence. In these areas, the old ways, for example in relation to the position of women, remained in force and had to be consciously overcome by a process of negotiated change. In this context, popular justice could not simply rely upon the spontaneous sentiments of the people but had to be mediated by central direction in the shape of party-created groups of local cadres who would act to 'dynamise' the local setting according to the principles of the new constitution. Thus from the beginning there existed a centre-periphery, party-people relationship which recognised the leadership role of the new state. Like the Cuban, the Mozambican 'new man' would not emerge spontaneously but through a process of socio-political development guided by the party and the new state.

It is hard to imagine it being otherwise. All Third World revolutions must reckon with the enormous dislocations in the social formations brought about by the history of imperialism and must seek to develop the society in a way that best defends the gains of the revolution and offers a viable path for national survival. The Mozambican Revolution, since its birth, has had to reckon with the hostility of its apartheid neighbour, a relationship that has put enormous stress upon the revolutionary process. White (G 1983) has identified a typical three fold development in Third World revolutions that is applicable to the Mozambican situation (cf Hanlon 1984; Egero 1987). The first of these is the period of revolutionary voluntarism in which the upsurge of popular power in the first years of revolution persuades the people and the party that a direct popular route to socialism exists. Thereafter, in the light of failures and the fading of the first enthusiasm, there grows up a belief in the necessity of state action on behalf of the revolution. This phase entrenches a 'bureaucratic voluntarism' in which a belief in the omnipotence of state bureaucracy replaces a belief in the power of the people. In the light of failings in the bureaucracy, a third 'reformist' phase is then adopted in which revisionist, market based policies emerge as part of an attempt to save the nation by any means possible.

Taken abstractly, the model is too mechanistic to identify the material and historic factors which underly a development that is by no means inevitable. The setting of commodity prices at levels that do not allow Third World countries to break the cycle of underdevelopment, and the granting of aid only on the basis of 'structural adjustment' and liberalisation packages together with unofficially sanctioned terrorist subversion of new regimes make it very difficult to maintain a socialist revolution. These factors provide a strong push towards the kind of reformist strategies that have been developed in recent years in Mozambique.

There is also however an internal organic set of contradictions which encourages the growth of a kind of class formation in the new regime, and which can also lead to support for reform strategies. The growth of bureaucracy in a Third World socialist revolution is a likely if not inevitable response to the uneven, underdeveloped nature of the social formation. But the establishment of a bureaucracy immediately raises the question of bureaucratic interests separate from those of the people, and of the adoption of wholly bureaucratic solutions to problems that would have admitted of more popular ones. As regards the latter, the adoption of a collectivist farming strategy under the tutelage of the East Germans in Mozambique is perhaps a case in point. More serious however is the adoption of authoritarian state policies of social control that mirror those of colonialism and neo-colonialism. The adoption of whipping and forcible removal of 'vagrants' from the cities reveal the socialist state dealing with 'its' people in a way that clearly identifies the people, or some of them, as the problem (Hanlon 1984). This is then legitimated in terms of demands for order emanating from the people as a whole (Sachs 1985), but if it is justified as a popular socialist measure instead of being acknowledged as a setback for socialist organisation in the fight against crime occasioned by the overall social context, then it is clear that bureaucratic, anti-socialist policies are being adopted in the name of socialism.[6]

The issue that then emerges as a development from within the revolution is the possibility of the emergence of a bureaucratic caste or proto-class, located in the cities and with access to power and resources, which objectifies the problems of the mass of the people and seeks to administer them in ways that are disconnected from their experiences. If it happens that the bureaucracy, pushed by hostile natural and social forces, becomes sufficiently remote, the way is open for the adoption of IMF-type reform packages which return the liberated country to the form of a neo-colony and transform the bureaucratic socialist elite into a compradorial state bourgeoisie along Tanzanian lines for example. It is impossible to say at this time what the ultimate fate of the Mozambican revolution will be, but it is clear that a process of change is being undergone at the present time in which the old socialist ways of doing things are being officially discarded. If the society is moving towards a more market-based and class differentiated form, the criminal justice system's initially progressive goals are likely to be further eroded. In this context, popular justice is either transformed into a legitimating ideology of state-bureaucratic repression, or is crushed for its opposition to that bureaucracy (cf Oloka-Onyango 1989; Fitzpatrick 1982; Paliwala 1982).

The Renewal of Capitalism in State Socialist Societies

This brings us finally to the question of criminal justice policies and the resumption of capitalism in the state socialist countries. There is a popular but mistaken belief amongst Western academics and, it appears, the intelligentsias of Eastern Europe, that the re-introduction of capitalism will also mean the development of democracy and the rule of law. But capitalism and market exchange have historically been compatible with widely diverse forms of political and legal organisation, often of a most brutal kind. The key to understanding democracy and the rule of law in the West, such as they are, is to recognise the pre-eminent position that the Western economies enjoy in the world as a whole. Western economic development, and hence democracy and legalism, has been bought at the price of economic underdevelopment throughout the Third World, for it is the dominance of the Western economies that allows the trickle down of wealth to the lower classes and cements the hegemony of capitalism in the metropolitan centre. It is no coincidence that it is when the West fights the fiercest of imperialist wars abroad that it reveals its kindest and most caring face at home.[7] Consensus at home and oppression abroad are closely connected.

In Eastern Europe, however, the re-introduction of capitalism will not occur in conditions ripe for it. The economies of the East, while more developed than those of the Third World, have an infrastructure developed in the 1930s, 1940s and 1950s. They are not able to directly compete on the world stage. There will have to be massive unemployment connected with a withering of the welfare services previously offered by the socialist state before the conditions are created for capitalist investment. These changes may generate considerable resistance, and therefore require authoritarian intervention if they are to be achieved.[8] Further, the socialist organisation of these countries embraced all forms of social relations and constituted the cement holding society together. Take that cement away without replacing it with a viable alternative, and all that is left to the elite is naked power in a situation of social disintegration, such as we witness today in the emergence of organised crime and drug abuse in the Soviet Union and Poland.

Some evidence for these claims can be drawn from the example of China, where for a decade now, a transition to capitalism has been underway in the hands of a bureaucratic elite. The privatisation of the land and the 'open-door' economic policy have increased wealth and production but in a divisive, inegalitarian way, giving rise to a resurgence of crime throughout the society and a cynically corrupt attitude within the party-state bureaucracy (Gittings 1991). The response to this has been a dramatic increase in both crime and the use of the death penalty with few legal safeguards. There has also been a decisive move away from forms of popular justice and an insistence on an authoritarian rule by law in place of informal methods of dispute resolution (Brady 1981; Clark 1985). The process of economic transition has fuelled popular criticisms of the state and party and expectations of democracy. These threaten both the hoped-for stability of the economic reforms that have been created and the state bureaucracy. Undermined by the process it has itself set in motion, the state has only been able to respond with repression (Gittings 1991; Findlay 1989; Findlay and Wing 1989).

Conclusion

I have argued that crime, criminal law and criminal justice are conditioned in their form and content, in their overall logic and shape, by their character as particular mediations of relations of production in historically different modes of production. In broadly different social formations, the rule of law is shaped by combinations of oppression, democracy, bureaucracy, popular involvement, authoritarianism and legality, which are themselves the product of the broad social and economic relations that govern a society's development. Law is a social and historical phenomenon assuming many different appearances depending upon the context within which it emerges and the social relations it reflects.

This position stands opposed to the general ideological thrust of much Western scholarship which takes its cue from the ideology of the 'end of ideology' and, for that matter, of history, a viewpoint that has been strengthened by recent developments in Eastern Europe. Viewed as a historical phenomenon within a changing world history, law must be seen as capable of assuming many different forms, and of being opposed by other means of social regulation, such as forms of informal popular justice. It then becomes important to evaluate the nature of different forms of regulation and the claims to virtue that are made on their behalf.

The Western 'rule of law' is a practical and ideological concept that emerged with capitalism in Europe and the United States. The key to understanding it is to see that it unites contradictory elements of oppression and freedom within one concept (Norrie 1991). On the one hand, the 'governance of laws' codifies and enforces the private property norms of a mode of production that is exploitative and oppressive for large sections of the people. This was particularly clear at the time of the birth of Western criminal law because the imposition of bourgeois property norms on the landless and the workless was newly explicit. It has become less apparent in the West because of the development at certain levels of the system of a relative political and ideological consensus across the social classes, although as social conflicts come to the surface, the consensual aspects of the rule of law diminish. It remains vividly apparent in Third World societies, where the distance between haves and have nots gapes transparently. There the rule of law can only appear, viewed from this side of the concept, as a form of oppression.

On the other hand, the 'governance of laws' establishes the promise of a realm of freedom from state authoritarianism. The individual has a claim that the state should not intervene in her life unless she breaks the law. In principle, the 'rule of law' in its Western garb establishes a field for the play of individual liberty. Thus in the criminal law, the rule of law enforces an exploitative and oppressive social system, but it does it in a way that proclaims its self-limiting character. It would be naive to think that the state will necessarily follow in practice the principles that it proclaims. Whether it does so is a matter of political and ideological contingency depending upon the security of elite power, and this is as true of the Western democracies as it is of the Third World dictatorships. Nonetheless, the rule of law remains a hostage to fortune and the basis for formal political and juridical claims around which the oppressed can organise their resistance. To the extent that they are successful in using the formal guarantees of the law to press their substantive social claims against the state, the oppressed will find the guarantees of the rule of law less available to them; however, viewed from this side, and even though it is attached to a system of wealth production that is the ultimate problem for the achievement of human liberation, the rule of law operates as a limited space of liberty, and as a defensive channel in the struggle for emancipation.

Popular justice is sometimes suggested as an alternative and conflicting means of achieving human liberation, although one that contains inherent dangers. It offers the possibility of a 'direct route' to emancipation. The people take power into their own hands, and use it to transform their lives. Law, it is recognised, offers a sphere of liberty, but one that is tied to inegalitarian structures of wealth and power so that to resort to law is to get bogged down in existing inequalities. Popular justice, it is true, runs the risk of an unregulated social development which can get out of hand, but that is a risk one has to take if emancipation is to be possible. One either 'rides the tiger' of popular justice, or gets bogged down in the mud of legal formalism and the inequitable system it protects (*cf* Spitzer 1982).

This 'either/or' approach to law and popular justice is a

Criminal Justice, The Rule of Law and Human Emancipation

mistake because it fails to recognise, first, the objective social and economic conditions within which popular forms of socialist transformation have occurred, and, second, as a corollary, the need for legal forms in the development of societies beyond a popular revolution. The successful popular socialist revolutions of the twentieth century have all occurred in situations of economic and political underdevelopment, where there has been a need to develop both the forces and the relations of production in a socialist direction, and where there has been a 'gap' between the ideology of the revolution and the practical experiences of broad sections of the population, and therefore between the party and state leadership on the one hand and the mass of the people on the other. For a revolution to succeed in such a situation requires the continued involvement of the people in the revolutionary process they have instigated, in a situation where that involvement will not necessarily occur spontaneously, or maintain its progressive direction (cf Deutscher 1967; Sachs and Welch 1990). It also requires a party and state leadership that works on behalf of the people and is selfless in a situation of serious material scarcity. The former condition points to the need for regulative legal forms that will guarantee but also channel popular decision-making (cf Isaacman and Isaacman 1982; Sachs and Welch 1990); while the latter indicates the need for legal forms which will control corruption within the party bureaucracy and the state, and also mediate relations with the people. Thus the location of popular revolution in underdeveloped social contexts reveals a set of sites for legal forms that both channel and give effect to popular involvement and control the state. Such revolutions contain the potential for enormous structural conflicts of interests, and it is these that require the existence of mediating and directing legal forms at the same time as they require the continued involvement of the direct desires and energies of popular forces. If these seem contradictory requirements, then the contradictions lie in the social contexts which generate the need for the particular forms of law that emerge.

In a context in which he did not foresee the conjunction of socialist revolution and political and economic underdevelopment, Marx wrote the words quoted at the beginning of this paper. I would argue that they are given added relevance and importance by the experience of the revolutions of the twentieth century. Marx (1968) foresaw a process whereby the inegalitarian bourgeois right would be burst apart by the achievement of a socialist revolution which could replace narrow, individualistic claims with a socially organised system for the satisfaction of all individual needs. The former represented a narrow horizon that the latter would transcend, but only after a period in which new advanced forms of social organisation would be put in place to replace the old individualistic forms. Third World revolutionary contexts require legal forms to regulate state and people precisely because they occur in contexts in which the economic and cultural structure still need development. For this reason, they cannot do without mediating forms of right. In a highly contradictory situation of Third World popular revolution, human liberation requires the co-existence of highly contradictory social forms - forms of direct popular involvement together with mediating and controlling forms of right.

Notes

1 This chapter was partly written while I was a guest at the Faculty of Law in Dar Es Salaam under a link arrangement funded by the British Council and I would like to thank Angelo Mapunda and Issa Shivji for their assistance. I would also like to thank Abdul Paliwala for saving me from some of my mistakes, while absolving him from any responsibility for those that remain.

2 I have in mind here the position of women comparatively within criminal justice systems. To mention three important features of this relation, there is first the question of particularly female forms of deviance that are constructed within the logic of the colonial and neo-colonial state such as prostitution (Bujra 1982; White 1987), illegal squatting (Unterhalter 1987), and female 'delinquency' (Paliwala 1982). Second there is the question of the ways in which the specific forms of oppression of women in the pre-colonial period are carried forward into the colonial and neo-colonial periods. The dominance of men over women was to a large extent connived at by colonial authority (Guha 1987), which sought to police women in relation to their husbands (Mbilinyi 1988), and access to their sexuality (Bujra 1982). The inferior position of women is maintained in the neo-colonial setting by the blind eye turned by the criminal justice system to bride murder, wife beating, and widow burning (Matsui 1989; Stein 1989), where it is not officially sanctioned by, for example, devaluing the evidence of women in relation to crimes such as rape (Mehdi 1990). Third, there is the question of the way in which criminal justice and popular justice in revolution-

ary contexts can assist in the liberation of women, an issue that requires an understanding of the fundamental dynamics of gender relations and how they can be transformed (Massell 1968; Sachs and Welch 1990).

3   The process of co-optation is of course one that takes place at a number of levels - ideological, political and cultural as well as economic. The important question, which I have discussed elsewhere (Norrie and Adelman 1989), is how one integrates the different levels within an historical account that both identifies their specificity and relates them to the underlying structural developments.

4   An alternative, I believe overstated and less historically grounded, way of explaining the existence of legal rights in the West is through Foucault's (1977) argument that the juridical forms are underpinned, and undercut, by the operation of behavioural disciplines which do the real work of control (cf. Garland 1990).

5   I address the issue of popular justice in the post-revolutionary situation, not that of 'dual power', and in connection with the transition to bureaucratic control in the context of economic underdevelopment.

6   This minor example of making a socialist virtue out of necessity, and thereby pushing bureaucratic interests against the people, finds its greatest, epochal, form in the Stalinist theory of 'socialism in one country' (Deutscher 1963).

7   Thus it was the Boer war that instigated the first moves to the welfare state in Britain (Semmel 1960) and the Vietnam war that instigated the 'war against poverty' in the United States.

8   The problems of carrying through a bourgeois revolution without a strong bourgeoisie are vividly revealed in the inability of the Polish government at present to carry through its privatisation policy in the face of popular antagonism. The Minister for Privatisation, Lewandowski, is quoted thus: 'There was much platonic love for the market in post-communist Europe, but people don't want really the real disciplines and the real verdicts of the market. There is only a verbal commitment.' (The Guardian 16.10.91)

5

Third Generation Rights and Social Action Litigation

Jill Cottrell

Introduction

In an article on 'The Environment, Human Rights and a New South African Constitution', Glazewski (1991: 172) argues that:

> In the last twenty years or so, the ambit of human rights has been further expanded to include a third generation or what have been termed People's or Solidarity Rights. The essence of these rights is that they cannot be exercised by individuals as individuals but rather as group rights. Environmental rights fall neatly into this category, appropriately also termed 'green rights', because often the essence of environmental problems is to impose public environmental interest onto individual private rights.

Glazewski goes on to discuss the use by the Supreme Court of India of what is variously known as public interest litigation (PIL) or social action litigation[1] in the environmental context, and it is this on which this paper focuses.

The Enforcement of Third Generation Rights

Limitations of space preclude a detailed analysis of 'third generation rights' or approaches to their enforcement (see Crawford 1988). It is nonetheless important to have some idea of the enforcement of such a system in order to assess the value of PIL. Such rights are responses to injustices affecting classes of people rather than individuals. Some may already be recognised, at least in principle, both as collective rights and as traditional individual rights: for example, a particular state may prohibit discrimination against women or members of ethnic groups in its constitution or other legislation. Others may be recognised in constitutional provisions that are aspirational rather than operational, such as the Indian Constitution's Directive Principles of State Policy. Yet others may be recognised in international instruments rather than domestic law, and some have yet to receive recognition anywhere. The types of interests which have been constituted as the basis of rights of this collective nature include the rights to self-determination, to environment, to development, and the right to exist (which may mean the right to a way of life, to a culture, and to freedom from genocide).

Within the domestic sphere, what is required is enforcement procedures that are accessible because they are not too expensive, obscure, or physically distant from groups which are by definition disadvantaged and alienated. The traditionally closed nature of most legal systems may be remedied by procedures in which the legal machine is activated by someone else on behalf of the disadvantaged. Recent literature has stressed the role of non-governmental organizations (NGOs) in activating the rights of groups (CHRI 1991, Steiner 1991), and an institutionalised role for NGOs in enforcement may indeed be desirable if not essential. And, to the extent that we are talking about the rights of existing groups, rather than of future generations (Weiss 1989), such procedures ought to be participatory rather than paternalistic. The ombudsman model has been advocated as a valuable means of protecting of many of these rights (Weiss 1989). In India, however, there is no federal ombudsman, and plans to create one have been viewed as a means of controlling corruption rather than maladministration (Saxena 1987). The development of PIL may be viewed in part as response to the absence of effective procedures of this kind.

Trigg (1988) is one of a number of writers who have pointed out that it is all too easy for groups, including the state, to use collective rights as a justification for restricting more traditional rights such as freedom of speech. An enforcement procedure must therefore be capable of taking into consideration the implications of the decisions made; it must be effective in giving remedies to those who have suffered and, more important, must be capable of changing the behaviour of those who infringe such rights; and it must be capable of resisting capture by those sections of society that it is designed to control.

What is Public Interest Litigation?[2]

Upendra Baxi (1988) wrote in 1988 that 'The Supreme Court of India is at long last becoming...the Supreme Court for Indians'. Kagzi (1987: 203) observed that:

> Those who lived in the past told us that the *Shudra (achut)*, the untouchables, were not allowed entry in the Vishwanath Temple in Banaras. These people could get *darshan* [sight of a god] of the Almighty God through an aperture made in the outer wall of the temple by the custodians of the Hindu religion. Much in the same way the bold judicial enthusiasm of the radicals among the Judges throws open the possibility of remote entry into the temple of the goddess of justice through social action proceedings, complaints and petitions.

Fully developed PIL jurisprudence is multifaceted, and it is the full pattern that makes the phenomenon uniquely Indian. At its core is an expanded concept of *locus standi* (the right to bring an action) embracing organisations and individuals who would previously have been regarded as busy-bodies. Defining PIL is however difficult: there are, for example, no special rules of procedure. Indeed, a major aspect of PIL is that existing or still evolving rules may be departed from or flexibly applied. Nor is there any rigidly defined content. The courts have sometimes emphasised not the subject matter but whose interests the litigation must seek to protect. In many instances cases are not explicitly referred to as PIL cases and courts may need to decide whether a case falls under this rubric only when and if a party challenges some relaxation of the normal rules of procedure. As a consequence, there are descriptions rather than definitions of PIL. Mr Justice Bhagwati (1985: 571) has stated that:

> Where a legal wrong or a legal injury is caused to a person or to a determinate class of persons by reason of violation of their constitutional or legal rights, and [persons are] by reason of poverty or disability in a socially or economically disadvantaged position and

unable to approach the Court for relief, any member of the public or a social action group acting *bona fide* can maintain an application in a High Court or the Supreme Court seeking judicial redress for the legal wrong or injury caused... This is no more than a radical generalization or extension of the technique followed in most countries in *habeas corpus* cases where the Court usually acts on letters written by or on behalf of such a person or determinate class of persons. (Bhagwati 1985: 571).

The United States model is, I believe, concerned more with civil participation in governmental decision-making, and it seeks to represent 'interests without groups', such as consumerism or environmentalism. These, no doubt, form the issues of public interest litigation in India also, but the primary focus is on State repression, governmental lawlessness, administrative deviance, and exploitation of disadvantaged groups and denial to them of their rights end entitlements. The public interest litigation model which we have evolved in India is directed towards 'finding turn-around situations' in the political economy for the disadvantaged and other vulnerable groups. It is concerned with the immediate as well as long-term resolution of problems of the disadvantaged. It also seeks to ensure that the activities of the State fulfil the obligations of the law under which they exist and function. The substance of public interest litigation in India is thus much wider than that of public interest litigation in the United States. (Bhagwati 1985: 569).

Venkatachaliah J was prompted in *Sheela Barse v Union of India* (1988 4 SCC at 233-4) to say:

While in the ordinary conventional adjudications the party structure is merely bi-polar and the controversy pertains to the determination of the legal consequences of past events and the remedy is essentially linked to and limited by the logic of the array of the parties, in a public interest action the proceedings cut across and transcend these traditional forms of inhibitions... The proceedings [are]...intended to vindicate and effectuate the public interest by prevention of violation of the rights, constitutional or statutory, of sizeable segments of the society, who, owing to poverty, ignorance, social and economic disadvantages cannot themselves assert - and quite often [are] not even aware of - those rights... The grievance in a public interest action, generally speaking, is about the content and conduct of government action in relation to the constitutional or statutory rights of segments of society and [such actions tend to be] sprawling and amorphous, to be defined and adjusted or readjusted as the case may be, *ad hoc*, according as the exigencies of the emerging situation...

Again, the relief to be granted looks to the future and is, generally, corrective rather than compensatory although it may be both. The pattern of relief need not necessarily be derived logically from the rights asserted or found. More importantly, the court is not merely a passive, disinterested umpire or onlooker but has a dynamic and positive role with the responsibility for the organisation of the proceedings, moulding of the relief and, this is important, also supervising the implementation thereof. The court is entitled to and often does seek the assistance of expert panels, commissioners, advisory committees, *amici*, etc. This wide range of the responsibilities necessarily implies correspondingly higher measures of control over the parties, the subject matter and procedure.

The Constitutional Basis of PIL

Virtually the entire development of PIL has occurred within the context of Article 32 (in the Supreme Court) and Article 226 (in High Courts) of the Indian Constitution. Article 32 provides:

> (1) The right to move the Supreme Court by appropriate proceedings for the enforcement of the rights conferred by this Part [i.e. Part III of the Constitution, containing fundamental rights] is guaranteed.
>
> (2) The Supreme Court shall have power to issue directions or orders or writs, including writs in the nature of habeas corpus, mandamus, prohibition, quo warranto and certiorari, whichever may be appropriate, for the enforcement of any of the rights conferred by this Part.

Article 226 provides that:

> every High Court shall have power...to issue to any person or authority, including in appropriate cases any Government... directions, orders or writs, including writs in the nature of habeas corpus, mandamus, prohibition, quo warranto and certiorari, or any of them, for the enforcement of any of the rights conferred by Part III and for any other purpose.

Bhagwati CJ noted in *M C Mehta v Union of India* (AIR 1987 SC at 1089) that 'It may now be taken as well settled that Art 32 does not merely confer power on this Court to issue a direction, order or writ for enforcement of the fundamental rights but it also lays a constitutional obligation on this Court to protect the fundamental rights of the people and for that purpose this Court has all incidental and ancillary powers including the power to forge new remedies and fashion new strategies designed to enforce the fundamental rights'. Elsewhere, Bhagwati (Sturgess & Chubb 1988: 432) has observed that under Art 32 'an appropriate proceeding need not be a written petition' and that even a letter to the Court would be sufficient to initiate proceedings. He argues that the fact that the Article does not refer only to the fundamental rights of the petitioner has enabled the court to interpret it as referring to the the fundamental right of everyone.

Some Illustrative Cases

Given the difficulties of defining PIL, it may be most useful to provide a sample of the cases that have come before the courts in this innovative form of litigation.

Hussainara Khatoon v State of Bihar (AIR 1975 SC 1360)

In 1978 a member of the national Police Commission toured the jails of Bihar and was appalled by the conditions of certain prisoners. Soon after Mrs Kapila Hingorani, a lawyer, filed *habeas corpus* applications on behalf of Hussainara Khatoon and the other prisoners, producing the Commission's newspaper accounts in support of the applications. She alleged that large numbers of men and women (and even children) were being kept in custody for years without trial. The root of the problem was identified by the Court as the bail system, which effectively prevented the poor from obtaining bail. It urged lower courts to use criteria relative to a person's community ties in assessing eligibility for bail. Problems in the bail system do not, however, explain the length of the legal process. A speedy trial is not an explicitly recognised fundamental right under the Constitution, but Bhagwati J argued that it must be viewed as an aspect of the right to life and liberty under Art 21.

The Court directed that the 18 people named in the petition should be released on personal bonds. It appears that the Court acted in the absence of any response from the State and on the assumption that the newspaper reports were accurate. However, the state responded by undertaking to complete expeditiously cases where the investigation had taken two years; the Court expressed its astonishment that police investigation should require as long as two years. Even more astonishing was the fact that some of the people named were not even awaiting trial but were women held in what was euphemistically termed 'protective custody' as victims or potential witnesses. The Court ordered these women to be removed to welfare homes and demanded reports on all individuals who had been committed for trial years previously but had not been tried. It directed that the Government should scrutinise its own records and identify those who had been in prison so long that prosecution was now time barred, for example in relation to offences punishable only with a fine or a maximum of three years' imprisonment. It also demanded enforcement of sect 167 (5) of the *Criminal Procedure Code* providing that 'summons cases' should be discontinued if the investigation is not completed within six months unless a magistrate is satisfied that there are special reasons requiring continued investigation.

The Court required the State to produce a record of all prisoners in custody pending trial. The Bihar Government found itself, quite rightly, in a no-win situation as compliance with the order revealed ever greater horrors. The State revealed that 70 prisoners listed by Mrs Hingorani had served longer periods on remand than the maximum possible sentences for the crimes they were alleged to have committed. The Court ordered their immediate release. It considered legal aid facilities and ordered the State Government to provide lawyers at state expense to represent prisoners on bail applications and to report its compliance to the High Court. The Court 'strongly recommended' the establishment of a comprehensive legal aid scheme. Lastly, the Court directed the Government to file details of all cases pending in magistrates' courts and, where appropriate, explanations of why such cases had been pending for more than six months. The State later reported that it had released the 70 prisoners who had served longer than their potential sentences but Mrs. Hingorani produced the names of 59 more. The State also revealed that in 5835 of 10339 'major' cases investigations had been pending for over six months, as had 7228 of 17887 'minor' cases. The Court found these figures 'staggering' and asked to be supplied with the norms for disposal of cases fixed by the High Court for magistrates and trial judges. The Court found a constitutional obligation to provide legal services for those at risk of losing their liberty and could not afford a lawyer and declared that future failure to comply might lead to trials being nullified.

Rural Litigation and Enlightenment Kendra, Dehradun v State of Uttar Pradesh (AIR 1985 SC 652, 1259, AIR 1987 359, AIR SC 2187, AIR 1989 SC 594)

> The Doon Valley is an exquisite region. Bounded by the Himalayan and Shivalik ranges and the Ganga and Yamuna rivers, its perennial streams and fertile soils yield a mix of unique crops like tea, basmati rice and lychees...Today, the valley is in danger because of uncontrolled quarrying for limestone. Mussoorie, often called the queen of hill-stations, is being stripped bare of its verdant cover. In the valley, the area under tree cover is now reported to be only 12 per cent as against the officially recommended 60 per cent. (CSE 1984-5: 22).

This, the so-called *Doon Valley* case, illustrates the potential in PIL for protection of the environment. It was begun by social action organisations in a letter to the Supreme Court in July 1983. In August the Court appointed a committee to inspect the limestone quarries. When it subsequently decided the case the Court had before it not only this report but also that of a Government Working Party under the same chairman. The Court's committee divided the quarries into three categories: Category A causing the least environmental impact, Category B having a more pronounced impact and, in Category C, those that should be closed immediately. The Court followed these recommendations, but extended the closure to some Category B quarries as well.

In March 1985 the Court decided that it required further information about the remaining quarries and appointed another committee to which lessees were to provide evidence of their compliance with the relevant legislation. Until the committee had reached a decision on a particular quarry it would not be allowed to operate. Conscious of the hardship this might cause, the Court directed the Union and State governments to give priority to displaced lessees as other areas in the State became available for quarrying. The government was also directed to reclaim the abandoned quarries, and provide employment to workmen thrown out of their jobs. The new committee approved none of the schemes for re-opening the quarries but the Supreme Court permitted certain quarries to continue operating.

In 1988 the Court's attention was drawn to sect 2 of the 1980 *Forestry Act* under which no state government could permit forest land to be used for a different purpose and on this basis decided that all quarrying should cease. However, in view of defence needs and foreign exchange earnings three quarries were permitted to continue operating for a certain period subject to specific conditions. Of these only one was in the Mussoorie area but it was outside the forest and municipal area, the minerals would not be taken through the city and the lessee undertook to rehabilitate the area at the end of the lease. Some months later a further petition came before the Court which satisfied it that no real distinction could be drawn between this mine and those which had been closed down earlier. This remaining quarry was therefore also ordered to be closed - six years after the case originally came to court. The court also directed the appointment of a rehabilitation committee for displaced mine owners and workers (the Ministry of Environment and Forests was to deposit 300 000 rupees in the Supreme Court registry for this purpose) which was directed to make an initial report to the court within eight weeks and a Monitoring Committee to which the Uttar Pradesh Government was ordered to provide Rs 500 000 by way of 'initial funds'.

Sheela Barse v Union of India (AIR 1986 SC 1773, AIR 1988 SC 2211)

Sheela Barse is a Bombay journalist and activist who has brought several PIL petitions. Her experiences in the courts have not all been happy ones (Barse 1987).

This case came before the Supreme Court in September 1985, when state governments were directed to supply information on children under 16 detained in jail. By July 1986 several authorities had failed to comply but the Court nonetheless gave specific directions about handicapped and desitute children in custody. The Court observed that every state but one had a Children's Act but many had not been brought into force and although 'ordinarily it is a matter for the State Government to decide as to when a particular statute should be brought into force', such states should file affidavits by the end of August explaining why their legislation had not been brought into force. The Court directed District and Sessions Judges to visit local prisons bi-monthly and to report violations of the law with respect to children and ordered the provision of lawyers for children on remand.

Barse volunteered to travel around the country collecting information, a role that the Court acknowledged ought to have been perfomed by the State, and it ordered that she be permitted access to homes and other institutions and that the Government should provide Rs 10,000 for her expenses. In mid-August, the Court stated that if investigations in cases involving children under 16 charged with offences punishable by a maximum of seven years imprisonment were not completed within three months, the cases should be dropped. It also held that the period from the filing of charges to the completion of the trial should not exceed six months. It urged state governments to establish Juvenile Courts and to implement the existing legislation and proposed that state legislation be replaced by a federal act in the interests of uniformity.

The case was scheduled for final judgment in December 1986 but the Chief Justice was otherwise engaged. By August 1988 Barse's patience was exhausted and she requested permission to withdraw the case. She complained, in language which the Court observed was not conspicuous 'for its moderation', that the court had become 'dysfunctional' by virtue of its repeated adjournments and the fact that it could not ensure compliance with its orders. She maintained that the citizen was co-equal with the Court in the PIL process, a contention which the court held to present 'some difficulties'. The Court found Barse scornful of its processes and, while acknowledging that compliance had been hard to achieve, implied that states had pleaded financial difficulties and stressed the importance of obtaining the willing compliance of the authorities.

In ordinary litigation it is open to a petitioner to withdraw a case he or she has started but PIL is different. Parties have less control because the rights of those bringing the litigation are subordinate to the interests of those on whose behalf it is brought. Barse was therefore not able to withdraw the case but the Court recognised that it could hardly compel her to continue to press the litigation. Her name was deleted and that of the Supreme Court Legal Aid Committee substituted as petitioner (*Supreme Court Legal Aid Committee v Union of India* AIR 1989 SC 1278). Subsequently the Court appointed a group of advocates to draw up a scheme for ensuring implementation of the Juvenile Justice Act, and appointed another advocate to ascertain the number of juveniles in the prisons of Bihar.

The Citizens of Simla v State of Himachal Pradesh (ILR 1983 HP 5)
This final example is typical of the cases brought before the High Courts. The complaint, aired in a letter, alleged that the State had granted licences for the sale of alcohol in locations which violated State's policy. Many were near places where the sale of alcohol might cause offence or offer temptation, including hospitals, places of worship, educational institutions, harijan residential areas or the national highway. The Court converted the letter into a writ petition and asked three advocates to argue it.

At the time licences were offered to the public, conditions were announced concerning the location of shops and as to prohibitions on the advertising of alcohol by loudspeakers or the display of bottles in shop windows. Neither the licencees nor the State wished the conditions to be enforced. In January 1983 the Court criticised the State for conniving at the breach of its own rules in the interests of increasing revenue, pointed out that Article 47 of the Constitution places an obligation on governments (though one not strictly enforceable by the courts) to prohibit the consumption of alcohol, and directed all shops in violation of the State's 'Announcements' to close. The state perceived it had an emergency on its hands and on March 12 the Governor passed an Ordinance repealing the conditions in question. For the following year the conditions were removed or modified *inter alia* obliging liquor shops to be at 'a reasonable distance' instead of the previously specified at least 200 yards from places of worship. In consequence the Supreme Court on appeal set aside the High Court's decision (*Satya Pal v Himachal Pradesh* ILR 1983 HP 1). However, certain determined Simla residents, including Muslims who objected to liquor shops near to mosques, returned to the High Court (*Himachal Pradesh Nashabandi Parishad v Himachal Pradesh* ILR 1983 HP 493). This time the Court was more forthright in its condemnation, holding that 'the change was only to ensure that the liquor barons were not affected irrespective of the feelings of the community'. What was a 'reasonable distance' could not be left simply to bureaucrats to determine but that two hundred yards would seem to be a reasonable distance in the circumstances. (It could not perform the same sleight of hand so far as the shops near the highway were concerned since the State had taken the precaution of deleting this provision entirely). It directed the closure of all shops which were at less than this reasonable distance and of two shops where bottles were visible (in one effectively through the door, the other having a totally glazed front).

PIL procedure

These cases illustrate most of the features of the PIL phenomenon. Many PIL cases are begun not by formal process, but by a letter written to a court, or even to an individual judge.[3] In some cases the court itself, usually on the basis of a newspaper report, has instituted the action (for example *Re Inquiry into Gang Rape* 1988 20 IJR Gauhati 92). In 1989 about 150 letters were arriving daily. Since Bhagwati's term as Chief Justice a committee headed by a judge has filtered such letters before they are submitted to the Court, developing its own criteria and giving priority to cases emanating from women and scheduled caste applicants.

The feature which justifies the description of public interest litigation is that the cases are brought by individuals not directly affected by the circumstances of which they complain (or are no more affected than the public at large), by an organisation representing its members or the general public.

PIL cases do not involve the fact-finding processes characteristic of the adversarial system such as the presentation of evidence in person for both sides and cross-examination. Sworn statements in the form of affidavits are the only factual material which usually accompanies these cases. But many PIL cases have involved complex issues of fact or the submission of large quantities of factual material. Where existing material and affidavits cannot supply the facts, the courts have frequently commissioned the parties themselves (such as Sheela Barse) to produce it, or have requested committees or individuals to carry out special studies. The authorities themselves, as in the *Hussainara* case, are also regularly asked to supply the necessary information.

Remedies in PIL cases also exhibit unusual features, not least their piecemeal character. As in *Hussainara*, courts satisfied that a particular abuse had been identified have given orders relating to particular individuals or to a class of cases without waiting until the case is finished. As Barse complained, some cases have gone on for years without any sign of finishing or any formal end to the proceedings. In many cases courts do not simply decide that the respondents ought to perform specific actions but require that they return on a set date to report on implementation. Although the remedies are not usually financial, compensation has been ordered in some cases, with courts going beyond what has traditionally been permitted under Articles 32 and 226, which are based upon prerogative writs. The Supreme Court has been cautious on this point, holding that compensation might be awarded for breach of fundamental rights if 'the infringement was patent and incontrovertible, the violation was gross and its magnitude was such as to shock the conscience of the court and it would have been very unjust to the person whose fundamental right was violated to require him to go to the civil court for claiming compensation' (*M C Mehta v Union of India* AIR 1987 SC at 1091, Joshi 1988). The High Courts have been less cautious, particularly in some cases that have been really tort or trust cases under Article 226 vehicle (e.g. *Jaram Singh v State* AIR 1988 HP 13, *Kalawati v State* AIR 1989 HP 5). In the *Gang Rape* case the Chief Justice awarded compensation to the affected women on the basis of the *prima facie* evidence produced by the Inspector General of Police (see also *R. Gandhi v Union of India* AIR 1989 Mad 205).

The pattern of relief granted does not necessarily derive logically from the rights asserted in the course of the case. Remedies may be imposed on the parties, but they may also be negotiated. In *Azad Rickshaw Pullers Union v State of Punjab* (AIR 1981 SC 14), for example, the Supreme Court worked out a settlement between the State, banks and rickshaw pullers enabling the latter to purchase their rickshaws, and in Gujarat the state was persuaded by the court to provide funds for drainage work (*Janki Natubhai Chhara v Sardarnagar Municipality* AIR 1986 Guj 49). Another feature of some cases has been the setting out of guidelines going beyond the circumstances of the case (e.g. *Lakshmikant Pande v Union of India* AIR 1984 SC 469, *Elumalai v Tamil Nadu* ILR 1984 1 Mad 312, 347 and *Khaitan v West Bengal* AIR 1985 Cal 208). In several cases the litigation has prompted administrative action intended to avoid the risk of losing on the substantive legal point (Baxi 1988: 404).

PIL cases also tend to be rhetorical and hortatory. In some instances the courts have felt themselves unable to make a specific order to the authorities, possibly because the issue is too technical or political, but this has not always stood in the way of urging the authorities to take action. Sometimes, as in *Hussainara*, courts have exhorted action over and above that which they were mandating. A certain rather high-flown rhetorical style has crept into the speeches of some of the judges that is sometimes at odds with the actual decision in the case (see *Olga Tellis v Bombay* AIR

1986 SC 180, *Sachidanand Pandey v West Bengal* AIR 1987 SC 1109).

In a number of cases the courts have gone beyond traditional practice and actually assumed the role of policy makers and administrators. In *Rakesh Chandra v State of Bihar* (AIR 1989 SC 348) the court effectively ordered that the running of a mental hospital be reorganised on the lines of another institution, and in *A.P. Adimajati Sewa Sangham v Guntur M C* (AIR 1987 AP 193) the Andhra Pradesh High Court went so far as to direct that licensed pigs should have tokens hanging round their necks! On other occasions, however, they have merely required the authorities to conform to proper procedures in reaching decisions, most notably in the *Olga Tellis* case.

A feature of the cases we have looked at has been the degree of control exercised by the court. We have seen courts transforming letters into writ petitions, appointing lawyers and refusing to allow a party to withdraw a case. In cases like *Hussainara* it is apparent that the court is setting the agenda as much as the petitioner. Thus persons or institutions who are not parties may be ordered to produce information or, as in the Doon valley case, funds. Similarly people who are not parties may ultimately benefit from the outcome of the case.

In attempting to elucidate the nature of PIL courts have suggested that the proceedings are not 'adversary' in the sense that this is conventionally understood. According to Bhagwati J in *Bandhua Mukti Morcha v Union of India* (AIR 1984 SC 802 at 811):

> When the court entertains PIL, it does not do so in a cavilling spirit or in a confrontational mood or with a view to tilting at executive authority or seeking to usurp it, but its attempt is only to ensure observance of social and economic rescue programmes, legislative as well as executive, framed for the benefits of the have-nots and the handicapped and to protect them against violation of their basic human rights, which is also the constitutional obligation of the executive. The Court is thus merely assisting it in the realisation of the constitutional objectives...The Government and its officers must welcome public interest litigation, because it would provide them with occasion to examine whether the poor and the down-trodden are getting their social and economic entitlements.

This is perhaps an optimistic view of the likely response of government, particularly as the Judge was bemoaning the fact that the Haryana State Government was resisting the petition in question. In an earlier case Bhagwati and Baharul Islam J suggested that PIL 'involves a collaborative and co-operative effort on the part of the State Government and its officers, the lawyers appearing in the case and the Bench for the purpose of making human rights meaningful for the weaker sections of the community' (*Upendra Baxi v State of Uttar Pradesh* 1986 4 SCC at 117). Elsewhere Bhagwati (1986: 186) has provided what is perhaps a more accurate reflection in arguing that 'The Government treats the petitioners as adversaries of the State. It denies all the violations in its affidavits and even tries to destroy the credibility of the petitioners'.

Substantive Law

Parmanand Singh (1989) has summarised the principles of judicial restraint in the Supreme Court as follows (the additional observations in square brackets being mine).

(a) The courts can be activated only if the executive is remiss in fulfilling its constitutional obligations to the poor or the disadvantaged.
(b) The courts can act as critics and monitors of the government but it is beyond them to usurp the administration or indulge in continuing surveillance of public bodies [I have the impression that in the post-Bhagwati years there has been more of a tendency for court directions to be more general and to require less reporting back, e.g. *Vishal Jeet v Union of India* (AIR 1990 SC 1412)].
(c) The courts will respond only if there is already in existence ameliorative legislation for the welfare of the poor and exploited. It is beyond them to initiate legislation [*Himachal Pradesh v Parents of a student at Medical College, Simla* AIR 1985 SC 910].
(d) The public mind might be greatly agitated or shaken by police brutalities, encounter deaths, custodial rapes and the like, but the courts cannot easily be activated and will be reluctant to order the setting up of a parallel investigation unless they are fully satisfied that the statutory agency is not functioning properly.
(e) The medium of PIL cannot be used for political gains or for inquiring into the role of the politicians. Nor can it be used to settle private disputes.

The necessity of bringing all PIL cases originating in the Supreme Court under the ambit of Article 32 apparently involves the satisfaction of two inescapable requirements (*S P Gupta v Union of India* AIR 1982 SC 149). First, the rights to be enforced are the fundamental rights in Part III of the Constitution, many of which forbid infringement by 'the State'. Second, in order for the article to be invoked, there must be an infringement of a fundamental right. These two requirements arise in any proceedings under Article 32 but in PIL cases courts have been particularly inclined to broad interpretations. Most interesting are the cases in which the human rights element is not self-evident and where the court has had to take an expansive view of Part III in order to embrace the cases.

Article 21, by far the most important vehicle for PIL cases in the Supreme Court, provides that 'No person shall be deprived of his life or personal liberty except according to procedure established by law'.

Indian courts are fond of quoting Anatole France to the effect that the law in its majestic impartiality prevents both rich and poor from stealing bread and sleeping under bridges. In *Olga Tellis v Bombay* (AIR 1986 SC 180) an attempt was made to establish a right to live on the streets of Bombay. The Supreme Court was prepared to hold that the right to live includes the right to livelihood and that since pavement dwellers required to live where they were in order to work, their removal would amount to a deprivation of the right to life. (Nothwithstanding this holding, the petitioners effectively lost the case).

In some judgments the Court does not even bother to identify what articles (other than Article 32) of the Constitution are involved. In some major PIL cases, such as the *Doon Valley* cases it is possible to infer that Article 21 is also involved, presumably on the basis that the pollution is hazardous to life.

The Indian Constitution originally included a number of fundamental rights (mainly civil and political rights) which were to be enforceable in the Supreme Court under Article 32 and Directive Principles of State Policy (akin to social and economic rights) which were to inform State policy but were not justiciable (Part IV). The first are essentially negative (actions which infringed these rights were unconstitutional) whereas the second are positive exhortations (things the state ought to do to improve the lot of its citizens). The situation is slightly complicated by the introduction (under the 42nd Amendment) of Fundamental Duties of the Citizen (Art 51A, Part IVA). The complex interaction between these provisions and the dialectic between legislature and court have been discussed by others. The important point to be made here is the way that Part IV (and Part IVA) have figured in the Supreme Court's application of Part III of the Constitution in PIL. This has occurred particularly through the expansion of the scope of Article 21. In *Bandhua Mukti Morcha* (AIR 1984 SC at 811-2), the Court suggested that the right to life means a life with 'dignity, free from exploitation' which 'derives its life breath' from the Directive Principles (especially Arts 39(e) and (f), 41 and 42 relating to conditions of work and children). Therefore, no State 'has the right to take any action which will deprive a person of the enjoyment of these basic essentials'. This does not place an obligation on governments to provide a guarantee of these rights, but it opens the door to the Court's ability to regulate State behaviour that does in fact infringe them. Similarly, in *Olga Tellis*, Chandrachud CJ relied on Article 39(a), which covers the duty of the State to 'direct its policy towards securing that the citizens, men and women equally, have the right to an adequate means of livelihood', and on Article 41 in holding that the right to life includes the right to livelihood.

The Deployment of PIL

With a concept as amorphous as PIL, and in the absence of judicial statistics, it is impossible to arrive at an accurate picture of its use. The table opposite (Table 1) is based on cases that I have collected (from law reports at national and state level and other sources).[4]

Not all judges or commentators have been enthusiastic about the development of PIL. Most appear to vary between sceptical enthusiasm or enthusiastic scepticism. It is, however, interesting to note divisions in judicial opinions. Although there was no dissent on the outcome of *Bandhua Mukti Morcha* it is this case that has created an impression that Pathak J (who succeeded Bhagwati as Chief Justice) was less than enthusiastic about PIL. His judgment in this case, contrasting with the many judicial and extra-judicial speeches that have advocated PIL, remains one of the most carefully expressed manifestations of the cautious view of PIL. For example:

> New slogans fill the air, and new phrases have entered the legal dictionary, and we hear of the 'justicing system' being galvanised into supplying justice to the socio-economic disadvantaged. These urges are responsible for the birth of new judicial concepts and the expanding horizon of juridical power. They claim to represent an increasing emphasis on social welfare and a progressive humanitarianism. (AIR 1984 SC 862 at 838).

Table 1

Major Issues in PIL Cases

Issue	High	Supreme	Total
Environment/planning	22	5	27
Bonded labour	1	5	6
Rights of workers etc. (unions, groups of professionals, pensioners)	12	8	20
Interests of weaker sections (Harijans [formerly 'untouchables', adivasis [original 'tribal' peoples], villagers, pavement dwellers	7	7	14
Jails and criminal trials	3	12	15
Fair administration	9	1	10
Information & entertainment media (films, TV, radio, books)	7	-	7
Corruption and abuse of power	5	1	6
Police abuses (some might come under criminal trials)	2	3	5
Children and women (some might come under criminal trials)	2	6	8
Drugs, alcohol & food (attempts to prevent sale, protect quality, etc.)	2	4	6
Public utilities	4	1	5
Education	2	1	3
Political questions (some corruption cases might fall into this category)	6	2	8
Other (includes Delhi riots case: *PUDR v Ministry of Home Affairs AIR 1985 Delhi 269*, which might equally fall under 'weaker sections' above)	6	-	6
Total:	90	56	146

Court in which case was brought.

He did not deny the need for a broader approach to standing or for more active judicial control over litigation than had been traditional. What seemed to exercise him was the necessity for the Court not to exceed the limits of its powers. He argued that the Court must ensure that it gives due notice to all who might be affected by its orders - which in the case of PIL often goes beyond the parties to the case. The Court must not bypass statutorily required procedures and it must be careful not to trespass on legislative territory or make political decisions - risks to which it is exposed because 'the citizen seems to find it more convenient to apply to the Court for the vindication of human rights than appeal to the executive or legislative organs of the State' (at 843). The Court should not forget the difference between the public debate characteristic of the legislature and the more secretive process by which judicial decisions are reached. It should avoid emotional appeals and rely on legal principle, especially 'when a few social action groups tend to show evidence of presuming that in every case the court must bend and mould its decisions to popular notions of which way a case should be decided' (at 844). Pathak J stated 'That we sit at the apex of the judicial administration and our word, by constitutional mandate, is the law of the land can induce an unusual sense of power. It is a feeling we must guard against by constantly reminding ourselves that every decision must be guided by reason and by judicial principles' (at 845).

Conclusion

The types of cases which have been brought as PIL indicate that this procedure has some significance for the enforcement of the rights of classes as opposed to individuals. Problems affecting prisoners, women, children and bonded labourers, in addition to environmental issues can all be described as collective interests which have received attention in the Indian courts in a way which few, if any, other countries approach.

I suggested earlier that an important requirement is that the procedure be accessible. In comparison with the general civil litigation in India PIL scores quite highly (see Baxi 1982). PIL is relatively non-technical and cheap. On the other hand, the locus of most PIL activity to date has been the Supreme Court, which sits only in Delhi. Even state High Courts are available only in the major towns. It would appear that in order to take off, PIL must be adopted by the lower courts, as has happened in a few cases and appears to be technically feasible (Suryawanshi 1987). Many cases have been brought by social action organisations, of which the disadvantaged groups are not necessarily members. Others have been brought by individuals such as journalists, lawyers, academics and 'social workers', or even instituted by the judges themselves on the basis of newspaper reports. This has made possible the activation of the courts on behalf of sections of the community who previously would never have thought of making use of them.

Evidence on the effectiveness of PIL is patchy. It is clear from the *Sheela Barse* case for example that many cases extend over long periods of time, although in several instances improvements have occurred in the conditions of the victims prior to the final outcome (if, indeed, there is a definitive outcome). This is particularly true of environmental litigation such as the *Doon Valley* case, which actually brought to an end the quarrying. In another case the Supreme Court appeared to have put some life into the Ganga Action plan to improve the River Ganges (*M.C. Mehta v Union of India* [1988] 1 SCR 279). The Indian courts have shown creativity in requiring the authorities to report progress on implementation, but they are not equipped to constantly monitor public authorities or private enterprises. The sort of determined pressure necessary to achieve change may require a determination on the part of the litigant that may ultimately falter. In the *Ganges* case, for example, the lawyer who brought the original petition returned to the Court complaining that some of the treatment plants installed by the tanneries under a Court order were not operating (Wijesinha 1991). Similarly, a series of orders requiring the improvement of a 'protective home' for women in Agra was nullified, causing the litigation to be virtually restarted, when the State moved the home to a new site (*Upendra Baxi v State of Uttar Pradesh* 1986 4 SCC 106). And, despite the numerous and much publicised PIL cases on prisons, writers like Gonsalves (1988) have bemoaned the fact that prison conditions remain as savage as ever. It is one thing for the court to say 'our door is open' and another to give any concrete remedy. Parmanand Singh (1987: 154) has observed that:

> It remains...unexplained what social purpose has been served by the court in unduly expanding and reconceptualising the right to life under Article 21 without carrying any burden to fulfil the enlarged commitment. Will such expansion of Article 21 not demote the right to life to the status of a non-enforceable directive principle?

Another matter of concern is the ability of the courts to consider all the implications of the decisions they hand down. Here again the *Ganges* case is relevant. Although it is undoubtedly true that the Ganges is highly polluted, the order of the court threatened to put a large number of small tanneries, and their owners and employees, out of business (Rao 1991). The risk of courts using PIL to override other rights seems to be more acute at the High Court level, where a vetting process similar to that established by the Supreme Court may not be in operation. 'Cultural' or 'minority' interests may therefore come into conflict with considerations of freedom of speech in High Court cases. For example, cases have been brought seeking unsuccessfully to stop television programmes because they would stir up communal disharmony or encourage superstitious beliefs (*Ramesh v Union of India* 1988 19 IJR 364, *Oddessey v Lokvidayana Sanghatana* AIR 1988 SC 1642); and to halt the importation of foreign films or the screening of television programmes undermining Indian culture, the broadcasting of vulgar songs, or the sale of foreign pornography (see Mridul 1986). In one instance the Madras High Court overturned the decision of the Board of Film Censors partly on the ground that the film in question insulted the 'backward classes' (*P Jagajeevan Ram v Government of India* AIR 1989 Mad 149).

The possible 'capture' of a procedure that is quicker, cheaper and simpler than the usual processes of litigation by the litigating classes is a risk to which the courts, and the Supreme Court in particular, are very much alive. A further risk is that the procedure will be used as a mask for personal interest, and it appears that a few cases of this kind still get through even the Supreme Court's net. In dismissing one case the Court attacked a litigant who 'In order to feed his fat personal grudge...has taken several proceedings against the respondent-company including the present proceedings' (*Subhash Kumar v State of Bihar* AIR 1991 SC 420, 423; see also *Chhetriya Pardushan Mukti Sangharsh Samiti v State of Uttar Pradesh* AIR 1990 SC 2060).

Some cases, especially at the High Court level, appear to have been motivated by political or sectarian considerations, with litigants 'trying it on' but receiving short shrift from the Court. A blatant example was the case of *Chadanmal Chopra v State* (AIR 1986 Cal 104) in Calcutta in which an attempt was made to ban the Koran on the basis that it stirred up communal disharmony. Similarly, attempts to persuade the Madras High Court to direct the Government of India to intervene in Sri Lanka (*Karuppan v*

Government of India 1985 II Mad LJR 504), or that of Andhra Pradesh to order the proclamation of Martial Law (*Chinta Subba Rao v Supreme Commander* AIR 1980 AP 172) are but two examples of cases summarily disposed of by the courts. In the *Judges' Transfer* case the Supreme Court said 'we must be careful to see that the member of the public who approaches the court in cases of this kind is acting *bona fide* and not for personal gain or private profit or political motivation or other oblique consideration' (AIR 1981 SC at 195). However, not all politically motivated cases have been dismissed. In *Dhronamraju Satyanarayana v N T Rama Rao* (AIR 1988 AP 144) the Andhra Pradesh High Court found a number of allegations against the Chief Minister proven, and the court decided that cases involving serious allegations could not be rejected simply because they were filed for political motives. In Madhya Pradesh the leader of the opposition brought a petition alleging the improper conduct of a lottery, and that it was protected by powerful people (*Kailash Joshi v Madhya Pradesh* 1989 Jab L J 127). His petition was successful despite the court's recognition that it had political overtones.

Another issue has been the use, particularly in the High Court, of PIL for the benefit of middle-class interests. By middle-class I have in mind, for example, cases concerning the use of land previously used or zoned for parks or similar purposes, for residential or commercial uses, the best known instance being the use of part of Calcutta Zoo's land for a hotel (*Sachidanand Pandey v State* AIR 1987 SC 1109). The ragging of freshers at university, the demolition of the elegant Attara Cutcherry housing the High Court in Bangalore, the failure to provide state funding for private law schools, the institution of a one-way system on a road leading to the High Court, and a challenge to the erection of a statue of Gandhi on the basis that it made him look 'depressed' are all instances of cases that may be characterised as representing middle class concerns rather than those of weaker sections of society.[5]

There is, of course, no reason why the 'collective rights' protected should only be those of the weaker sections, and environmental rights in particular have a universal impact. But there is some reason to be concerned if remedies intended for the disadvantaged are appropriated by those who have traditionally had less difficulty in mobilising the legal and political systems in their interests. In fact, there is a somewhat paternalistic tendency in the PIL movement. Parmanand Singh (1989: 45) has written that:

Typically, PIL is initiated and controlled by elites and is governed by their own priorities and choices. These activists have different agenda and ideologies. Most of them lack sustained commitment to any specific victimised groups. Nor have they any enduring relationship with such groups.

The courts do refuse to allow classes to have remedies thrust upon in the absence of any indication that they desire them or are unable to seek for them themselves.[6] The NGOs and middle-class activists who espouse the causes of the underprivileged in India are no more paternalistic than their counterparts elsewhere, and this is presumably an inevitable corollary of a strategy which uses an establishment institution like the courts, and does so by allowing the initiative to be taken by those other than the underprivileged themselves.

Whether PIL achieves more than ameliorative or symbolic measures is difficult to gauge. As Parmanand Singh (1989: 45) has argued, 'The effectiveness of PIL in fostering social change remains unknown and unassessed'. Bhanumurthy (1986: 90) believes that the courts have a more modest role in PIL:

> the new role that the courts have assigned to themselves must be seen as their attempt not to correct the social reality, but to correct the legal system. Trying to redeem the system of not having kept up its laudable objective - justice for all...

> Once it is recognised that the courts cannot bring about social change, or at any rate, cannot replace social movements, the only role they can play is to aid social movements...The courts can only free an ailing Naxalite prisoner, or bail out a labour leader, or free one group of the endless stream of bonded labour.

PIL has, therefore, been a means by which the courts have extended their limited powers. In many of these cases, as we have seen, they have endeavoured to release more than one prisoner and to wipe the tears from many eyes.[7] The obvious answer to the criticism that this is not the role of the courts is provided by Justice Chinnappa Reddy's contention (1983: 39) that 'It is not the Judiciary, but the Parliament and the Executive that have failed the people'.

Whatever the contradictions of PIL, the bold and imaginative steps taken by the Indian courts have, not surprisingly, attracted attention throughout the world, though often not as much as they merit. In a few countries, such as Malaysia[8] and the Philippines[9], they have been emulated. The Indian model may thus inspire lawyers in some other jurisdictions, or even the occasional judge. But there remains some doubt as to how far PIL has become institutionalised even in India, where its development has depended upon certain peculiarities in the Constitution such as the Directive Principles of State Policy (which have become a familiar feature of constitutions elsewhere in recent years, e.g. Papua New Guinea, Nigeria and Namibia). More than anything else, perhaps, the possibility of PIL developing elsewhere depends upon whether judges are prepared to be as creative as their Indian counterparts. The Indian judiciary is almost certainly the most activist in the common law world, for reasons which are arguably peculiar to India itself and the traumatic impact of the 1975 Emergency in particular (see Das 1987). The judges have been important, but PIL also requires a strong and civil liberties movement to prompt such cases, even India, where there is a longer tradition of NGO activity than elsewhere in the South, does not have a sufficient number of such organizations (Bhanumurthy 1986). Thus, although PIL at first sight offers exciting and progressive possibilities, its future both in India and elsewhere remains uncertain.

Notes

1   The more common expression is public interest litigation - as is evidenced in the index heading in the *All India Reporter* and the regular chapter in the *Annual Survey of Indian Law* (Indian Law Institute, Delhi). The main advocate of the expression 'social action litigation' is Baxi (1985, 1988).

2   There is now a considerable literature. See for example Baxi (1985, 1988), Gupta (1988), Massey (1985), Parmanand Singh (1985), Agrawala (1985) and Craig & Deshpande (1989). Less has been written about the High Court, but see Cottrell (1990) and Mridul (1986).

3   There is of course a formal procedure for petitions under Article 32 that are commenced in the normal way. One of the features of PIL that have generated particular controversy has been the commencement of proceedings by letter. During the mid-1980s these became a positive flood, many of them being addressed to Chief Justice Bhagwati, who was perceived as the main proponent of PIL. In one

of his last judgments, *Bandhua Mukti Morcha* (AIR 1987 SC 1030), Bhagwati argued that letters should not be rejected simply because they were addressed to a particular judge, provided that they came from someone in custody, from someone representing them or on 'behalf of a woman or child or a class of deprived or disadvantaged persons' (see Singh 1987: 143 and, for a critical view, Agrawala 1985).

4   The tables were compiled up to three years ago, but subsequent cases do not appear to change the overall picture - although there may be some states in which PIL cases have been brought that had not previously witnessed them. It should be noted that in many of these cases the court rejected the petition as an inappropriate use of PIL.

5   Respectively *State of Himachal Pradesh v Parent of Student of Medical College* AIR 1985 SC 910, *B V Narayana Reddy v State* AIR 1985 Kant 99, *Manubhai Pragaji Vashi v State* AIR 1988 Bom 296, *Ram Sahai Verma v State* AIR 1989 MP 334, and *Babubhai Jashbhai Patel v State* AIR 1988 Guj 1.

6   A recent example is *Satish Chandra Mishra v State of Uttar Pradesh* (AIR 1990 All 119), in which the High Court refused to allow a petition by a (presumably) private practitioner against the imposition of a condition on State Counsel that they should not engage in private practice.

7   The phrase was Gandhi's. Its most frequent judicial user was Krishna Iyer J in, for example, the *Azad Rickshaw Pullers'* case above.

8   *Jau Jok Evong v Marobong Lumber Sdn Bhd.* Kuching High Court Civil Suit KG 256 of 1988 (challenging the sanctioning of logging), and *Woon Tan Kan v Asian Rare Earth Sdn Bhd* Ipoh High Court Civil Suit No. 185 of 1985 (residents challenging a plant which they accused of causing radiation) (Nijjar 1991).

9   'On March 20, 1990, 45 children/minors from all over the geographic regions of the country, legally represented by their parents/ guardians - acting on behalf of their generation and for generations yet unborn - instituted a legal action against the defendant Secretary of the DENR (Dept of Environment and Natural Resources). The prayer for mandatory injunction is to enjoin the cancellation of all Timber License Agreements in the Philippines' (Oposa 1991).

6

Rights-struggle, Class-struggle and The Law: Reflections on Experiences at the University of Dar es Salaam

Issa G. Shivji[1]

Introduction

During the three decades of its existence, a marked feature of legal teaching and theorisation at the Faculty of Law at the University of Dar es Salaam has been its linkage with larger social theories on the one hand, and practical student struggles on the other. Where one of these links has been broken or non-existent, the debate has tended to take either a demagogic or an eclectic form.

The debates of the 1960s and 1970s have been variously recorded (Ghai 1987, Kanywanyi 1989, Shivji 1986a), so this paper focuses on the issues and politics of the Eighties in order to draw some conclusions about broader questions of law, rights struggles and class struggles. I begin by tracing the immediate precursors to these developments.

Law & Development versus Historical & Socio-Economic Method

Law and Development, like the modernisation theories from which it sprang (*cf.* Adelman & Paliwala *infra*), was not the result of local debates or struggles on the Dar es Salaam campus. In the Faculty of Law it came as part of a North American package. Where modernisation had a local manifestation, as in the 'African Initiative' school in History, it had a greater influence. Law and Development, however, made little positive impact on student consciousness.[2] Although it continues to appear in the University Calendar it has not been taught for two decades. Instead, a course on the *Social and Economic Problems of East Africa* developed locally and had a marked impact. It was organised as a response to the expulsion of 300 students in 1966 (the result of student demonstration against National Service) in the context of the Arusha Declaration (see Picciotto 1986, Kanywanyi 1989).

The course was located within traditions of radical scholarship and was particularly influenced by the bourgeoning 'development and underdevelopment' school which was gaining sway on the campus. Whatever its shortcomings, the underdevelopment school dealt a fatal blow to both modernisation and Law and Development. In the Faculty of Law the debate culminated in the formal adoption and inclusion in the University Calendar of the 'historical and socio-economic approach' as a method of teaching (Tenga 1986, *cf.* Mabirizi 1986). The socio-economic approach was never clearly defined or debated theoretically by the radicals who adopted it. In practice, it involved some version of Marxist political economy and historical materialism for the radicals. Others, without declaring so, continued to adhere to the American sociological school or the 'black letter' law tradition.

Within radical scholarship, two currents emerged in the early 1970s concerning the meaning of the historical and socio-economic method. Both took Marxist political economy as their point of departure, but there were considerable differences in their approach to the teaching of law. One current rigidly applied the economic base-superstructure dichotomy. Law, as part of the superstructure, was viewed as a reflection of the determining economic base. Law would ultimately reflect social changes which resulted from changes in the economic base. Adopting the historical and socio-economic method meant tutoring students in the Marxist classics and in historical and dialectical materialism. Most courses began with discussion of the five modes of production, etc. and ended with a textual and doctrinal analysis of the rules in the positivist tradition.

The other current argued that law should be regarded as a significant bourgeois form in its own right and should be analysed to reveal or expose its substance, namely its exploitative class character (Shivji 1972). Adherents to this current never explicated their approach in a lucid manner and were still groping in the dark when a new factor intervened.

In the mid-Seventies, the globalist school emerged (Shivji

1990a: 56-8). Taking Lenin's *Imperialism* as its point of departure, it viewed 'international finance capital' as the all-pervasive phenomenon to which everything else, including law, was subordinated. It influenced the nature and conduct of the debate and, to a certain extent, marred creative thinking in the Faculty in the late Seventies (Mahalu 1986: 89-90). People were reluctant to express themselves for fear of being identified with one or the other position or being accused of departing from orthodoxy. In the absence of practical student struggles, the so-called 'debate' of the period regrettably degenerated into a sterile regurgitation of fundamental texts (see Tandon 1982, Copans 1991 and, for a veiled critique, the late Prime Minister Sokoine 1983).

Meanwhile, a small group slowly crystallised and galvanised around practical concerns under the umbrella of legal aid. Legal aid activities were based on a very broad and somewhat woolly theorisation of democracy. Most participants, particularly younger members, consciously avoided discussion of larger social theories for fear of being pigeon-holed. Nonetheless, legal aid activities constituted a form of struggle for rights within the broader struggle for democracy (Shivji 1991b, Peter 1991, Mwaikusa, 1991, *cf.* Lugakingira 1990). It was during the Eighties that the broader struggle for democracy gradually came to the fore, and it is to this that I now turn.

The Struggle for Democracy

The 1980s may be conveniently divided into two periods. In the early part of the decade the student body continued to suffer from the proscription of the Dar es Salaam University Students Union (DUSO) following a demonstration by students against increased privileges for Ministers and Members of Parliament in 1978. This marked an end to an autonomous students organisation in Tanzania. They were now organized under MUWATA (*Muungano wa Wanafunzi, Tanzania*), a 'students union' controlled by the youth wing of the ruling party. As a consequence student debates took a low profile. In 1980 the academic staff formed UDASA (University of Dar es Salaam Academic Staff Assembly). Having no place under the *University Act*, UDASA is formally a standing committee of the Convocation although in practice it functions fairly independently. Debates about teaching and broader social theories were deeply affected. Activists were still smarting from the vitriolic debates of the late seventies. Although some members of staff were active in legal aid and in seminars and discussions organized outside the University, there was no direct link or effect on their day-to-day teaching or on wider student politics on the campus.

On the theoretical level, there was increasing awareness of 'democracy as the central question in the African revolution' (IDS 1983).[3] In the Law Faculty, this translated itself into a struggle for rights, albeit in a relatively unarticulated form. For example, Faculty members were in the forefront of the challenge to the draconian *Economic Sabotage Act* of 1983.[4] The Legal Aid Committee was the first to protest against the killing of four Kilombero workers by the Field Force Unit (FFU) in 1986. The Committee's most important input was, however, in the constitutional debates of 1983-84. Paradoxically, this input came in the Tanganyika Law Society Seminar held in downtown Dar es Salaam in July 1983. Neither the broader student nor the staff bodies were involved in the debate, underlining the fact that the debates of this period took place in absence of practical student politics.

Three issues dominated the Law Society seminar. First, the question of the Union of Tanganyika and Zanzibar and the right of the latter to self-determination.[5] Second, demands for a Bill of Rights and, third, demands for freedom of association, in particular the right to form autonomous mass organizations. The latter demand was admittedly a minority current emphasised by academics, with practitioners displaying little interest. These issues would subsequently become the focus of deeper debates in later separate seminars and conferences. Another facet of Zanzibar's right to self-determination, namely democratisation on the island, attracted a lot of discussion at a seminar organised by the Institute of Development Studies in Zanzibar in January 1984. The dominant trend in this seminar was the demand for greater autonomy for Zanzibar. New technocrats reared during the post-Karume era argued that Zanzibar had suffered economically as a result of the Union; and that the absence of direct contact with aid donors etc. meant that Zanzibar was ignored in the allocation of aid and other largesse.[6] This somewhat perverted nationalist argument failed to comprehend the fact that the mainland's contacts with donors had increased the country's debt and thereby served to integrate more closely into the world capitalist system.[7] A minority argued in favour of strengthening the democratic initiatives of the Jumbe period.[8] In this, the law faculty once again had a significant input.

Rights-struggle, Class-struggle and The Law

The constitutional debate came to an abrupt halt when the Party National Executive Committee announced in January 1984 that the 'political atmosphere had been polluted', particularly in Zanzibar. Aboud Jumbe, then Vice-President of the Union and President of Zanzibar, was forced to resign and the question of the Union was once more swept under the carpet. Nonetheless the constitutional amendments of 1984 did include a *Bill of Rights* in the Union Constitution as did the Zanzibar Constitution of the same year. The *Bill of Rights* came under close scrutiny at the next available opportunity, the Faculty of Law Silver Jubilee Seminar in October 1986.

Most of the twelve papers concentrated on the limitations of the rights as they were formulated in the Constitution. There were arguments in favour of expansive drafting so far as rights were concerned and calls for the judiciary to interpret the relevant clauses liberally (Mbunda 1980). The seminar sent an urgent telex to the leader of government business in the National Assembly calling upon it to desist from presenting the *Bill on Emergency Powers* to the Assembly as this would violate the *Bill of Rights*.

Zanzibari autonomy was also a focus of discussion at a conference in December 1986 organized to mark twenty years of the Arusha Declaration (Hartman 1991). Members of the Faculty of Law again played an active role in discussions centered on multi-party democracy (echoes of which are being heard in the 1990s), separation of the state and the party, and the freedom to form autonomous civil organisations (see *Eastern Africa Social Science Research Review*, Vol.III, No.1, January 1987; Shivji 1986b). Unfortunately, as noted earlier, there was little attempt at theorising the concerns and practices of the activists during this period or at situating them within larger social theories. The result of such theoretical eclecticism was to fall back, often unconsciously, on liberal perspectives. For this reason the concept of democracy was never concretely interrogated as a mode of politics in civil society. Instead, it was conceived merely as a form of the institutional organisation of the state and/or the relation of the citizen to the state (Shivji 1991e).

Although there was broad debate on (human) rights, the liberal philosophical and political premises underlying the dominant human rights discourse were taken for granted. For those who attempted to theorise at all it was with the traditional preoccupations of lawyers that they were concerned: the role of the judiciary, the effectivity of administrative law remedies, modes of constitutional interpretation, and the comparison and classification of rights in the fashion of analytical jurisprudence. Some fine pieces of scholarship were produced by younger members of the Faculty within this tradition (see e.g. Peter 1990a), but the question of rights as struggle was not addressed in any rigorous fashion; neither was legal aid activity explicitly theorised or located within popular democratic struggles.

The external activities of academics were not effectively translated into definite approaches to teaching or the production of progressive teaching materials. This further reinforced the absence of any link with the larger student body. By default if not design, teaching began to fall back on traditional doctrinal and textual analysis in the positivist tradition.[9] In the second half of the eighties, for reasons that will become clear, positivist teaching appears to have succumbed to shoddiness and lack of concern.

In addition, the deterioration of the academic infrastructure and the living and working conditions of lecturers dealt a severe blow to the activist tradition of the Faculty of Law. Participation by members of staff in general discussions on the campus declined while debates, research and writing at the Faculty virtually disppeared. The agenda of academic work and legal aid activity began to be set by the demands of consultancy services and the predilections of donor agencies. Such criticism is not specific to the Faculty of Law; but reflects tendencies that can be witnessed in the University as a whole. Thus far, the relative inactivity of 'lawyers' has not manifested itself in right-wing approaches to campus struggles. This brings us to the second half of the Eighties, which witnessed a dramatic turn in the practical struggles of the student body.

The 'Ideological Tiananmen': 1986-90

The hesistant moves towards economic liberalisation initiated in 1983-4 became full-blown by 1986, in which the national budget was an undisguised IMF budget (Campbell & Stein 1991). Cuts in social welfare expenditure resulted, for example, in the imposition of school fees. The shilling was dramatically devalued. By the late 1980s a University professor's salary amounted to no more than US $50 while the student book allowance covered no more than two standard text-books. The University infrastructure deteriorated to the point at which even chalk, dusters and mimeographed material became scarce. In 1986, UDASA had drawn the attention of the relevant authorities to these pathetic conditions and the resultant flight of teachers to greener pastures but had been cold-shouldered by the bureaucracy (Sheriff 1990). Students began to comprehend that their grievances would not be addressed without some form of organised protest, which was virtually impossible under the heavily controlled MUWATA. It is believed that there were rumblings for the formation of an autonomous student organisation in 1986 and matters came to a head when students boycotted classes in protest against the rise in food prices, the so-called 'food strike' two years later. A more militant student leadership emerged which set to work on the formation of an autonomous organisation amongst other things.

In 1989 events moved even faster. In the early part of the year two student leaders were arrested, detained for three weeks and interrogated, apparently because they had dared raise questions about the use of funds by the 'leaders' of a trip to a youth festival in North Korea (*UDASA Newsletter*, No.9, October 1989). A Committee appointed by the University Council to investigate found the arrests and detentions to be illegal and recommended that the Government institute an official investigation and take appropriate disciplinary and legal actions against the perpetrators of these acts.[10] Nothing happened. In the privacy of his chambers, the then Prime Minister (who at first ignored the issue) blamed the students involved and the organs of the state equally and asked all to forgive and forget!

The influence of the changing international context became more marked with the collapse of the 'communist' regimes in Eastern Europe and the emergence of movements towards democracy. The Dar es Salaam campus, which had hitherto been relatively passive, suddenly burst into life. Numerous well attended seminars and symposia were organised to discuss these changes and their impact on Africa and generated heated debate. At the same time, the President of the Republic declared a 'war on corruption' and called for greater accountability by the ruling party and the state in response to their rapid loss of public credibility (Shivji 1990c). The Party Chairman announced that discussion about a multiparty system was no longer a 'sin', his declaration coming in the wake of deliberations by the Party National Executive Committee on the changes in Eastern Europe. Consequently, albeit haltingly and selectively, the controlled media began to allow greater expression of opinion about corruption and democracy.

An autonomous student organization, Daruso (Dar es Salaam University Students Organisation), emerged with a constitution approved by the University Council. It elected an interim government even as recognition by the Chancellor under the University Act was pending, and convened a *Baraza* (General Assembly) on 7 April 1990 to discuss their own academic and living conditions amongst other things. The *Baraza* developed into an extended session lasting ten days as student demands began to be pressed at various levels. Lecturers, while expressing reservations about the methods adopted, such as a boycott of classes, to press demands and raise issues, gave their support. In an unprecedented move, lecturers joined the *Baraza* through UDASA and joint discussions ensued. On 12 May 1990 the President of the University closed the institution for eight months.

The New Democratic Form: Issues as Rights-Struggle

The debates that took place at the *Baraza* and the formal demands which they generated have three broad rights themes.

1. *The right to education*

Students emphatically criticised the falling share allocated to education in the national budget. The figures they repeatedly quoted in their statements showed that this had fallen from some 20 per cent in the 1960s to approximately 5 per cent in the late 1980s, an amount lower than that spent on education in neighbouring countries like Kenya and Uganda. They argued that unproductive sectors like defence and administration received larger and ever-growing allocations which reflected a skewed sense of priorities and bureaucratic neglect of a very important social sector.

It was in this context that the deteriorating University infrastructure, extremely low academic salaries and inadequate book and other allowances were highlighted. Underlying these demands was the assertion, not only of the right to education, but the right to *wholesome* education. The *Dar es Salaam Declaration on Academic Freedom and Social Responsibility of Academics* adopted by the six staff associations of Institutions of Higher Education in Tanzania at this time also emphasised the 'right of every resident to wholesome education'.[11] Article 9 of the Declaration demands that:

The State should make available an adequate proportion of the national income to ensure in practice the full realisation of the right to education. The State shall bind itself constitutionally to provide a nationally agreed minimum proportion of the national income for education.

2. *The right to call and recall administrators (the essence of accountability)*

In an innovative move, the *Baraza* summoned four administrators, including the Chief Administrative Officer and the University medical officer, to appear before it and explain alleged incompetence, negligence and corruption in their offices. Hitherto officers might have been called by their superiors or organs such as the University Council to justify their actions, but having to explain and exculpate themselves before a mass assembly of the academic community was unprecented and was not appreciated by the administrators. In the absence of legal powers, the *Baraza* 'fired' the Estates Manager and withdrew recognition from the Chief Administrative Officer in an important act presaging a new mode of politics. What was being asserted was the right of the community to demand accountability and recall, if necessary, those appointed to serve it but who, in law and practice, lorded over it. As the *Baraza* proceeded it became extremely sceptical of established parliamentary methods of representative democracy such as the appointment of committees and delegations to discuss, negotiate and decide on behalf of the community. Instead, the Principal Secretary in the Ministry of Education was invited to attend the *Baraza*. Dissatisfied with his explanation, the *Baraza* called upon him to convey an invitation to the Chancellor. When the Chancellor sent a message to the effect that he was prepared to see a delegation, the *Baraza*, after initial reluctance, agreed. The delegation was given a specific, limited mandate: to give the Chancellor a broad view of the issues and questions raised by the *Baraza* and invite him to the campus for an exchange of views. It had no mandate to 'negotiate' or take any decisions. This was later construed by the media and state spokespersons as insolence and an act of disrespect on the part of students to the Head of State). In the same spirit, the *Baraza* elected a joint student-staff committee with technical powers and no political mandate to prepare a comprehensive statement to be presented to the Chancellor during his visit.

3. The right to discuss and debate national issues

In both its debates and statements the *Baraza* raised a number of what students called 'national issues', which included the gutting of the Central Bank in a fire which remained unexplained, the purchase of a second-hand pontoon that had broken down within days of its arrival and for which no one had been held accountable, the deteriorating conditions of workers and peasants and the increasing income differential between the rich and poor, and the dumping of waste by the Tabata City Council resulting in health and environmental hazards.[12] Whatever the merits of these issues, their significance lay in the assertion by students of their right to debate national issues *openly*[13] and the right of any sector of the community to demand and receive explanation and information on issues of national concern (Tegambwage 1990). Underlying these propositions is the evolution of a mode of politics which resists capture within established institutions and procedures.

Admittedly, this process of democratic struggle was contradictory. A number of aspects betrayed non-democratic attitudes and internalised state ideologies. There was, for example, considerable intolerance of unpopular views which may have precluded full debate of all issues, not least tactics, by the *Baraza* and limited its ability to arrive at mature and rational decisions. Threats of violence rather than persuasion were often resorted to in attempts to impose certain lines of action. In addition, there was a limited appreciation of the distinction between the methods of the state (logic of force) and the methods of the community (force of logic) in resolving differences.

Another shortcoming, particularly in comparison to previous student struggles, was the virtual absence of a grand ideology, democracy proving too equivocal and ambiguous to play this role. This created a lack of direction and meant that the struggle lacked a tactical dimension embodied in the consolidatation of gains, the evaluation of one's strength, the ability to make strategic retreats, and particularly to preserve the broadest possible organizational strength and unity. Militant students persistently and naively tended to over-estimate their strength and to take the slogans of 'student power' literally and simplistically. Bridge-building and networking with potential sympathisers in the community at large was virtually absent, and little effort was made to establish independent means of disseminating information to the surrounding community. For this the students paid dearly when the state launched a massive ideological campaign against them, facilitated by the lack of public awareness of the issues. Unlike their brethren of the Tiananmen Square, for whom freedom of expression and the right to disseminate information were priorities, such demands were not explicitly made by the Dar es Salaam students.

The State Reaction

During the week in which the University was closed there was a poster campaign maligning the Head of State. Some of these were regular political cartoons while others were indefensibly filthy, abusive and insulting pornographic drawings. The latter probably originated on the extremist fringes of the student body but the actions of *agents provocateurs* from state organs could not be ruled out. The Committe of Enquiry appointed by the University Council and headed by a High Court judge (the Mrosso Commission) failed to find any substantial evidence against the students.

The official reasons given for closing the University were many and various. They included protecting peace on the campus, forestalling physical clashes between students, and imposing (collective) punishment for disrespect, indiscipline and insubordination. In any event, the ideological campaign against the students, which is what concerns us here, began almost two weeks before the poster episode. It was intensified after the poster episode, but this was clearly the motive behind it.

The 1990 struggle of Dar es Salaam students at the Nkrumah Hall and the subsequent closure of the University bear little comparison with the gruesome massacre of the Chinese students Tiananmen Square, not least because there was virtually no physical violence on the campus. In spite of efforts by *agents provocateurs* to incite violence, students remained peaceful even when they were hounded out of the campus on Black Saturday (12 May), at four hours' notice. What is comparable, however, is the vehemence with which the two states reacted against the students, probably for the same underlying fears. If the Chinese tanks rolled over the bodies of thousands of students in Tiananmen Square, the Tanzanian media rolled over their souls in Dar es Salaam. It was 'an ideological massacre'.

The two daily newspapers in Dar es Salaam, owned by the party and the government, and state radio launched a massive propaganda campaign against the students beginning on 18 April following a government ultimatum ordering the students to return to classes. The ultimatum was essentially obeyed but was accompanied by face-saving proclamations from the students. The students were variously depicted as traitorous, unpatriotic internal enemies, agents of external enemies, rude, disobedient and hooligans. No evidence was produced against them (and none were taken to court), and they were given no platform to air their grievances. In fact, the Mrosso Commission almost totally exonerated the students but its report was conveniently ignored by the Government. Editorials and the views of citizens solicited by the press (one does not know how much of this was downright fabrication), called upon the Government to punish the students severely, including whipping them, and to make them pay for their education. In the midst of serious flooding and the campaign against corruption, state and party resources and the energies of the public were diverted to stage demonstrations all over the country to condemn the students and congratulate the President for closing the University. This unprecedented media war was calculated to drive a permanent wedge between the students and the public and to strike fear in the University community, the only remaining bastion of critical thought in the country. That it did not totally succeed was not due to lack of effort from the powers that be.

How does one explain the vehemence of this concerted and irrational ideological onslaught? The Government may have feared the democratic movements in Eastern Europe, Gabon, Ivory Coast and Burkina Faso would have a domino effect in Tanzania. Students are an important sector of the community and the issues they were raising were on the lips of the masses, even if they remained unspoken. As important as the content of the issues was the *form* in which they were raised. Open debate and discussion in a mass assembly looked like a harbinger of the mass politics long forgotten since the fight for independence. The *Baraza* appeared to be turning the official version on its head, giving the campaign for accountability (launched by the President himself) new meaning and content. Its actions indicated that accountability from officers of the state and the University should be to the people in mass assemblies. The students complained about corruption to the relevant authorities and demanded that it be weeded out, thereby threatening many in the power elite. The media and the state accused the students of usurping the role of Parliament and subverting the election of superiors every five years in accordance with electoral laws. Equally important were the fears of both state and party that the example provided by an autonomous student organization might become contagious. Even in officially sponsored 'mass organizations' calls for autonomy and the right to freely elect leaders without party intervention (such as the 'filtering' of nominees) were beginning to be heard.

What was at stake were of two different forms of politics. In the established mode, politics took place within the confines of the law. In an authoritarian one-party system this meant the usurpation by parliament of the role of the people, the usurpation by party of the role of parliament, the usurpation by the party National Executive Committee of the role of the party and its bureaucracy/leadership, and the ultimate usurpation of power by the cabinet and the state bureaucracy. In contrast, student activism represented a different mode of politics (Wamba-dia-Wamba 1990), originating at grassroots level and heedless of both the laws and The Law,[14] and charging the 'leaders' with usurping the role of the people. The students did not articulate nor theorise their politics in this way, but their actions did raise the fundamental issue of the meaning and content of accountability which state control did not allow to be fully discussed. Later events, particularly the Mrema phenomenon, demonstrated the centrality of this issue in the struggle for democracy.

At the conclusion of the election in October 1990 it was clear that the credibility of the Mwinyi Government would hinge on the President's election promises to effect accountability and to crack down on corruption and bureaucratic inefficency. Mwinyi appointed Augustine Mrema, hitherto a vocal bank bencher and former security officer, to the post of Minister for Home Affairs. Mrema mounted a high profile one-person campaing to expose and bring corrupt elements to book. He offered large sums of money to anyone who would volunteer information, intervened in matters as diverse as matrimonial affairs and taxation, acting as investigator, conciliator, prosecutor and judge, and became enormously popular. In reality his actions undermined any sense of accountability from below. Like other populist demagogues, people viewed him as a messiah who would deliver them from political and social evils. His popularity signified a form of protest against inefficient and corrupt state institutions, including the police, the judiciary and the private bar, and resulted in part from the truism that unorganised alienated masses tend to seek a saviour onto whom they can displace their hopes and who substitutes for their lack of organised strength. The Mrema phenomenon reiterated the contradictory nature of the struggle for democracy. Accountability, it seems to me, is at the heart of that struggle. The question, as ever, is the extent to which accountability by subordinates to superiors is prescribed by law while the accountability of rulers and bureaucrats to the people is masked by that same law.

Another significant and unprecedented feature of the 1990 struggle was that the lecturers' organisation, UDASA, joined the student *Baraza* on an equal footing despite the fact that teachers were even more divided in their approaches than the students. Adherence to state ideology and authoritarian/disciplinarian orientations among lecturers regularly marred the dialogue. The authorities took every opportunity to condemn this unity despite the positive role played by teachers.

There were, finally, other minor factors which influenced events. These included the fact that 1990 was an election year, internal contradictions in the 'palace', and the currying of favour by individuals with the Head of State by attempting to outdo each other in their condemnation of the students. The vehement malice of the propaganda was designed to create a moral panic calculated to distract attention from other national issues. Even at this early stage it would appear that the *Baraza* was an important milestone in the struggle for democracy generally and the struggle for rights in particular. The adoption and the ratification of the *Dar es Salaam Declaration on Academic Freedom and Social Responsibility of Academics*, sponsored by UDASA, is as an important appendix to these struggles despite having only an indirect relationship to them. It captures, in an innovative fashion, some of the central theoretical problems surrounding the question of rights (Shivji 1991c).

Since the University was re-opened in January 1991 the debate on democracy has taken a new turn. In the following section I therefore recapitulate some of the more important issues because of the bearing which they currently have on the debate amongst African intellectuals about the question of democracy (Shivji 1991d).

The University and the Debate on Democracy

In June 1990, after stepping down from the leadership of the CCM Party (*Chama cha Mapinduzi*), Julius Nyerere opened the debate on multi-party democracy. Official newspapers began to publish opinions critical of the ruling party after the first salvoes were fired by the Tanganyika Law Society in a two-day public seminar in September 1990 on *The Party System and Democracy in Tanzania*. Three groups played a leading role in these deliberations, which were attended by over 300 people: University academics, several private law practitioners, and former politicians from the independence era. With the University still closed, students were conspicuous by their absence. The seminar, which voted overwhelmingly for multi-party democracy, and stimulated a number of disparate advocates of a multi-party system to form groups and committees demanding immediate installation. After a short period, during which the debate continued in the newspapers, President Mwinyi appointed a commission to gather views of the public on the issue. The Nyalali Commission recommended that Tanzania adopt a multi-party system despite the fact that approximately 80 per cent of the people it interviewed favoured the retention of the one-party system (Nyalali Commission 1991, Fimbo 1992, Shivji 1992a). The CCM unanimously endorsed this recommendation and the National Assembly passed the *Eighth Constitutional Amendment Act* in 1992 to enable the registration of political parties (Shivji 1992b).

As soon as the University re-opened students were confronted with two major issues: the proposed introduction of cost-sharing and the debate on multi-party democracy. The issue of cost-sharing came in the wake of the IMF structural adjustment programme (known euphemistically as the economic recovery programme, or ERP) imposed on the country involving, *inter alia*, reductions in government expenditure on social services in particular. Students have generally opposed cost-sharing, but they have not seriously discussed its wider implications, such as the effects on the social composition of the student body. Similarly, they have given little serious scrutiny to imperialist role of the IMF in the Third World and the broader implicatiaons of multi-party democracy. Nonetheless, student activism once again resulted in a boycott of classes in January 1992 following the expiry of an ultimatum to the President demanding the withdrawal of cost-sharing. Once again, the students failed to place the issue in a wider social context and therefore were unable to mobilise public support. The Government and the new University administration resorted to a series of suspensions and expulsions while academics involvement amounted to issuing contradictory statements.[15] Academics were effectively neutralised through increased salaries and perks, and UDASA's leadership proved incapable of responding to events. By means of both carrot and stick the University administration brought an end to the cost-sharing strike.

Despite this, groups advocating multi-party democracy found the campus to be a fertile recruiting ground. Aggrieved at their treatment by the ruling party and the state during the University closure, students overwhelmingly but uncritically joined the multi-party bandwagon. A minority sought to raise broader issues such as different forms of democracy, the nature of mass-based politics, the adequacy of liberal and constitutionalist perspectives conflating democracy and multi-party rule, and the character of both domestic and international social (class) forces advocating a multi-party system (Shivji 1991e, 1991f; Wamba-dia-Wamba 1991). These issues did not, however, receive widespread attention on the campus. Multi-party democracy is uncritically regarded as an unqualified human good, an inherent human right which does not require further historical and social interrogation. The danger inherent in uncritical acceptance of liberalism in an imperialist-dominated social formation is that it inevitably degenerates into compradorial politics, as appears to be occurring in Tanzania.

In contrast, student struggles of the 1960s and 1970s were theoretically linked to larger questions. To whom does the University belong, the compradorial class or the people? What is the character of the state and how does it control ordinary citizens? In what directions are state and society moving? Participants in those struggles believed, perhaps presumptuously, that they were participants in the African Revolution. Some of the theoretical debates of that time were admittedly conducted in a polemical style that alienated many potential supporters and, with the benefit of hindsight inevitably but understandably reveals the mistaken and sometimes immature views of the students involved. They were, however, unequivocally committed, passsionate and intellectually critical. Moreover, they sought to act in the interests and from the standpoint of workers and peasants. It was this that made the Dar es Salaam campus, and the the Faculty of Law in particular, the envy of many African universities.

Despite these changes, the University continues to occupy an intellectually influential place in the Tanzanian polity. As Parliament was preparing to pass the 1992 *Organisation of Trade Unions Bill* and other measures designed to limit freedom of association and exclude judicial review of administrative action, the Faculty of Law produced a petition which was sent to members of Parliament urging them to reject the legislation. The bills were eventually enacted with several amendments following heated opposition and the denunciation by the leader of government business of the petitioners (mainly academics) as 'internal enemies'.

The University also had an important influence on the multiparty debate. When the Presidential Commission came to hear submissions from the student body, every participant eloquently denounced authoritarian and the undemocratic nature of both the state and the ruling party. This event was carried live on radio and was transmitted several times on Zanzibar television. It was recorded and replayed in public places like bars. It aroused such sympathetic interest amongst the public that it was rumoured that the cassettes were eventually removed from the radio library by state intelligence.

Conclusion: Law as an Arena of Rights-Struggle and Class-Struggle

The debates and struggles that have taken place at the University of Dar es Salaam bring into sharp relief the contradictory nature of democratic struggles in general and the tensions inherent in rights struggles in particular, and it is to an examination of these questions that I turn by way of conclusion. Limitations of space preclude a full survey of contemporary debates on law as an arena of struggle, on its potential and limitations, or on the role of law in authoritarian African legal orders (see, however, Ghai 1986, 1991 and *infra;* Thomas 1984). Instead, I will draw some conclusions derived from the rights struggles that have taken place on the Dar es Salaam campus.

These experiences have thrown into sharp relief the proposition that the juridical form leads inevitably to a politics on a terrain defined by law, the state and the ruling class. It is an error to ignore the law-form *per se* and concentrate exclusively on the content of law in order to elucidate its class character (this is the shortcoming of Owori's (1982) otherwise interesting thesis). The juridical form contains characteristics that tend to facilitate the reproduction of law as a vehicle of domination rather than liberation. Among these charactersitics are the individualisation of class and other collective grievances; the disguising by formal equality of the laws of material and social inequalities and the hegemonic hold of this ideology on subordinate classes; the procedures and institutions which construct procedural fairness as 'natural' and thereby reduce material oppression to metaphysical categories; the apparent consensus in The Law that mystifies the real (state) coercion behind it; the illusion of state apparatuses as divided against themselves which is derived from the 'separation' of powers and the 'independence' of the judiciary and deflects attention away from the *unity* of state power; and, finally, the translation through The Law of ruling class unity into the 'general will' - an all-inclusive unity of individuals abstracted from their class that hides the role of state in dividing subordinate classes.

The question of rights is also contradictory. From one perspective, rights originate in a legal category controlled by the state, which grants them at its discretion. They are standards and norms which are defined and embodied in law and ultimately the outcome of the activity of lawyers. Another perspective views rights struggle as the assertion of popular politics. They are regarded as symbols around which people may be mobilised. In this sense rights struggle is a constant activity, a vehicle for expression rather than a means of self-censorship (see Shivji 1989b, 1990d). To some extent, the 1990 student struggle reflected these contradictory perspectives on rights.

In an authoritarian African legal order the liberal perspective on rights has to be modified because the law itself is largely what I have termed elsewhere right-less law (Shivji 1989a). In such a system coercion is undisguised by apparent consensus, legal procedures have little regulatory or restraining effect on the exercise of power (Mwaikusa 1990, Nyange 1990, Peter 1990a, Shivji 1990d), and legal ideology has no hegemonic effects on the powerless. In these conditions, the liberal perspective appears to be a 'natural' an ideal to struggle for and the struggle for democracy is easily reduced to a struggle for *liberal* democracy.[16] It is therefore important to distinguish between the two perspectives. Rights struggle in the context of popular democracy has to be distinguished from the struggle for (legal) rights under liberalism. This is not to belittle struggles for rights, particularly in authoritarian systems, as a tactic to the greater end of meaningful democracy. Victories in the struggle for rights (for example, to have a Bill of Rights in the constitution in Tanzania) often de-energise and marginalise popular forces by the focus on courts as the core arena of struggle and on lawyers as the central actors. Many of Corrigan and Sayers's views about The Law applies to Rights in the Tanzanian context. For example:

> Class victories at law are articulated in forms which actively, insistently and rigorously denigrate their class character and origins. Law must indeed be taken seriously. But a major part of that taking seriously must lie in recognising that law as such is an alienation of social power that needs to be reappropriated if the people are to rule. When the latter keep their distance from The Law, it is a class distance. (Corrigan & Sayers 1981: 41-2).

Rights must also be taken seriously. But it must be recognised that rights as such are an ideology legitimising the politics of the state. Rights ideology has to be reconceptualised as rights struggle in order to legitimise the people's politics of resistance. The student struggles at the University of Dar es Salaam that we have discussed are a small part of that ongoing process of redefinition and reconceptualisation. Unfortunately, this process has been crippled in recent years by a lack of societal vision and a renunciation of social theory. Liberal and popular democracy have not been historically and socially differentiated and the concept of democracy has not been linked to any project for social emancipation. If the struggles of the 1960s and 1970s erred by overemphasising class struggle at the expense of rights struggle, the struggle of the 1980s erred in the opposite direction. The struggle for democracy was not understood as a mode of politics in which class struggle is crystallised. In the absence of such a theoretical perspective the struggle for democracy courted the danger of degenerating into compradorial politics. The uncritical acceptance by the intelligentsia on the Dar es Salaam campus of the liberal multi-party agenda is a reflection of this tendency.

While the demand for a multi-party system may be a necessary condition for the transition to democracy, it is not sufficient to generate a democratic *movement*. The immediate response to the multi-party movement in Tanzania has been the resurgence of compradorial elements whose politics are largely a vulgar replica of IMF structural adjustment programmes. The local flavour added by some of these groups comprises calls for the indigenisation of local commerce, the tourist trade, the service sector and real estate businesses hitherto in the hands of state agencies or Asian capitalists. Interestingly, none of the thirty odd proto-parties which had emerged at the time of writing could be regarded as left of centre or even left of the ruling CCM. The fact that these developments have received little intellectual analysis other than euphoric acceptance or individual cynicism vindicates the misgivings expressed in this paper about rights struggle on the campus. One of the periodic strengths of the struggles on the Dar es Salaam campus has been the link forged between student struggles and broader theoretical perspectives. In the current conjuncture the immediate danger is not simply that such a link is non-existent but the very renunciation of theorisation and contextualisation. In the longer term, the danger may be the 'recompradisation' of the African intellectual. The least that may be expected of committed intellectuals is that they will alert the people to the real dangers of the new world (dis)order.

Notes

1 This essay is based on an earlier paper, Shivji (1991a).

2 In the 1968-9 Faculty of Law crisis Law and Development was one of the subjects most heavily criticised by students (see Shivji 1990a).

3 See, for example, the proceedings of the Symposium on Marxism held under the auspices of the Institute of Development Studies on the occasion of Marx's centenary (IDS 1983).

4 Some members of staff made a substantial input in the Tanganyika Law Society's memorandum against the *Economic Sabotage Law*. The Law Faculty also organised a moot in which the constitutionality of the Economic Sabotage Tribunal was challenged. See Peter (1983).

5 Since its formation in 1964 the Union has had a turbulent history. At various times Zanzibaris have expressed concern about the retention of their separate identity and have demanded greater autonomy. While placating Zanzibar politically, the mainland authorities have continued to add to the list of Union matters in the Constitution, effectively constricting the former's powers (see Shivji 1990b).

6   Abeid Karume became the first president of Zanzibar after the 1964 revolution led by his party which overthrew the oligarchic Arab regime in power. Karume's rule was marked by intense political repression and uncompromising nationalism in relations with mainland Tanzania. Karume was assassinated in 1972.

7   Figures produced by Zanzibar government officials showed that during the Karume era Zanzibar had no external debt, a good foreign exchange position and a more internally integrated economy. This is not to condone the fact that Karume's idiosyncratic and autocratic rule failed to ensure that the relative prosperity of the economy was extended to the whole population.

8   Aboud Jumbe came to power with significant mainland support after Karume's assassination in 1972.

9   Kanywanyi (1989) draws attention to this retrogression, although he unnecessarily constructs strawmen like 'civil society'. The return to the positivist tradition is epitomised in most of the essays on the Court of Appeal published in the *Eastern Africa Law Review*, Vol.16, No.2. My own Inaugural Lecture (Shivji 1990b) uses traditional doctrinal and textual analysis to argue for greater autonomy for Zanzibar.

10 Report of the Sarungi Committee (*UDASA Newsletter*, No.10, February 1990). The Legal Aid Committee again acquitted itself honourably by taking the case of a detained student leader to court. At the time of the judgment the student had been released and the court therefore did not feel obliged to decide the merits, see *R. v Kashaju Ludovic Bazigiza* Misc. Criminal Cause No. 38 of 1989, High Court at Dar es Salaam (unreported).

11 Shivji (1991c). The Declaration subsequently became the basis for the *Kampala Declaration on Intellectual Freedom* adopted by some 200 African academics under the auspices of the Council for the Development of Economic and Social Research in Africa (CODESRIA) in November 1991.

12 A series of successful court cases, popularly referred to as 'dampo', were brought against the City Council challenging its environmentally hazardous practices. Some of these cases were advocated by legal aid lawyers at the University on behalf of neighbourhoods

involved. See for example *Festo Balegele and 794 Others v Dar es Salaam City Council* Misc. Civil Cause No. 90 of 1991, High Court of Tanzania at Dar es Salaam (unreported).

13 Authoritarian systems controlling mass media function in utmost secrecy. Most issues of national significance get discussed in rumours based on half-truths for lack of information. For an interesting account of media reportage in Tanzania see Tegambwage (1990).

14 I am using this term to imply the various characteristics of The Law as a bourgeois juridical form explained so well in Corrigan & Sayer (1981).

15 The former Vice-Chancellor, Professor Mmari, whose democratic inclinations proved unacceptable, was unceremoniously removed from office and several academics were transferred to government commissions or sent on sabbaticals (*UDASA Newsletter* Nos. 12, 13 and 14).

16 There is an ongoing debate among African intellectuals on the contradictions of democracy. See *Southern African Political and Economic Monthly* (SAPEM, Harare) and *Codesria Bulletin* (Dakar). See also Nyongo (1988) and Shivji (1990d).

7

International Business and Global Development

Sol Picciotto

Introduction

Despite radical changes in the global political climate during the 1980s, the problems facing the world's peoples have become more acute. Despite four decades of global economic growth since the Second World War the vast majority of the world's population still live below a reasonable subsistence level (World Bank 1990). The deceleration of global growth during the 1980s has not prevented the continued expansion of the Transnational Corporations (TNCs), the dominant elements in international business. Yet these power-houses have, with few exceptions, turned their faces further away from the world's poorer regions and countries, and concentrated even more on the established over-developed centres, especially in Europe, North America and Japan. Politicians, activists and intellectuals concerned with the problems of global uneven- and underdevelopment have been plunged further into the dilemma of how to deal with the institutions and groups which control these powerful concentrations of capital. Attempts to establish a degree of social accountability through any form of state intervention not only results in the drying-up of private investment, but also in the flow of development finance from public sources slowing to a trickle. Especially for countries whose former status as colonies has distorted their economies and made them highly dependent on world markets, self-reliance is not a solution.

Policies for dealing with international trade and investment are an essential component of any development strategy. Yet it is perhaps in this area that the gap between law as mere rhetoric and law in practice is the greatest. Lawyers are centrally involved the nuts and bolts as well as the broader strategic aspects of global business transactions. The major commercial law firms, which are themselves becoming transnational businesses with substantial turnovers, play a central part in structuring transnational business operations, and control an immense amount of specialist expertise in myriad areas of transnational corporate law, taxation, contracting, intellectual property, financing and other areas of law. Equally, although lawyers are perhaps not so influential in international policy discussions as are economists, legal questions are central to the consideration of the regulatory framework for global commercial activity. Yet the work of international lawyers on the role of law in development too often gets lost in a miasma of discussions about abstract principles such as the right to development, permanent sovereignty over natural resources, the common heritage of mankind, and so on.

While the formulation of such general principles may in some contexts be valuable, their utility is seriously diminished by several factors. Such formulations are either too vague and/or contradictory due to the many compromises necessary to obtain agreement by any organization with adequate global political and geographical representation. As a result, the general principles have little relevance to the more specific and practical issues of the legal framework for international economic relations. The second basic flaw in such formulations, in my view, is their tendency to state that rights belong to people (or peoples) while their implementation depends on the state (or states). This results in an emphasis on state action, or sometimes cooperative action by states, while ignoring the role of social groups, both within the state and internationally. This tendency satisfies the prevailing nationalist ideology of ruling groups in underdeveloped countries; but it also provides an acceptable international framework for TNCs, who have preferred to deal with national governments individually (and play them off against each other), and to become 'good citizens' in each country, rather than be subjected to regulation on a global basis (see Picciotto 1991).

This paper develops these arguments by looking at the issues and developments of the past 15 years or so in relation to the regulation of global business, especially TNCs. In the late 1960s and early 1970s considerable political attention was focussed on TNCs as they emerged as the dominant private institutions in the world economy. This is not just a matter of sheer size, since the wilder predictions that global economic activity would be subsumed by a mere 200 or so such entities within a very few years have inevitably proved ill-founded. However, the internationalisation of business has accelerated, with new trends towards internationalisation in the finance, services and retailing sectors, and internationalisation of medium and even smaller-sized firms (UNCTC 1988). As a form of capital, the TNC has reinforced its global domination. This is directly exercised through the common management of related companies within the group, although centralisation of strategic direction must be balanced against the need to decentralise other aspects of management to ensure flexibility and encourage initiative (Bartlett & Ghoshal 1989). It is important to note that there may also be effective control of related entities without an ownership link but through contractual relations: thus franchising arrangements enable firms such as MacDonalds and Benetton to control outlets which are owned and perhaps financed by small entrepreneurs; equally, supplies may be purchased from firms or even small artisanal producers which, although independently-owned, are tightly controlled as to quantity and quality of production and other factors.[1] Large firms often establish joint arrangements amongst themselves for production, distribution and, increasingly in recent years, for strategic research and product development. They are also interrelated through cross-membership of Boards of Directors; and in some countries, notably Japan and to a lesser extent Germany, banks or trading companies play an important role in encouraging long-term strategic planning and coordination between firms in a network (Scott 1986). Hence TNCs are important not only because of their own absolute size but through their dominant role in such corporate networks (see Dunning 1988).

Symbolic Battles over Ownership and the Substantive Limits to National Sovereignty

The substantive issues raised by the control and accountability of business have been largely obscured by conflicts over the symbolic issue of ownership. While nationalisation, particularly of natural resources, was the touchstone of radical development policies in the 1960s and 1970s, the trend in the 1980s was towards the privatisation of many state-owned enterprises. This ideological transformation has, however, made little difference to the substantive issues involved in ensuring that transnational businesses contribute to national development.

Nationalisation

In the earlier period the dominant ideology stressed the necessity of moving from formal political independence to a more substantive economic independence, which was regarded as essential to true self-determination (Brownlie 1979). An important element of this was the assertion of the right to national ownership of natural resources, and in many cases of firms engaged in other major economic activities. Such policies were formally legitimised in international legal instruments, notably UN General Assembly Resolution (UNGA) 1803 of 1962 on *Permanent Sovereignty over Natural Resources* and reached an apogee with the principles establishing the New International Economic Order (NIEO) (UNGA 3171 of 1973) and the *Charter of Economic Rights and Duties of States* (CERDS) of 1974. Article 2(a) of the CERDS asserts the primacy of national jurisdiction and denies the existence of any obligation to grant 'preferential' treatment to foreign investment. Article 2(c) states that 'appropriate' compensation shall be paid in the event of a nationalisation, but such compensation is a matter for the host state 'unless it is freely and mutually agreed by all the states concerned that other peaceful means be sought on the basis of the sovereign equality of states'.

These resolutions establish the principle that under general international law the nation state has the right to assert total regulatory power over economic activity within its borders, to assume or limit ownership rights, and to determine the amount and form of compensation if it is deemed appropriate.[2]

On the other hand, both politicians and academics from developing countries have placed too great an emphasis on the principle of the supremacy of national jurisdiction in general international law. National jurisdiction is not unlimited, for the national state does not exist as a hermetic unit but as part of an interlocking and overlapping system of jurisdictions. As global economic and social life have become increasingly integrated it has become increasingly difficult for the state to exercise exclusive unilateral jurisdiction over major economic activities. Although the state may have the formal legal right to nationalise assets or enterprises within its borders and to decide for itself questions of compensation, states have generally carried out such nationalisations after negotiation with owners and have paid compensation, even if based on book rather than market values or in the form of lump-sum payments after lengthy negotiations with home countries.[3]

Even more interesting has been the growing movement, that has coincided with the assertion of the right to economic self-determination in formal declarations and ideological statements, towards the negotiation of Bilateral Investment Treaties (BITs) (UNCTC 1988a). The importance of these is that they convert any private or domestic public law undertakings made by states to foreign investors into obligations under international law.[4] Since the first modern BIT was signed between West Germany and Pakistan in 1959, some three hundred such agreements have been concluded between about 80 underdeveloped countries and almost all developed countries. However, some of their advocates concede that their importance is primarily symbolic, since the absence of such an agreement does not necessarily deter investment.[5] In negotiating such agreements, capital-importing countries are still unwilling to give up the supremacy of national jurisdiction as a general principle: only sixteen per cent of the agreements analysed by Peters contained a 'stabilisation' clause, even though the three judge tribunal in *Kuwait v Aminoil* (1982)(66 ILR 518) held that such a clause should not be interpreted to restrict national sovereignty. Nevertheless, they do commit themselves to obligations which actually restrict the broad assertions of national sovereignty: almost all agreements contain arbitration clauses for disputes between state parties, and many cover state-investor disputes as well. They also include undertakings limiting the right to nationalise and accepting an obligation to pay compensation.[6]

While some commentators have viewed the negotiation of these treaties as an expression of the sovereign will of states and a progressive development of international law (Bergman 1983: 34), it is more accurate to say that governments have conceded the necessity of concluding such agreements in order to attract investment. They are therefore an expression of the inability of underdeveloped states to give substantive economic content to their formal assertions of national sovereignty and internal jurisdictional omnipotence. In contrast, it is significant that some developed countries (e.g. Germany and Switzerland) have been unwilling to accept such limitations over their internal jurisdiction, such as an obligation to accept arbitration of investment disputes, because they argue that they cannot constitutionally oust the jurisdiction of their courts (Peters 1988: 141). Equally, developed-country oil producers such as Britain have established licensing regimes that are almost entirely localised: licensees are required to be incorporated and resident in the UK, and the terms of the licence are subject to the virtually complete discretionary power of the government, provided the Minister acts in the 'national interest'. Indeed, the 1975 *Petroleum Act* retrospectively imposed a production control system (Higgins 1982: 312, 349-50). When such positions are adopted by underdeveloped countries they are regarded as evidence of hostility to private investment. However, developed country governments are also restricted by the political and economic pressures generated by business. In legal terms, attempts have been made to limit their national jurisdiction over business by developing the right of property in human rights law.[7]

While underdeveloped countries have pressed strongly for formal legal statements of economic sovereignty and the right to national ownership of assets, they have been unable to give effective substance to such claims. In many, if not most cases, nationalisation has amounted to a formal transfer of ownership with the foreign investor retaining effective control through management agreements and other contractual relations. Nationalising states have, to be sure, acquired property rights, especially over natural resources, but they have discovered that in an interdependent world economy such rights may amount to liabilities rather than assets. First, the ability to export the product of a nationalised enterprise usually necessitates an agreed settlement with the former owners that generally involves compensation based on estimated future profits. However, the acquisition of property rights also entails the assumption of risk, especially of declining world prices, and in well-known cases such as the copper nationalisations in Zambia and Zaire, the nationalising state has borne the brunt of declining world prices while the TNCs whose assets were seized were able to use the compensation payments to diversify their investments and reduce their exposure to risk (Shafer 1983). Nationalisation certainly offers the possibility of integrating economic activities of nationalised sectors into a national development plan, but this possibility has not been effectively realised.[8]

Privatisation and Investment Incentives

It is therefore not surprising that the 1980s has witnessed the reverse movement towards state divestment of ownership or 'privatisation'.[9] This was triggered after 1980 by global shifts in terms of trade and onset of the debt crisis, ending the access of states to funds with which to sustain large public sectors that were generally in deficit through inefficiency, bureaucratic incompetence and corruption, the heavy financial demands of restructuring for development, or a combination of these. However, the privatisation movement has been as symbolic as that of nationalisation. The lack of active capital markets in underdeveloped countries has made the very concept of privatisation problematic. What has in fact often taken place has been the sale of a proportion of the equity of the enterprise or even the conclusion of leasing or management contract arrangements with foreign firms. Where complete sales have taken place, the price has generally been less than the full value, i. e. less than the realisable value of the assets. Hence there is a short-term net loss for the state, while medium-term benefits depend on often non-existent efficiency gains from market pressures (see Bouin & Michalet 1991).

What private investors seek is the minimum risk and financial outlay in relation to the probable return, an aim compatible and in some ways more easily achieved with state ownership. Nevertheless, nationalisation has been feared and attacked by business due to its symbolic implications and political motivations.[10] Some governments that have carried out nationalisation programmes designed to produce a mixed economy have found not only that they have they failed to establish an efficient state sector integrated into national development planning but have simultaneously acquired a reputation for hostility to private business that has frightened investors.

A stark example is provided by Tanzania, which carried out a highly publicized series of nationalisations after 1967. Care was taken to negotiate agreed compensation (see Green 1978), to leave untouched enterprises which held a commanding world market position (notably Williamson Diamonds, part of the De Beers group), and to define areas in which foreign investment would continue to be welcome. Nevertheless, the nationalist and populist ideology motivating and justifying the nationalisations (Kitching 1989) resulted in an international image of Tanzania as hostile to foreign investment. For example, Peters (1988: 135), a former adviser to Royal Dutch Shell, refers to Tanzania together with Burma and Albania as countries aiming for total self-reliance and rejecting foreign investment. This international reputation eventually led Tanzania to send new signals through the enactment of a *National Investment Promotion and Protection Act* in 1990 which goes further than necessary to attract foreign investors. To cite one example, it offers tax holidays, even though most foreign investors can credit foreign tax paid against home country liability.[11]

In general, investment incentives merely operate as a subsidy for TNCs. The World Bank has concluded from a consultants' study that, 'other things being equal', incentives may affect the decision where to invest (World Bank 1985: 130) - but where, as is more common, they are not equal, the granting of incentives is merely distortive and a drain on national resources. It is only because of competition between states to attract investment projects, especially those which are relatively mobile, that incentives can be said to have any effect.[12] Given that the least developed countries, which are least attractive to investors, also have least resources to compete in offering incentives, it should be a high priority for institutions such as the World Bank to use their powers to end such incentives rather than tolerating them as a 'fact of life' or encouraging them as a symbol of commitment to private investment.

While symbolic struggles are not unimportant, the danger is that the substance is lost from view. High-profile conflicts over state or private ownership of business have frequently obscured substantive questions of how to establish an optimal framework for ensuring managerial efficiency at the level of the firm combined with responsiveness to social needs. The remainder of this chapter addresses the question of regulation of TNCs to ensure accountability to social concerns.

Establishing an International Regulatory Framework for Transnational Business

The issue of effective regulation and accountability of transnational business, highlighted since the late 1960s, has become increasingly acute. Most importantly, it has revealed the limitations of a strategy of social control of business reliant largely on state power and the exclusivity of national jurisdiction. It has become increasingly evident that what is needed instead is a perspective that is genuinely internationalist and directly involves social groups and organizations. A considerable body of practice of such transnational regulation has developed in the international system, although with substantial limitations. These limitations result first from the ambivalence of business managers and representatives who, while regularly conceding the need for transnational regulation in concrete cases, always prefer that it not affect *their* company and argue in principle for a mythical freedom for market forces.[13] Second, government representatives have remained attached to the equally mythical sovereignty of the nation state and therefore reluctant to concede any power to inter- or supranational bodies. This has made officials of intergovernmental organizations extremely cautious in developing their activities. Third, social movements and organizations themselves have often reflected limited sectional interests and been reluctant to develop the broader alliances which would allow them to reinforce each others' strengths.

Denationalisation, or International Supervision, of TNCs

Strong political pressures for effective international regulation of business, particularly TNCs, developed in the period 1967-77. Although proposals were put forward for a single political entity to oversee the operations of TNCs, what resulted was a series of disjointed and partial initiatives, many of which have become bogged down in political quicksands. As early as 1967 George Ball, US Under-Secretary of State and representative at the United Nations, and later Chairman of Lehman Brothers International (investment bank), proposed the 'denationalisation' of TNCs. He argued that supranational citizenship for TNCs should be provided by treaty, since in his view the pragmatic policy followed by TNCs of obeying local laws would not resolve the 'inherent conflict of interest between corporate managements that operate in the world economy and governments whose points of view are confined to the narrow national scene' (Ball 1967: 28-9). Ball's proposal was renewed in 1974 (Ball 1975: 167-73). More modest versions were subsequently put forward. Charles Kindleberger argued for the establishment of a General Agreement on Multinational Enterprise (GAME) modelled on the General Agreement on Tariffs and Trade (GATT), but with a greatly reduced regulatory role in relation to TNCs than that proposed by Ball (Kindleberger 1980). Both Ball and Kindleberger envisaged an agreement amongst countries of the Organization of Economic Co-operation and Development (OECD) establishing a consensus on a minimum core of principles. Although Kindleberger rejected the idea of global citizenship for TNCs, he argued that it was important to establish procedures for case-by-case adjudication of complaints against them or disputes between governments over corporate regulation in order to build up international case-law. These ideas failed to receive support from transnational business or underdeveloped countries, both of which, albeit for different reasons, disliked the notion of a single forum dominated by OECD governments dealing with issues such as restrictive business practices, transfer pricing, bribery and compliance with export controls or unilateral embargoes.[14]

Developed countries have indeed dominated the process whereby international regulatory procedures and principles for business have emerged, mainly by developing common positions through the OECD and using these to influence or block agreement in the United Nations and its specialised agencies. In 1974 the UN established the Commission and Centre on TNCs which, although it has done much excellent work, has only an advisory function. Kindleberger had envisaged a body with jurisdiction to decide disputes concerning international business and issue authoritative rulings, although without formal sanctions. Work on a general Code of Conduct for TNCs, which was given the highest priority when the Commission was established, is still not concluded. UNCTAD had more success in obtaining agreement on a set of rules for the control of restrictive business practices, but its work on a code for transfer of technology is also not yet complete.[15] In the meantime, several other organizations have agreed codes of conduct for international business generally or covering particular issues, so that there is now a plethora of such codes.[16]

Enforcement and Dispute-Settlement

These codes have, however, proved difficult to agree and consequently have been expressed in very general language. More seriously, there has been strong resistance from some developed countries and TNCs themselves to the establishment of any mechanism for supervision or monitoring of compliance or a dispute-settlement mechanism. This issue has been misleadingly expressed in terms of whether such codes should be legally binding.[17] The argument for legally binding codes is based on the view that the effectiveness of rules depends on sanctions, which require state action. The national state is the traditional linchpin of the international legal system. A binding code therefore requires the voluntary assumption of obligations by states under public international law; but the enactment of the rules and the monitoring of compliance by firms and individuals remains a matter of domestic jurisdiction. The result is to shift the spotlight from the international to the domestic arena and to put enforcement in the hands of state officials. On the other hand, even a non-'binding' international code can provide an important focus for direct action by pressure groups, trade unions and other non-state actors.

There are two significant examples of international action by social movement organizations using codes of conduct as a focus for attempts to ensure social accountability by TNCs. One is the campaign by various pressure groups against the indiscriminate and unscrupulous marketing of breast-milk substitutes. As part of this campaign, the World Health Organization (WHO) adopted a *Code of Marketing of Breast-Milk Substitutes*. But it was the actions of non-governmental organizations[18] which gave the Code some teeth. This was done by developing an internationally organized campaign which systematically monitored the activities of the companies, backed by the threat of informal sanctions such as product boycotts (see Chetley 1986, WHO 1990). The effectiveness of the campaign was to some extent due to particular circumstances such as the emotive nature of the breast-feeding issue. Pressure groups have also played an increasingly important role in other areas, for example in relation to policies on the sale of pharmaceutical drugs in developing countries. In some developing countries, social action groups have developed effective campaigns focussing on issues like the impact of TNC activities on consumers, the environment and their employees. A prime example is the Consumers' Association of Penang, in Malaysia, which has published a lively newspaper and organized campaigns using both social action and legal procedures.

The other example is the role of trade unions in using the OECD Guidelines.[19] Possibly because they were formulated at the start of a period of major restructuring by TNCs, trade unions were motivated to use the Guidelines to raise a number of cases of TNC misbehaviour, such as the international transfer of workers as strike-breakers (the Hertz case), parent company responsibility for employees in the case of bankruptcy of a subsidiary (the

Badger case), and informing and consulting employees prior to plant closure (the Phillips-Finland and Ford-Amsterdam cases) or disinvestment (the Viggo-British Oxygen case).[20] When the OECD's Committee on International Investment and Multinational Enterprise (CIIME) was established in 1975, its task included the formulation of 'intergovernmental procedures for dealing with possible complaints' against enterprises, but the OECD Council's *Decision on the Inter-Governmental Consultation Procedures* which accompanied the Guidelines firmly stated that the Committee 'shall not reach conclusions on the conduct of individual enterprises'. The cases referred to the Committee by trade unions (joined, on a few occasions, by a government) provided opportunities to raise issues of principle and interpretation of the Guidelines, and it became accepted that the CIIME could issue 'clarifications'. Nevertheless, the unions have taken the view that the prime responsibility for enforcement lies with governments through 'binding regulations at the national level' (Blanpain 1979: 52). In the hope of such firm action by governments and of co-operation from enterprises, they refrained from public denunciations of bad behaviour by enterprises in breach of the Guidelines or from conducting campaigns aimed at their trade union members or public opinion generally (Blanpain 1979: 104). The debate about TNC behaviour and the principles laid down in the OECD Guidelines was thus confined to a small circle of initiates within the relatively arcane procedures of the CIIME. The trade unions also supported the establishment of National Contact Points as the first point of reference for complaints, in the hope that this would prompt a more active government attitude to enforcement of the Guidelines, but most of the Contact Points have remained totally passive, serving to defuse further the effectiveness of the Guidelines.

While trade unions have perhaps been over-optimistic in seeking an active government intervention, they have accurately identified the central issue relating to codes of conduct, that of enforcement. There are many ways of inducing compliance and increasing adherence to the standards contained in codes, such as publicising them, encouraging firms to include statements in their Annual Reports on the extent of their compliance, negotiations at company level and pressures from national governments. There must, however, be a role for a procedure allowing specific complaints about firms to be brought forward and adjudicated upon (Pursey 1980), even if the body empowered to do so has little direct authority to impose sanctions. It is, after all, these firms themselves who have insisted on provisions for the arbitration of investment disputes, both in national investment codes and in the BITs discussed above. It is hardly logical for them to continue to oppose a similarly open procedure for the evaluation of complaints against them.

Over-reliance by international trade union bodies on action by governments has also led them to neglect the possibilities of building a broader political basis from which to direct their critiques of business mismanagement. Many issues impinge not only on workers employed by the enterprises but also the communities around major plants or the consumers of their products. Major environmental disasters such as the gas leak from the Union Carbide plant at Bhopal in India have clearly shown the importance of joint action involving both community and workers' organizations. While this type of cooperation can often be found at the grassroots, there is unfortunately too often suspicion and hostility at the official level. This is to some extent the result of organizational differences: official trade union bodies have a formal structure which in many ways ensures accountability to the membership but which can be hindered by formalism and bureaucratisation. In comparison, although social action groups are often self-selected and indisciplined they can also be much more flexible, highly-motivated and capable of swift decisions and action. It should be a high priority of those involved in such bodies to seek ways of harnessing and combining the strengths of each for common ends.

Towards More Open and Effective Transnational Business Regulation

The merit of the proposals put forward by Ball and Kindleberger two decades ago was that they entailed a comprehensive and international approach to the regulation of transnational business. Their suggestions were minimalist, emphasising progress through consensus and focussing on developed countries. In many respects business representatives and leaders would prefer a stronger degree of international co-ordination of business regulation. For example, they have pressed within the OECD for a procedure for resolving problems arising from the conflicting requirements placed on TNCs.[21] Similarly, on the question of the prohibition of illicit payments or bribery they would generally prefer a more effective internationally co-ordinated approach. In relation to the taxation of income or profits from international business, they pressed early on for international treaties preventing double taxation. These treaties have developed into a wide network, especially under the aegis of the OECD, are incorporated into and often override national law, and grant tax exemptions which minimise exposure to international double taxation either of the same or related business entities (see Picciotto 1992).

While business has pressed for international legal provisions and procedures to establish rights and guarantees for investors, it has generally resisted the establishment of internationally enforced globally-oriented standards, preferring to comply with domestic legislation. In relation to taxation, business has insisted on the 'arm's length' principle of national taxation of subsidiaries or branches as if they were separate enterprises with separate accounts and has strongly resisted the idea of taxation of a globally-integrated group of companies on a consolidated or unitary basis. It has become increasingly clear, however, that the arm's length principle is unworkable and TNCs themselves have pressed for acceptance of formula apportionment of overhead or fixed costs such as research and development expenditure or management and service costs. They have also pleaded for an international arbitration procedure to resolve conflicting views of national authorities on appropriate transfer prices.[22]

Another example, of crucial importance to developing countries, is the state-protected monopolization of new technologies, usually referred to as Intellectual Property Rights (IPRs). Control of the application of science and technology for industrial processes has been a key element in the emergence and growth of big business. In some industries an important aspect of this was the legal protection granted by the state in the form of patent, copyright and other rights. The *quid pro quo* for this protection was the publication of the innovation (by disclosure in a patent application or actual publication of a work for copyright protection) and acceptance of limits to the monopoly. These limits are temporal (specific periods), social (the exclusion in many cases of food and pharmaceutical drugs), economic (compulsory licensing or revocation for non-use), and scientific (protection of the application and not the idea and exemption for 'fair dealing'). The 1883 *Paris Convention* (for patents) provided the right of national treatment of foreign applicants and a one-year right of priority, while allowing each state to regulate the limits of protection (subject only to protection in Article 5 for patent holders for a few years from the invocation of compulsory licensing or forfeiture). This liberal system was workable so long as the global exploitation of technology, mainly by TNCs, appeared to be of general benefit and posed relatively few questions about the limits of the protection provided. It came under great stress from two interrelated factors. First, the political perception, particularly in less developed countries, of the unequal benefits deriving from technological development. Second, the increasing complexity and pace of innovation raised new and difficult questions about the appropriate limits of protection. No appropriate forum has been found to discuss these issues. Having resisted strong pressures from developing countries for revision of the *Paris Convention* to permit obligations to work a patent locally, developed countries shifted the ground of the negotiations over IPRs to the GATT, where they have greater bargaining power, particularly over many of the export-oriented economies of South-East Asia and Latin America, whose lax or protectionist approach to IPRs has helped stimulate local industry (Raghavan 1990 Ch. 6). Their aim appears to be to secure and legitimise the protective arrangements allowing TNCs to dominate the appropriation of technological innovation and control its international diffusion while avoiding full discussion of the limits to protection and social accountability in the development and application of technology (UNCTAD 1990b).

The main reason advanced for rejection of a more global approach to regulation has been the lack of political consensus at the world level. Political divergence, so the argument runs, would inevitably produce conflicting regulation unless each state can be confined to its own sphere of jurisdiction. Increasingly, however, the overlapping areas of state jurisdiction have grown along with the increasing global integration of economic and social life. The solution found by business has been to use the flexibility offered by the freedom to incorporate and contract in different national jurisdictions to minimise its exposure to conflicting regulation or what it regards as unfair regulation. The use of regulatory havens of various kinds (offshore financial centres, tax havens, nationalities of convenience for shipping, etc.) was sometimes tolerated and even encouraged by the regulatory authorities of leading states, particularly during the post-War global economic expansion. Since the increased competition and restructuring of the mid-1970s there has been greater concern about the avoidance of international regulation. The rapid growth of offshore finance and banking from the early 1960s was largely unsupervised. It was only in 1975 that a minimal arrangement was established, through the semi-formal Basle Committee of Bank Supervisors, for allocation of responsibility and co-ordination of bank supervision; not until 1988 did this Committee reach an agreement on common capital adequacy standards (see Kapstein 1989; Pecchioli 1983: 96-111 and 1987: 37-9). The abrupt closure in July 1991 of the Bank of Credit and Commerce International (BCCI), which was suddenly found to have been used as a systematic cover for fraud and money-laundering despite having been under scrutiny by a specially-established college of bank regulators for several years, starkly revealed the holes in the network of supervisory co-operation.

While developed countries have, paradoxically, resisted pressures for more comprehensive global approaches to business regulation, there has been considerable activity in specific areas in attempts to strengthen co-operation between national regulators. This, however, has taken an essentially bureaucratic form, and has been highly secretive and technicist. What is required is to open up these processes to public discussion and debate. It is also important to involve developing countries in these arrangements, if only because they might otherwise be used as regulatory havens.

Conclusion

For nearly three decades TNCs and the governments of many less developed states have been suspicious of or hostile towards proposals for the establishment of even a minimal framework of regulation of business at the international level. As we have seen, however, regulators in developed countries have comprehended the need to strengthen the arrangements for the international co-ordination of business regulation. Nonetheless, the procedures and mechanisms which have so far developed in various fields are likely to prove less than efficacious for two major reasons. First, they generally involve few countries, which are almost inevitably developed countries. Second, they generally take the form of *ad hoc* committees or groups of administrators operating secretively. Relatively mild proposals made more than two decades ago for the establishment of a multilateral agency with general responsibility for supervising international investment and business were brushed aside. Developed countries have, within the context of the Uruguay Round of the GATT, now begun to stress the need for international agreement on investment regulation. However, the proposals put forward in the *Punte del Este Declaration* inaugurating the Uruguay Round focus on *trade-related* investment measures. Essentially, this entails an attempt merely to dismantle any national regulatory measures which powerful countries consider to be distorting trade. This ignores the necessity of taking joint action to regulate the even more distortive use of economic power by TNCs (Raghavan 1990, Ch.7).

If we are to have any chance at all of directing the use of the world's resources for the benefit of all peoples in ways which are both more equitable and less harmful there is a strong need for more active popular involvement at the international level. There is no shortage of awareness and enthusiasm, as is evidenced by the strong international support obtained by the myriad globally-oriented social action movements focussing on issues such as the environment, political prisoners, women, gender, and so on. In practice, it is only through this type of direct awareness and involvement that a climate can be created in which to secure active compliance with legal obligations or codes of conduct.

Notes

1   Lawyers and economists have recently become interested in analysing long-term contractual relations between firms, a form mid-way between corporate integration and independent contracting (see Hadfield 1990, Joerges (ed.) 1992, Williamson 1988).

2   Commentators have shown some surprising confusion over this. Some, like Peters (1988) refuse to accept that the CERDS (Art. 2) means what it says, i.e. that under general international law a state may assert total power over internal economic activities, although it may by agreement restrict this freedom. Others, like Higgins (1982: 311), despite accepting that clear statement, see the assertion of the primacy of national jurisdiction as an irresistible force meeting the immovable object of *pacta sunt servanda*. Surprisingly, she seems to view concessions or rights of establishment granted to private entities such as TNCs as constituting such *pacta*, apparently placing private or domestic public law obligations on a par with duties under public international law - a view which developing country scholars rightly criticise (Khan 1988).

3   For state practice see Lillich & Weston (1975 and 1988) and Akinsaya (1980). However, academic commentators remain divided about the implications for legal principle. Some consider lump sum settlements as a matter of expediency and prefer to prioritise arbitral decisions as the main source of law over both state practice and official statements. On this basis, Norton (1991) argues that decisions of arbitral tribunals have reaffirmed the rule of full compensation based on market price. In order to do so he discounts the opinions of judges such as Mahmassani and Lagergren. Although he concedes that the actual sums awarded by tribunals have generally been small (Norton 1991: 495), he regards this as a 'realist caveat' rather than an indication of the *opinio juris*. Even on its own ground, the decisions of international courts and tribunals, the argument for a general rule of full compensation is weak (see Schachter 1984). Others contend that the overwhelming state practice of lump sum settlements should be taken as evidence of the creation of a rule of international law (Lillich and Weston 1975, Vol.1: p.43; Lillich and Weston 1988). The implication is that something less than 'full' compensation is payable, at least in the case of lawful nationalisations as part of state policy. Lillich and Weston (1988) accept that academic opinion is divided and that the views of arbitrators have differed (see e.g. the separate opinions of Lagergren and Holtzmann in *INA v. Iran*, 1985). However, it is not always clear what 'full', or 'market' value might be (see Green 1978 and Hu 1980 for an analysis of the effect of uncertainty on market valuation). Clearly, the payment of compensation is directly linked to a state's desire to remain in or return to the capitalist world economy, as in the US - Hungary claims settlement of 1973 (US - Hungary, 1973), which was expressly tied to the development of trade between the two states and the granting of Most Favoured Nation status. This is conceded by Schachter (1984: 129), who argues that the rule of 'just' compensation will prevail as long as states need foreign technology and capital. Akinsaya points to the incidence of overt or covert political interventions by home states to protect their investors, although this has been more demonstrative than effective (Akinsaya 1980, 1987). Dolzer has argued that state practice and formal declarations show the demise of the Hull formula (prompt, adequate and effective compensation) and the Calvo doctrine (supremacy of national jurisdiction), and that the variations of compensation agreements and practices can be explained by taking into account political expediency and economic factors on the basis of a principle of balancing of public and private interests. In my view, the statement

in the CERDS is the clearest reflection of practice, i.e. that states do not accept a general obligation to pay compensation according to any clear minimum standard (hence the word 'appropriate'), but are willing to negotiate specific terms in the particular economic and political circumstances of each case.

4   Peters (1988) found that 60% of the 301 treaties he studied explicitly entailed acceptance of such an obligation. See also UNCTC (1988a), which provides a (non-exhaustive) list of the treaties, as well as several samples and model treaties, including those drafted by the Asian-African Legal Consultative Committee. Dolzer (1981) notes that the European Community's Lome II agreement with developing associated states has an appended *Declaration on Investment* which is equivalent to a multilateral investment agreement.

5   Salacuse (1990), points out that between 1978 and 1989, 350 US companies invested some $3.5 billion in China although there was no US-China BIT following five years of unsuccessful negotiation.

6   See UNCTC (1988a), Peters (1988). This has led to the surprising and opportunistic argument from capital-exporting states that such treaty obligations should be treated as a source of customary international law affirming an obligation to pay compensation (see e.g. Mann 1981: 250). This argument was effectively demolished by an eminent US international lawyer who pointed out that 'the repetition of common clauses in bilateral treaties does not create or support an inference that those clauses express customary law', not least because a state conceding such a commitment by treaty does so in exchange for specific benefits (Schachter 1984: 126).

7   See Higgins (1982, Chs. IV and V), who explains how the opposition of the British Labour government blocked wording implying a general right to compensation in the *European Convention on Human Rights* leading to a compromise in the form of the inclusion of a reference to the principles of international law in Article 1 of the First Protocol. As predicted by Higgins, the European court, in a case brought by former shareholders of aircraft and shipbuilding firms nationalised by the British Labour government (Lithgow Case 1986 75 ILR 436), held that it does not apply to claims by nationals. However, the Court went further and stated that even in relation to nationals a general right to compensation is inherent in Article 1, although it would not be violated unless there were a clear and

substantial disproportion between the interference with the individual's rights and the public interest justifying the state's action.

8 Bolton's study (1985) of Tanzania's nationalisation of sisal tells a familiar tale: it was undertaken for populist and economic-nationalist motives, and lip-service was paid to socialist ideology in the management of the industry, both at the national strategic level and on individual sisal farms. There was no evaluation of the role of sisal in the economy, so that the industrial policy of investment aimed at reducing dependence on the world market was contradicted by the Treasury's insistence on short-term profitability. This could only be satisfied by higher productivity, but the populist ideology required economic concessions to labour, without conceding effective participation.

9 The term 'privatisation' is a misnomer since it implies that the operation of major economic assets by firms which are not state-owned is a 'private' matter. In fact, business activities are regulated everywhere, whether operated by 'public' companies (i.e. those whose shares are quoted on a stock exchange) or not.

10 Nationalisation or other unexpected political interventions can cause dislocation costs which TNCs sometimes anticipate by planned 'divestment' (Boddewyn & Torneden 1973) or by establishing new investments as joint ventures with local state or private partners, or otherwise trying to minimise the value of assets vulnerable to takeover (Stansbury 1990).

11 For an account of the new Tanzanian investment code see Peter (1990b). For a tax holiday to be of net benefit to investors, there must be a treaty allowing a credit for tax 'spared' (although where a company has excess foreign tax credits a tax holiday may be preferable). The reluctance of developed countries to concede a credit for tax sparing is but one of the reasons why there are few tax treaties between developed and developing countries. TNCs have in any case developed the use of intermediary companies based in tax havens to minimise tax liability at source (in host countries) and optimise the 'deferral' of home country taxation (Picciotto 1992).

12 This study found that incentives were the dominant factor in the location decision in 24 of the 74 cases studied. However, this was based on responses by executives to the question whether the

investment would have been made if the chosen country had withdrawn all its incentives while others had maintained theirs (Guisinger *et al.* 1985), which largely explains why the study's conclusions contradicted others that have generally found that incentives have a marginal effect compared to factors such as market size. Although the methodology of the World Bank study has been criticised (Farrell 1985), its interest lies in the detailed industry and country case-studies (Guisinger *et al.*, 1985). These show that competition between countries to attract investment has led to a trend towards flexible and discretionary incentive packages, which TNCs often negotiate at the highest levels within the state.

13 I say mythical because market relations cannot exist without regulation: first, to establish and protect property rights; second, to maintain conditions for exchange; and finally to intervene to re-establish competition and fairness. For a discussion of the historical and theoretical analysis of capitalist relations of production and the state, see Holloway and Picciotto (1977).

14 See comments by D L Guertin of Exxon and A Jimenez De Lucio, of the UNCTC, in Kindleberger (1980).

15 *The Restrictive Business Practices Code* is UNGA, 1980, RBP. The latest version of the *Transfer of Technology Code* is UNCTAD (1990a).

16 A selected bibliography on codes (up to 1979) is provided by Bruce Seymour in Horn (1980), a selected table in Picciotto (1984). A recent, rather optimistic, evaluation of the progress made in establishing an international framework for regulation of international investment is given in Hansen & Aranda (1991).

17 Due to resistance from business and from some states, notably the USA, codes often explicitly state that they are 'voluntary and not legally enforceable' (*cf*. OECD Guidelines, Introduction, para. 6). States have used the formula of 'voluntary guidelines' in preference to a decision or recommendation of relevant international organisation like the OECD and the ILO. Nevertheless, this does not prevent codes from being 'sources' of law, e.g. by being enacted by governments, embodied in BITs, or referred to by courts or tribunals (see Baade 1980). More importantly, some type of 'follow-up' measures to monitor and encourage compliance has been established for most codes, although political resistance has often explicitly excluded

consideration of individual complaints (see e.g. UNGA 1980, para. G.4).

18 Supported to a significant extent by UNICEF which is a UN agency but is funded by voluntary and charitable contributions and therefore has more independence from governments and a stronger relationship with non-governmental organisations, especially development-oriented bodies and pressure groups.

19 OECD governments went to great lengths to avoid any suggestion of binding status for the *Guidelines for Multinational Enterprises*, which were annexed to an inter-governmental Declaration (and not a Decision). They were, however, accompanied by three Decisions, which in OECD practice are considered 'binding' on members, covering National Treatment, International Investment Incentives and Disincentives, and Inter-Governmental Consultation Procedures on the Guidelines. The latter has been especially important, since it required the Committee on International Investment and Multinational Enterprises (CIIME) to review periodically the experience of application of the Guidelines, with the involvement of its Business and Industry and Trade Union Advisory Committees (BIAC and TUAC respectively: the former basically represents TNCs, the latter trade unions and their international secretariats).

20 The functioning of the Guidelines in their first, and most active, phase has been extensively documented by Professor Blanpain, who was a member of the Belgian delegation to the CIIME (Blanpain 1979, 1983). Although these works are hard to assimilate, they provide a valuable insight into an otherwise surprisingly opaque process. The official sources are the periodic review reports of the CIIME, published by the OECD.

21 Following the highly damaging conflict in 1982-3 between the United States and its allies over the US application of 'export' controls to foreign firms licensing technology from the US and supplying equipment for the Siberian-European gas pipeline project, the best that the OECD could come up with was a statement on 'General Considerations and Practical Approaches' for minimising such conflicts (see OECD 1987 and Lange and Born, 1987 for a business viewpoint). The US passed the 1988 *Omnibus Trade Act* making possible the imposition of sanctions on foreign firms for breach of other countries' trade laws (applied against Japanese firm

Toshiba and the Norwegian company Konigsberg for sales of high-technology milling machines to the then USSR). With the end of the Cold War it seems that controls over the diffusion of advanced technology on the grounds of potential military use will be transferred to targeted developing countries (sse Peter Montagnon, *Financial Times*, 30 August 1990).

22 On the worldwide unitary taxation controversy, see Picciotto (1989, 1992, Ch. 9). For a detailed examination of the administration of the arm's length criterion and the attempts to co-ordinate this through mutual assistance between tax authorities, see Picciotto (1992, Chs. 8, 10).

8
The Debt Crisis, Underdevelopment and the Limits of the Law

Sammy Adelman with A. Caesar Espiritu

Introduction

'On August 20 1982, Jesus Silva Herzog set in motion an international crisis of grand proportions. The Mexican finance minister announced to an audience of bankers, gathered at the Federal Reserve Bank of New York, that repayment of principal on bank loans was to be halted for three months. Debt payment problems quickly spread to Brazil, Argentina and several other countries. Ten years later, none of the loans has been repaid' (*The Financial Times*, 30 July 1992). Mexico informed its creditors that its foreign reserves had been so depleted that it could not meet the repayments on its $80 billion external debt.[1] It requested a further loan from foreign governments and banks, a moratorium on payments of principal to banks, and a rescheduling of its debt so that accumulation would not be completely undermined, not least by rising social and political discontent as expenditure was throttled back in order to service the debt. Mexico approached the IMF for a loan and a stabilisation programme and launched the South on the path towards structural adjustment. A decade later, the social and political effects of Mexico's indebtedness are intensifying for the poor, who ultimately bear the cost of repaying the loans.

Expenditure has been slashed on health and education in order to meet the conditions imposed by creditors, unemployment has escalated and the agricultural sector, historically a major source of foreign exchange, has been devastated by the decline in infrastructural spending, forcing many farmers to become tenants on land now owned by foreign agribusiness.[2]

Mexico is not alone. In the final decade of the twentieth century development in many less developed countries (LDCs) is overshadowed by the consequences of indebtedness. In 1990, the World Bank classified 69 of the 111 countries reporting to it as moderately indebted. Together they owed $913 billion of the total LDC debt of $1300 billion (ODI 1990). Frank (1989: 34) estimates that there was a net transfer of approximately $500 billion from the poorest to the richest inhabitants of the planet between 1982 and 1987: $200 billion through debt service *per se*, $100 billion through capital flight, another $100 billion through lower export prices and terms of trade, 'plus the usual $100 billion of remittances of profits and royalties on foreign investment and technology'. According to the IMF, the net resource transfer from indebted to industrialised countries was $27.9 billion in 1980 and $57.7 billion by 1988. For Latin America alone debt service payments totalled 46.1 per cent of GDP in 1986 (Krugman & Obstfeld 1991: 655). This chapter examines the genesis of the crisis, analysing how and why less developed countries (LDCs) became so hugely indebted, and some of the methods that have been advocated for its resolution. We look in particular at the role of law, arguing that the legal responses put forward, ranging from the establishment of an international debt commission to attempts to lessen the burden on the citizens of the South through the imaginative use of international law, are generally limited because they do not address the underlying causes of the debt. Law has generally been deployed to manage rather than resolve what Frank (1989: 34) calls 'this enormous haemorrhage of the Third World'. We contend that the crisis can be resolved only through some form of cancellation of the debt, a solution implicitly recognised by Western governments, lending banks and other financial institutions (most notably the World Bank and the International Monetary Fund (IMF),[3] but whose logical consequences they have thus far refused to embrace. Despite its profound developmental implications, they have dealt with the crisis either in terms of the threat that a wide scale default ostensibly poses to Western financial institutions, or as a problem of accumulation. What has been absent is a willingness to transcend the narrow economism that has historically characterised developmentalism (see Adelman & Paliwala, *infra*).

The Genesis of the Crisis

The contemporary debt crisis is not unique. LDCs defaulted on their debts in the 1890s and again prior to World War I. Those countries that defaulted prior to the Great Depression were largely shut out from international lending markets until the outbreak of World War II, and it was not until the 1970s that private lending to the South reached pre-Depression levels.[4] During the past two decades lending has consisted primarily of official lending by governments, short-term trade credits granted by foreign exporters (many of which became official loans through government guarantees designed to facilitate Northern exports), and direct foreign investment. LDCs borrowed heavily to finance the infrastructural expansion dictated by the modernisation paradigm (Adelman & Paliwala, *infra*), the development of their military/security capabilities against real or constructed external threats and local resistance, in shoring up their often narrow political bases, as a cynical but effective means of increasing employment, and as a distraction from the realities of mass impoverishment, endemic corruption and chronic underdevelopment. Throughout and beyond the Cold War the superpowers and major arms exporters used regional conflicts in the South for proxy battles and the testing of military hardware, bleeding the South in more ways than one.

The willingness of LDC governments to incur large external debts was matched by that of Western governments and financial institutions to make the necessary capital available.[5] Until the quadrupling of the oil price in 1973 financial institutions had not engaged in substantial lending to LDCs, but the glut of funds on the Eurodollar markets and from investments by OPEC countries in Western banks led them to seek new debtors. American banks in particular found themselves with huge resources and, faced with negative domestic real interest rates, were eager to lend to LDCs at higher levels. LDCs borrowed even during the global recession in 1974-75 in pursuit of expansionary policies aimed at improving their relative output growth rates. The total debt of non-oil exporting LDCs almost tripled from $130 billion in 1973 to $336 billion in 1979. After the 1979 oil price rise their collective indebtedness rose to more than $600 billion by 1982. By this time, however, oil exporting countries were themselves sliding into deficit and were unable to fund the deficits of non-oil exporters (Krugman & Obstfeld 1991: 646).

The 1981-83 global recession led to a collapse in commodity prices and in the demand for LDC exports. Severe anti-inflationary monetarist policies adopted by Western governments resulted in substantial interest rates rises which 'set the stage for a widespread developing country debt crisis comparable only with that of the 1930s' (Krugman & Obstfeld 1991: 647). High real returns encouraged banks to lend internally, making it difficult for LDCs to borrow from the very institutions which had so eagerly facilitated their indebtedness. The US dollar rose sharply and since much of the debt is denominated in dollars, an increasing number of LDCs found themselves unable to meet their interest payments. When short-term loans taken out immediately prior to the recession fell due, LDCs were confronted with the dilemma of repaying or refinancing them at historically high interest rates.[6]

The effect of the debt crisis on the South can be gauged from *Table 1*, which shows that real growth rates in the developing world never recovered to the levels of the 1970s: for example, the 2.7 per cent growth rate in the countries of the Western Hemisphere in 1983 was a direct consequence of the debt crisis.

Table 1

Growth rates of output for developed and developing countries, 1971-81 average and 1981-88 (per cent per year)

Country Group	1971-80 average	1981	1982	1983	1984	1985	1986	1987	1988
Industrial Countries	3.2	1.5	-0.3	2.8	4.9	3.4	2.6	3.4	4.1
Developing Countries	5.5	1.9	2.2	2.2	4.1	3.6	4.2	3.3	4.3
Africa	3.8	1.9	2.5	-0.9	0.5	3.5	2.2	1.2	1.7
Asia	5.3	7.8	5.4	7.8	8.2	6.7	6.6	7.2	9.0
Middle East	7.2	-1.3	1.3	1.7	0.1	-1.4	0.9	-1.6	3.9
Western Hemisphere	5.9	0.3	-0.8	-2.7	3.7	3.6	4.1	2.6	0.9

Source: International Monetary Fund, *World Economic Outlook*, April 1989, Table A1. Output measures are real GNP for developed countries, real GDP for developing countries; reproduced in Krugman and Obstfeld (1991: 650).

Countries which went into deficit or threatened to default risked losing commercial credit and concessional finance facilities, exclusion from IMF and World Bank borrowing facilities, the seizure of their assets and reductions in potential gains from international trade (Krugman & Obstfeld 1991: 653-4). Many debtor countries experienced a negative resource transfers of 5 to 6 per cent of GNP and 30 to 50 per cent of export earnings (Frank 1989: 34). Arrears on principal and interest reached approximately 6.9 per cent of all LDC debt by 1989; and by 1991 the collective debt of sub-Saharan Africa amounted to $175,836m, a net outflow of $1,005m resulting in a ratio of debt to GNP of 106.1 per cent (Earth 1990: 20). Debt-to-export ratios rose in practically all debtor LDCs. The annual debt service payments of 19 severely-indebted middle income countries (with annual per capita incomes above $500) have typically ranged between 20 and 40 per cent of their total external receipts, and close to 50 per cent among the 26 most severely indebted low income countries (annual per capita incomes below $500) (Goel 1989).

Responses to the Debt Crisis

Liberal economists like Sachs (1989) and Dornbusch (1988) have ascribed the origins of the crisis to a combination of policy actions in the debtor countries, macro-economic shocks in the world economy, and unrestrained bank lending between 1979 and 1981 followed by the abrupt withdrawal of new credits in 1982. From a Marxist perspective, Cleaver (1989: 19) traced the origins of the crisis to 'an international cycle of working class struggles which ruptured global capital accumulation' and located its continuation 'in the failure of capital to overcome those struggles and to restore conditions for a new cycle of accumulation'.

This disparity in explanations of the crisis has been paralleled by the equally wide range of proposals for its resolution. From the liberal perspective the basic preoccupation has been to manage the debt, primarily in order to limit the damage to Western financial institutions. A more radical demand has been for the cancellation of the debt. Others, like Wachtel (1986: 210-11), have called for sacrifices by all parties if greater monetary stability is to be achieved.

Managing the Debt Crisis

The West has sought to manage the crisis by controlling the expansion of LDC debt in order to limit the threat to its financial institutions and keep alive the possibility of repayment. Third World debt has therefore been treated in the same manner as any other contractual arrangement, forcing debtors to yield to a degree of Western control over their political economies unprecedented since the days of direct colonial rule. Amongst the methods imposed on debtors have been corporate restructuring, buybacks in the market of debt, debt-for-debt equity swaps and debt-for-debt swaps (in which loans are swapped by banks for bonds or other higher quality obligations).

The first phase of the Western attempt to manage the crisis involved 'concerted lending', under which creditor banks were required to lend new funds to debtors in proportion to their initial exposure in those countries.[7] Concerted lending was envisaged as a temporary measure enabling debtor LDCs to reduce their debt-output ratios, the expectation in Western financial and government circles being that debtors would be willing and able to make full repayment - an indication of the Alice in Wonderland nature of the crisis. By 1984, however, the current account deficits of non-oil exporting debtor states had fallen well below the levels of the early 1980s, and all debtor LDCs were making substantial reverse resource transfers to their creditors. Negative output growth rates became common, accompanied by high unemployment, falling real wages and growing social and political unrest.

After several rounds of debt restructuring many of the creditor banks began decreasing or removing loan facilities. After 1984 most of the funds obtained by debtor LDCs came from direct investment, the IMF or the World Bank. By 1986 calls for some form of debt relief were being heard more frequently. Many banks were selling off LDC loans, these 'securitized' assets being traded at discount prices reflected the growing belief that non-payment was inevitable. In America the Citicorp bank set a pattern by writing off a major segment of what it was owed, tacitly accepting that it would not be repaid.[8] The pursuit of full repayment continued nonetheless. Although the plight of the 26 most severely indebted low income countries (mostly in sub-Saharan Africa) was far worse than that of middle income LDCs, the banks targeted the latter in the expectation that some form of repayment was more likely from them. The combined debts of the low income countries amounted to $116 billion - less than 10 percent of Third World total of $134 trillion at the end of 1990 (World Bank 1992).

Despite this, Western creditors continued to treat the crisis as a transitory liquidity problem in a few indebted countries due to special circumstances, the solution to which was structural adjustment, including a reduction of overborrowing, leading to the restoration of the creditworthiness of debtors in an otherwise unchanged international financial order. Creditor governments used their leverage to ensure that the rescheduling of bank debts owed by foreign governments involved neither an interruption of interest payments to the banks nor a reduction in the present value of the debtors' future obligations to those banks.

By 1985, however, it was clear that this strategy was failing. During the preceding two years indebted LDCs paid back more in interest and principal than they received in new loans. Real commodity prices continued to decline and negative growth was widespread amongst debtors. It became apparent that the crisis was more than a problem of mere transitory liquidity. In October 1985, US Treasury Secretary James Baker unveiled a three-point plan designed to replace the ad hoc nature of the Western approach to the crisis. Debtors would be required to implement severe austerity measures, including the reduction of their debt burdens through increased exports, there would be a $20 billion increase in commercial bank lending over three years, and a continuing role for the IMF along with an enhanced role for multilateral development banks. Baker's plan was aimed primarily at Latin America, but failed because banks were reluctant to continue lending and because higher export earnings were absorbed by the rising cost of debt service. Critics viewed the Plan as nothing more than a political initiative designed to defuse resistance amongst debtors to debt servicing (Hall 1988: 10).

Creditors succeeded in coercing debtor countries into servicing their foreign debts until 1986, when Peru unilaterally declared that it would cap its interest payments at 10 per cent of its export receipts.[9] Two years later, Brazil also began to seek a way out of the debt trap. By 1989, however, fears that widespread default might precipitate an international banking collapse had abated sufficiently to enable the Comptroller of the Currency to declare that 'the vulnerability of the US banking system to LDC debt performance has loosened considerably'.[10]

However, the persistence of the debt problem led the US Administration to announce a new initiative named after Baker's replacement, Nicholas Brady. This shift in US policy was prompted by a fear of increased social and political unrest in the 'American' hemisphere, especially in the fledgling democracies. The Plan incorporated official US backing for debt reduction schemes involving enhancements from the international financial institutions. It implicitly recognised that full repayment was no longer a realistic expectation and that there was a growing awareness of the lack of parity of sacrifice between creditor banks and debtor countries.

The Plan sanctioned the growing pattern of structural adjustment by linking debt relief to economic reform. The logic was that policy reform required financial support to succeed, but financial support without policy reform amounted to throwing good money after bad. The Plan provided some relief, but to only five of the 19 most severely indebted middle-income countries, those which accounted for more than 80 per cent of the exposure of the nine US banks most heavily involved in lending to the 42 debtor LDCs that had rescheduled their commercial bank debts by 1989. Commercial banks were encouraged to provide a broader range of financial support to debtors, the IMF and the World Bank were urged to supply funding for debt or debt service reduction, and the IMF was asked to modify its practice of delaying disbursements to debtors until commercial bank creditors had agreed on their own lending commitments. The Plan also supported market-based debt reduction, an illusion which appeared to offer a cheap and easy way for debtors to reduce their indebtedness by buying back their own debt at low market prices. This was possible because by 1987 loans to problem debtors were being traded below face value in the secondary market. As Krugman and Obstfeld (1991: 662) point out, 'a careful examination of exactly what happens when a country uses its own resources to buy back its troubled debt reveals that the country's creditors are the only ones who benefit!' Another possibility is for third parties to buy the debts, and some observers have indeed interpreted the Brady Plan as suggesting that the World Bank and the IMF provide funds for this purpose. Even in this scenario, however, the outcome is likely to be a minimal gain for the LDC in question but large windfall gains for creditors (Krugman & Obstfeld 1991: 667).

Apart from the clear message that market-based debt reduction should be promoted by official agencies, the Plan was vague in describing how its recommendations were to be effected. It was greeted sceptically.

Twenty months after the Brady Plan was launched Third World arrears on interest payments to commercial banks had tripled to $24 billion. In December 1990, Latin America's foreign debt amounted to $429 billion, $1 billion more than it had been before agreements were concluded with Mexico, Venezuela, Costa Rica, and Chile under the Plan.[11]

Debt Forgiveness and Debt Cancellation

The realisation that full repayment by all, or even a majority, of debtor LDCs is unlikely forced Western governments and financial institutions to consider the only viable alternative, debt forgiveness or cancellation. Radical proposals for cancellation of the debt came from those less concerned with the viability of the international financial system than with the costs to the people being exploited to pay the debt. Notable among such groups are the Debt Crisis Network (DCN) in the United States and the International Counter-Congress which met in Berlin in 1988 to protest against IMF and World Bank policies. In its statement of principles the DCN declared its support for 'the call by some non-governmental organizations and governments in the south to cancel payment of the debt' (cited in Cleaver 1989: 19). In its declaration the Counter-Congress called not only for 'a global cancellation of debt' (rather than conditional cancellation of debt relief) but also for reparations for past damage.

The UN Centre on Transnational Corporations (UNCTC 1988b: 147) has argued that debt relief is required because the crisis is so widespread and systemic that its resolution is in the nature of a public good. An internationally negotiated programme, based on legal principles, is desirable because '*De jure* debt relief, as against *de facto* defaults, offers a far better prospect that coherent adjustment programmes can be negotiated'. Krugman and Obstfeld (1991: 668) point out that debt relief benefits both creditors and debtors:

> A special case of an externally financed buyback is debt forgiveness, in which creditors simply cancel or forgive part of the debt. In effect, funds for the 'buyback' of the cancelled debt are provided by the creditors themselves. Our analysis implies that it would cost creditors *as a group* less than it seems to cancel the debt of problem debtors...In July, 1989, for example, Argentina's debt was traded on the secondary market at a price of only 17.5 cents on the dollar. This

low price meant that much of Argentina's debt had very little chance of ever being repaid, so that creditors could forgive at least some of it at virtually no real cost to themselves. Such forgiveness would benefit debtors, not only by reducing their expected payments of debt, but also by lowering the costs and penalties due to ongoing friction with creditors (their emphasis).

And the case for debt forgiveness becomes almost overwhelming when Lawrence Summers, the chief economist at the World Bank, advocates substantial forgiveness of the debt owed by low-income African countries (*Financial Times*, 3 and 7 August, 1992).

Griffith-Jones (1989: 8-10) has argued that any proposal for dealing with the crisis must meet certain criteria: it must eliminate net transfers of resources from South to North; any resources freed by concessionality on debt or interest relief must be utilised within a development plan leading to sustained economic growth and increased social welfare; the package must not be biased in favour of large or middle-income debtors; and it should have a positive effect on the world economy.

While debt default is not historically unusual, the differences between the present crisis and those which preceded it render comparisons difficult. What is apparent from previous crises, particularly those of the 1890s and 1930s, is that creditors must expect to write off such debts if a global resolution is to be achieved. The reluctant acceptance of this reality was reflected in the differences between the Baker Plan, which envisaged full repayment through concerted lending, and the Brady Plan, which implicitly acknowledged the impossibility of achieving this - and was later reflected in the Toronto and Trinidad terms. In September 1988, the 10 major OECD countries concluded the *Toronto Agreement*, a menu of options for Paris Club governments to soften rescheduling terms on non-concessional debt, mostly owed to export credit agencies.[12]

Facing up to reality might have been quicker if the lessons of previous debt forgiveness had been learned. In the 1930s, there 'was a cut of between 50 and 70 per cent in required interest payments and 20 to 30 year maturities' (Snowden 1985: 268). This arose not from a sudden altruism amongst creditors but from the realisation that debt overhang is the most crippling factor facing any country wishing to stimulate renewed foreign investment. Creditors may theoretically benefit from unpaid debt in the form of increasing interest payments, but as Lindert and Morton (1988:

232-33) argue, forgiveness and longer maturity periods bring 'gains in world wealth by avoiding destructive penalties by the creditors, the damage value of which would not be fully recaptured by them'. That forgiveness is viable is illustrated by the fact that realised returns from country bondholders in earlier crises were sufficiently high prior to default to prevent creditor disaster. The contemporary validity of this proposition was illustrated by the Dominican Republic, which could have defaulted on approximately 70 per cent of its publicly guaranteed debt to private creditors in 1986 and left them with 'as high a return as if they had lent to the United States all along' (Lindert 1989: 255). In fact, Western banks have done very well out of the debt crisis.[13]

By contrast, in the bond era, when banks merely issued and brokered bonds, the burden of default was spread more widely, posing a greater threat to global financial stability. This concentration led to the second major difference in the current crisis, the intervention of governments (often as creditors themselves), the World Bank and the IMF. In contrast to the Toronto and Trinidad meetings, previous crises were characterised by direct negotiations between debtors and committees representing bondholders.

There are, however, five basic objections to debt relief: '(a) affected countries will not regain their access to new credit; (b) a 'moral hazard' problem arises which might encourage countries to borrow irresponsibly in the future; (c) a precedent would be established which could lead other countries to renege on their debts; (d) the banks cannot afford it; and (e) taxpayers of home countries of banks should not have to 'bail out' banks and their customers. All of these objections are either exaggerated or miss the point' (UNCTC 1988b: 146).

The Debt Crisis and the Limits of the Law

Law, such as the international law of contract, has inevitably played a role in attempts to manage the crisis. Legislation in LDCs has also been substantially affected through the changes required by SAPs: debtor states have been coerced into passing legislation on the privatisation of public enterprises and financial contributions from parents to the education of their children in countries like Kenya and Tanzania. Law has been resorted to primarily in order to manage the crisis, and has thus appeared to be largely epiphenomenal. International law has, however, been of limited use in enforcing repayment, indicating that the law is contradictory for both debtors and creditors. Indeed, some writers argue that international law provides a basis for cancellation of the debt.

The Role of Law in Managing the Crisis

The UNCTC's observation that 'If there is a lesson to be learned from the debt crisis, it is that the international community lacks a legal framework to deal with situations in which countries are unable to continue to service their debts. At present, the only alternatives that a country has are protracted negotiations with its creditors or default. What is needed is an international legal framework for rewriting contracts when unforeseen developments make it impossible for sovereign borrowers to honour their commitments' (UNCTC 1988b: 150) is therefore apposite. Such a possibility, based on the expectation that the debt can and will be repaid, has been addressed in various ways, ranging from relief on part of the principal and/or interest rates, to a cap on the amount of gross domestic product used to service the debt (UNCTC 1988b: 148-9, Commonwealth Secretariat 1990: 90-1). UNCTAD has explored the possibility of applying the principles of domestic bankruptcy laws to sovereign debt (UNCTC 1988: 150). More specifically, it has been suggested that some of the provisions of the *US Bankruptcy Code* (11 U.S.C.A.) should be internationalised (Raffer 1989).

It may been objected that Chapter 11 of the Code, which covers corporate bankruptcy and reorganisation, is inappropriate on the technical ground that a state cannot discontinue its operations. Chapter 9, however, covers the insolvency of municipalities. Both affected individuals and employees of the municipality have a right to be heard in defence of their interests. Creditors receive what can be 'reasonably expected' under the given circumstances, and the living standard of the local population is protected. Under Section 904, unless the debtor consents or the plan so provides, a court may not interfere with the political or governmental powers of the debtor, with its property or revenues, or the debtor's use or enjoyment of any income-producing property. This, it is argued, provides a model for dealing with LDC debt.

An alternative suggestion is the creation of an international debt commission. In 1990, the UN Secretary-General appointed former Italian Prime Minister Bettino Craxi as his personal envoy to seek solutions to the debt crisis. This development indicated the need for a more formal body which might seek to follow Sachs' proposals (1986: 397) that relief should be granted, on a progressive scale, to countries whose per capita incomes have dropped 15 per cent or more relative to previous peaks. Such relief would comprise a suspension of interest payments for a given period, without capitalisation of missed payments. Countries with a decline in living standards of more than 25 per cent would be permitted to forego all interest payments for five years. All principal payments could be fully rescheduled for a period of several years.

The Organisation of American States Group has argued for joint negotiations by debtors in order to achieve a coherent framework which could then apply to particular cases. Such proposals might be relevant to middle-income debtors, but they are unlikely to have any effect on chronically indebted low income countries that have no realistic prospect of repaying their debts. The Trinidad Terms would represent an important extension of concessionality for middle income countries, they would still be inadequate for severely-indebted low income countries.

The poverty and economic underdevelopment of sub-Saharan African countries, for example, make it impossible for them to emerge from their debt problem without external assistance. Their indebtedness often exceeds their GNP, and is several times that of their annual exports. In a 1989 report on sub-Saharan Africa, the World Bank (1989) claimed that both productivity and outside aid would have to be doubled by 2000 if the region is to achieve sustainable growth.

The Limits and Potential of Private International Law

The fact that countries, unlike companies, 'do not go bust' has historically posed substantial legal problems for creditors in debt crises. '[F]ar from being a comfort to the lender, the impossibility of forcing a country into liquidation or installing a court-appointed receiver (the IMF, for example), is the reason why sovereign lending is inherently riskier than normal commercial banking' (Kaletsky 1984, *cf.* Kaletsky 1985). This is so because in sovereign lending the creditor's ultimate lines of defence - collateral and legal protection - either do not exist at all or not in any form commensurate with the sums of money involved. Some have even argued that sovereign lending is a form of gambling - a wager on the sovereign debtor's willingness to pay up. Sovereign loans used to be referred to as 'aleatory contracts', aleator meaning 'dice-player' in Latin.

It was only in the late 1970s, well after the lending boom which facilitated the current crisis, that British and American legislation was strengthened, but even with such laws the few cases which have come to court suggest that bankers face an uphill struggle winning any significant legal redress against sovereign creditors. Despite this, leading authorities like William Cline argue that: 'Foreign creditors could attach any of the foreign assets of a defaulting country, as well as its exports abroad (commercial airlines, ships, bank accounts, shipments of commodities, and so forth)'.[14] Kaletsky (1984) considers it unlikely that a defaulting debtor will ever be sued because 'the risks of provoking an outright repudiation or of having questionable loans declared formally in default by the courts would outweigh the possible benefits of litigation for the big banks'. He points to three general problems which make legal redress extremely difficult.

The first is that of jurisdiction: there is nothing to prevent debtor states introducing new legislation to make their debts uncollectable, for example by imposing exchange controls or converting debts into local currency. Courts around the world will generally judge such agreements on the basis of the laws under which they were made, so that a bank suing in the West would nonetheless have the loan agreement decided on the basis of the legislation passed by the debtor state. Most contemporary loans are, however, made either under New York law (for dollar loans to Latin America) or English law. Private trade credits, however, are usually subject to local governing law.

The second problem is that of sovereign immunity. It was not until the passage of the *Foreign Sovereign Immunities Act* of 1976 in the United States and the *State Immunity Act* of 1978 in Britain that the rights of private litigants were fully recognised. Such legislation made it possible for foreign nations to waive their immunity from suits in American and British courts, and such waivers have subsequently been included in most loan agreements. Colombia, Brazil and Venezuela have sometimes refused to sign such waivers on constitutional grounds, but even in these cases alternative wordings have usually been agreed. It is therefore possible in principle to obtain a default judgement against a defaulting government.

In such an occurrence a third problem would arise, that of enforcement. Generally, courts will not allow governmental property such as embassies and military equipment to be seized under any circumstances. Central bank property can be attached in the US and UK only if it is covered by a specific waiver. In the US the protection of central banks goes even further: their assets can never be attached before a judgement is rendered, making it possible for a nation to remove its foreign exchange reserves from US jurisdiction even after it has been sued. As far as other assets like airliners and ships are concerned, most governments do not own major foreign assets in their own names. In addition, nationalised corporations, fully owned by governments, have separate legal personalities and cannot usually be drawn into suits against the government which owns them. Much of a country's trade can be protected by ensuring that legal title to commodities passes to foreign importers immediately upon delivery.

> In summary, bankers could probably administer no more than 'pinpricks' through the legal system to a country which carefully organised its default...The only really effective sanction they have is the denial of future credits. But few major debtors can reasonably expect new credits remotely comparable with the annual interest they pay, however well they behave. (Kaletsky 1984).

Private lenders are therefore forced to rely on their governments for protection. However, such an approach is merely likely to result in seizures of foreign assets by debtor governments and possible trade wars.

International law has generally been regarded as a means of enforcing debt repayments. For this reason few writers have considered whether debtor states might also be protected. Seeking to establish an objective basis in international law that would enable debtor LDCs to cancel their debts, Frankenberg and Knieper (1984) consider whether the principle of *pacta sunt servanda* (agreements are binding and must be implemented in good faith, often said to be a rule of customary international law) must today yield to different criteria in the interpretation of international contracts, even when one of the parties is a nation-state. They argue that the general principles of international law 'are not tailored to the situation of debtors. Nevertheless they call into question the sanctity of treaties by admitting exceptions to and modifications of the categorical obligation to fulfil contractual obligations' (Frankenberg & Knieper 1984: 424).

Pacta sunt servanda has never, they argue, been applied to contractual obligations considered 'odious' (*dette odieuse*) and states have been released from such obligations on the basis that

The Debt Crisis

not all international agreements are subject to strict fulfilment.[15] The notion of odious debts developed in the context of the doctrines of state succession (O'Connell 1956, 1964, 1967) to preclude certain obligations assumed by a state from devolving onto its successor. The general view is that a change of government, as opposed to a change of sovereignty, is legally irrelevant and, moreover, that the protection of creditors under international law should extend only to public debts. However, binding the protection of creditors to concepts

> such as the 'national interest' or 'a governmental purpose' on the part of the debtor country is not only a breach of the principle of *pacta sunt servanda*...[but] modifies the abstract attribution of rights and obligations in international law according to the concept of state sovereignty and thus points beyond the particular problems of state succession. If a society organised under a state cannot be absolutely bound collectively for all contractual promises made by its political representatives, and if, for want of a national interest, obligations are attributed *ad personam*, then there is no objective reason to exclude change of *government* from this category (Frankenberg & Knieper 1984: 427).

They argue, therefore, that not only a successor state but also a government (at least one resulting from political overthrow) must be able to plead that a contract entered into by the preceding regime cannot be legitimated by assertions of national interest. The core of their argument is that odious debts, which cannot be characterised as public, are excepted from the obligation of fulfilment because they are contracted under an abuse of rights (Frankenberg & Knieper 1984: 428). Such debts constitute an unjust exploitation of the people, are *ultra vires* in a moral sense and should not therefore provide protection for creditors.[16]

This is an attractive argument, but the doctrine of odious debts has generated controversy over how such debts can be distinguished from state debts and fears of arbitrary and unilateral annulment to the detriment of international commerce. The burden of proof lies with the debtor state, which must show that the debt was incompatible with the interests of the people and that the creditor must have been aware of this fact. If this is proved, the onus then shifts onto the creditor to demonstrate that the funds were used in the public interest of the debtor economy.

Frankenberg and Knieper then argue that there is a duality of norms in international law which favours a particular category of LDCs, and take the somewhat dubious step of relying on the right to development and the UN General Assembly's *International Development Strategy for the Second UN Decade* (Resolution 2656 (XXV), October 24 1970) as authoritative legal sources. Although the latter was adopted unanimously, General Assembly resolutions are not generally accepted as authoritative sources of international law. On this basis they argue that consideration must be taken of 'the specific development problems which actually constitute duties of co-operation. Therewith, it would be incongruous to hold firmly to the customary priority of protection of creditors, and commensurately, to allow the question of devolution of debts only in the case of a 'change of sovereignty' and not equally in the case of a 'change of government'. It follows then, that it contradicts the premises not only of an international development law, but also of an international law of co-operation to orient the fulfilment of obligations for (bilateral) loan agreements...on reciprocal relations between private, autonomous business partners' (Frankenberg & Knieper 1984: 432-3). Their final step is to argue for a redistribution of risk to control and curb the misapplication of credits. In addition to showing that the credit was in the debtor's interest, creditors should also have to show that the agreement does not contradict the consensus on development reflected in General Assembly resolutions.

Conclusion

Unsurprisingly, Frankenberg and Knieper's provocative argument has not found much favour with international lawyers, jurists or courts. While political leaders like Alan Garcia of Peru attempted to mobilise Latin American debtors into collective action, progressive lawyers in the South failed to develop such arguments in ways which might have proved politically useful. The role of the law in the debt crisis has generally been to oil the wheels of international capitalism. Despite widespread calls for an international commission, court or arbitration forum, ten years after the onset of the crisis *The Financial Times* (30 July 1992) was able to declare that 'Improvisation worked. The collapse of the financial system that threatened did not occur. Notwithstanding the endeavours of the commercial banks, it has still not occurred. The case-by-case approach to the problems of indebted countries has also succeeded'.

For the West the crisis may have been averted, but for indebted LDCs, particularly those in sub-Saharan Africa, its consequences will endure for many years. As Mayo (1992) has put it,

> On this view of the 'end of the debt crisis', the Third World is never supposed to stabilise or pay off its debt but just to keep paying more out in interest than it borrows or gets in development aid. This is a debt trap...The interest Africa pays on its debts now amounts to more than its spends on the health and education of its people. As a result, diseases once eradicated, like yaws and yellow fever, are reappearing in countries such as Ghana...The result of the debt in the Third World has been increasing economic dependency, with more and more people forced to live on the margins of survival, on degraded rural lands or in burgeoning city slums. Famine, war and local environmental collapse are symptoms of this.

Attempts to manage the crisis have merely deepened and prolonged the economic, social and political problems of indebtedness. Forgiveness or cancellation is the only realistic means by which the citizens of debtor countries can envisage a future in which development is more than chimerical. The chief economist at the World Bank has admitted that 'troubled low-income debtors cannot grow out of their debt problem, the core of which lies in official debt - that is, government-to-government bilateral loans. For many countries, a resolution will involve substantial debt forgiveness, frequently going beyond the 50 per cent reductions of recent agreements under the Paris Club of official bilateral creditors' (*The Financial Times*, 3 August 1992).

Forgiveness is necessary because one of the major consequences of the West's response to the crisis has been the imposition of structural adjustment programmes on virtually every debtor state with dire effects. Reflecting neo-conservative economic dogma, SAPs have a simple aim: increase revenues, reduce expenditures (George 1988: 52). The measures 'recommended' to LDCs are designed to suppress demand (and hence inflation), devalue exchange rates, lower wages, eliminate tariff protection, facilitate privatisation, and promote greater freedom for transnational corporations. They are aimed at increasing foreign exchange earnings in order to service the debt while limiting government expenditure, particularly on social welfare and food subsidies. This 'liberalisation' - the Thatcherism which failed in Britain imposed on the South - has been accompanied by the imposition of extensive conditions on the granting of aid (Hill 1991). According to the World Bank, there is a crisis of governance in Africa (World Bank 1989: 60), of which the failure of public institutions is a root cause (World Bank 1989: xii). What is required to cure these ills is a reincarnation of the modernisation paradigm in the form of 'good governance'. This involves multiparty democracy, the rule of law, accountability, and free market institutions, all of which are, unsurprisingly, to be found in the Bank's friendly SAPs (for an extended critique see Beckman, 1990, Adelman & Paliwala *infra*). These are often unobjectionable on face value; their consequences for the majority of citizens in debtor LDCs are, however, dire: George (1988: 53) cites a study of IMF objectives between 1964 and 1979 in which the aim of protecting the poor against possible adverse effects of its programmes occurs exactly once. Structural adjustment is an ideology designed less to facilitate development in the South than to address the crisis of accumulation in the North. As Susan George (1988: 47) has put it:

> As watchdog and messenger, the IMF helps to ensure that overexposed banks will be repaid, that even major borrowers like Mexico will be prevented from destabilizing the system as a whole. As alibi, it allows the major industrialized countries and their banks to offload the consequences of their own shortsighted policies and financial recklessness on to the Fund's shoulders. The IMF helps them to consolidate their power over poor nations. At the same time, and in exchange for co-operation, it generally allows the elites of these same nations to maintain their affluence and perks at the expense of the majority of their fellow citizens. The IMF is a sort of Godfather figure - it makes countries offers they can't refuse.

Responding to such criticism of the negative social and political impact of its policies, the World Bank and the IMF have since claimed to be taking human rights into consideration in the formulation of SAPs. In May 1992 the World Bank published a handbook in which it is stated that 'Sustainable poverty reduction is the overarching objective of the World Bank. It is the benchmark by which our performance as a development institution will be measured'. What remains to be seen is whether the obvious link between the increase in poverty and SAPs will result in any modifications to the latter. The Bank has regularly prioritised issues like women's career development and the environment with few positive results. One Bank official stated that this policy change 'is yet another burden on our shoulders when we lack resources, which will mean a half-hearted effort. We'll take a quick trip to a poor neighbourhood and collect a few statistics to show that something is being done' (*The Guardian*, 11 May 1992). Given that the primary aim of SAPs is the restructuring of LDCs in order to safeguard the interests of the Western banking system and to facilitate the extension of capitalist relations in the South, there is an irreconcilable contradiction between the function of these international economic institutions and the protection of human rights and dignity.

The 1980s were a lost decade in much of the developing world. If the 1990s are to be different, debt forgiveness or cancellation is essential. Mayo (1992) points to a role that law might play: 'If the economic system is stacked against people, you have to change the rules...Debt repayments, for example, could rank below the rights of people to food, shelter, clothing, work and health'. The problem, as ever, is that he who pays the piper calls the tune.

Notes

1 Only Brazil, with a foreign debt of nearly $88 billion, was more indebted than Mexico in 1982. In 1991, Mexico paid more than $16 billion to service its debt, more than its total export revenues.

2 The claim by *The Financial Times* (London, 30 July 1992) that the debt crisis in Latin America is over now that capital has begun to flow into the region appears premature in light of the fact that Mexico's foreign debt has been reduced to a 'mere' 31 per cent of GDP, public foreign debt to 24 per cent of GDP, and total public debt to the equivalent of 38 per cent of GDP. When Angel Gurria, undersecretary for international financial affairs in Mexico's Ministry of Finance declares that 'For us, the debt crisis is over', it is not to Mexico's poor that he is referring. Even if the debt crisis were over in Latin America, it is certainly not in Africa, which has had only $7 billion of a total debt of $270 billion cancelled, and $1 billion 'swapped' into funds for investment or environmental projects (Mayo 1992). In addition, a new and potentially larger problem looms in the countries of the former Soviet Union.

3 The World Bank and the IMF are the key managers of the crisis on behalf of the West. Frank (1989:37) refers to the latter as 'the Institute

for Misery and Famine'. With their controlling votes on the world's two most powerful financial agencies, the World Bank and the IMF, the Group of Seven (G-7) industrialised countries dominate these agencies both directly and indirectly through their control of the financial and technical resources they need to operate.

4   Krugman & Obstfeld (1991: 644). 'The New York stock market crash of October 1929 and the ensuing worldwide depression caused foreign finance to dry up almost entirely. No longer able to borrow abroad, developing countries were forced to cut imports, a move that accentuated the decline in aggregate demand facing the developed world. As industrialized countries erected higher barriers to imports, it became nearly impossible for international debtors to earn the export revenues needed to meet debt payments. Bolivia defaulted on January 1, 1931, and it was followed, within three years, by almost every other country in Latin America' (*Ibid.*: 643).

5   It would be more accurate to refer to Northern governments and financial institutions as Japan is also involved in substantial lending to the South. However, the vast majority of lending which led to the debt crisis came from North America and Europe and it is for this reason that the term 'West' is more often used.

6   This problem was compounded by the fact that these floating-rate loan contracts with private banks were calculated on the London Interbank Offered Rate (LIBOR), the rate London banks charge each other for dollar loans.

7   Concerted lending arose from a meeting between Mexican finance officials and representatives of the numerous US banks from which the country had borrowed aimed at co-ordinating continued lending. An advisory committee was established to represent the banks, many of which were reluctant to increase their exposure and were coerced into concerted lending (Krugman & Obstfeld 1991: 656).

8   This section is derived from Krugman & Obstfeld (1991: 656-60).

9   Peru failed in its attempt to developed a co-ordinated strategy amongst all Latin American debtors, not least because of actual or implied threats concerning future credit from Western lenders.

The Debt Crisis 193

10 Robert L. Clarke testifying before The Banking Committee of the House of Representatives, *International Herald Tribune*, Jan. 7-8, 1989.

11 By 1992, little headway had been made with Brazil and Argentina, holders of nearly 40 percent of the Third World's debt and more than 60 percent of its arrears (*The Economist*, Jan. 25, 1992).

12 The formation of the Paris Club in 1956 was prompted by Argentina's debt difficulties. It provides a forum for negotiations between debtor and creditor governments under the chairpersonship of a French Treasury official, and consequently has no set membership. An important principle informing negotiations is the symmetrical treatment of all creditors. Debtors are usually required to approach the IMF for a loan and an approved adjustment programme prior to approaching the Paris Club. Creditors can choose from or combine three options: (a) cancel 33% of debt service covered by the Agreement; (b) reduce interest rates by 3.5 points or 50%, whichever is the less; or (c) extend grace periods to 14 years and maturity to 25 years (8 and 14 years in the other two options). Grace periods and maturity on aid loans can also be extended to 14 and 25 years.
Under the so-called Trinidad terms, agreed in 1991, the poorest 40 debtor countries are entitled to have up to two thirds of their official foreign debt written off and the remainder rescheduled over a period of up to 25 years. Those terms represent a significant improvement on the Toronto Terms, which give low income developing countries the choice of cancelling only a third of their debt, stretching their repayment terms or reducing their interest payments.

13 'To date, almost 40 per cent of private bank debt in highly indebted countries has been covered by comprehensive debt reduction deals. Arrangements under negotiation for Brazil and Argentina will raise that figure to almost 70 per cent' (Lawrence Summers, Chief Economist at the World Bank, *The Financial Times*, 3 August 1992).

14 *Ibid.* For case law on the treatment of act of state doctrine by American courts see Underhill v Hernandez 168 US (1897), Banco Nacional de Cuba v Sabbatino 376 US (1964), Libra Bank Limited v Banco Nacional de Costa Rica 570 F. Supp. 870 (SDNY 1983), Allied Bank v. Banco Credito Agricola de Cartago 757 F.2d 516 (Second Circuit 1985) and Weston, Falk and D'Amato (1990: Ch. 5).

15 *Clausula rebus sic stantibus* is the doctrine that a treaty is intended by the parties to be binding only as long as there is no vital change in the circumstances which obtained at the time of its conclusion. Frankenberg & Knieper (1984: 422) point out that debtor LDCs cannot rely on their insolvency in order to suspend or terminate a loan agreement. It would therefore appear that under this principle debt will not constitute a change of circumstances so substantial that fulfillment of the contract can no longer *bona fide* be expected. Article 62 of the *Vienna Convention on the Law of Treaties* provides that an unanticipated but substantial change in the circumstances present at the signing of an agreement can only be permitted as a reason for suspension or termination if (a) these circumstances present a substantial basis for the consent of the parties, and (b) the change of circumstances radically alters the extent of the contractual obligations yet to be fulfilled. Nonetheless, 'this "undue burden" conception of the *clausula* would...allow the debtor country the opportunity of raising the point about the socio-economic and political conditions surrounding the situation. However, the general recognition of changed circumstances does not guarantee that they will be legally taken into account (p. 423). The fact that the *clausula* is often appealed to in the practice of states does not mean that it is in fact recognised as a rule of customary international law. The International Court of Justice, in the fishing conflict between Britain, the former West Germany and Iceland (ICJ Reports, 1973) took the view that a partly executed contract which has benefitted one of the parties does not permit the other party to plead the *clausula*.

It is also in this context that the situation and capability of the obligated party is appraised. Most international agreements include hardship or escape clauses in case fulfillment is temporarily or indefinitely impossible. However, as Frankenberg and Knieper (1984: 423) argue, 'the international law doctrine of impossibility of performance remains theoretical in regard to problems of overindebtedness'.

16 Feilchenfeld (1931: 450*ff.*, 862*ff.*). See also Sack (1927: 127), who argues that a debt incurred by a despotic regime aimed at strengthening itself rather than serving the interests of the people is odious for the entire population: 'This debt is not binding for the nation; it is a debt of the regime, a *personal* debt contracted by the ruler, consequently it goes down with the demise of the regime'.

9
The International Labour Code and The Exploitation of Female Workers in Export-Processing Zones
Sammy Adelman

Introduction

One of the most significant features of the global economy during the past two decades has been the emergence of export processing zones (EPZs) throughout the less developed world as many countries have sought to emulate the success achieved through the export-oriented industrialisation (EOI) policies of newly industrialising countries such as the 'Four Little Dragons', Singapore, Taiwan, South Korea and Hong Kong. This tendency has been given further impetus by the structural adjustment programmes imposed by the World Bank and the IMF on debtor states in the South (*cf.* Adelman & Espiritu, *infra*), which have required the reorientation of these economies towards production for export as a means of debt service and repayment.

Nationalism, international competition and developmentalism (the ideology that subordinates democracy to development) are amongst the factors that have combined to limit the rights of workers throughout the South. Petras and Engbarth (1988: 109-10) note that 'Whenever development has been a transcendent goal to which trades unions and workers' rights are seen as a subordinate element, states have generally endeavoured to integrate trade unionism into official administrative structures and thus control it'.

This chapter examines the position of female workers in EPZs, focussing in particular on Malaysia, and analyses the reasons why women predominate, the quality of working conditions, and the efficacy of the International Labour Organization's (ILO) international labour standards as a legal framework for their protection. In Asian EPZs, for example, women comprise 70 to 80 per cent of the workforce subjected to what has justly been termed 'super-exploitation'.[1] In particular, the viability of the inclusion of a social clause in the General Agreement on Tariffs and Trades (GATT) is examined.

Export Processing Zones

The denial of trade union rights and poor working conditions have characterised the development of EPZs, which have been defined as a relatively small, geographically separated area within a country, the purpose of which is to attract export-oriented industries by offering them especially favourable investment and trade condidtions as compared with the remainder of the host country. In particular, the EPZs provide for the importation of goods to be used in the production of exports on a bonded duty free basis.[2] Above all it is the abundance of cheap labour power in LDCs which attracts foreign investment in EPZs.

All but two of the EPZs worldwide have been established since 1971. In 1986, 90 per cent of EPZs in the developing world were located in Latin America and the Caribbean (48 per cent) and Asia (42 per cent). They are now appearing in Africa as well, where Kenya and South Africa provide two examples.[3] By 1986 74 LDCs had established EPZs or were planning to do so. These zones 'vary enormously in size, ranging from geographically extensive developments to a few small factories; from employment of more than 30 000 to little more than 100 workers...Asia contains 60 per cent of all EPZ employment in developing countries' (Dicken 1992: 183). Employment in these zones grew from around 50 000 in 1970 (Maex 1983) to over 1.3 million in 1986 (Botchie 1984), a rate of some nine per cent per annum in the decade from 1976 to 1986 (ILO 1988: 1).

> EPZs appeared to many as the ideal solution. Segregated as they were form the rest of the local economy, they were unlikely to have the economically and socially damaging consequences which a sudden transition from high protection to open international com-

petition would probably have entailed. Oriented as they were to export, they would create far more jobs than would ever be possible through simple import substitution. And the presence of sophisticated foreign enterprises was viewed, rightly or wrongly, as one of the most effective means of acquiring sorely needed foreign technology. (ILO 1988: 54).

LDCs anticipate that EPZs will serve to alleviate unemployment and assist in the acquisition of technical and managerial skills (Dror 1984: 70; Froebel et. al. 1980: 366), but whether they stimulate widescale economic development is less certain. These zones are often physically and geographically isolated, so that their forward and backward linkages with other sectors of the economy are tenuous.[4] Nevertheless, the growth of EPZs has been an important feature in the industrialisation of several Third World economies, and is therefore closely associated with the global process of industrial relocation and the new international division of labour (NIDL) (ILO/UNCTC 1988: 68; Nash 1983: viii).

In the early 1980s, several theorists discerned a change in global patterns of accumulation under which production was shifting from the developed core to the less developed periphery where conditions were relatively more conducive to profitability. Under the traditional international division of labour, peripheral countries were integrated into the world economy primarily as suppliers of raw materials and agricultural products. Industrialisation usually took place in a defensive mode behind high tariff barriers, with import substitution being the primary goal. Southall, for example, wrote of a 'widespread recognition that a fundamental transformation is taking place in the conditions of accumulation and the expansion of capital on a world-historical scale' (Southall 1988: 1). This change encouraged numerous LDCs to adopt EOI as their developmental strategy and to establish EPZs.[5] This new, or changing, international division of labour (CIDL) led to the integration of industrial production on a global scale, based on a new relationship between industrialised and less developed countries (Henderson 1986: 91-117, Nash 1983: 3-37). Transnational corporations (TNCs) took advantage of their ability to isolate highly labour-intensive processes and transfer them to areas where labour could be exploited with equal intensity but at a lower cost (Gomez & Reddock 1987: 138). Relocation was made possible because complex production processes were fragmented into simpler separate processes which could be carried out with minimum levels of skill easily acquired in relatively short periods (Froebel *et.al.* 1980: 13; Southall 1988: 8). LDCs are collectively viewed by TNCs as an 'inexhaustible reservoir of disposable labour', which is 'cheaper, abundant and readily available, equally productive, [and] more easily subjected to discipline, hard work and longer hours' (Froebel *et. al.* 1980: 13; see also Southall 1988: 10). They have therefore become sites for industries manufacturing for the world market as TNCs sought to take advantage of extremely good investment climates. Fiscal, financial and commercial incentives are provided to attract foreign investment, including tax and customs exemptions and the provision of infrastructural facilities such as transport, communications and banking.[6] Kenya, for example, provides a tax holiday for the first ten years, a reduced tax of only 25 per cent for the following ten years; permission to maintain offshore hard currency accounts; exemption from all withholding taxes on dividends and other payments to non-residents during the first ten years; exemption from import duties on machinery, raw materials and intermediate inputs; no exchange controls; no restrictions on management or technical arrangements; exemption from value added tax; advantageous customes treatment; and no restrictions on the employment of foreigners in managerial, technical and training positions.

Above all, however, the development of EPZs has been predicated upon the exploitation of cheap labour power, and one of the major incentives offered by LDCs pursuing this strategy has been the provision of 'favourable' industrial relations systems which inevitably redound to the disadvantage of workers.[7] For TNCs, the possibility of using cheap labour has been the decisive factor determining decisions to relocate (Gomez and Reddock 1987: 138). The Sameer EPZ in Kenya sees no need for trade unions, but recommends that TNCs pay wages at levels at least 30 per cent above the country's minimum wage.[8] In fact, EPZs have everywhere been hostile to unionised labour. The labour process in EPZs has been characterised by Lipietz (1982) as 'Bloody Taylorization', in which repressive state control and the regimentation of workers are strong features. Inexperienced rural recruits who are more likely to be obedient, healthy and compliant are preferred by employers.

The transnationalisation of production requires repressive political institutions and social formations in the Third World whose role is to educate, discipline and mobilize the potential and actual labour force for servitude. This has resulted in 'the development and maintenance of highly repressive regimes in NICs precisely because the international mobility of capital dictates that the peripheral state maximizes its attractiveness as a site for investment by minimizing the cost of labour and ensuring its quiescence and its adaptability' (Southall 1988: 12). Similarly, Bjorkman *et. al.* (1988: 71) argue that:

> Because of the intense competition for investments, EOI broadly speaking seems to require a firmly controlling, indeed politically repressive state...Hence it is that control of unions, minimum wage regulations, prohibitions of strikes by law, and other more direct measures related to unions, and union activities are typical state activities intimately associated with this type of industrialization.

Malaysia: A Case Study

The importance of EPZs varies according to levels of development, natural resources and state policies. For some LDCs, EPZs have not been the main engines of industrial growth and technological development, whereas for others they have formed the very basis of the industrialisation process. Malaysia, along with Singapore, Sri Lanka and the Dominican Republic, falls 'somewhere between these two extremes, and exemplif[ies] what is perhaps the more usual process whereby EPZs can foster industrial development, while industrial development in turn stimulates the growth of EPZ industries' (ILO 1988: 23).[9] In almost every country which has established EPZs there is usually a dominant industry, usually electronics or garments. For example, while total exports from Malaysian EPZs are significant, they amount to no more than 5 per cent of Malaysia's total exports;. they have nonetheless accounted for more than 60 per cent of new manufacturing employment in Malaysia since they were established (ILO 1988: 56).

The importance of EPZs inevitably varies according to levels of development, natural resources and state policies. For Brazil, South Korea and Taiwan, EPZs have not been the main engines of industrial growth and technological development, whereas for Macau and Mauritius EPZs have formed the very basis of the industrialization process. Of the 74 enterprises in Malaysian EPZs in 1988, 64 per cent were foreign owned, 31 per cent were joint ventures, and only 5 per cent were domestically owned (ILO

1988: 26). Of the foreign owned enterprises, 47 were from industrialised countries and 7 from developing countries (6 of which were from Hong Kong) (ILO 1988: 32). In almost every country which has encouraged the establishment of EPZs there is usually a dominant industry, and in the case of Malaysia this is electronics, which constitutes three-quarters of all EPZ activity.[10] While total exports from Malaysian EPZs are significant, they amount to no more than 5 per cent of Malaysia's total exports:

> with its electronics monoculture [it] has a low net export ratio...[which] suggests that the net export performance of EPZ industries has little if any connection with the types of industries operating in the EPZs...and probably has a lot to do with government policy and with the presence of a pre-existing industrial basis in the host country. (ILO 1988: 46).

Nonetheless, it has been calculated that EPZs have accounted for more than 60 per cent of new manufacturing employment in Malaysia since they were established (ILO 1988: 56). In 1986 employment in the 11 Malaysian EPZs totalled 81 688 (Dicken 1992: 183), most of these jobs filled by women.

Malaysia's Political-Economy

In 1988, Malaysia's per capita GDP was US$2,034 (*The Financial Times*, 28 September 1989). With a real growth rate of 8.1 per cent, it is an upper middle-income country in the World Bank classification (World Bank 1988). Under British colonial rule its main economic activities were the production of tin and rubber for western markets. Since independence in 1963, the government has promoted a policy of industrialisation to reduce the country's dependence on commodity exports. At first a policy of import-substitution industrialisation (ISI) was pursued, but this was unsuccessful and aggravated political and economic differences and racial tensions.[11] In 1970 the government formulated a New Economic Policy designed to restructure Malaysian society and correct the economic imbalances between the races. In particular, the NEP was intended to bring more Malays into the industrial labour force, where they have historically been underrepresented (Ong 1983: 429).

Malaysia's economy remains primarily based upon plantation agriculture, but EOI is increasingly part of its long-term economic strategy - with electronics being particularly important. The country became a popular location for labour-intensive industries in the late 1960s and early 1970s because of its good economic infrastructure.[12] The first EPZs were established in 1972 and by 1986 eleven were in existence (Froebel *et. al.* 1980: 308; ILO/ UNCTC 1985: 8), taking advantage of the fiscal and financial incentives offered to foreign investors: industries can apply for 'pioneer status', which qualifies them for tax relief for up to ten years, there are minimal customs fees for the import and export of materials, and free transfers of capital and profits.[13]

Guarantees of stable labour relations in its labour legislation is part of Malaysia's strategy for attracting foreign investors. Thus a Federal Industrial Development Agency (FIDA) investment brochure advertises that 'adequate legislation in industrial relations ensures the maintenance of industrial peace and harmony, ...thereby guaranteeing the smooth operation of production without undue disruption' (Ong 1983: 429).

The foundations for repressive labour relations were laid between 1947 and 1960, under British colonial rule and when collective bargaining became prevalent following independence in 1963, the government enacted a comprehensive statutory framework for the conduct of labour relations in the form of the *Industrial Relations Act* of 1967. Together with the *Employment Ordinance* of 1955 and the amended *Trade Union Ordinance* of 1959, this Act constitutes the basis of the Malaysian labour relations system. It covers the rights of workers and employers and their organizations, recognition of trade unions, collective bargaining, the settlement of labour disputes, and strikes and lockouts. A central position is occupied by the Industrial Court, which can issue binding awards for the settlement of labour disputes. For industries in which workers are not sufficiently organized, tripartite wages councils, first introduced in 1947, are empowered to lay down minimum wages and conditions of employment (Schregle 1982).

Towards the end of the 1960s, government policy shifted towards EOI in pursuit of rapid industrialisation. In 1969 the *Industrial Relations Act* was amended to make certain personnel decisions, including recruitment, transfer, promotion and dismissal, management prerogatives which would no longer be subject to collective bargaining. Section 15 stipulates that trade unions may not make proposals for a collective agreement regarding questions such as the promotion or internal transfer of workers, staff recruitment, retrenchment, and the assignment of duties. The aim of these provisions is to protect pioneer industries from 'unreasonable' demands by trade unions.[14] In 1975, the Malaysian Minister of Labour and Manpower, apparently a man with little sense of irony, stated that these provisions

> seek to place the terms and conditions of employment on a more equitable basis, where employers are given greater expectation of securing a more contented and industrious labour force, which in turn, contributes to stability and productivity, while workers are assured of minimum standards of protection and benefits. (Froebel *et. al.* 1980: 363).

The *Free Trade Zone Act* was passed in 1971, providing that there could be no improvement of working conditions in pioneer industries over and above the minimum standards laid down by legislation without authorisation from the Ministry of Labour (ILO 1972: 29). In 1980, the *Industrial Relations Act* and the *Trade Union Ordinance* were amended to allow the Ministry of Labour and Manpower to suspend a trade union for reasons of internal security, prohibit the use of trade union funds for political purposes, limit the exercise of the right to strike and to control the international affiliations of Malaysian trade unions. Under the *Ordinance*, the Registrar of Trade Unions has wide discretionary powers to reject applications by new trade unions and to suspend or withdraw the registration of existing bodies. The Act also gives the Minister of Labour the power to suspend a trade union for up to six months if in his opinion it is being used for a purpose prejudicial to or incompatible with the interests of state security or public order (Wangel 1988: 294). The Act stipulates that unions may be established only by workers engaged in the same or similar trades or occupations, and gives the Registrar discretionary power to refuse the federation of separate unions.[15]

Malaysia has ratified the ILO *Convention on the Right to Organize and Bargain Collectively* (No. 98) and is therefore obliged to respect the right to collective organization and bargaining. Despite this, by restricting registration, placing controls over the structure of unions, and limiting the nature of demands that may be articulated in collective agreements, labour legislation in Malaysia effectively restricts the right of workers to organize and bargain collectively.

Strikes do occur in Malaysia, but most disputes appear to be referred to arbitration and to be settled through conciliation, whether real or enforced. Complaints of unfair labour practices are filed with the Ministry of Labour, which presides over conciliation and mediation procedures. Strikes are prohibited during the course of such proceedings. If the parties fail to reach an agreement after such proceedings, either side may refer the dispute to adjudication by an independent tribunal. These compulsory procedural limitations are tantamount to a prohibition on the right to strike.

In 1986, only 8.7 per cent of the 5.9 million-strong workforce was unionised. EPZs employed 81 668 people, constituting only 1.5 per cent of the total labour force. The estimated unionisation rate in EPZ industries, excluding workers in the textile and garments sector (who account for only 14.2 per cent of the total workforce in EPZs), was 5 per cent (ILO/UNCTC 1988: 20). The rate of unionisation in Malaysia as a whole is very low, no doubt due in some measure to state hostility, and is particularly so in EPZs. The structure of the Malaysian trade union movement has thus been weak and fragmented (ILO 1972: 3). While legal standards pertaining to workers' rights are generally low throughout Malaysia, they appear to be even less favourable in EPZs and other off-shore production zones where TNCs are most active.

The Malaysian government argues that it is necessary to impose restrictive labour practices and laws which limit workers' rights so as to achieve the goals of economic growth and industrial development. The Government's position was made clear in the following statement issued on behalf of all Asian Labour Ministers:

> The concept of freedom and rights held by developed countries, especially European countries, is different from the one held by developing countries...[ILO] Coventions...invite resentment and resistance from developing countries, including Malaysia, because they are not practical to their political systems and the security of their countries...[I]mproving the wage earning population through the implementing international standards would only increase the disparites between the 'haves' and the 'have nots' in these economies and thus create social and political instability (ILO/ARPLA 1982 cited in Wangel 1988: 301).

Female Workers in Malaysian EPZs

TNCs have developed specific 'management techniques' adapted to local conditions 'determined by a number of factors, including the degree of poverty of the general population, the patterns of family organization, standards of education and the degree of state repression and support for these industries' (Gomez & Reddock 1987: 148). Froebel *et. al.* (1980: 359) discuss the 'super exploitation' of workers in these zones in general, while Lim (1983: 80) has argued that in addition to being subjected to capitalist exploitation women workers in LDCs are also subjected to what she calls 'imperialist' and 'patriarchal' exploitation. The labour force in the electronics, and textiles and garments industries is overwhelmingly female and accounts for more than 80 per cent of employment in EPZs globally.[16]

This preponderance of women in low-skilled employment in EPZs is explained by Wong in terms of 'capital-labour dynamics' (Wong 1983: 31): in order to reduce labour costs, maximise profits, and enhance accumulation, foreign-owned enterprises prefer female labour power because it is cheaper and more productive than male labour power (Wong 1983: 31-37). Those parts of the electronics and textiles industries which have, for example, been relocated in LDCs are highly labour-intensive, with standardised and repetitious production processes requiring little skill. Young, inexperienced rural women are the preferred choice in EPZs (Maex, 1983) as they are considered to have naturally nimble fingers and keener eyesight than men, to be naturally more diligent and docile, and more willing to accept tough work discipline (Elson & Pearson, 1981). They are also considered to be more reliable and less troublesome than men, and less likely to organize and generate or participate in labour disputes aimed at achieving higher wages and better working conditions. Amongst the enticements offered in the FIDA brochure referred to above are 'The manual dexterity of the oriental female [which] is famous the world over. Her hands are small and she works fast with extreme care. Who, therefore, could be better qualified by nature and inheritance to contribute to the efficiency of a bench-assembly production line than the oriental girl?' (Quoted in Elson & Pearson 1981: 149). Gomez and Reddock (1987: 149) argue that the 'main characteristics of female participation in the labour force ... advantageous to capital are (with the exception of youth, which could be said to apply to both men and women) their relatively subordinated and repressed character; acceptance of work discipline and experience with delicate monotonous work; dispensability, flexibility and the lack of the necessity of paying a 'family wage".

Wages and working conditions are generally accepted to be better in those enterprises owned by TNCs than in domestically-owned firms in LDCs (Lim 1983, Dror 1984, ILO/UNCTC 1988). Wages in EPZs are comparable to, if not higher than wages for the same categories of workers in similar industrial employment outside EPZs in Malaysia (ILO 1985: 42). However, wages earned by workers in TNCs in LDCs are generally much lower than those employed by the same corporations in industrialised countries, and the average wage for women is generally lower than that of men. This is true in Malaysia, where women in the manufacturing sector receive wages that amount on average to only two-thirds of those received by males in the same sector (ILO 1985: 43).

Lim (1983: 80) argues that these sex-wage differentials reflect patriarchal exploitation of women, derived from the sexual division of labour which accords women a socially and economically inferior status as secondary income earners. Women are therefore paid lower wages usually insufficient to support a family as they are primarily intended to supplement the income of the male breadwinner who cannot get employment in the industry precisely because of the facile ideological pretexts employed by TNCs to employ women rather than men.

Women also tend to predominate in production which requires low skill levels. Even where they are more productive than men they are usually paid less. Hence wages in female-intensive industries are usually lower than in male-intensive industries with comparable skill levels (Lim 1983: 80). The cheapness of womens' labour power, and their subordinate position in the sexual division of labour (overdetermined by the international division of labour) can be explained in terms of womens' lower social and economic status, which is not just a result of patriarchal and religious traditions and attitudes, but also of the unequal sexual division of labour in society (Wong 1983: 42).

The low wages, stressful and hazardous working conditions and minimal or absent social security benefits that are characteristic of employment by TNCs in EPZs in Malaysia and elsewhere are evidence of the exploitation of workers in general and women in particular (Lim 1983, Froebel *et. al.* 1980). Froebel *et. al.* (1980: 359) write of the 'superexploitation' of the labour force in EPZs and describe this phenomenon as:

The interaction of the working conditions found in enterprises in EPZs - the low wages, long hours, high intensity of work, social insecurity, additional burdens such as shift work with the lack of safety constitutes the superexploitation of the labour force in EPZs...Superexploitation in this context means essentially working conditions and a level of exploitation which actually impairs the reproduction of the labour force.

Women comprise more than 80 per cent of total global employment in EPZs, and predominate in the electronics and textiles industries in particular. In 1980, employment in EPZs amounted to about 23 per cent of total manufacturing employment in Malaysia (ILO/UNCTC 1988: 20, 53), of which women constituted 85 per cent.[17] EPZs thus play an important part in generating industrial employment, particularly for Malay women.[18]

We have already referred to the repressive legal-political regime controlling industrial relations in Malaysia. It is therefore interesting to observe that despite the restrictive labour laws and practices workers have nonetheless tried to organize to protect themselves and to change the terms and conditions of their employment. The Electrical Industry Worker's Union's (EIWU) efforts to organize workers in the electronics industry in EPZs in Malaysia have, for example, met with continuous government repression (Wangel 1988: 294). Government resistance to the formation of unions by workers in EPZs has meant that women workers in these industries are generally non-unionized and therefore mostly excluded from such organized resistance as exists (Ong 1981: 431).

Patriarchal and religious control inclines Malaysian women to be respectful and obedient to male authority and means that they are less likely to involve themselves in labour unrest (Wong 1983: 38). These factors mean that women continue to be exploited both domestically and in the workplace, rendering them far less likely to resist in the latter sphere for fear of being divorced from the former - a factor which employers are not slow to exploit. Moreover, the often limited and temporary nature of female employment makes women far less prone to unionization. Together, these factors combine to give women workers in EPZs the weakest bargaining position in the labour market (Ong 1983: 431; Lim 1983, Gomez & Reddock 1987).

The predominantly female character of employment in EPZ enterprises thus appears to have had an impact on the organization of trades unions in Malaysia, which are fragmented, weak and have low membership. However, women workers in EPZs have resorted to 'oblique strategies of resistance' to express their anger and dissatisfaction at their conditions of work (Ong 1983: 434, 436). Ong documents newspaper reports of outbreaks of mass hysteria and views this as instances of 'ritualized rebellion'. Other strategies include the constant obtaining of permission to go to the toilet or, if they are Muslim, to worship. Malay women have also carried out 'covert protests by damaging the components that they had painstakingly assembled' (Ong 1983: 436).

> [T]he overwhelming predominance of female labour in these industries raises questions not only about the viability of the traditional conceptions of the development of an industrial proletariat and the appropriate forms of workers' struggle, but also wider issues of the implications for gender relations in society as a whole. (Froebel *et. al.* 1980: 134).

Lim poses the pertinent question as to whether the

> employment of women factory workers by multinational corporations in developing countries [is] primarily an experience of *liberation*, as development economists and governments maintain, or one of *exploitation*, as feminists assert, for the women concerned. (Lim 1983: 70; emphasis in the original).

She argues that the increase in opportunities for employment generated by TNCs in LDCs results in partial economic and social liberation for women - liberation from the confines and dictates of traditional patriarchal society. At the same time, however, she acknowledges that in such employment they are subject to both capitalist and patriarchal exploitation (Lim 1983: 83-4). It would appear that exploitation rather than liberation has been the predominant experience.

Ong points out that while there has been an increase in employment for Malay women owing to the limited and temporary nature of employment and the high turnover rate, these women are soon released from employment and become part of the reserve army of labour. Being unskilled, or semi-skilled at best, they can only find alternative employment as shop assistants, seamstresses, food vendors, petrol pump attendants and prostitutes - if they manage to find employment at all (Ong 1983: 433-5, Lim 1978).

Safa expresses the view that the temporary nature of employment, low wages and poor living conditions that women working for TNCs in EPZs have to endure does not support the argument that such employment results in economic and social liberation. The impact of such employment on the economic status of women workers in the family, and/or in the community generally is minimal.[19] However, the overall impact of increased employment opportunities for women is variable and complex:

> A job may give a woman a degree of economic autonomy and loosen the bonds of a patriarchal family, but it also exposes her to a new form of capitalist exploitation and state control (Safa 1981: 429)...EPZs may serve to integrate women into the development process by providing them with large numbers of new industrial jobs; it also enhances their possibilities for exploitation. In assessing the advantages and disadvantages of export processing as a development strategy in Third World countries it is important to assess its impact on women (Safa 1981: 432).

Thus the advantages brought by the creation of new jobs in the Third World must be viewed in the light of their contradictory effects on the people who fill them, and women in particular.

The International Labour Code

The ILO Constitution states that the primary objective of the labour standards formulated in the conventions and recommendations passed by the International Labour Conference is the promotion of social justice and peace.[20] In 1958 the Conference legislated against discrimination on the basis of race, colour, sex, religion, political opinion, national extraction or social origin in the Convention (No. 111) and Recommendation (No. 111) on *Discrimination (Employment and Occupation)*. The Convention has been ratified by more than 100 states but not by Malaysia.[21] A 1975 Plan of Action called for equality of opportunity and treatment for women workers, and Convention 156 of 1981 calls on states to 'make it an aim of national policy to enable persons with family responsibilities who are engaged or wish to engage in employment to exercise their right to do so without being subject to discrimination and, to the extent possible, without conflict between their employment and family responsibilities' (ILO 1987b: 247). Further conventions cover maternity protection (No. 3), night work (No. 4), the employment of women in unhealthy or dangerous occupations (No. 45) and equal remuneration (No. 100). By January 1, 1990 Malaysia had not ratified any of these conventions.

It was recognised at the formation of the ILO in 1919 that countries which abolished rest periods, used child or forced labour, or paid inadequate wages would enjoy substantial competitive advantages. The fear of unfair competition was so great that the first convention passed by the International Labour Conference was the *Hours of Work (Industry) Convention* (No. 1), designed to standardise the length of the working day. It is therefore arguable that the 'regulation of competition between capitalists remains a fundamental reason' for the existence of the code (Adelman 1990: 564; *cf.* Hansson 1983: 166). Indeed, the Preamble to the Constitution states that 'the failure of any nation to adopt humane conditions of labour is an obstacle in the way of other nations which desire to improve the conditions in their own countries'.

Concern about the comparative advantages derived from unfair labour practices is long-standing.[22] The problem facing LDCs is that while the cheapness of their labour power is considered by the industrialised countries to be an unfair advantage, the technological advantages enjoyed by the latter are not. The idea of a social clause was first put forward by Charles Frederick Hindley in 1833 and the idea was resuscitated in the early 1970s, when poor working conditions in many LDCs led to repeated suggestions for the insertion of a social clause into Article XIX of the GATT, which covers exceptions to the main provisions of the Treaty.[23] The European Community doubtless had unfair competition (and labour costs) in mind when it proposed the inclusion of a social clause in the second *Lomé Convention* of 1979 designed to grant trade preferences to LDCs party to the treaty which satisfied minimum labour standards. Ultimately, however, the EC and ACP countries agreed not to introduce a conflict between human rights and labour standards. In 1980 the Economic and Social Council proposed a 'social agreement' reflecting Third World opposition designed to make respect for labour standards part of EC policy towards the South, but this too made little headway (Wangel 1988: 292). Two decades later, it is, if anything, more relevant than ever in a world in which export-oriented industrialisation is increasing, accompanied by widespread legislation limiting or prohibiting workers' rights. Industrialised countries have long argued that the the poor quality of working conditions in LDCs, and EPZs in particular, enables the costs of production to be depressed below their market level and is tantamount to the kinds of export subsidy which may invoke import restrictions under Article XIV. As Charnovitz (1986: 73) points out however, it is difficult to distinguish between tax relief and the denial of trade union rights in deciding what constitutes a subsidy.

What constitutes an unfair labour practice has never been defined, but it is assumed that a social clause would embrace fundamental rights (the right to organize, non-discrimination, and forced labour); working conditions (health and safety, labour inspection); and the Conventions on *Equal Remuneration* and *Child Labour*. The social clause was discussed by the ILO between 1972 and 1974, but foundered on the opposition of Third World governments and employers. In theory, a social clause would enable parties to the GATT to restrict imports produced under working conditions which fail to meet the minimum standards in the international labour code. Countries which permitted the existence of such conditions would have to meet the minimum standards or risk increased trade barriers or embargoes. If it can be demonstrated under GATT rules that low wages and/or poor working conditions are the *decisive* cause of enhanced competitiveness, the goods thus produced may be subject to import restrictions.

The central question as far as LDCs are concerned is, therefore, whether the cheapness of their labour power constitutes a violation of the international labour code because wages are depressed below what Marx demonstrated to be their socially determined level. It is doubtful that this could be easily determined and it is for this reason amongst others that the idea of a social clause has been criticised by LDC governments fearful that it would operate as a hidden form of protectionism. Consistent with their developmentalist orientation, they have argued that North-South relations should remain purely economic. To this end, some of the more cynical regimes have argued, as we have seen, that the international labour code is inimical to their social, political and cultural values and, more legitimately, have questioned why so many industrialised countries have failed to ratify and enforce ILO conventions. In addition, they point to the poor working conditions which characterised early industrialisation in the West and under Stalinism in the former Soviet Union. It has been argued that obliging LDCs to adhere to the international labour code would discourage investment in development projects by increasing production costs and thereby adversely affect both international competitiveness and profits (Zeytinoglu 1986: 60). Calls for a social clause therefore bolster the developmentalist argument that placing priority on improving labour standards in LDCs would undermine economic growth at this stage of their development. In addition:

> the clause affects only industries, disregarding the fact that the worst examples of exploitation and suppression of workers are often found in other sectors. [E]ven in the hypothetical case that an effective clause might lead to increased wages in the export sector, a government would be inclined to impose higher taxes on these workers in order not to introduce imbalances in the economy. Generally speaking, it is difficult to imagine that a negative sanction against a proven occurrence of exploitation would produce an improvement of bad working conditions and low wage levels. What remains in the mode of operation of a social clause is a basically protectionist justification. (Wangel 1988: 292).

In the absence of comprehensive analysis, the implications of a social clause remain unclear. Not all labour standards will necessarily increase labour costs; indeed, some may have a positive effect through increases in productivity or savings in other cost areas. However, when the formulation of such a clause would appear to redound to the advantage of LDCs it often leads to Western claims that there is no economic justification for it, and that social and economic issues should be kept separate - an argument popular in both the World Bank and the IMF, who 'fear that the use of such criteria could be viewed as mitigating the cold calculus of economic viability' (Alston 1988: 18). This, however, 'ignores the reality that social and economic issues are inextricably intertwined and that policies in one sphere have a very direct effect on results in the other' (Alston 1981: 459).

Finally, a social clause has been objected to on the basis that it would constitute interference in the internal affairs of sovereign states. Not only would a clause affect trade policies in LDCs, it would also be tantamount to forcible ratification of ILO conventions by sovereign states which, if members of the ILO, have made a sovereign choice not to ratify. Moreover, the imposition of the international labour code could not reflect the different cultures, histories and stages of development of individual countries.

Wangel (1988) therefore argues that a social clause can only be justified as a unilateral measure of foreign policy towards countries flagrantly violating human rights and thereby also basic trade union rights. In such cases of 'social dumping', a trade embargo against the country in question could be a relevant instrument in weakening its government and pressurising it into changing its policies.

The broader issue to which the proposal for a social clause gives rise is the nature of the global political economy, in which LDCs suffer from a myriad structural imbalances so that the form of their insertion 'into the world capitalist economy dictates the need for ultra-exploitation of the workforce' (Adelman 1990: 567) if their competitive disadvantages are not to multiply. The problem, however, is that it is Third World workers (and women in particular) who suffer twice over, from the subordinate status of their countries within the global economy and from the depradations of developmentalism. Faced with the lack of protective national legislation workers are forced to turn to the ILO for support in resisting violations of union rights and bad working conditions: 'Although the ILO system of international labour standards only provides an additional measure in a strategy for international trade union solidarity, it becomes a decisive factor when faced with these challenges of export-oriented industrialization. The demand for the inclusion of a social clause in the GATT Treaty is a demand for a procedure of negative sanctions against the labour-related effects of this change in the international division of labour' (Wangel 1984: 411).

Conclusion

The only viable way in which a social clause could operate would be on the basis of a *quid pro quo* in which LDCs adhere to the international labour code in return for easier access to markets in industrialised countries. However, the Uruguay Round of the GATT suggests that the structural imbalances which characterise the global economy are likely to be perpetuated. Picciotto's chapter in this volume indicates the difficulties involved in securing the accountability of TNCs within an undemocratic international order. This lack of democracy is compounded by the inherent weaknesses of the ILO.

As far as EPZs are concerned, the only relevant convention which Malaysia has ratified is No. 98 on the *Right to Organize and*

Bargain Collectively. Despite this, it effectively denied the EIWU such rights in its struggle for recognition - a struggle in which the support offered by the ILO was marginal: 'The main reason of the EIWU for filing the complaint cases to the ILO was to publicly embarrass the Malaysian government' (Wangel 1988: 300).

The ILO has a comprehensive supervisory machinery which seeks to ensure the enforcement of the international labour code, but in the absence of a sanctioning mechanism it is arguable that negative publicity is the only weapon which the code provides for workers in struggle. The Organization's tripartite structure encourages consensus in the setting of standards, but the presence of employers and governments alongside workers limits both the scope and implementation of the standards. The tripartite structure also encourages a narrow technicist and legalistic approach to the realities of labour disputes and workers' struggles (Cohen 1987: 11).

> The authority and legitimacy of the ILO is closely related to the independent and objective functioning of procedures which imply that only a strictly legal point of view can be applied...[T]he continuous process of monitoring the labour market situation and industrial relations in the member countries and of presenting recommendations when complaints are brought before ILO committees makes this contradiction between universal standards and unequal development continuously evident. (Wangel 1988: 303).

A second objection raised to the code is that the standards contained in it are Eurocentric due to the influence of that continent in the ILO's history. Third, the contradictions of global legislation have prompted the International Labour Conference to permit the flexible implementation of standards subject to local conditions so that these protections have been extended to much of the Third World in rhetoric alone (Wangel 1988: 289). In fact, the ideal of universal labour legislation is contradicted by EOI as TNCs seek to exploit unequal development and reinforce the disadvantages of dependent capitalist states. The increasing 'flexibility' of labour in the changing global economy undermines the organizational base of traditional trade unionism and the power of workers to resist. For these reasons the international labour code appears to be an important but insufficient form of protection for women suffering 'superexploitation' in EPZs. The limitations of the law in this regard in domestic legislation are well documented (see Stewart *infra*); at the international level these limitations are more apparent.

In an increasingly interdependent world characterised in part by a developing consensus on the importance of human rights (recognised in the *Universal Declaration of Human Rights* and the two 1966 Covenants) it is inevitable and acceptable that Third World states be required to adhere both to these standards and to the rights contained in the international labour code. What is not acceptable is that the protection of human rights should take place at the expense of development in the South.

The international labour code therefore provides an important yardstick by which workers can measure the efficacy of domestic legislation in protecting their rights. There is, however, a great difference between rights provided in law and the actual enjoyment of those rights. Because the exploitation that occurs in EPZs is a reflection of social relations within particular LDCs, the search for the means of removing it must initially be located there as well. Just as the level of protective labour legislation is a reflection of the balance of class power within states, so the efficacy of the international labour code is contingent upon the state of such relations at the international level. While law is therefore an important weapon for workers, the solution to the conundrum of development and democracy appears to lie elsewhere.

Calls for a New International Economic Order are heard less frequently today than in the 1970s, but the need for it arguably remains as urgent as ever. Ultimately, the limitations of EPZs as a path to industrialisation may be the decisive factor in limiting their effect on workers' rights. According to an IMF study 'there are a number of qualifications and requirements associated with the EPZ concept that should actually limit its wider use substantially'.[24] Inevitably, the study sees no option to increased liberalisation of LDC economies, a process which has proved during the 1980s equally as damaging to Third World citizens.

Notes

1   A term used by Gomez & Reddock (1987), derived from Frank (1981). See also Froebel *et. al.*, 1980, Elson & Pearson 1981, Nash & Fernandez-Kelly 1983, Gomez & Reddock 1987.

2 UNIDO (1980: 6). The *Kenya Export Processing Zones Act*, No. 12 of 1990 defines an EPZ as 'a designated part of Kenya where any goods introduced are generally regarded, insofar as import duties and taxes are concerned, as being outside the customs territory but are duly restricted by controlled access and wherein the benefits provided under this Act apply'.

3 South Africa does not, at the time of writing, have any EPZs but is in the process of establishing approximately a dozen in the country's major ports.

4 A 1990 IMF Working Paper argued that 'Regarding the emergence of forward and backward linkages with the host economy, expectations should...be rather guarded. Forward linkages are unlikely to be created as long as EPZ companies are obliged to export their production completely. The potential for backward linkages is...limited' (Alter 1990: 26).

5 Despite the fact that capital accumulation has always been spatially, sectorally and temporally uneven and that there are obviously numerous continuities between the 'old' and the 'new' international divisions of labour and the fact that the volume of goods produced by *all* third world countries towards the end of the 1980s amounted to no more than 10 per cent of global output, CIDL theorists identified a global trend with significant implications for labour and development. Hong Kong exemplifies the success of the strategy: with virtually no natural resources and a population under 5 million, it has climbed to fifteenth place on the table of manufacturing producers (Cohen 1987: 20).

6 But see Froebel *et. al.* (1980: 245-7), where they dismiss the basic UNIDO document on "Industrial Free Zones as an Incentive to Promote Export-Oriented Industries".

7 More recently some writers have begun to lay greater emphasis on the flexibility of labour power in the South rather than its cheapness. (eg Standing 1989).

8 Given that this would amount to less than a fifth of what workers earn in industrialised countries (Sameer EPZ recommended $50 per month in 1992), the burden on TNCs is not particularly large.

9 In Malaysia, of 74 enterprises in EPZs, 64 per cent were foreign owned, 31 per cent were joint ventures, and only 5 per cent were domestically owned (ILO 1988: 26).

10 The others being textiles and garments; instruments and optical products; rubber products; metal products and machinery which, along with electronics, account for all but 5 per cent of Malaysian EPZ activity (ILO 1988: 38).

11 Malaysia has a population of 17.02 million, approximately 40 per cent of which are urbanised (*The Financial Times, op. cit.*). It comprises indigenous Malays (50%), and Chinese (40%) and Indian (10%) immigrants, who were imported as what is now Malaysia industrialised because Malays resisted wage labour when the colonial power sought to develop the rubber and tin industries. Thus, while Malays constitute the majority of the population, they are relatively marginal in terms of economic influence. Today, they are largely employed in the rural areas and public service, Chinese in industry and commerce, and Indians on the plantations. This racial divide. which has aroused strong resentment amongst Malays, dominates Malaysian life, including labour relations, and the moulding of Malaysian nationhood has been a central preoccupation of successive regimes (Schregle 1982: 28).

12 Ong (1983: 429). Fuentes and Ehrenreich (1983: 41) note that Malaysia became a low-wage haven for the electronics industry with assistance from the United States Agency for International Development (USAID).

13 Ong (1983: 429). These incentives are set out in the Free Trade Zones Act of 1971, for a discussion of which see Wangel (1988: 293).
The Malaysian Government also markets its labour resources to potential investors. In particular, female workers are marketed by laying emphasis on their productivity, skill, availability and the low wages which they are prepared to accept. Froebel *et. al.* (1980: 341) note that the marketing is done 'using the same modern advertising techniques employed in promoting or selling any other commodity'.

14 They apply for a five year period from the date on which a pioneer industry commences operation, but can be extended for an indefinite period by the Minister (see Wangel (1988: 294).

15 Froebel *et.al.* (1980: 364). See Wangel (1988) for a discussion of the struggles of the EIWU, which sought to organize workers whom the Government argued were not in a similar trade or occupation to that for which it was registered, and denied recognition. In 1988 the Malaysian Government surprisingly announced that the country's 85 000 electronics workers would be allowed to form and join trade unions, but stipulated that this largesse applied only to 'in house' unions and not to national or industry-based unions (Rosa 1991: 13).

16 In the early 1980s, the electronics industry accounted for 74.5 per cent of total world employment in EPZs, textiles for 14.2%, instruments and optical products 3.7%, rubber 2.7%, metal products and machinery 1.8%, the remaining 5.8% accounted for by other industries (ILO/UNCTC 1988: 38-39).

17 This compares to an average of 33 per cent in non-EPZ industries. The respective figures for South Korea were 75 and 37.5 per cent; 60 and 49.3 in Hong Kong; 74 and 48.1 in the Philippines; 88 and 17.1 in Sri Lanka; and 90 and 47.9 per cent in Indonesia. The average age of workers in Malaysian EPZs is 21.7 years, amongst the lowest in Asia (ILO 1988: 60-1).

18 Ong (1983: 429). Conversely, this means that EPZs do not appear to have had any significant effect in reducing the rate of male unemployment, a major goal of NEP; instead, they have introduced more young women into the industrial market (Safa 1981:427).

19 However, 'the withdrawal of young single women workers from the rural peasant settings has significant implications on processes within the household economy' (Safa 1981: 428-9). For a discussion of these implications see Chan *et. al.* (1983: 398).

20 Conventions create mandatory legal obligations for member states upon ratification, obliging them to incorporate the provisions of the convention into national legislation. Recommendations are intended to guide state policy in a particular field of labour law, and are often associated with particular conventions.

21 Compared to other regions of the world, south-east Asia has the lowest level of ratification of ILO standards.

22 '[W]e have had historical pictures of farseeing individuals, the large capitalist lobbying for safety regulations, patently not in his immediate interests, because he could see it as serving his long-term interests by wiping out smaller competitors who could not afford to comply' (McBarnet 1984: 237). Since 1983 the trade and investment policies of the United States have been linked to the implementation of minimum labour standards in the form of the *Carribean Basin Economic Recovery Act* (1983), the *General System of Preferences* (1984), the *Overseas Private Investment Corporation Act* (1985) and omnibus Trade and Competitiveness legislation (1988). Social clauses are also contained in the *International Tin and Cocoa Agreements* of 1975.

23 For a historical review of attempts to link labour standards and trade policy see Hansson 1983 and Charnovitz 1987.

24 Alter (1990: 26). Amongst the problems identified are the difficulties of preferential external market access, the potentially substantial costs of EPZs, stronger international competition, and problems relating to linkages with the rest of the economy.

10
The Dilemmas of Law in Women's Development

Ann Stewart

Introduction

The growing ascendancy of market economics during the last fifteen years has coincided, since 1989, with the collapse of the Eastern bloc. Liberal democracy, with its emphasis on law and constitutionalism, is taking centre stage. International agencies and Western governments now emphasise the importance of 'good', 'accountable' and 'democratic' government in their negotiations with states in the South. For those countries that have been subjected to structural adjustment programmes and conditionalities, good government and the rule of law are demanded as necessary adjuncts to the market. A British government official at a seminar I attended recently summarised the position succinctly: 'You cannot have a market economy without a law on insolvency and a debt collection system'.

These changes have inevitably affected the position of women and present a major challenge for feminism. Governments are becoming aware of the barriers to economic development caused by women's often limited legal capacity. Non-governmental organisations increasingly recognise the importance of gender differences. At the international level women's concerns have been recognised in anti-discrimination conventions and are being transformed into human rights. At a time when legal reformism is being pushed on to the agendas of many nation states by a variety of different constituencies, including women, Western feminism is intellectually distancing itself from political and social action; at a time when international organisations are promoting women's rights as human rights, Western feminism is becoming deeply sceptical of the value of legal rights; at a time when governments are being exhorted to adopt Western legal frameworks, Western feminism has begun to argue for non-engagement with law because the power it wields over women is considered to be too substantial.

This chapter explores some of the dilemmas raised by law in women's development. The first section considers whether there are any analytical tools available to enable constructive exploration of differences in contrast to the constraints imposed by theories that do not seem to 'fit' the variety of women's experiences. The second section examines specific examples of the relationship between law and women's development in East Africa and Iran in order to draw some general conclusions about the impact of law on women's lives.

The Limits of Western Feminism

Feminists have developed a variety of theories, most of which are predicated on gender rather than biology. A decade ago it was possible to point to three major strands of analysis in Western feminism. The liberal and Marxist/socialist strands had their roots in established world views, and feminists sought unsuccessfully to transform these theories into viable options for action for women (Beechey 1987, Jagger 1988, Pateman 1988, Barrett 1988). Radical feminism, broke free from the constraints of these theories and sought to fashion an understanding of women's position by analysing power relations between men and women and evolving the concept of patriarchy. More recentlty, there has been a tendency to re-order these categories; to distance them further from their origins and to address methodological questions.

Sandra Harding (1987) develops two main categories in examing the problem of how research can be validated if 'feminism is a political movement for social change'? She describes feminist empiricism, which has its roots in the methodological norms of scientific inquiry, but points to 'recent tendencies in the philosophy and social studies of science to problematise empiricist epistemological assumptions'. Alternatively feminist stand-point theorists argue that knowledge emerges 'for the oppressed only through the struggles they wage against their oppressors. It is through feminist struggles against male domination that women's experience can be made to yield up a truer (or less false) image of social reality than that available only from the perspective of the social experience of men of the ruling classes and races' (Harding 1987: 184, 185). Both feminist epistemologies stretch their 'paternal discourses' and seem to be 'locked into dialogue' with each other. 'The empiricists and stand-point theorists are both attempting to ground accounts of the social world which are less partial and distorted than the prevailing ones. In this sense, they are attempting to produce a feminist science - one that better reflects the world around us than the incomplete and distorting accounts provided by traditional social science' (Harding 1987: 187). In Harding's words they are therefore 'transitional epistemologies'.

Into this debate emerged a third force, namely feminist postmodernists sceptical of the enterprise. They reject universalist concepts and the metatheories that accompany them, and argue that "reality' can have 'a' structure only from the falsely universalising perspective of the master. That is, only to the extent that one person or group can dominate the whole, can 'reality' appear to be governed by one set of rules or be constituted by one privileged set of social relations' (Harding 1987: 188, citing Jane Flax).

> So at any moment in history there are many 'subjugated knowledges' that conflict with, and are never reflected in, the dominant stories a culture tells about social life. There can never be a feminist science, sociology, anthropology or epistemology, but only many stories that different women tell about the different knowledge they have. (Harding 1987: 188).

This new seam of understanding reflects the political context of Western feminism. Liberalism has yielded rights but little progress for women, who still operate in highly segregated labour markets and earn less than men. Pornography and violence against women proliferate. Socialist feminism has become engrossed in abstract categorisation in its attempt to change the world even as Western governments have been engaged, at least at an ideological level, in transforming the state so as to make this much more difficult.

Accounting for and coping with the differing experiences of women have proved politically painful. The category woman seems to fragment into women of colour, working class women, women with disabilities, lesbians and women with children, and to be characterised by an intense individualism. In the United States black women like Bell Hooks insist 'that what makes feminism possible is not that women share certain kinds of experiences, for women's experiences of patriarchal oppression differ by race, class, and culture...Thus there could not be 'a' feminist stand-point as the generator of true stories about social life. There could, presumably, only be feminist oppositions, and criticisms of false stories' (Harding 1987: 188). Analysis thus becomes as uncertain as politics.

These debates have generally focused on the concerns of Western women and have reflected the anxiety caused by the need to account for racism. Women in the South have therefore participated in these debates to a very limited degree. Liberal feminism has blended with modernisation theory to produce the *Women in Development* school which has largely been confined within traditional world views and tends to assume that 'underdevelopment in the Third World is caused by traditional values and social structures; that the basis for development lies in the diffusion of values, capital, technology and political institutions from the West' (Bandarage 1984: 497), and that the benefits of the Western development model have accrued only to men (Boserup 1970). The term development, however, has been drained of any coherent meaning (Adelman & Paliwala *infra*), so that for women the basic question is whose development?

There is now a large body of literature which documents the impact of development policies on women's lives, much of which makes gloomy reading. Time and again it reveals that the failure to recognise what women do and to value their contributions, particularly in agrarian subsistence economies, leads to a worsening of womens' relative social positions. Industrialisation has not proven to be an unmitigated blessing for women, who are generally incorporated into economic activity not as 'free productive workers' but at the margins, in the informal sector, and as housewives.

Marxist anthropologists have sought the origins of sexual inequality in class societies. In their accounts of the exploitative nature of women's incorporation into global capitalism they have revealed the diversity and complexity of women's integration into the processes of capitalist development (Bandarage 1984). History, however, has demonstrated that there is a large gap between Marxist theory and practice, and there is clearly no longer any justification for a model based, however loosely, on the old Eastern bloc despite the gains made by women in socialist states like Cuba. Wheareas Marxism has consistently underestimated the cultural and psychological dimensions of sexual stratification, radical feminism has offered an analytical framework for issues such as rape, wife battery, prostitution, genital mutilation, dowry murders and sex tourism, all of which demonstrate the global reach of patriarchy, if not an international male conspiracy. On the other hand, this strand of analysis lacks sensitivity to forms of oppression such as class, race and nationality.

Within the discourse of development studies the emphasis appears to be on refining familiar categories in order to account for changing social realities both in the West and the Third World. Bandarage has argued that *Women in Development* is an esoteric and peripheral sub-field within feminist discourse.[1] In the past decade the competing world theories have been challenged by new social movements, most notably those concerned with peace, the environment and women, but theoretical progress has been slow.

Chandra Mohanty (1988, 1991) opened the post-structuralist debate within Western feminism on the production of 'Third World Woman' as a singular monolithic category. She argues that Western feminist scholarship assumes a privileged ethnocentric universality when analysing women in the Third World, that much of this work produces the 'Third World difference' which fails to understand the complexities of women's lives, and is itself an exercise in power. Mohanty warns of a Western feminist colonialism that silences the millions of women who are eternal victims of violence, subjugated by religious ideologies or universal dependents. In response, Indian scholars influenced by post-structuralist theory are attempting to develop an understanding of the interaction between gender and colonialism, amongst other things (Sanyee 1989, Sangari & Vaid 1990).

Both Harding and Mohanty are concerned with the relationship between academic and political practice. Mohanty sees a necessary and integral connection between the two and points to an 'urgent political necessity of forming strategic coalitions across class, race, and national boundaries' (Mohanty 1988: 61). She uses a post-structural framework to show the potential that feminist discourse may have in constructing a particular image of women. Harding is concerned with the political consequences of postmodern philosophy, which appears to encourage political paralysis by failing to recognising the value of women's experience and celebrating a relativism antithetical to collective politics. She asks whether feminists should be

> willing to give up the political benefits which can accrue from believing that we are producing a new, less biased, more accurate, social science?... Should women - no matter what their race, class or culture - find it reasonable to give up their desire to know and understand the world from the stand-point of their experiences *for the first time*? As several feminist literary critics have suggested, perhaps only those who have had access to the benefits of the enlightenment can 'give up' those benefits. (Harding 1987: 188, 189; emphasis in the original).

To quote Barbara Ehrenerich (in Jagger 1988: 118) 'there is a difference between a society in which sexism is expressed as female infanticide and a society in which sexism takes the form of unequal representation on the central committee'.

Legal Dilemmas

Western feminists, particularly in North America, have placed considerable emphasis on law because of the central position it appears to occupy in women's lives through its impact on their capacity to act and its perceived potential for change. Naffine (1990) and Smart (1991a) have periodised and categorised the ever increasing corpus of feminist legal theory. Naffine suggests that feminist legal theory has advanced 'its understanding of its subject by a similar set of intellectual moves' to that which has occurred in other disciplines. She describes three phases. The first phase focuses on the perceived male monopoly of law, 'where the principal concern is with how the male personnel of the law have operated upon sexist principles to the detriment of women' [and have] endeavoured to preserve their own power and to keep women in their place' (Naffine 1990: 2). The second phase extends this argument to encompass 'what is seen as a deep-seated male orientation in law which infects all its practices'. Law embodies a male culture and the feminist task is therefore to devise an entirely new law for women (Naffine 1990: 2).

> Third phase feminists challenge the very concepts law invokes to defend itself as a just and fair institution. While law...professes to be

rational, dispassionate, value neutral, consistent and objective, it is in fact none of these things...the actual relation between law and the patriarchal social order is complex and variable... It is therefore too simple to characterise law as uniformly masculine in its orientation and its practices... [T]he problem of law for women therefore goes beyond the sexism of its representatives or any legal culture of masculinity... Rather the problem is that law presents itself in a way which is specifically designed to demonstrate its essential neutrality in relation to the sexes...while in fact the very mode of its self-presentation is deeply gendered... [T]he concepts invoked by law to demonstrate its essential justness - concepts such as 'impartiality', 'objectivity' and 'rationality', are gender biased in their very construction' (Naffine 1990: 2-3).

Mirroring developments within feminist thinking, Smart has developed an analysis which starts to dissolve some of the categories of legal analysis discussed so far. Informed by post-structuralist thinking and Foucault in particular, she argues 'we can begin to analyse law as a process of producing fixed gender identities rather than simply as the application of law to previously gendered subjects' so that the key question is how gender works in law and how law works to produce gender. She argues that 'Woman is a gendered subject position which legal discourse brings into being' (Smart 1991b: 9). In other words law constructs Woman even as it discriminates against her by dealing with her using male concepts such as impartiality. From this perspective, feminism itself constructs Woman and the woman of legal discourse is different from the woman of feminism. Emphasis is therefore placed on investigating the discourse itself as a form of social practice. No overarching theory is necessary because the point of departure is not women and their experiences. Rather, the aim is to chart the construction of the woman of legal discourse historically by focusing on particular instances such as rape trials or deaths from abortions.

While women's issues have increasingly figured on the agenda of both academic and social development programmes, they have rarely surfaced in analyses of the law. Indeed feminist contributions have until recently been conspicuous by their absence at a time when attention is being focused on a variety of national and international legal regimes. Women are beginning to look at the ways in which law affects their lives and are taking action on this basis. Policy makers are beginning to see the legal barriers to women's activity in particular and to economic development in general. The challenge is therefore to develop an analytical framework that offers a broader horizon than that thus far provided by the concerns of Western women about law.

Women, Law and Development

These developments aroused a range of activities. Within the first phase of Naffine's periodisation, that covering demands for women's rights on the basis of liberal legality, was activity stimulated by international conventions. The United Nations has adopted a variety of human rights instruments over the years, the most important of which is the 1979 *Convention on the Elimination of All Forms of Discrimination Against Women* (CEDAW), which came into force in 1981. The Convention sets out the right to equality in all aspects of women's lives, and places special emphasis on the position of rural women in Articles 14 and 15. It obliges parties to report to the UN Committee on the Elimination of Discrimination against Women on legislative and other steps taken to implement its provisions (Pietila & Vickers 1990).

In 1985, women involved in legal struggles throughout the world held a five day Third World Forum on Women, Law and Development in Nairobi.[2] This spawned the US-based *Women, Law and Development* (WILDAF) organisation that published numerous contributions to the forum (see Schuler 1986) and created a regional structure to act as an information exchange and training base.[3] The organisation's perspective is that law functions as an instrument of control by promoting or inhibiting access to certain resources while supporting attitudes and behaviours that maintain oppressive social structures and relations. Law is seen as regulating access to economic and social resources such as land, jobs and credit and to political power. Schuler (1986) constructs the traditional liberal dichotomy in arguing that laws touching the public arena have been modernised and brought into line with more enlightened thinking but that family and personal laws have been left untouched by the state.

With their focus on international activity such perspectives inevitably describe an unproblematic view of law in general and rights in particular. Law is viewed as a tool which, in the right hands, can be used to improve women's position both symbolically (as an educational tool) and instrumentally (to bring about reforms). Adherents to this perspective share with many of their

The Dilemmas of Law in Women's Development

more analytically radical North American jurisprudential colleagues a focus which seldom questions the construction of the law itself. There is little consideration, for instance, of the impact of plural legal systems on analyses which assume a public/private dichotomy. The implicit assumption that family and personal laws are in need of reform is also problematic, not least because of the uncritical acceptance of the need for modernisation. Because the state is regarded as a source of enlightenment the nature of the nation state and the role it plays in post-colonial societies is largely ignored. Transposing Western concepts of divorce and maintenance into wholly different contexts such as those in Africa is highly problematic as evidenced by the research undertaken by the Women and Law in Southern Africa project (see Paliwala *infra*). The limitations of the highly individualised liberal rights framework are becoming increasingly apparent in the West in situations in which the content of individual rights seem to evaporate or are challenged by more powerful individuals using the same framework. This is illustrated by 'women's right to choose' in the area of reproduction where a variety of challenges are being made on behalf of the foetus and the father, some of which receive considerable support from the state, particularly in circumstances where the mother can be held responsible for the situation. A particularly acute conflict may arise when the foetus is endangered by a woman's lifestyle: for example, if she takes drugs or smokes during pregnancy. This framework is even more inadequate in dealing with issues like female infanticide (facilitated by amniocentesis) in India, or the difficulties caused in a kinship-based society such as Zimbabwe by the individual rights framework contained in the *Legal Age of Majority Act*.

In contrast, a creative partnership between feminist legal thinking and African women scholars and activists has developed in southern and eastern Africa involving highly innovative collaboration at both analytical and practical levels. Tove Stang Dahl (1987), working in the Institute of Women's Law at the University of Oslo, has developed a distinctive jurisprudential approach called *Women's Law*. She takes women's experiences as her point of departure in a method that involves establishing 'the needs and wants of women in general and their opinions about what is fair and just' (Smart 1991a: 147). Values are thus important and do not merely emanate from experience. Dahl considers justice, integrity and self-determination to be central to the enterprise. Her approach deploys the methods of social science to determine the basis for women's law. Her concern is with the 'grassroots', with the application of laws that affect women directly rather than with the jurisprudence of appellate courts. She is therefore relatively unconcerned with legal method. As Smart (1991a: 148) points out, because Dahl does not develop a theory of power or the state she can be described as a 'feminist Fabian' concerned primarily with 'the idea of promoting science as a value free and superior form of knowledge whose results can be applied to improve society and eradicate social problems' (1991a: 149).[4]

The strength of the *Women's Law* approach lies in means that it provides for women to make sense of the world through a legitimate concentration on gender issues and the creation of growing body of literature in an area where none previously existed. To reiterate Harding's argument (1987: 188), it is difficult to abandon a women's standpoint where none has existed. Dahl's use of social science methodology to persuade and educate is attractive within the African context because its appeal to science and rationality fits easily into the dominant modernisation paradigm and thereby provides legitimacy for women's research and campaigns. On the other hand, the application of the theory and method of *Women's Law* to the concerns of women in southern Africa also highlights its weaknesses. As in Dahl's own work, women's interests are generally treated in an unproblematic fashion. The presumption is that there is a set of values that women aspire to and that determining what women want will provide these in practice. But which women and what values? The urban women who are employed as professionals, are relatively independent of kinship structure and have resort to updated and universalised colonial laws; rural subsistence farmers who rely on customary or traditional law and, to a large extent, rely on kinship structures; women who work as prostitutes servicing migrant workers; or the wives of white settler land owners? The emphasis in *Women's Law* on (an undifferentiated) women's experience, on an homogenous women's standpoint and the neglect of both state and power may be appropriate in the context of the relatively benign Norwegian welfare state but in post-colonial Africa this approach is problematic.

Analyses of the state are common in Marxist and neo-Marxist approaches to law in development, but gender issues have received rather less attention. This gap has begun to be filled in the African context by contributors to the volume on *Women and the*

The Dilemmas of Law in Women's Development

State in Africa (Parpart & Staudt 1989). The aim of the book is to investigate the relationship between women and African states through analyses of the formation and operation of classes and particular states under colonialism and post-colonialism. The authors repeatedly point to the need for specificity rather than abstract categorisation. Fatton (1989), for example, argues that the state in Africa is not hegemonic in Gramscian terms because it ultimately rules by coercion rather than consent. Individual nation states are often arbitrary, corrupt and heavy-handed so that women, as several contributors demonstrate, have chosen or been forced to engage in economic activity outside the embrace of the state and to avoid political action or protest directed at the state. Illegal trading, co-operatives and informal groups are the basis of women's resistance, methods that reflect attempts by women to find a limited freedom or at least a means of existing outside the power of the state and its laws. This is a long way from the treatment of the state in Dahl's analysis, where it is regarded as a neutral institution open to persuasion and change.

Although several contributors deal in some detail with women's relationship with the law, their focus is primarily on the way that the state orchestrates divisions based on class and gender. Law is again viewed instrumentally, as an important means by which these divisions are promoted. Law does more than this however. It structures and constructs gendered existences that differentiate women's experiences into good mothers, bad women, married women, illegitimate daughters and widows. By failing to address the ideological power of law it is possible that the methodology of *Women's Law* unintentionally serves to legitimate this process. This is not necessarily to argue for less law but rather to displace the centrality that law occupies in this approach. In order to examine the position of women at the grassroots, where the law operates indirectly and where, to use Fatton's term, they have exited the state, it is necessary to comprehend the role, form and content of the law in a wider social, political and economic context.[5]

Guha's (1987) Foucaultian analysis of the web of power relations operating in the death of a woman from an abortion administered by her female relatives in nineteenth century India demonstrates the possibilities of studies that go beyond the law. Whereas her relatives considered the abortion an act of solidarity designed to prevent the woman being made an outcast because of the illicit intercourse, colonial law constructed it as a criminal activity, as an act of homicide. Moreover, the actions of her impregnator, who insisted on the abortion, went unpunished under both the colonial and community legal regimes. At a simple level, such accounts merely represent the way in which state law and community law discriminated against women, but Guha's analysis is more profound than this. It unravels the ways in which this event was interpreted: whose account is recorded, whose is not, the nature of the reporting process and the different stories told about the event. It reveals the construction and workings of discourses, and contemporary legal discourse in particular. The problem that several writers have identified that it is difficult to discern the connection between this type of approach and the practices of political and social movements, not least because it offers no prescriptions for action. Thousands of abortions continue to take place in Indian clinics after amniocentesis indicates the presence of a female foetus which the deconstruction of power relations does little or nothing to halt. The concentration by some feminists on violence against Indian women in the form of dowry deaths or femicide within the context of a worldwide male power structure leads to a view of all Indian women as hapless victims and ignores other forms of oppression such as caste, religion and economic status (Mies 1986).

Despite such studies, gender has not figured significantly in studies of law in development, in large part because most feminist theory has evolved at the hands of Western women, whose concerns it overwhelmingly reflects. Feminist legal theory has generally revealed a similar bias. There is thus an urgent need to develop analytical tools appropriate to an understanding of the interaction of women and the law in developing countries. To this end, I now turn to a consideration of the 'law as a process of producing fixed gender identities rather than simply as the application of law to previously gendered subjects' (Smart 1991: 9). In particular, I analyse the meaning of marriage, the construction of prostitution and the development of the concepts of housewife and worker in two specific social and political contexts. The first example is drawn from British colonial Africa and is based on a substantial body of work that examines the impact of colonialism on 'traditional' practices. My second example is drawn from post-revolutionary Iran and is based on a small body of literature which focuses specifically on the legal position of women in Islamic societies. Both cases illustrate the way in which categories have been constructed within and by the law and how the boundaries between the public and the private, and the married and the unmarried evolve in different contexts: what it means to be a 'housewife' or a 'prostitute' in Africa or Iran. My aim is to offer insights for women on the power of law in a global context in which the dogma of constitutional and legal reform predominates.

British Colonial Africa

Marriage is a form of social regulation of women's capacity to produce and reproduce (Hirschon 1984: 10). However, marriage is a term that contains many meanings. It can reduce or extinguish a woman's capacity to act independently and can render her labour valueless. The concept of marriage distinguishes prostitution and structures divorce, and the history of British colonial Africa between the 1920s and 1950s reveals a range of interpretations advanced by different interested groups. Women in particular were trying to create their own understanding of marriage and to do so, in the main, by avoiding the legal construction of marriage produced by customary and colonial regulation. Eventually, the power of law prevailed but for a while a range of meanings was available, those of the colonial administration, the elders of kinship groups, capitalists and women.

State intervention in east, central and southern Africa under British colonialism provides an illuminating example of the process of creating married women and regulating their relationship to the labour market. Lovett (1989) argues that women's experiences of the colonial state differed very substantially from those of men: 'This difference ultimately was rooted in the gendered nature of class formation in that under a colonial capitalist system largely predicated on male migrant labour with subsistence wages, production increasingly came to be gendered male, while reproduction conversely became gendered female' (Lovett 1989: 23). Crudely, women were to remain in rural areas as subsistence farmers while men were to work for settlers on plantations or down the mines. The wages of these migrant male workers were subsidised by women's labour in agriculture. Women were also to be responsible for the welfare of the young and old, and the reproduction of labour power in particular.

In the pre-colonial era, both women and men engaged in productive activities, with women taking primary responsibility for agricultural production. Access to and control over basic resources was differentiated. For men access and control were based on patrilineage. Women possessed no independent right to land; their 'access was mediated through men - either their fathers, adult sons, or most notably, their husbands' (Lovett 1989: 25). Colonialism transformed these patterns of authority, 'catalysed by expanding cash-crop production, and with the active cooperation of the colonial state, men's supervisory rights over land increasingly were transformed into ownership rights... Under the same conditions, however, women's usufructuary and trusteeship (for their sons) rights in land became increasingly threatened and vulnerable' (Lovett 1989: 25). Women had few, if any rights, but their labour was vital to the colonial system.

In the early days the colonial administration created courts to resolve disputes. These, however, recognised and sought to enforce individual rights rather than those of the corporate kin group. Women were given access to courts, leading to divorce rates high enough to cause unease amongst state officials. The introduction of the cash economy affected marriage arrangements and threatened the control of male elders over women and young men (Lovett 1989: 30), although it was the former who became the focus for attention as elders sought the support of the state to keep 'uncontrollable' women in their rural homes. This response reinforced gender differences. 'Whereas men were directly controlled within the wider 'public' sphere as actual or potential wage labourers or peasant producers, the state sought to regulate women indirectly through the language and authority of kinship' (Lovett 1989: 28). A rather unsubtle way of keeping women in their place was through restrictions on their movement: 'Chiefs and headmen giving evidence to Northern Rhodesian district officers seeking to establish the jurisdiction of the new Native Courts...invoked 'tradition' to justify their claims that under customary law they possessed 'total powers of control over people's movement" (Lovett 1989: 29). On the basis of this evidence, chiefs were permitted to issue legislation restricting women's freedom of passage out of the rural areas - although women easily overcame these restrictions.

Preventing the reconstruction of marriage, however, proved more difficult. A new 'customary' law of marriage emerged after the state gathered evidence from male elders on the problem. Bridewealth was to be proof of the existence of a legally recognised 'traditional' marriage.[6] Native Courts were created and given jurisdiction over marital cases. Urban Native Courts on the Copperbelt were established between 1936 and 1938 to stabilise urban marriages by bringing them within the ambit of 'tradition'. In the 1940s all such marriages had to be contracted and registered in the rural areas. In 1947 the *Northern Rhodesia Draft Marriage Ordinance* made registration compulsory and by the 1950s only registered marriages were considered legal (Lovett 1989: 30). The objective was to construct a view of women as daughters and wives within a kinship system bolstered by colonial legal authority.

Women, however, were avoiding the power of chiefs, headmen and the colonial authorities by creating their own interpretation of marriage. In the 1920s and 1930s they moved in increasing numbers to the newly developed mine compounds and urban townships of the Copperbelt where they lived with men without payment of bridewealth or sanctions from kinship groups. As these 'marriages' were outside the control of urban courts women could leave when they proved unsatisfactory and enter new arrangements as they wished. Mine owners were not adversely affected; indeed, because the presence of 'wives' encouraged greater efficiency and productivity amongst mineworkers, the owners recognised relationships of a week's standing as legitimate unions. They distinguished between married and unmarried women in denying rights to single women, thereby 'persuading' the latter to enter termporary marriage arrangements.[7] The mine owners' definition of marriage therefore varied considerably from that of chiefs.

Alternatively women could run away, not in order to marry, but to the towns where they could let rooms, brew beer and provide sexual services to the migrant population. Here again in the 1930s women were beyond existing controls. These women provided a wide range of reproductive labour - cooking, washing clothes, offering baths and a bed. They were thus able to develop entrepreneurial skills outside marriage that enabled them to accumulate property. The relative freedom that these women acquired led to a reaction in the form of attacks on their rights as property owners and single women. Women property owners resisted state attempts to undermine their ability to own private property by transforming them into location tenants. However, in the dichotomy constructed by the state between the urban and the rural, women were firmly placed in the rural areas and since residence in urban areas for all Africans was construed as temporary women seeking permanent urban residence were doubly burdened.

One consequence of women's attempts to become economically independent was pressure to change the meaning of prostitution, which was to be tolerated only if it served to reproduce male labour on a daily basis but not as a means of accumulating wealth. Prostitution came to carry a number of meanings, but essentially involved women living relatively independently in towns as occupiers of urban housing with the potential to accumulate property. These were privileges denied to men and to married women. This construction of prostitution as the province of the unmarried independent woman has had profound and enduring effects, including stigmatising all single women living in towns (Jacobs & Howard 1987).

The growth of unplanned urban settlement and economic activity has presented various African governments with major difficulties. In this climate of informal, and sometimes illegal, change women have often found the space to challenge traditional roles and to earn and control (usually paltry) incomes for themselves. In turn they have also been faced with some of the most vociferous and violent attacks from state machineries delivered to any sector of the population (Jacobs & Howard 1987: 38).

This has taken the form of clean up campaigns in a number of countries. During the 1983 round up in Zimbabwe, women were accused of prostitution although the area targeted in Harare was occupied by young professional people. Women were arrested because they were young, single, and showed evidence of earning their own living (Jacobs & Howard 1987: 42).

Beer brewing provided another relatively lucrative economic outlet for women. In the 1920s and 1930s the colonial state created a monopoly over the preparation and provision of liquor and declared illegal the brewing, sale or possession of beer. Lovett (1989: 35) suggests that the ban on individual beer brewing predominantly affected women who were at least nominally married but a majority of the women used this activity to increase their own economic autonomy. With women becoming more firmly situated within increasingly stabilised urban marriages it is likely that beer brewing was primarily a means of supplementing their husbands' wages.

Parpart (1989) argues that independent women were easy targets in the courts and were regularly fined or repatriated. Women who lived with men under informal arrangements were victimised by urban courts, which refused to recognise unregistered relationships. These women were therefore placed beyond legal control. In the 1940s and 1950s pressures for properly registered marriages increased and more urban couples acquired legitimate marriage certificates. Freedom to change partners became more difficult. Parpart argues that women maintained a degree of flexibility in constructing grounds for divorce by presenting themselves as good and faithful wives victimised by neglectful husbands. They were nonetheless obliged to cede to the power of law by constructing arguments framed within the parameters of the 'private' sphere of marriage as good wives rather than as owners of rooms or as economic entrepreneurs.

These different constructions of marriage and prostitution provide an instructive example of the power of law. Being a married woman has ultimately meant limited independent access to the labour market, economic dependency on a man and confinement to the rural areas.

Post-Revolutionary Iran

State support for an outwardly consensual and temporary form of marriage that allows women and men access to sexual intercourse but does not presume a joint household and is not regarded as prostitution has developed in post-revolutionary Iran, in a context very different to that of colonial Africa. *Mut'a* (temporary marriage) in Iran is an extremely flexible arrangement in an otherwise inflexible Islamic theocracy that has had profound effects on the position of women.

As in other parts of the world, the early part of the twentieth century was a period marked by the efforts of Iranian women to obtain freedom. Afshar documents the emancipation struggles through which women obtained access to education in 1910 and the abolition of the veil in 1936. She views the departure of the Qajar and the coup by Reza Shah in 1922 as crucial because 'the country moved to a new phase of modernisation, which included a demand for the paid labour of women in the newly installed textile industries and provided a place for educators to staff the rising number of state financed girls' schools and training institutions' (Afshar 1987: 24). Afshar maintains that royal patronage led to the enfranchisement of women in 1963 and the reforms contained in the *Family Protection Laws* of 1967 and 1975 that curtailed polygamy, limited automatic paternal rights to custody of children and provided for payment of maintenance on divorce (by imposing conditions in the marriage contract). Abortion was legalised in 1978. Afshar acknowledges that these often amounted to paper rights not backed by political action. Despite the fact that the 1979 Islamic Revolution swept away even these nominal rights, women strongly supported the revolution and many still do. The most vociferous opposition to the theocracy has come from the intelligentsia and middle class women.

Haeri (1989: 65) argues that 'the concept of contract...is not simply a dominant feature of interpersonal obligations and commercial transactions in a Muslim society, it is also a model for the interpersonal male-female relationships in Iranian culture and thus is the backbone of marriage institutions' (see also Mallat & Connors 1990). She describes the two marriage forms available in Shi'i Islam: permanent (*nikah*) and temporary (*Mut'a*, known colloquially as *Sigheh*) marriage. Haeri (1990) argues that Islamic family law is based on three determinisms: legal, biological and divine. Legally, marriage takes the form of a contract in which husband and wife are the principal transacting parties. The wife must consent if the contract is to be valid and under law the woman receives the full amount of *mahar* (payment of which in permanent marriage is usually deferred until divorce).

> Ironically, however, the very same structure that gives her the right to exercise her decision-making power deprives her of it as soon as she uses it. Prior to signing the contract of marriage an adult Shi'i Muslim woman is accorded relative legal autonomy, but after the conclusion of the contract she is legally associated with the object of exchange, and hence she comes under the jural authority of her husband... This association of women with the object of exchange is at the heart of the Islamic doctrinal double image of women (naive-cunning, sexually insatiable-innocent) as well as at the root of the ideological ambivalence towards them... For in a permanent marriage women sell their sexual and procreative capacity/organs and themselves as the inevitable vessel. Intercourse is intertwined with monetary exchanges. As purchasers in a contract of marriage, men are 'in charge' of their wives because they pay for them, and women are required to submit that for which they have been paid (Haeri 1990: 57, 58).

Under biological determinism male sexuality is regarded in Islam as unrestrained and desire must be satisfied on demand. It is accommodated by polygamy and unilateral divorce. A Shi'i Muslim man is permitted to marry up to four permanent wives but he can legitimately contract an unlimited number of tempo-

The Dilemmas of Law in Women's Development 237

rary marriages simultaneously or serially. Temporary marriage (*Mut'a* or *Sigheh*) is similar to a contract under which a woman's sexual organs are leased in exchange for a reward which is paid immediately on the formation of the contract. The parties agree to marry under a verbal contract for as short or long a period as they desire. No divorce is necessary; children are legally protected but socially stigmatised (Haeri 1990: 60). Women may only *Sigheh* serially and must observe a period of sexual abstinence of two menstrual months on termination. Both forms of marriage require women to be obedient, which is not merely a culturally accepted behaviour for women but is 'rather a binding legal obligation' (Haeri 1990: 61). If a woman does not obey she has no right to clothing, housing or sleeping facilities.

The third determinism, the divine, reinforces the obligation to obedience in that the *Qur'an* gives the husband a unilateral right to divorce his wife or wives. The logic of the contract gives him the right to return the 'goods' (women's sexual organs) when he no longer wishes to keep them. The marriage contract is thus simultaneously revocable and irrevocable since the wife has no such right to unilateral determination.

> Shi'i Islam views women's sexual and reproductive organs as an object, a commodity...separated from the woman's persona. Women's sexuality however is perceived by the dominant male ideology to represent her whole being... Women are thus...perceived not only as symbols of sexuality but as the very embodiment of sex itself...[who must be jealously controlled] objects of desire to amass, to discard, to seclude, and to veil, objects of indispensable value to men's sense of power and virility...[S]exuality...is simultaneously perceived as precious and treacherous to its original master (Haeri 1989: 70).

The law relegates women to the realm of 'nature' and considers them to lack self control even as it acknowledges 'the urgency, vulnerability, and unpredictability of male sexuality by legitimatizing sexual gratification through various institutions such as permanent marriage, temporary marriage, and slave ownership' (Haeri 1989: 70). Female sexuality is not constructed *per se* but is derived from its significance to men: 'It is because of this inextricable interconnectedness that the Shi'i ideology imputes a strong sense of power to female sexuality, not as something powerful in and of itself, but powerful in the sense of what it signifies to men and in the reaction it presumably provokes in them' (Haeri 1989: 71).

Temporary marriage is defined as marriage but involves sex in exchange for payment. It is sanctioned by Islam on the basis that it serves men's sexual appetites in a manner which avoids prostitution and is viewed as the unacceptable free association of the West. Women's motives are deemed to be economic in that they hire out their sexuality. Legally a Shi'i Muslim woman can be a commodity either owned (permanent marriage *Nikah*) or leased (temporary marriage *Sigheh*). She is also able at certain stages of her life to negotiate contracts, control their outcome and exchange gifts. Sometimes she is a decision-making adult, sometimes a minor (Haeri 1989: 199). A *Sigheh* woman thus attracts cultural and legal ambivalence. She will have been married and divorced, and have more experience than other women. As a divorcee her legal status is the 'closest that a Shi'i Muslim woman can come to having legal autonomy. But autonomy is not a trait socially approved of for women in Iran' (Haeri 1989: 200). Because the objective of temporary marriage is sexual enjoyment it has a 'close structural association with prostitution' (Haeri 1989: 200). Women who engage in *Mut'a* are perceived in a morally ambivalent manner. Haeri found that men are clear that it is religiously sanctioned to facilitate their sexual satisfaction. Women's understandings, however, reflect its inherent ambiguities. Some adhere to the dominant view that such marriages are religiously motivated and support it on this basis. Others emphasise the religious foundation but have 'recognised the underlying assumption of sex-as-an-object in the marriage law and manipulated it for their own benefit' (Haeri 1989: 205). Yet others 'view themselves as individuals interested in establishing meaningful and mutual interpersonal relationships, which they had apparently not enjoyed in their failed marriages' but were disappointed by the cultural ambivalence displayed towards them and therefore felt insecure (Haeri 1989: 206).

Haeri's research indicates that polygamy is regarded as a way of dealing with perceived male desires in a culturally acceptable way that allows the possibility of legitimating offspring. The purpose of *Mut'a* is, however, sexual gratification rather than procreation. Because it involves sex for money it appears to Western eyes to be a form of 'prostitution'. It places women in an ambiguous position yet it is not morally proscribed. For women it offers the possibility of subsistence (depending on the terms of the contract) but limits their potential earnings by requiring them to *Sigheh* only one man at a time and to undertake a period of two months abstinence between marriages (*Idda*). Clearly this obliges women to be economically dependent on a single man, precludes meaningful control over their earnings and pressurises them into accumulating through prostitution. Significantly, *Mut'a* is constructed in the private sphere; in public, prostitutes face the possibility of stoning.

As has historically been the case in the West, women are generally firmly positioned within the private sphere and opportunities for paid employment outside the home are limited. Women need men for economic support and marriage is the means to achieve it. Marriage is central to Iranian society and is important to both sexes: 'It is the most significant rite of passage in Iran, and not only does it confer status and prestige on men and women, it also establishes the only legitimate channel for association between the sexes, erotic or non erotic' (Haeri 1989: 208). Within this inflexible framework temporary marriages permit a degree of flexibility in interactions between women and men. Marriage may be a core institution in Iranian life but it carries with it a multitude of meanings that generate ambiguities and different realities for women and men. This is partly a consequence of segregation and partly the result of the legal, economic and social context in which marriage occurs. The law, which exists in a symbiotic relationship with religion, thus exercises a powerful influence in the construction and reinforcement of gendered realities.

Conclusion

In this concluding section I summarise some of the themes that have emerged from my discussion of the ways in which law constructs gendered beings. In Britain the development of the nuclear family with the man as head of household and breadwinner and the woman primarily performing the role of economically dependent homemaker took place within the framework of marriage laws. The married woman emerged as a legally incapacitated being, constructed by law predominantly in the private sphere. It was, paradoxically, only when women began to enter the workforce in substantial number in the twentieth century that women's services as wives and mothers began to be valued in the law (see Brophy & Smart 1981). All women who enter the labour market are perceived by employers as actually or potentially married. In a labour market highly segregated and segmented on gender lines, married women overwhelmingly occupy part-time positions in the service sector. Although a majority of women are engaged in formal employment, they are regarded primarily as housewives and mothers rather than 'free' workers. Bennholdt-Thomsen (1990: 159) argues that 'housework as performed by housewives does not represent a set of tasks which women have always carried out because of some natural predisposition, but is the product of a particular history. Nor did the housewife emerge, as it were, spontaneously, in response to the dictates of an economic system. She was created - by the church, through legislation, medicine and the organisation of the workforce (protective legislation, the 'family wage')'. The 'private' and unregulated sphere is however being reconstructed through a range of legal measures including the recognition of marital rape. At the same time the regulated 'public' sphere is being further fragmented into more casualised, temporary and part-time occupations.

Just as the battle over the construction of marriage in British Colonial Africa led to women's legal capacity and economic activity being tied more to their husbands than their kin, so too is marriage an important element affecting the position and perceived value of women in the British labour market. In contemporary Iran the institution of marriage plays an even more dominant role in placing women in the private sphere than in Britain or post-colonial British Africa. Far fewer women work outside the home and gendered sexuality is heavily reinforced through the different forms of marriage. The boundaries of public immorality and private marriage are strictly drawn and temporary marriage, although akin to a form of prostitution in Western eyes, is legitimated and construed as marriage - with all the economic limitations this brings. A *Sigheh* woman receives payment from her husband for sexual services but is not normally expected to be a 'housewife' and carry out domestic responsibilities (although this does occur in longer contracts). Marriage is not so all-encompassing a concept in Britain, where cohabitation outside marriage is common despite ideological assaults against it by the state. Prostitution is hedged around with criminal sanctions but is not illegal and provides a means of economic support for a minority of women.

Whatever the form of marriage, it is apparent that women's access to the formal labour market is limited throughout the world and that their activities in the informal sector tend to be viewed as extensions of their 'domestic activities'. In Iran, where sexuality is accommodated through serial polygamy which legitimates offspring but leads to culturally ambivalent perceptions of women. In Africa, polygamy ties women and their offspring to kinship structures in rural Africa while in urban areas prostitution is the form through which sexual and other reproductive services are provided. In the former instance women are controlled through their confinement in the domestic sphere whereas in the latter case prostitution leads to the construction of women 'outside' society and therefore as dangerous, and as the mothers of illegitimate children. Particularly in the South, the informal sector is often perceived as dangerous and illegal, especially if women operate independently. Women's work becomes valued as domestic labour even if it involves tasks which if organised in the 'public' domain would be regarded as skilled and highly remunerated.[8] The construction of the 'modern urban marriage' may bring individual rights but it also creates a particular type of woman.

In each of these situations it is necessary to analyse the way in which the law creates gendered boundaries and categories and the impact that this has on the position of women. Understanding the ways in which conceptions of marriage control women and their access to work is the first step in dissolving boundaries between law and other aspects of society and facilitating creative thinking about the power that law exercises in women's lives. By combining some of the insights of postmodernism with an understanding of the social and economic structures of particular societies it becomes possible to transcend instrumentalist conceptions of law and avoid the assumption that there are universal truths about either law or women. In confronting the law's power to construct gendered categories we need to be concerned as much with law's symbolic functions as its content.

Notes

1 Bandarage (1984: 507). Staudt (1986), in a response to Bandarage, argues for a concentration on the bureaucratic workings of the state, its gendered application and for greater analysis of different state forms.

2 The Forum was one of the activities held by non-governmental organisations alongside the *World Conference to Review and Appraise the Achievements of the UN Decade for Women* which adopted forward-looking strategies for the advancement of women into the twenty-first century.

3   WILDAF's headquarters are in Harare, from where it undertakes these activities to the extent that its limited resources permit.

4   The ideas and methods of *Women's Law* have been used as a basis for a diploma course for women from Southern and Eastern Africa which has run annually since 1986 with funds provided by Norwegian Overseas Aid. The course was first held in Oslo but is now provided at the University of Zimbabwe. Many, although not all, of the women who have taken the diploma are now engaged on a regional project entitled *Women and Law in Southern Africa* (WLSA), its purpose being to investigate and, if necessary, reform laws relating to women. The first two-year research topic covered maintenance laws and their application within the region (see Paliwala *infra*), the second will look at inheritance. Two books have appeared which document women's position within the law and provide invaluable source material (Armstrong & Ncube 1987, Armstrong & Stewart 1990). The research project has also produced a working paper on research methodology (WLSA 1990) which includes a wide range of approaches all of which are, however, firmly within the boundaries of 'traditional' social science methodology.

5   I listened to a debate between feminist activists in which a woman from Botswana argued that the 'modern' law had created illegitimate children. Many agreed but argued that the answer was to seek alternative legal terminology such as out of wedlock. Such a response implicitly legitimates the power of law to construct social (and in particular gendered) categories that perpetuate rather the resolve the problem.

6   According to Chanock, 'Custom regarding a basic institution, already irrevocably altered in its working was to be 'established' by a series of hypothetical enquiries from those who had been adversely affected by the change' (quoted in Lovett 1989: 30).

7   They were not allowed access to company land in which to plant a garden or access to company market. After 1944 unmarried women were required to possess a pass in order to enter mining compounds.

8   This is the case, for example, with carpet weaving and lace making in India and embroidery in Spain (see Weston 1987, Mies 1982, Lever 1988).

11
Gender and Legal Change in Zimbabwe: Childless Women and Divorce from a Socio-Cultural and Historical Perspective

Anne Hellum

"True learning must not be content with ideas, but must discover things in their individual truth."
Umberto Eco 1984: 317

Introduction

Seeking to describe, understand and improve the position of women in law and society, women's law scholars in the North and South share common values.[1] The principle of taking women as the starting point represents common methodological ground. It is, however, important to have in mind that Northern and African scholars operate within different historical, legal, social, economic and cultural contexts. The methodologies of Western women's law studies have to a large extent been developed in the context of formally unified, ostensibly gender neutral legal systems within more or less developed social welfare states. In African societies, theories and methods which analyse the positions of women within plural legal systems, where imported Western law operates in conflict or interplay with African customary laws, are required.[2] African women's law researchers propose to take up this challenge and to use activist research in order to: '... discover new ways that women can use the law as a tool to improve their lives, and to combine research with active strategies to enhance the position of women.' (WLSA 1990).

The rapidly growing body of African women's law research has largely taken imported Western legal concepts as its starting point. Within areas such as child custody, maintenance and matrimonial property rights, the focus has been on the 'gaps' between the increasingly unified, gender neutral national law and women's position at the 'grass-roots' level (Maboreke 1987; May 1983, 1987; Ncube 1986; Armstrong and Ncube 1987; Stewart and Armstrong 1990; Tsanga 1990; WLSA Zimbabwe 1992). When problems and disputes are resolved locally, gender specific traditional customs and practices often overrule national law. It has consequently been assumed that women occupy a weak position within the family and the local community.

The aim of this chapter is to draw a picture of the varied and complex interplay between coexisting normative structures which determine women's positions at different levels of problem and dispute resolution. The chapter is based on a case study which takes the life situations of childless Zimbabwean women in the process of divorce as its starting point. Childlessness has been chosen as the thematic focus because it reveals basic conflicts and contrasts between coexisting notions and norms relating to womanhood, personhood and status. As far as the regulation of marriage and divorce is concerned, childlessness represents a meeting point between family-based custom and individualistic statutory law. A central theme is the effect of colonial and postcolonial law on the dissolution of the marriages of childless partners. In addition, the selection of the case material has been guided by an assumption that the position of childless women in the process of divorce is influenced by an interplay between gendered and fertility-centred custom on the one hand, and gender neutral and fertility-indifferent statutory law on the other.

My intention is not to give a comprehensive, nationwide description of the social and legal situations of childless women in Rhodesia and Zimbabwe, but to illustrate what a multilevel and multifactor approach can contribute to the analysis of gender and legal change in the context of plural legal systems and multicultural societies.

Childless Women : A Multilevel and Multifactor Approach

The interplay between custom and statutory law is in turn assumed to be influenced by two factors, namely the procedural mode of the problem-solving forum and the socio-cultural and historical context of the involved parties. Consequently, the cases have been selected from different levels of law with different procedural modes, in terms of varying degrees of rule-orientation, pragmatism and flexibility. In order to gain an impression of the impact which such factors as religion, world-view, kinship structure, habitation pattern and the social position of the actors have on the interplay between the coexisting normative structures, the cases have been selected from different socio-cultural contexts. This approach enables us to examine the divorce practices of childless women and men in situations characterised by the presence in one social field of more than one legal order. It implies a deconstruction of the concept of a unified system of law. Sources of various practices on different levels are not ordered and harmonised within a methodological hierarchy, as is usually the case in Western jurisprudence. These sources are described in their own right as a process of different practices in interplay on different levels.

In order to assess continuity and change regarding the positions of childless women and gender relations, cases from both the colonial and the post-colonial period have been selected. Particular attention is paid to linkages between the position of childless women, gender relations and the procreative beliefs inscribed in attitudes, values, customs and laws (Delaney 1986; Stölen 1991). The procreative beliefs of the patrilineal and patrilocal Shona implied a more hierarchical structuration of gender relations than those of the matrilineal and matrilocal Tonga. The transformation of these beliefs, as childless women and men seek new strategies for coping within changing social, economic, cultural and legal environments, is illustrated through historical and cross-cultural comparisons.

The first part of the chapter investigates the position of childless women in the process of divorce among patrilineal Shona and matrilineal Tonga groups within customary law as 'living law' in the colonial era. Marriage and divorce was negotiated by male family elders on behalf of the extended family. Family and third-party mediation was characterised by pragmatic, flexible and negotiation-oriented modes of problem and conflict resolution. These shifting and varied practices were a part of oral tradition and everyday life. They have been termed 'living customary law'. Anthropological records provide the main source of divorce practices at the family and village level in the colonial period. The actual case studies in this chapter are drawn from Elizabeth Colson's monograph *Marriage and Family among the Plateau Tonga of Northern Rhodesia* (Colson 1958) and J.F. Holleman's *Shona Customary Law* (Holleman 1952).[3]

The second part of the chapter describes some of the implications of the creation of 'state customary law' for the position of childless women and for gender relations among Shona and Tonga groups. Colonial state legislation and the establishment of local and central colonial courts resulted in a shift from family to state jurisdiction. The customary law which applied in the state courts has been termed 'state customary law' or 'lawyers' customary law' (Woodman 1985). It is a written, codified and rule-oriented abstraction of people's 'living customary law'. African women who, according to 'state customary law', lacked legal capacity, were under the guardianship of their fathers, elder brothers or husbands. From the level of national colonial law, I have selected divorce cases concerning childless marriages from the records of the Native Court of Appeal of Southern Rhodesia for the period 1928-80. Cases from local colonial law are drawn from Colson's and Holleman's monographs.

In the third part of the chapter the amalgamation of substantive and procedural customary and general law, which has taken place since independence, is analysed from the perspective of childless Shona women. Upon independence, African women achieved majority status. Formally, a shift occurred from a contractual, family and fertility-centred mode of reproduction regulation to a statutory, individualistic and fertility-indifferent mode. As far as the post-colonial period is concerned, interviews with paralegal workers attached to Seke Paralegal Scheme are the main sources of agreements and solutions on the family level. From the central state court level, divorce cases concerning childless marriages have been selected from the records of the Supreme Court of Zimbabwe. At the local state court level, divorce and *lobolo* (brideprice) cases concerning childless marriages have been selected from Seke and Kariba Community Courts for the period 1981-1989.

Cross-cultural and historical comparisons demonstrate that women and men, as well as different groups of women, are differentially affected by changes in social and legal regulation. It is argued that women's law researchers, whose aim is to improve women's positions in law and society, must always take this complex social and legal reality into consideration.

Fertility Centred Practices in the Family and the Village

Anthropologists have described the marriage contract as an important regulator of sexuality, fertility, birth and labour among both patrilineal Shona and matrilineal Tonga groups in the colonial period (Holleman 1952; Colson 1958). Within both groups, the fertility and continuity of the lineage were central values embedded in the marriage contract. The status of women and men was linked to marriage and fertility. The marriage contract and its dissolution was, however, negotiated by male elders on behalf of the extended families and the young couple and their extended families.

The Shona are the largest population group in Southern Rhodesia. Social relations have historically been defined through patrilineal kinship: descent defined through male ancestors. In rural areas, patrilocality was common - that is, a married couple took up living with the husband's family. The matrilineal and matrilocal Tonga are an ethnic minority. Matrilineal descent is 'that which is traced through females; thus children are affiliated to the group of their mother, or, as it is sometimes expressed, of their mother's brother, since in matrilineal societies power and position are generally held by men, though transmitted through women. The kinship group formed by persons linked by matrilineal descent to a known common ancestress is termed a matrilineage' (McLennan 1986: 185).

This fertility-centred family mode of reproductive regulation existed in the context of a dual colonial legal system made up of native and tribal courts applying indigenous customary laws and European courts applying imported Western law. On the basis of racial choice of law criteria, customary family and personal law applied to natives while Western imported law applied to the white minority. African women were regarded as minors under customary law. The Royal Charter of 1890, whereby the British Parliament empowered the British South Africa Company to govern Southern Rhodesia, laid down that in the administration of justice to the African: '... careful regard shall always be had to the customs and laws of the class, tribe or nations to which the parties respectively belong ...'

The following case studies describe the dissolution of childless marriages at the family and village levels among Shona and Tonga groups. Within 'living customary law', folk definitions of procreation, kinship organisation and habitation patterns provided an influential normative and social structural context. Comparisons between divorce practices at the family level between patrilineal Shona and matrilineal Tonga in the colonial period illustrate how these so-called 'open, flexible and pragmatic' negotiations were often strongly influenced by gendered norms and prescriptions. Perpetuation of the male lineage of the wife's or the husband's family was a basic consideration.

Patrilineal Shona Practice

According to Holleman, Shona customary law developed in the context of 'open, flexible and pragmatic' discourses. He describes the process of contracting and dissolving marriage as guided by broad principles aimed at establishing a balance between the two families involved. If the considerations which guided the dissolution of childless marriages are re-examined from women's perspectives, it will be seen that they were coloured by the reproductive interests of male elders. It seems to have been through actions rather than discourse that childless Shona women influenced the outcome of the process.

According to Holleman in order to reproduce itself a Shona patrilineage had to obtain wives from another unit. The traditional marriage contract, symbolised by *lobolo* payments, was a contract between the families of the bride and the groom. In *lobolo* marriages, women and cattle were exchanged as equivalent reproductive potentialities (Holleman 1952: 148 - 185). The cattle received enabled the 'wifegiving' family to obtain a wife from another unit. The essential contractual implication of the agreement was that the woman, who was transferred against the delivery of *lobolo*, should raise a reasonable number of children for her husband and his family. If these expectations were not met, the contract could be reconsidered.

In the context of a patrilocal household, the marriage contract would subsequently be interpreted in the light of patrilineal procreative beliefs. The wife was expected to fulfil the reproductive expectations of her husband's family. Personhood and status were, in the Shona view of the world, linked to fertility and procreation (Aschwanden 1982). A person was someone that would one day become a *mudzimu*: the spirit of a dead parent or grandparent. Without children, a man or a woman could not become a *mudzimu*. Ties established through blood, lineal, spiritual and ancestral connections put the individual under an

Gender and Legal Change in Zimbabwe 249

obligation to relatives. Male superiority was established through a monogentic theory of procreation under which procreation was attributed to one main procreator -the man. Through contributing semen, he was seen as sowing his seed in the field which was the woman's uterus. The man's spirit was passed on to the child through his semen. The husband's mother also held a strong interest in the couple's procreativity. It was by becoming mothers and grandmothers that women achieved status as ancestral spirits in their husbands' family (Bourdillon 1987). In the event of childlessness, the hierarchically structured gender relations which were established through monogenetic procreative beliefs, could be reproduced through conflicts between the husband's mother and the childless wife. In a patrilocal context, it was thus often assumed that the young wife was the cause of the fertility problem. If the wife's family failed to find a solution to the problem, for example by providing another daughter as a second wife, it was often claimed that the union should be dissolved. Male sterility, on the other hand, was not seen as a justifiable ground for a claim of divorce from the wife's family (Holleman 1952).

In practice, however, women would find ways of manoeuvering out of a childless marriage. From the cases it would appear that they manoeuvered through action rather than argumentation and negotiation. The following case illustrates how a woman, through adultery, created a situation which forced her husband to give her a divorce:

> A wife rejected her husband (with whom she had no children) 'because she loved another man.' Her new suitor gave five head of cattle and 9 pounds, the exact amount the husband had paid so far. Upon receipt of this payment the first marriage was liquidated (Holleman 1952: 303).

Dissolution took place through the return of *lobolo*. The husband of the childless wife could claim return of *lobolo* cattle. The wife's father could, on the other hand, claim that the value of his daughter's services, in terms of labour and sex, should be deducted from the returnable *lobolo*.

The childless wife had no direct claims in connection with dissolution of the marriage. Female contractual entitlements were linked to motherhood. They were seen as spiritual rather than legal. According to the marriage contract, the bride's mother was entitled to a cow. This payment was termed *ngombe yomai -*

the motherhood beast - because she had cradled the bride in her womb. This cow was not returnable in the event of divorce, even if the wife proved to be barren. To claim the return of the motherhood beast was seen as inviting disaster. It was usually dedicated to the spirit of the bride's mother as a tribute to the female ascendants of the wife's matriline. According to Holleman's informants, a son-in-law, however strong his claim was, would never be so foolish as to pursue a claim against his mother-in-law:

> A husband in the Wedza area had given one of the *rovoro* cattle of a daughter to her mother because the woman badly needed a cow to dedicate it to her mother's spirit and the husband's family had not as yet been able to provide one. The daughter deserted her husband after a short while (no children borne yet) and the husband's family claimed all their cattle back. The husband (the father of the deserting wife) told his wife (the mother of the deserting wife) that he wanted the cow back, arguing that it could not properly be regarded as *ngombe yomai* But the woman threatened to become *ngozi* (revengeful spirit) after death if he took the cow away from her. He allowed her to keep it, replacing the animal out of his own stock when he returned the *rovoro* to his daughter's husband's family. (Holleman: 183)

At the village level disputes were resolved by chiefs and headmen. The dispute resolution process of chief's or headmen's courts in Southern Rhodesia was also, according to Holleman, characterised by informality, openness and flexibility (Holleman 1979). The *Native Regulations Act* of 1937 empowered the Native Governor to constitute African courts presided over by duly appointed chiefs and headmen, with the task of deciding civil cases between Africans 'in accordance with African law and custom' and in conformity with traditional 'practice, procedure and law of evidence'. The tribal courts - chief or headmen's court - did not have jurisdiction in any action where dissolution of a marriage was sought. However, in practice, disagreeing families often let the tribal courts decide divorce cases instead of using the District Commissioner's Court, which had formal jurisdiction.

The divorce process in these courts has been described as a combination of legal consideration and practical tactics, often aimed at determining the question of guilt and refusal. There was no rigid division between fact and law. According to Holleman (1952: x) Shona customary law did not make up a clear pattern of strictly defined rules, but 'a collection of broad concepts and guiding principles, the practical application of which varied with so to speak every case.' He saw them as giving content to a form of justice in which a satisfactory solution of the conflict between the parties often mattered more than a correct interpretation of the legal principles involved.

Numerous cases illustrate how childless women in the process of divorce made strategic use of the tribal courts. The fact that the High Court of Southern Rhodesia in 1928 had ruled that the wife of an impotent and sterile husband had an individual right to divorce is hardly reflected in 'living customary law'. Women did not argue that they had a right to divorce. For Shona women, whose status in society was based on marriage and fertility, it was of great importance to get a new husband before manoeuvering out of a childless marriage. In order to get out of a childless marriage, it was not unusual that a woman committed adultery. Her lover would be obliged to compensate her husband through adultery damages. On this basis, the parties often regarded the old marriage as dissolved and a new marriage as established.

The following case illustrates how childless women through their actions created situations which led to legal conflicts between men, namely the wife's husband, father and lover. It would be the husband or the father who would bring these cases to court. The women, it seems, preferred to manipulate facts through actions rather than take the matter to court and argue in terms of the newly achieved individual divorce rights. In this respect the lack of a strict division between fact and law seems to have given women room for manoeuvre:

> In Wedza Reserve a complainant charged his wife with adultery. The woman did not deny that she had slept with a lover but refused to be held guilty of adultery. She explained that her husband had blamed her for the fact that she had remained childless, while she believed him to be sterile. In order to 'prove him wrong', she had solicited another man to have intercourse with her. Her explanation did not exculpate her and the court found reason to rebuke her severely. But the circumstances mitigated her act to such an extent that the case remained undecided: the court considered the husband's claim for damages (his condition for reconciliation) excessive, and did not agree with his alternative suggestion that the woman's family should be held responsible for an immediate return of rovoro cattle. The result was that the woman went home with her parents pending further developments. In the words of the court:

'the husband will now be able to find out whether she still loves him. If she does not love him she will run away with another man (Holleman 1952: 294).

Matrilineal Tonga Practice

Tonga social organisation, conflict resolution procedures and customary principles have been characterised as a loose and flexible framework (Colson 1958). Where the parties agreed, a marriage would be dissolved through family jurisdiction. In matrilineal and matrilocal households, it was the wife's family who controlled the legal status of the marriage. This allowed a Tonga wife considerable reproductive freedom, which is reflected in case studies of the dissolution of childless marriages.

A wife's barrenness could not, in the opinion of her family, justify a husband's wish to repudiate her. On the assumption that it was the husband's duty to make his wife pregnant, her family often felt free to return the bridewealth and announce that they considered the marriage terminated, irrespective of whether the husband wanted a divorce or not. In the context of the matrilocal organisation of society and the matrilineal definition of kinship, the emphasis was on the right to offspring of the wife and her family, rather than that of her husband and his family (Colson 1958: 149). According to Colson, no part of the marriage contract guaranteed the husband that his wife would produce children for him. The woman's primary obligation to procreate was directed towards her own matrilineal group, not the husband's lineage as was the case among the patrilineal Shona. When a man had provided his wife with children, he would acquire new status with his wife's matrilineal group because he helped to ensure continuity. According to Colson, the Tonga said: 'It is through our affines that our matrilineal line is perpetuated. When a man has given us children we feel that he has become a member of our *basimukowa*' (Colson 1958: 345).

In the context of matrilineality and matrilocality, the marriage contract allowed women considerable sexual and reproductive freedom in so far as the aim was to have children. In line with the matrilineal nature of society, the emphasis fell on 'the wife's right to fertility', not 'the man's right to offspring' (Colson 1958: 148). If the reason for childlessness was that the husband had absented himself by labour migration or other reasons, it would be accepted that a woman simply took action and remarried. A woman was not expected to waste her child-bearing period waiting for an absent husband to return. The husband was expected to be present and fulfil his functions. If he failed in this and could not provide a substitute, his rights in his wife lapsed. She was regarded as free to find a husband who could provide her with children (Colson 1958: 154). Any circumstance which wasted a woman's child-bearing years was wrong and should be corrected. The wife's family would, on the basis of this moral principle, support action taken by women, as in the following case:

> A widow inherited by her husband's brother left him within a few weeks with comments about her chances of having children by him. He was generally reputed to be sterile, though his first wife continued to live with him. A few months later the widow married a bachelor from a nearby village. As the months passed by she did not conceive, she became more and more impatient though her husband had met her demand that he move to her village where they could live near her relatives. Finally one day he returned home to find a letter pinned to the door which demanded, 'Why do you waste this woman's time when you cannot give her children?' He complained to his wife; she immediately repeated the charge and told him to leave so that she might find a more virile husband. (Colson 1958: 153)

Among the matrilineal Tonga, the value of the wife's reproductive and sexual capacity was also the cause of conflicts between the male members of the two families. As already mentioned, the most powerful party when it came to dictating the terms of dissolution was the wife's family. When the former husband demanded that the brideprice should be returned since he no longer had the wife in his homestead, her relatives would refuse and argue that he himself had driven her away.

Fertility Considerations within 'State Customary Law' under Colonialism

The establishment of colonial state courts led to levels and new meanings for customary laws. The so-called *Native Regulations* of 1898 and 1910 conferred considerable legal powers upon the Native Commissioners with regard to customary law jurisdiction. Through the establishment of District Commissioners' Courts with appeal to the Native Court of Appeal of Southern Rhodesia and a final appeal to the Appellate Division of the High

Court, European judicial officers became interpreters of African customary laws. The practice of the appeal courts, colonial legislation, Western considerations of justice and morality, anthropologists' empirical descriptions of customary laws and the argumentation of male African chiefs and elders were merged into 'state customary law'. As already mentioned, African women were regarded as minors and generally had no access to the colonial courts in their own right.

The position of childless women was, in some respects, slightly improved through legislative intervention and court practice.[4] These changes, however, seem to have had slightly different implications for matrilineal/matrilocal and patrilineal and patrilocal kinship societies. Individual rights and colonial state court jurisdiction strengthened the position of childless Shona women while the position of Tonga women was weakened. Among both Shona and Tonga the position of husbands and fathers was strengthened as male contractual claims for the return of *lobolo* were transformed into legal claims which could be sanctioned by the colonial courts.

The Patrilineal Shona

In the case of *Chawa* v *Bwuta* (1928 SR 98), the High Court of Southern Rhodesia laid down that women had an individual right in Shona customary law to divorce an impotent and sterile husband. In this case Chawa, an African woman, had claimed divorce from her husband, Bwuta, on the grounds of his sterility. The husband admitted sterility, but opposed the divorce. The finding of the Native Commissioner in Mutoko was:

1. Defendant is sterile as well as impotent.

2. In my opinion this question was correctly stated in the High Court in Bulawayo in *Rex* v *Sigiwe* (1918 SR 68) i.e. 'A man may always divorce a woman but a woman may never divorce a man'. Later, 'But a woman cannot get a divorce at all by pure native law'.

The case was stated for the opinion of the High Court by the Native Commissioner because:

The point upon which I am in doubt and upon which I desire the High Court's opinion is whether recourse to such a course of action is repugnant to natural justice and morality and whether on such grounds the claim of the plaintiff should be granted.

The High Court concluded:

> The rule that a marriage is void and voidable when the husband is proved to be impotent is of very wide application. It obtains in the Roman and Roman Dutch law; in the laws of England, Scotland and many of the states of the American Union; in German, Austrian-Hungarian, Italian and Spanish law and in the Canon law, but not in French law. The law of this country is the Roman Dutch Law which is only ousted in civil cases between natives by native custom where such custom is not repugnant to natural justice and morality. In the opinion of this Court it is contrary to natural justice that she should be compelled to have recourse to her husband's brother; if she agrees, good and well; if she does not agree the Court considers that she is entitled to relief and that it would be contrary to natural justice and morality to refuse her.

During the colonial period, the Native Court of Appeal of Southern Rhodesia dealt with numerous cases concerning dissolution of marriage. In a few cases Shona women claimed divorce in their own right. However the individual right to divorce did not imply corresponding individual economic rights, such as the right to a share of the matrimonial property or maintenance after divorce. The majority were claims by divorcing husbands for return of *lobolo* and counterclaims by the fathers of childless wives for deductions in the amount of returnable *lobolo* from the childless wives' fathers. Fathers, husbands and lovers fought over the value of childless women's sexual and productive capacities through claims concerning cattle and cash.

On the basis of Native Court of Appeal practices, judges, administrators and legal scholars constructed general principles for evaluating of women's sexual, productive and reproductive services (Bullock 1913, 1928; Child 1965; Goldin and Gelfand 1975). Upon divorce, husbands were deemed to have a right to return of *lobolo*. Factors which were taken into consideration in claims for reduction of the amount of returnable *lobolo* were whether the wife had properly performed her marital duties, the length of the marriage, the number of children born in the marriage (dead or alive), the number of daughters for whom the father could receive *lobolo* and the conduct of the parties. The value of the reproductive, sexual and domestic services of the wife were among the factors which determined the amount of returnable *lobolo*.

The creation of 'state customary law' has been seen as strengthening the position of men in law and society (Chanock 1982, 1985; Rwezaura 1990). Chanock understands the creation of a central colonial legal order as enabling men to transform negotiable claims into enforceable legal rights (Chanock 1982). As the colonial legal intervention loosened the legal control of male elders over sons and daughters, the former strategically fed their claims into the colonial courts in order to regain control over age and gender relationships and, therefore economic resources. With regard to the position of women he states:

> The introduction of Western legal modes in the form of the colonial legal order had the effect that woman were not able to take advantage of a period of redefinition of relationships which were legitimated as 'customary law'. Because recognition of custom was virtually the only way in which Africans could impose their social aims upon the colonial order, women's claims were almost by definition non-traditional, and could not be effective. (Chanock 1982: 67).

When divorce was established as an individual right it was, as Chanock points out, an important issue for the bride's father to regain control of his daughter's reproductive capacity by transforming the negotiable claim of deduction of returnable *lobolo* into a legal claim. In this way his position as party to the *lobolo* contract was integrated in marriage as a legal institution under the jurisdiction of the colonial legal order. The following cases are illustrative:

> In *Japondi* v *Elisa and Jack* (1945 SRN 315) the Native Court of Appeal allowed the wife's guardian to deduct £5 pounds from the returnable brideprice. Divorce was granted on the ground of the wife's malicious desertion. The marriage was childless but the court did not state which of the spouses was the cause of the childlessness. The judge reasoned that the husband, Japondo, had enjoyed certain services and marital privileges and that he, by his long delay in bringing the divorce action, had ruined his wife's possibilities of remarriage:

Japondi has sued for divorce four years after registration of marriage and I have no doubt that, like most Natives, he lived some considerable time with Elisa before the marriage was registered. During this period he has had certain services and marital privileges from Elisa though she bore no children and by his delay in suing for divorce he has debarred her from possible remarriage.

The Native Court of Appeal, however, sought to prevent what it understood as 'economic traffic' in divorcing women. In the case of *Lucia and Chakanyuka* v. *Gandidzanwa* (1953 SRN 388) the childless wife was sent back to her husband. The Court moralised over the father's apparent contentedness with the fact that his daughter, whilst she was living with him, was keeping herself by what the Court regarded as prostitution. The Court did not approve of the fact that he had received *lobolo*, allowed his daughter to maintain herself by prostitution, and then claimed compensation from her husband for not maintaining her.

The Matrilineal Tonga

Between 1928 and 1980 the Native Court of Appeal of Southern Rhodesia did not deal with any cases concerning the dissolution of childless marriages under Tonga custom. At the district level, it is possible to trace in the decisions of the Native Authority Courts a shift in the balance of power between the wife and her family and the husband and his family. As already mentioned, family jurisdiction implied that the wife's family, by controlling the return of the brideprice, had considerable bargaining power to dictate the terms of dissolution. According to Colson, the Native Authority Court would, presumably in line with Tonga custom, grant a divorce in any cases where it was shown that the continuation of the marriage conflicted with the woman's right to bear children. If the husband was impotent or incapable because of an illness, or if he was away for any length of time, the court would grant a divorce (Colson 1958: 192). However, the imposed state jurisdiction and the introduction of the Western principle of guilt enabled men to argue their divorce cases in a more favourable manner than had been possible in the context of family negotiations. The court insisted that one of the parties must be to blame for the divorce, usually the one who insisted upon divorce. A woman who had already taken action by going to live with a man she believed capable of making her pregnant was viewed by the court as guilty and immoral. Both of these factors supported the husband's claim for return of bridewealth in court. Colson never observed a man claiming divorce in court. Instead, a man would provoke his wife to leave him. When the wife brought the matter to the court he would swear that: 'I still want my wife but what can I do if she refuses to return to me. They must return my bridewealth but I still want my wife.' (Colson 1958: 148)

Gender-Neutral Statutory Law and Fertility-Centred Custom on Independence

Upon independence the Zimbabwean Government adopted a law reform strategy aimed at gender and race neutralization through substantive, procedural and institutional legal unification (Ncube 1989).

Through changes in personal, marriage, maintenance, and divorce law, an individualistic mode of regulation of human reproduction has been implemented so that contemporary statutory marriage regulation is fertility neutral. It presumes marriage to be based on romantic love and individual consent. Women's legal status is linked to age rather than fertility and marriage. The *Legal Age of Majority Act* of 1982, which gave women and men over 18 years of age full legal capacity, has implied a shift of formal reproductive power from fathers to sons and daughters, and from husbands to wives. The new divorce law contained in the *Matrimonial Causes Act* of 1985, which came into force in 1988 applies equally to marriages contracted under general law and those contracted under customary law. Customary grounds of divorce such as sterility, barrenness and impotence are replaced by the principle of 'irretrievable breakdown'.

The *Customary Law and Primary Courts Act* of 1982 has laid an institutional foundation for an amalgamation of the substantive customary and general law through the creation of community courts (Cutshall 1991). The community court is a local forum where women can exercise their individual rights.

Formally, the position of a divorcing childless woman depends on what type of marriage she has contracted. There are three types of marriages: civil marriage in terms of the *Marriage Act* of 1964 (Chapter 37), registered customary marriage under the *African Marriages Act* of 1951 (Chapter 238), and customary unregistered unions which are established through *lobolo* payments.

Fertility-centred *lobolo* considerations and fertility indifferent

Gender and Legal Change in Zimbabwe

statutory rules still coexist and interact. This is reflected in the process of divorce. The varied practices at different levels and in different socio-cultural contexts show that despite formal unification and neutralisation there is still considerable interaction between the various forms of regulation of marriage dissolution. A couple usually enters a customary marriage before they formalise the union through registration. If the wife does not conceive, the parties will usually handle different aspects of the problem within the framework of the existing normative structures. The interested parties pick and choose parts of these structures to suit their own needs. This underlines the importance of studying legal reforms, 'state customary law' and 'living customary law' as continuous processes of interplay on different levels rather than as separate systems:

> [The rules] emerge from many individual transactions and choices which culminate in new norms and values. But norms are also legislated by governments or dictated by administrative and judicial decisions, or imposed in other intentional ways by private agencies. These impinge on the semi-autonomous social fields which already have their rules and customs. (Moore 1973)

Family and Village Court Settings: The Patrilineal Shona

Unregistered customary unions are dissolved by agreement between the individual parties, their families or by the village court.[5] Childless Shona women who have entered into unregistered customary unions lack formal individual legal protection. With regard to divorce they fall outside the jurisdiction of the community court and the application of the *Matrimonial Causes Act*.[6]

Many childless Shona women who have contracted unregistered marriages appear to be negatively affected by the loosening of extended family obligations. Modern practices regarding premarital sex and cohabitation have loosened paternal control and protection in the process of marriage and divorce. Before the wife has given birth to at least one child, a man is often unwilling to pay *lobolo* or register the marriage. Fearing that their boyfriends will leave them if they do not give birth, some women go to the extremes of babystealing.[7] The marriage register in Seke Community Court shows that most marriages are registered up to four years after the couple have started living together and after the wife has given birth to between one and four children.

Through interviews with nine paralegal workers in Seke and Chitungwiza, I was informed of the various types of family arrangements concerning dissolution of childless marriages among the Shona-speaking population.[8] In the process of urbanisation and sexual liberation, folk beliefs, which link procreation to perpetuation of the male lineage, still seem to be a factor which operates to the disadvantage of childless women.

It is often assumed that the wife was the cause of the couple's childlessness. Wives who had not fulfilled the fertility expectations of their husbands and his family are often chased away from the matrimonial home. This is often the case when the couple is living with the husband's family:

> My first husband died long ago. He was killed in a car accident. I tried to remarry. I stayed with that man who I remarried and his family. His family disliked it because I did not give birth. They did not want to have someone who did not make children staying. So I was chased away. It was not a registered marriage. It was just to walk away.'

Husbands often argue that a wife who has failed to give them a child is not entitled to any share of the matrimonial property. According to one respondent:

> Most of the childless women, they are being divorced. They go away with their kitchen things. Their husbands say that she came without giving anything. They think she should suffer if anything happens. Instead they should say that they were the wrong person and that they will give her something to leave with. But they are jealous and think that once they give her something she will take it and go to stay with another man. But the man himself goes to stay with another woman. That is where women are being cheated.

Many childless women feel they get a rough deal. They say they should be allowed to enjoy the fruits of the work they have invested in building up the matrimonial home. Divorced childless women complain: 'How can I have nothing when I did so many things in that home?'.

In practice, some childless Shona women manage to invoke both systems of regulation to their own advantage. In a written report from one of the village courts in Seke, I noted that the court had applied a combination of *lobolo* based fertility principles and

Gender and Legal Change in Zimbabwe 261

new legislation regulating the division of matrimonial property between the individual parties:

> Claim: I divorced in February 1989 and I was married in 1977. No child. My husband charged $1100 and 7 head of cattle as *lobolo*. I stayed as his wife for 12 years.
> Judgement: The court ruled that he will pay $500 and 4 head of cattle, 2 goats plus sharing the property they bought together.

This case illustrates that the open and flexible 'living customary law', which operates at the village court level, also is open to social and legal change. Modern legal principles are taken up and merged with custom. Recent research in the area of women and maintenance law illustrates that the pragmatic approach which characterises 'living customary law' is capable of bringing about improvements in the social and legal position of women. In Botswana single mothers are awarded lump sum maintenance for their children within the concept of seduction damages in local chiefs' courts. This is a significant change, as seduction damages were originally meant to compensate the father for the reduction of his daughter's brideprice value (WLSA Botswana 1991). Chuma Himonga's research in Zambia illustrates how maintenance claims have been accommodated within the concept of compensation in local courts (Himonga 1985). On the basis of a study of a popular tribunal outside Maputo, Berg and Gundersen have concluded that this informal and common sense-oriented institution has enhanced women's access to law in Mozambique (Berg and Gundersen 1991). But, as Gundersen has emphasised, access to a legal institution is not in itself sufficient to achieve social justice and gender equality (Gundersen 1992). With the wide discretionary power accorded to the lay judges, the identities and identifications of the male and female judges strongly influenced the interplay between the political, moral, customary and modern legal sources and arguments which determined the actual cases. Traditional attitudes towards gender roles persisted to a large extent in the tribunal, in some cases to the detriment of women.

Family and Village Court Settings: The Matrilineal Tonga

Whether the lack of access to a neutral court granting individual legal protection has the same implications for Shona and Tonga women remains unanswered. The Kariba Community Court has jurisdiction over several Tonga-speaking areas. According to the records, none of the divorce cases examined originated from Tonga-speaking areas. The court staff informed me that in these areas, divorce cases were decided at the family level or by the adjudication of the chief. This was presumed to be the case because the Tonga did not register their marriages. According to the presiding officer, the Tonga did not trust Shona-speaking court staff unfamiliar with Tonga custom.

The persistence of the practices described by Elizabeth Colson in the 1950's which gave childless women a relatively strong position in relation to the dissolution of childless marriages remains to be investigated locally. We know that integration of Tonga societies into the colonial-capitalist economy led to increased economic independence for younger men. According to Colson, this created new clashes between the nuclear family unit based on marriage, and the matrilineal kinship unit based on descent (Colson 1958: 63). Geographical mobility, the diffuse character of the kinship system and the emphasis upon individual independence strengthened the nuclear family unit headed by the husband. Among Tonga couples who had established nuclear households, the wife was expected to reproduce her husband's lineage. This shift may have influenced the matrilocally based fertility expectations and assumptions and thus the position of childless women in the process of divorce.

However, according to Colson, matrilineality and matrilocality still prevailed among the Tonga of the Gwembe Valley in the 1970's (Colson 1980). During her fieldwork in the nearby Tonga-speaking areas of Omay and Gache Gache in 1989, Reynolds observed that a great number of married couples still took up living with the wife's kin (Reynolds 1991).

Local State Courts

Registered customary marriages under the *African Marriages Act* of 1951 (Chapter 238) are contracted and dissolved by the community court. A registered customary marriage is potentially polygamous.[9]

Until 1987, customary law regarded barrenness, sterility and impotence as grounds for divorce (Ncube 1989). Today, the *Matrimonial Causes Amendment Act* of 1987 overrules customary law. It defines 'irretrievable breakdown' and 'insanity of the spouse' as the sole criteria for dissolution. On the basis of the *Maintenance Act* of 1971 and the *Matrimonial Causes Amendment*

Act of 1987, a childless wife may claim maintenance and a share of the matrimonial property.

In the community court, cases are decided by presiding officers who are civil servants. In practice, divorce cases often appear to be decided on the basis of consensus between the parties. In both the written court records and the judgements, the distinction between facts and law is blurred and rules are seldom referred to.

A study of divorce and *lobolo* cases in Seke Community Court, which has jurisdiction within the communal lands and the Chitungwiza High Density area, provides insight into practice concerning dissolution of childless marriages. For the period 1982-1989, I found eight divorce cases and one *lobolo* case concerning the dissolution of childless marriages. Four divorce complaints were initiated by the wife and four by the husband. In five of these cases, women were awarded a share of the matrimonial property. In only one case was maintenance awarded. In one of the divorce cases, which was initiated by the husband, the wife's sister, on behalf of the family, claimed that the unpaid *lobolo* still had to be paid.

This litigation pattern indicates that Shona women are now taking an active part in the legal process of the distribution of rights and obligations between women and men which has accelerated since independence. A number of factors appear to be influential. The granting of legal capacity to women is important. Changing habitation patterns are another factor. Most cases in Seke Community Court come from Chitungwiza High Density area where married couples often buy or rent their homes instead of living with the husband's family. The importance of habitation patterns in relation to family law practice has also been demonstrated in Greenland and in Mozambique (Bentzon 1990).

The outcome of the cases indicates that childless Shona women are in many respects treated less partially in the community court than within patrilineal nuclear or extended households. Women are not automatically assumed to be the cause of the couple's childlessness. In five of the eight divorce cases childless women were awarded a share of the matrimonial property. In two of these cases the court found it proven that the woman was barren. In such cases the reproductive capacity of the parties was not taken into consideration in relation to the division of matrimonial property. The cases indicate that childless women who live up to what is expected of a good housewife are met with sympathy. Several cases illustrated that childless women who had affairs with other men were treated less sympathetically than childless men who took a mistress in order to get a child.

In one case a childless wife was awarded divorce on the grounds of her husband's cruelty. She was also awarded a share of the matrimonial property and maintenance (SCC 150/89):

> My name is Maggie Z. I reside in Zengesa II. I am staying with my uncle - my mother's brother. I am married to the defendant and our marriage is registered. We have no children. I have decided to divorce because he is very cruel to me. He has assaulted me and injured me on my head with a knife saying I am barren. Then he chased me from the house. He sacked me from his home. He took all my clothes. I therefore claim my clothes; 1 black dress, 1 red dress, 1 blue dress, 3 petticoats, 5 blouses, 1 skirt, 1 blue blouse. I am claiming the kitchen unit worth $700, sofas worth $1600 and a fridge worth $1700. I do no longer want to stay with the defendant because he is very cruel and would not like to support me.

> Judgement in default: The case has been postponed more than one time. The defendant is giving very petty reasons. Therefore I decide to give judgement in default.

> 1) Divorce granted on the ground of cruelty
> 2) Defendant to return the belongings of the plaintiff with $686
> 3) Sharing of property, kitchen unit $700 and fridge $1700
> 4) Plaintiff's maintenance $80 per month

In three cases the wife did not claim any share of the matrimonial property. These cases should be understood in the light of the two sets of entitlements which may be invoked when a *lobolo* marriage is dissolved. The interplay between individual maintenance and matrimonial property rights and claims for return and deductions in *lobolo* payments need to be studied more closely. Whilst the marriage union may be dissolved by the court, economic matters are often resolved through negotiations between the two extended families. The following case illustrates a situation in which the wife's sister, on behalf of her family, raised a claim for payment of *lobolo* in the course of the dissolution process (SCC 241/82):

> In his address to the court the husband claimed: 'I no longer love the defendant because she has been telling me I am barren - causing me great pain - she even injured me. She refused to go home. They are not trustworthy - including the parents.'

> The wife opposed the divorce. She maintained that she still loved her husband. She admitted that she had been violent, but argued that this was because her husband had got a new girlfriend: 'The day I beat him was because he had gone to his girlfriend and he had told me this. I got angry and beat him with a hammer. Only one man came who took him to hospital. And when he came home the following morning my sister-in-law was the one who commented he was a coward. And that was when he poured paraffin over me.'
>
> She did not claim any share of the matrimonial property. The wife's sister appeared in court as a witness. On behalf of the wife's family, she disputed that the marriage should be dissolved and claimed that the rest of the *lobolo* should be paid: 'I dispute the marriage to be dissolved - because the defendent did not finish paying *lobolo*. I only wanted him to pay a part of the *lobolo* since he stayed with her. I know they did not get a child. If he could give me half of the *danga*, that is the half of 7 head of cattle which was asked for.'
>
> The court found it proven that the husband had paid $70 *rutsambo* and granted divorce on the grounds of cruelty and that there had been no child.

In order to understand why some women leave matrimonial property behind, systems other than the legal regulation and control of relationships law ought to be examined. Studies of community court cases indicate that women, to a greater extent than men, resort to spiritual powers in order to gain control of the relationship (Cutshall 1991). According to one of the leaders of the Zimbabwe National Healers' Association (ZINATHA), women often fight over men through resort to traditional medicine. To leave the matrimonial property behind is seen by some childless women as a way of gaining control of the husband and his new girlfriend or the new wife's sexuality and reproductive capacity:

> I was divorced. My husband and I grew apart. I left everything. I wanted to start afresh - to be out of his control. By leaving my things with him - he will not be able to free himself from me. I will always be there in control. My husband married again. He does not have any children with his wife. The family says that I am still there, that is why they are childless. The new wife is sleeping in the old wife's blankets. That can make her barren. In a way I am in control. Although I have never spoken to her.'

National State Courts

A civil marriage under the *Marriage Act* (Chapter 37) is contracted and dissolved by the High Court. A civil marriage is monogamous.[10] A case in the Supreme Court of Zimbabwe illustrates a significant difference in the legal position of childless women within customary and civil marriages. Childless women who have contracted civil marriages are not expected to put up with the fact that their husbands take a mistress or a new wife in order to have a child (SC 54/87):

> The husband's case is that his wife failed to get a child. He wanted her to ask one of her nieces to come as his 'second wife' but 'this failed'. His evidence continues:

> 'I told her I was going to get another wife and we agreed. I found one, consulted her and she told me she was not happy about her and I abandoned her. I then looked for a girl and had a child. After we had stayed for some time, she said love cannot be shared and said (she) was going back to her home'.

Now the evidence was clear that this was a Christian marriage and not a marriage under customary law. It follows therefore that the wife was entitled to regard the taking of a 'second wife' as an act of adultery constituting constructive desertion. Therefore it makes no difference whether she left him for the reason she gave, or the reason he gave. In either case she was a deserted wife, entitled to refuse to come home and to ask for maintenance.

Conclusion: Gendered, Ethnic and Class Responses to Legal Unification

The cross-cultural and historical comparisons of divorce practices in childless marriages among the matrilineal Tonga and patrilineal Shona demonstrate a wide variety of male and female responses to the coexisting procedural modes and sets of norms and considerations. It has been shown that the interplay between coexisting procedural modes, norms and cultural perceptions are spatially and temporally specific (Geertz 1983: Benda-Beckman 1991). This implies that women and men, as well as women within different social and ethnic groups, are differently affected by changes in social and legal regulation. The different implications of the amalgamation of 'lawyers' customary law' and general law which has taken place through changes in substantive and procedural divorce law since independence is an example of this. Women's legal reproductive position has been improved. Full legal status has been accompanied by substantive divorce rights. The community court has improved women's access to law. Women are responding to these improvements. At the level of the community and village court a number of childless women claim divorce and a share of the matrimonial property. However, very few claim maintenance for themselves. Male claims for return of *lobolo* are more rare in the courts than in the colonial period when lack of individual legal status was a factor which prevented women from participating directly in the process of reformulation of male and female rights and obligations. Male elders dominated the redefinitions of customary rights and obligations taking place in the colonial customary courts. Among both the patrilineal Shona and the matrilineal Tonga, the control of male elders over women's work was perpetuated and strengthened.

These reforms have, however, had varying implications for different groups of women. In order to grasp complexities and variations we must pay attention to the interplay between gendered and fertility-centred custom and neutral state law in different socio-cultural and legal contexts. Although some childless women are able to combine different sets of legal and cultural considerations to their own benefit, a great number of women fall between these different sets of regulation. The case studies illustrate how coexisting modes of regulating reproduction through different types of marriages in different fora, interact with existing structures of inequality based on ethnicity, habitation patterns and social and economic factors. Inequities between childless Shona women who have registered their marriages and those who live in customary unregistered unions is a striking example. Dissolution of unregistered, customary unions is not an object of state court jurisdiction. These unions are dissolved at the family level. In the context of patrilineal nuclear or extended family households, patrilineal fertility assumptions and expectations often operate to the disadvantage of childless women. On this level they seem to be more influential than the fertility-indifferent divorce laws which have been passed since independence. The result is a tendency to perpetuate a hierarchical structuration of gender relations, particularly among the Shona.

Notes

1. In the course of the last 15 years, action-oriented women's law teaching and research has emerged at universities and independent research and documentation centres and networks. Women's law was introduced as an academic discipline at the Faculty of law at the University of Oslo in 1975 (Dahl 1987, Hellum 1990b). The NORAD Diploma Course on Women's Law for lawyers from Southern and Eastern Africa and the School of Law in Warwick offer comparative perspectives on women, law and development (Hellum 1990b, Stewart *this volume*). In Africa, courses have been introduced at the Universities of Zimbabwe and Nairobi (Maboreke 1990; Kabeberi 1991). African based research and development projects include the *Women and Law in Southern Africa Research Project* (WLSA) (Armstrong and Ncube 1987; Stewart and Armstrong 1990) and the *Women in Law and Development Africa Programme* (WILDAF), a network of female lawyers from Southern, Eastern and Western Africa aimed at empowering women through the law (OEF 1990).

2. The legal situation in many post-colonial African states is characterised by a combination of *de jure* and *de facto* legal pluralism. *De jure* legal pluralism refers to a situation in which several legal orders are formally recognized within the state legal order. *De facto* legal pluralism refers to situations where some of the coexisting legal orders are not recognised by the national legal order. This situation is often referred to as legal pluralism in a descriptive or sociological sense. It is characterised by '... the presence in one social field of more than one legal order.' (Griffiths 1986: 1). In *Children of the Fence* Athaliah Molokomme (1991) analyses the maintenance of extra-marital children under law and practice in Botswana within such a paradigm of legal pluralism.

3. When written down, 'living customary law' is transformed into the more static 'anthropologist's customary law'. When adapted by state customary courts it is further abstracted from time and place (Bentzon 1992). In this chapter I use anthropological records as a source of divorce practices on family and tribal levels. Both Colson and Holleman refer to a number of cases concerning childless marriages. A problem of using anthropological records as a source is that the factual descriptions and interpretations of the anthropologists are often closely interwoven.

4 Legislation was passed which required that females must 'freely and voluntarily consent' to their marriage (*Native Marriages Act* Chapter 79).

5 Statistics from 1982 show that 26.3% of the rural Shona and 68% of rural Tonga population did not register their marriages (Weinrich 1982). In rural areas, 35% of the population did not register their marriages, while only 1.5% of the urban population did not register.

6 However they are deemed to have a right to maintenance which may be claimed in the community courts (Ncube 1989).

7 See HC-H-47-83.

8 Seke is a Shona-speaking communal land area 30 kilometers outside Harare. Chitungwiza is a Shona-speaking high density area on the outskirts of Harare.

9 According to statistics from 1982, 51.2% of the Shona-speaking population and 29.7% of the Tongas contracted customary registered marriages (Weinreich 1982).

10 In 1982, 22.6% of rural civil marriages were contracted by Shonas and 2.3% by Tongas. Civil marriages made up 17.2% of marriages in rural and 23.6% in urban areas (Weinreich 1982).

12
Family Transformation and Family Law: Some African Developments in Financial Support on Relationship Breakdown

Abdul Paliwala[1]

An Absent Problem?

What happens on breakdown of family relationships in African societies? An idealist traditionalist perspective suggests that relationships are harmoniously reallocated. The wife goes to her parents' home[2] where she is supported by them with the assistance of the extended family. She may be provided with a plot of land and can start a new life. Unencumbered by her children, she has good prospects of remarriage. The husband, provided he has paid brideprice, keeps the children and stays in the family home. He is likely to start his new life by marrying again. Until then the children will probably be looked after by his mother or sister(s), but his new wife will subsequently be expected to look after the children. In this scenario, there are no financial obligations to maintain and no or minimal transfers of property. The only economic issue of significance is the refund of brideprice. There is no state involvement because the continuing support provided by the extended family obviates the need for such intervention.

This ideology underlies the statement made by Udo Udoma J. in a decision made before he became Chief Justice of Nigeria: 'It is almost unprecedented in this country for a wife having divorced her husband to turn rough and seek maintenance from the same husband. The very idea of maintaining a wife after divorce appears to be foreign to the African conception of marriage and divorce'.[3]

Such attitudes are not unique to Nigerian male judges in the seventies. As Kazembe (1990) illustrates in relation to a recent study of maintenance in Zimbabwe, a majority of males have negative attitudes towards the new maintenance and custody laws. Most men claimed that women abuse maintenance provisions by making unnecessary and exhorbitant claims, proceeds from which are appropriated by mothers instead of being used for child support. Even some community court judges were of this view (Cutshall 1991). This phenomenon is not of course confined to Africa: the emotive concept of 'the alimony drone' has had a strong influence on policy on post-divorce finance in the United Kingdom (Smart 1984).

Whatever the merits of traditionalism, a number of questions are raised about spousal support in the contemporary situation. Is it possible to continue to rely under the so-called 'African' conception of post-divorce support on the wife's extended family? If not, does maintenance from the spouse constitute an adequate substitute? What should be the role of mothers in post-divorce child care? What should be the role of the State when family relationships break down?

I argue in this chapter that while remedies such as private law maintenance may be relevant, they provide too narrow a focus for the resolution of the implications of family breakdown. On the one hand, it is necessary to explore wider areas of law than maintenance or property redistribution. On the other hand, while law is important in constituting family relationships and regulating the position of men and women in society, it is necessary to de-centre the law and to look at wider political, social and economic concerns and relations of power in exploring the problem (cf Smart 1989). In this respect, Sally Falk Moore's notion of law as part of semi-autonomous social fields (Moore 1973) is an interesting point of departure. Equally significant is the pluralist conception of law -not merely of formal sate recognised legal pluralism, but the existence of plural legal orders as sociological phenomena (Merry 1988). Underlying these questions are issues of great significance for family law in African societies, issues which cannot be resolved without recourse to an analysis of African family systems in their changing socio-economic contexts. Much theorisation of these changes has been in terms of the inevitability or even desirability of modernisation of family systems. It is therefore necessary both to explore the social changes and to deconstruct the accompanying ideology of modernisation (Fitzpatrick 1992 and this volume).

The purpose of this chapter is therefore to use post-divorce financial arrangements as a focus for analysing several significant issues in family law. This focus is chosen because while pre-divorce customary and general law place support obligations largely on the husband, the post-divorce situation requires us to examine the roles of the extended family and the state. What I hope to present is a schematic view of recent developments using examples taken from Nigeria, Tanzania, Zimbabwe and Mozambique. These examples are chosen for two reasons. Firstly, these countries represent a wide variety of approaches in recent state policy with Nigeria representing a continuation of the customary law and general law dichotomy, Tanzania and Zimbabwe representing a measure of unifying reform, and Mozambique providing an example of the radical abandonment of legal pluralism. However, a second and more pragmatic reason is the existence of socio-economic analyses in each society on the effects of changes in family and social structures on the financial consequences of relationship breakdown.[4] While certain common issues become apparent, it is of course not my intention to suggest that African families are all similar or that one can even talk about an 'African' customary law. As Hellum's chapter in this volume indicates, it is necessary to consider divergencies between societies within each state as the same policy may result in different consequences.

The Nature of the Problem

In many countries, economic consequences of relationship breakdown were, apart from the question of brideprice refund, legally invisible for state law. There was no legislative provision for property distribution and financial support on divorce, particularly for those married under customary or Islamic law, the main forms of marriage for everybody but the elite and the expatriates. This has changed in a number of countries, with the *Tanzania Marriage Act* of 1971 and subsequent legislation in Zimbabwe, Mozambique and Zambia. Despite such changes, recent studies point to the lack of financial support for women and children as a growing problem (Usman 1989; WLSA Zimbabwe 1992; WLSA:Zambia 1992; Rwezaura 1985; Armstrong 1992). Thus

Usman (*Ibid*: 193) gives an interesting account of the link between prostitution and divorce in Maiduguri in Northern Nigeria (see also White L 1983; Bujra 1982; Stewart this volume). He also provides evidence gleaned from social welfare offices of the problems faced by women on breakdown of relationships. In Tanzania, where post-divorce maintenance is possible for those married under customary law as well as under the general law, Rwezaura (1985: 141) provides evidence of the extent of claims made by separated and divorced women. In particular, he suggests that women view access to state courts as an important resource, a means of escape from the relatively more patriarchal traditional dispute settlement mechanisms.

Perhaps the most interesting evidence is provided by the Reports on Maintenance by various teams involved in the Women and Law in Southern Africa Research Project (WLSA) (WLSA: Botswana 1992; WLSA: Zimbabwe 1992; WLSA: Zambia 1992; WLSA: Lesotho 1992; WLSA: Mozambique 1991; Armstrong 1992). In Zimbabwe it was found that 20.6% of a sample including both urban and rural informants had maintenance problems. The sample included both married and unmarried women and men with no filter for matrimonial conflict. In Harare in 1989, 1181 maintenance cases were brought before community courts and 1348 before magistrates courts (the jurisdiction depending on whether the relationship was customary or general law based)(WLSA: Zimbabwe 1992: 70). The studies clearly indicate that there is limited recourse to court-based remedies even when they are available. As the WLSA and other studies point out, factors such as cultural inhibitions, ignorance and lack of access to the law obscure the real extent of the problem. While support is a growing problem, there is no universal expectation of support from the husband after divorce (WLSA: Zimbabwe 1992; Usman 1989; Rwezaura 1985; Rwezaura & Wanitzek 1988).

Formal Legal Pluralism: The Colonial Pattern and Post-Colonial Transformations

The pattern of state-based family law established in the colonial period was one of formal legal pluralism. This formal pluralism itself did not supplant but coexisted with a wider social plurality of legal discourses (Merry 1988, Arthurs 1985, Griffiths 1986). In particular, Hellum's chapter in this volume emphasises the need to examine the interaction between peoples', anthorpologists' and lawyers' laws because each has an impact on the operation of state law and policy within this sea of discourses. It is therefore necessary to analyse the nature of state-based plural legal orders within this context.

A 'general' or 'ordinance' based family law was originally established to provide for the needs of expatriates. This was later extended to 'modernised' Africans (or in the case of Mozambique, the *assimilados*). The general laws were based in the case of Nigeria and Tanzania on English Law[5], in the case of Zimbabwe on Roman Dutch Law as modified by British and South African inspired legislation and in the case of Mozambique by Portuguese law (Morris 1979; Read 1979; Usman 1989; Ncube 1989; Sachs and Welch 1990). In principle, these general laws followed the provisions of metropolitan laws in regulating the consequences of relationship breakdown, providing in particular for maintenance on divorce. However, English family law underwent fundamental statutory reforms during the nineteenth and twentieth centuries[6] which have been part of worldwide trends in divorce reforms based on principles such as the judicial divorce based on the ground of breakdown of marriage, a wide judicial discretion on maintenance and reallocation of property irrespective of fault and more recently, the shift of emphasis to the principle that there should be no enduring rights to financial support for spouses on breakdown of marriage, but instead there should be an emphasis on child support (Eekelaar 1991, Weitzman and Maclean 1992). Sometimes, English legislation was imported as a consequence of provisions in the local legislation providing for automatic adoption of English statutes, on other occasions such legislation had to be specifically adopted[7]. While there have been attempts to follow English trends, these have been fitful and often with very little thought to their relevance in African conditions (Usman 1989; Ncube 1989; *cf* Rwezaura and Wanitzek 1988). A further constraint was that this legislation was applied only to the degree permitted by local jurisdiction and circumstances. The nature of the general law therefore depended on the nature of the enabling law, local legislative reform and the approach of the national judiciary. The impact of these laws on indigenous African populations is open to question. As a result of Christian influence, many Africans married in Church and thus became subject to general law marriage regimes. Nevertheless, most also carried out rituals appropriate to customary marriages, such as payment of brideprice. A general law marriage required a general law divorce, but very few Africans used this cumbersome and expensive process. Instead they chose to divorce and remarry under customary law, thus committing bigamy, a crime which as a matter of practice went unpunished. Read (1979: 1) has therefore suggested that '...the marriage laws in question have had little formative impact on the direction or character of social change in Africa'. Usman (1989) on the other hand contends that while the impact of the laws may have been limited in terms of judicial activity, they nevertheless promoted the ideology of modernisation. This Christian concept of marriage was part of the civilising mission promoting the construction of an elite African family which, while not completely abandoning traditional ways, was nevertheless a hybrid modernised family. It led to new forms of discipline in family relationships which, as the example by Snyder (1981) below illustrates may, *inter alia*, have had an effect in transforming the family division of labour to the advantage of men.

Where Asians had also settled in substantial numbers, separate family law provision was made under *Hindu Marriage Ordinances*. For the bulk of the Africans, a system of pluralism prevailed (Hooker 1975: 129). This pluralism took several forms, commencing with a general enjoinment to officials to have 'regard to the customs and laws of the class or tribe or nation' (*South Africa Charter* 1890) followed by the establishment of Native Courts under systems of 'Indirect Rule' (Morris & Read 1972; Woodman 1985). In addition, formal attempts were made in Nigeria under the *Native Authority Ordinance* of 1945 to write down the 'native customs' (Usman 1989: 56). This and the work of Hans Cory in Tanganyika (Cory & Hartnoll 1945; Cory 1953) constituted a precursor to the *Restatement of African Customary Law* project of the School of Oriental and African Studies in London. Islamic law took its place within this pluralist framework as the law applicable to muslims, often raising intricate questions of conflict of laws between Islamic and customary laws.

The significance of the formal legal pluralism for our purposes was that while most laws recognised a duty for husbands to maintain wives during marriage, there existed a variety of solutions to post-divorce distribution of property and maintenance. Whereas the English-derived general laws provided for separate property and discretionary maintenance on divorce, various customary and Islamic law solutions stopped short of providing that what was regarded as the husband's property could be given to the wife. More significantly, any obligation to maintain ended on divorce. What happened to the divorced wife was therefore a welfare issue for her natal extended family. Moreover any flow of funds was usually a refund of brideprice from the wife's family to that of the husband, with most divorce litigation being about the refund of brideprice (Rwezaura 1985; Usman 1989). This often constituted a strong disincentive to divorce on the part of the wife and her family, a disincentive which became greater with the impact of the money economy on brideprice (Rwezaura 1985). There were however some ameliorative influences in certain societies. The wife could get a rich new suitor to 'untie the knot' of marriage by refunding brideprice (Rwezaura 1985; Harrell-Bond 1977; Hellum this volume; Stewart this volume). Alternatively, some women were able to walk away with their property by informal separation without divorce. Perhaps the most significant factor was that in principle, under most patrilineal customary laws, custody of children went to the father. This generally ensured that there was no need to pay maintenance to the wife on behalf of the children.

Islamic law provides in principle for separate property. It also provides for limited maintenance in the short period of *idda* before the divorce becomes absolute, but not thereafter, and for prepubertal children to be with the mother. However, as Usman (1989: 249) points out, in these matters customary and patriarchal influences often seem to prevail over religious law.

Upon independence African governments were left with a range of choices on the question of formal legal pluralism. First, should the dichotomy between 'general' laws on the one hand and customary and Islamic laws on the other be maintained? Should customary laws themselves be left plural? What should happen to colonial courts and processes?

Nigeria

Nigeria, Tanzania, Zimbabwe and Mozambique adopted four different approaches. The prevailing approach appears to be that followed in Nigeria, which has in turn substantially followed the colonial approach. The dichotomy between general law and customary and Islamic laws has been retained. In the case of the general law, the Nigerian legislature enacted the *Matrimonial Causes Act* 1971 to implement reforms similar to those in the United Kingdom, but borrowed also from Australia and New Zealand. The consequence is that while a separate property regime prevails until divorce, a court thereafter has a broad discretion to re-allocate property and provide for maintenance. Nevertheless, as Usman (1989: 271-5) points out, unlike the United Kingdom where the courts have been relatively adventurous on property redistribution, the Nigerian courts, possibly influenced by customary law and by the attitudes of both men and women, have tended not to give the property 'belonging to the husband' to the wife. The courts have an absolute discretion to award maintenance, but they have to consider the partners' means, earning capacity, conduct and any other relevant circumstances. Usman (*Ibid*: 308-22) suggests that while there does not appear to be any consistency in the judicial exercise of discretion, the courts appear markedly reluctant to consider post-divorce maintenance as a right and may be influenced by customary notions in this regard.

Customary law retains its plural nature, with separate *Declarations of Native Law & Custom*. Nevertheless, the very process of writing down these declarations, as well as the role of court officials and lawyers in customary disputes, must provide a tendency towards regional unification (*cf* Woodman 1985). According to Usman (*Ibid*: 283), while women in Borno State in Northern Nigeria have a right to their separately acquired property, general discrimination in inheritance laws and inequality of opportunity leave them much worse off than men on divorce. In addition, the women's side of the family have to refund brideprice. While there are principles of maintenance during marriage, there does not appear to be any customary principle of maintenance on divorce. In practice, few women have recourse either to the general law or to customary law courts. Instead, social welfare offices increasingly provide the venue for dispute settlement. Officers appear to try and reach reasonable settlements between the parties without straying too far from prevailing social attitudes, and without too much regard for the letter of the law.

Tanzania

While Nigeria has retained a continuity with the colonial period, Tanzania attempted a form of unification. In 1963 the *Declaration of Customary Law* provided a uniform customary law in relation to bridewealth, marriage, divorce, maintenance and the status of children. This could be adopted by Districts (and was by most) subject to minor reservations. The process of unification went further with the *Law of Marriage Act* 1971 (Read 1976; Rwezaura and Wanitzek 1988). The Act provided a uniform law relating to marriage and divorce, while at the same time retaining elements of relevant religious and customary practices where relevant. Marriage became the voluntary union of a man and a woman, but polygamy was permitted in the case of customary and Islamic unions with the consent of the first wife. Brideprice ceased to be a requisite for customary unions, but was not made illegal. More significantly, a regime of separate property was provided for all on marriage, but the court had jurisdiction to redistribute on divorce any property acquired or developed by the joint efforts of parties. On divorce, courts could award maintenance to a wife where there were 'special reasons', and the wife could be ordered to pay maintenance to a husband who was incapable of maintaining himself. The paramount consideration for custody was the welfare of the infant, and it could be granted to either father or mother or, in exceptional circumstances, to a third party or institution.

Rwezaura and Wanitzek (1988) and Rwezaura (1985) suggest that these radical innovations have had limited impact. There has been a small but steady number of claims for property redistribution. But the approach of the courts has been mixed, with lower courts often ignoring women's claims for property redistribution and higher courts applying the law somewhat more rigorously. Nevertheless, the issue of whether housework could constitute 'contribution' and thus entitlement to a share in the family assets was only resolved by the Court of Appeal in 1983.[8] The normal expectation that wives will return on divorce to their own families has prevailed, and wives have generally not claimed rights in the family home. Custody still continues to be awarded to fathers. This applies even in urban areas. Courts have assumed that the duty of the husband to provide maintenance for the wife ceases on divorce, and have refused to make orders for maintenance unless there are 'special reasons' going beyond subsistence needs. This suggests a slow process of change furthered by a few determined women, mainly though not exclusively in urban areas. But this process is constrained by cultural factors, problems of access and the attitude of a male-dominated judiciary.

Zimbabwe

Zimbabwe had a similar colonial plural legal system, but with a Roman-Dutch law background. Customary law governed Africans but was substantially modified by the *Native Marriage Act* (No 23 of 1950) which required a divorce in a Native Court to effect dissolution, and provided specific grounds for such a divorce (Ncube 1989; May 1983). The post-colonial approach has been to retain the dualist structure with customary law applicable under the *Customary Law and Primary Courts Act* 1981, but with signifcant reforms which transcend the customary/general law divide in order to provide enhanced rights for women (WLSA: Zimbabwe 1992; Ncube 1989; Armstrong & Ncube 1989; May 1983; Cutshall 1991). While the independence Constitution does not specifically prohibit sexual discrimination, a number of enactments including the *Legal Age of Majority Act* 1982 (end of minority status for African women), the *Labour Relations Act* 1985 (prohibition of discrimination in employment) and the *Immovable Property (Prevention of Discrimination) Act* 1982 have reduced such discrimination (Maboreke 1987). The *Matrimonial Causes Act* 1985 recognises a woman's direct or indirect contribution to property and enables the court to redistribute property on divorce. The *Maintenance Amendment Act* 1985 provides for maintenance for spouses and children both during marriage and on divorce. There have also been significant developments in both general and customary law relating to the custody of children, and it is arguable that father right no longer prevails on breakdown of marriage and women tend to have custody of children. Yet, the actual impact of this changing legal position is unclear (Maboreke 1987; WLSA: Zimbabwe 1992).

The Report of the Zimbabwe team on the WLSA Project (1992: Ch V) suggests that while a significant number of maintenance cases are being heard, just as in Tanzania there are considerable obstacles in the path of women making such claims. These include problems such as ignorance of law, court procedures and expenses, the fear of victimisation and other social and cultural factors. Even greater problems exist in relation to the enforcement of maintenance. While machinery has been provided for the attachment of earnings, this has proved to be cumbersome. On the other hand, it appears that considerable sums of money paid into court under such orders are not collected. Nevertheless, the WLSA Zimbabwe team report (1992: 62) that 101 out of 216 interviewees support the law providing for maintenance after divorce. Understandably the support is strongest among women (90 out of 155) and weakest among men (11 out of 61). Seventy-nine interviewees (42 women and 37 men) were opposed to the law with he main reason for opposition being that it ran counter to cultural expectations which require women to return to their natal home and no longer to be the responsibility of the man.

Mozambique

Post-liberation Mozambique represents an attempt at a radical departure from a colonial pluralism which distinguished between white Portuguese and black *assimilados* on the one hand and natives on the other. The regime for non-natives was governed by a civil code which was heavily male-dominated. The natives were governed by a system of fascist authoritarianism but with the laws relating to family, succession and property governed by native custom (Sachs and Welch 1990: 79-85). The Constitution provides for sexual equality and, unlike other African constitutions, does not exempt traditional family law and land use from its application. Article 29 declares that the liberation of women is one of the essential tasks of the state (Sachs and Welch 1990: 65). The solution to the existence of a great plurality of traditional systems of family law was to empower elected popular justice tribunals and community courts to do justice in accordance with the facts of the case and any applicable uniform state norms rather than to apply any principles of customary family law. In particular, the composition of the tribunal requires at least one woman member. According to Sachs and Welch (1990: 73) there is no attempt to penalise practices such as polygamy and *lobolo* which are regarded as being incorrect, nor to prevent people from constituting and dissolving their families according to religious beliefs or traditional ideas: 'The State does not interfere. It does not recognise, but it tolerates. The court does not intervene on its own initiative, but only when one of the parties invokes its aid. Then it will apply the uniform state norms...'

The project for the provision of uniform state norms is incomplete as yet. A draft Family Law Code was prepared in the late Seventies. A few of its basic provisions have been brought into force, particularly new criteria and procedures for divorce, maintenance and property. However, the relationship between this new uniform family law and what happens in the popular justice tribunals is not clear. Many tribunal members do not know about the new law. The question of women's rights on breakdown is therefore much more dependent on the democratic nature of the tribunals.

Family Transformation and Family Law

How democratic these tribunals remain in the face of the enormous disaster of war, economic catastrophe and the retrenchment of socialist principles in the face of pressures from international lending agencies remains to be seen. Nevertheless, the catalogue of cases presented by Sachs and Welch (1990) indicates the development of solutions based on the actuality of problems. On the one hand the tribunals set their face against easy divorce without reconciliation. On the other, when divorce is inevitable, they are not averse to adopting radical solutions such as ordering the husband to build a house for the wife and to pay maintenance (Sachs and Welch 1990: 76-8). The WLSA study concludes that the popular justice tribunals should continue 'so long as a single and homogeneous body of civil law does not exist' (WLSA: Mozambique 1991).

Tradition v Modernisation

Recent legal developments in these countries have therefore left the situation in a kind of limbo. First, there is an effective division in most countries between the general law, which applies in the main to the elite, and customary and Islamic laws which apply to the vast majority. Even for the elite, courts generally interprete the obligation to maintain in a restrictive way. The majority of wives have to rely on their own resources or on those of their natal family as there is no duty to maintain, nor does the state provide support. If they can have custody of children, they might be able to obtain support, but in general custody resides with the father. While in some countries there is an attempt to shift financial obligations from the extended family to the husband, this shift is at best limited, being constrained by factors such as ignorance, attitudes and lack of access to court processes.

A simplistic approach to the issue of finance on breakdown is to see it in terms of tradition against modernisation. Tradition is here represented by attitudes such as those of Udo Udoma (above cited), the persistence of customary law under legal pluralism and extended family support systems. Furthermore, we have noted that even Western based modernising laws have received an interpretation which presumes the persistence of the extended family system. Modernisation theory perceives such changes in terms of the decline of the extended family and moves towards the nuclear family system (Goode 1963). The shift in responsibility for post-divorce support to the husband is therefore seen as a natural consequence of modernisation. Modernisation also demands that under the principle of the 'welfare of the infant' custody should normally be with the mother and for both children and their mothers to be maintained by the father/husband.

The tradition/modernisation dichotomy raises various problems, not least of which is the ideological nature of the debate. The idea of traditionalism represents a form of African populist romanticism, a reaction to the colonial law which is held responsible for a myriad of wrongs (cf Sachs & Welch 1990). However, the notion of a return to pure tradition is itself problematic because, as Snyder has vividly established, traditional law was itself a colonial construct, with pre-colonial practices being deeply transformed into a colonial customary law through the development of customary courts run by colonially appointed officials and manipulated by colonial decrees and laws (Snyder 1981a; Woodman 1985, Fitzpatrick 1980, 1983; Sachs & Welch 1990). Thus tradition often represents feudal, sexist and reactionary structures. As Fitzpatrick suggests in this volume and elsewhere (1992), the ideology of modernisation also stands for a crude and unsubtle progressivism, a form of shift towards nuclear family systems which ignores the real relevance and persistence of traditional family structures. Traditionalism and modernity are therefore part of the same mythical embrace, each ideologically sustaining the other.

The Extended Family System

A more appropriate approach may be to consider the significance of the changes affecting the extended family system. The growth of a money economy leads to a decline in extended family ties and changes in the relationships between men and women within the family.

Snyder's (1981) study of the colonial impact on the Banjal in Senegal suggests that capitalism transformed both the traditional economy and traditional family structures. Economic change was not merely restricted to urban areas because the introduction of taxation and cash cropping in the rural economy and economic links between urban and rural societies impacted equally on family structures. He suggests that the stimulus of taxation in particular affected family relationships between male elders and their dependents and between men and women:

Initially, elders both relied upon the migration of dependents as an economic necessity, consistent with rural production and colonial imperatives, and encouraged it as a potential means of extracting surplus labor from dependents in money form. Inevitably however, capitalist migration tended to accentuate contradictions between elders and dependents, especially as the production of commodities, including labour power, competed with rice production. (Snyder 1981: 201)

He further suggests that these factors accentuated patrifiliation (father-child relationships) at the expense of extended family ties, and gave greater economic and sexual independence to dependents. These changes had further implications for relationships between men and women. The endogamous culture of the Banjal involved the allocation of rice land by each spouse's group to the husband and the wife. With commodity production, changes in endogamy, and the development of Christian marriages, rice land allocation and the use of the rice produced changed. In the case of Christian marriages rice from the wife's land was either used first or stored in the husband's granary, leaving the husband's granary as the surplus storehouse - a significant change in power arising from altered property rights.

Rwezaura (1985) has developed a similar analysis in his study of Kuria family relationships in Tanzania in which the introduction of commodification had contradictory effects on power relationships between elders and the younger generation. While, elders use their power over land allocation and marriage to obtain maximum cash and labour benefits from younger family members, the latter use economic power derived from matters not under the control of elders to reduce their dependency. By the same token, women attempt to use state courts to escape male power. Himonga, Munachonga and Chanda (1988) describe how the modernisation of the agricultural sector, with the development of a greater emphasis on cash cropping has resulted in discrimination in land allocation to women in Zambia. The impact of capitalist change on family life is particularly dramatic in those Southern African regions because they provide a pool of labour for South Africa's mines and other industries and therefore give rise to a significant number of female single parent households.

Despite these trends, the attenuation of extended family ties cannot be compared to that in Western societies. In the WLSA Zimbabwe study (1992: 113), 63 per cent of respondents were in favour of supporting extended family members and only 19.4 per cent against. Significantly, 15.3 per cent believed that the extended family should be supported only after consideration of the needs of the nuclear family. While there is clear evidence that the influence of capitalist change leads to a weakening of extended family ties, extended family forms are not without means for their own survival.

It is therefore not surprising that courts should respond in contradictory directions when faced with the tensions between extended family culture and individualisation (Bakari 1991). The *S.M.Otieno* case[9] (Egan ed 1987; Van Doren 1989; Bakari 1991) is an excellent example of the conflicts courts face when dealing with the apparently 'modernised' African who in fact maintains his links with his rural community. The issue in the case was whether a prominent Kenyan lawyer should be buried in accordance with Christian ceremonies as desired by his Kikuyu wife or in accordance with the customs of the Luo group to which he had belonged. The lower court decided in favour of Christian customs, but the appellate court, no doubt impressed by the fact that he had continued his Luo links and even attended burial ceremonies, decided that he should be buried in accordance with Luo customs.

Fitzpatrick (1980) suggests the presence of a dynamic of preservation/dissolution in which a multiplicity of forces affect 'traditional' society in contradictory directions, but produce social forms which represent neither one nor the other. He argues that the continuing application of customary family, land and succession laws and a variety of administrative measures constitute forces for the preservation of extended family forms. While colonial capitalism constituted a force for transformation, and colonial governments used the stick of taxation and other measures to promote such change, the same colonial interests required the preservation of the extended family for the cheap maintenance and reproduction of labour power and in the interests of political stability. The rural extended family could raise and care for children, the unemployed, the retired and the divorce women. This constitutes significant savings in social costs which would otherwise have to be provided by the state or employers. Subsequently, Fitzpatrick (1983) has argued that while colonialism may have operated to create in traditional law modernity's own alterego, sites of resistance which retain their own power dynamic persist which cannot be entirely explained by their functionalism for colonial and neo-colonial interests.

The extended family thus continues to be a means of mutual social support in the event of calamity or retirement. In principle, this support transcends urbanisation. While urban family members are viewed as a more generalised means of support, the rural family provides a means of retreat during disasters or retirement. Both separated fathers and mothers call upon the extended family to provide child care. Nonetheless, the nature and impact of this support has been considerably weakened as a consequence of economic changes. Whereas the divorced wife might previously have found it natural to return to her home, where she would be given a plot of land to cultivate, today such expectations have weakened because of cash cropping and land shortage and thus vary from society to society. Rwezaura suggests:

> [Women] prefer going to an urban centre where they expect to start a new life. Others who return to their natal homes soon realise that they are not considered by their parents or their father's heirs as belonging there. They are seen rather as 'transit lounge' travellers waiting for their next flight into a second marriage (1985: 126).

These preservation/dissolution forces affecting the extended family system are part of the chemistry of relationship breakdown. Authoritarian colonial society carefully managed these issues, but the post-colonial period has witnessed even greater unevenness in the extension of capitalism. Everywhere in Africa, IMF/World Bank dominated strategies promote even greater advance of market forces with enormous implications for extended family based support (Beckman 1991; Adelman and Paliwala this volume). The consequence has been to undermine the general expectation of extended family support, which increasingly is performed inadequately or not at all. Yet, practically everywhere, the alternatives to extended family support, whether in the form of state welfare, private maintenance or a true liberation of women's economic capacities, are undeveloped.

The Position of Women

This leaves women in a difficult situation. The subordination of women is part of traditional society but is contradictorily exacerbated by the development of capitalist relations (Stewart this volume). The traditional extended family based system leaves them in a subordinate relationship both within the family of marriage and within their natal family. The payment of brideprice by the husband's family leaves them in a subordinate position in his family. As Fitzpatrick (1980: 230) suggests:

> A wife's base in the group was further fragmented in that most often she was an outsider who married into the group via an exchange transaction involving her natal group, with which she retained significant ties. Because of this indeterminate position of women and because this sexual division was close to an antagonistic class division, men considered women a threat and, in the face of divisions in their own ranks asserted a solidarity in opposition to the female (See also Armstrong 1992: 145).

At the same time women provided the labour power which maintained her husband's social status, a factor which underpinned a widespread practice of polygamy (Rwezaura 1985). The potential loss of brideprice on marriage breakdown ensures that her natal family would be keen to avoid a divorce or arrange a quick remarriage on divorce. Underlying this whole position are women's restricted property, succession and general economic rights compared with those of men.

Colonialism had a contradictory impact on women's position. On the one hand, colonial courts provided a limited avenue of escape from undesirable marriages, even if this interfered with custom (Rwezaura 1985: 132). On the other, the economic impact clearly privileged men, who dominated commodity production either as peasants or migrant workers, while women continued to be associated with subsistence and reproduction. Women's structural position as reprodcutive labourers therefore subsidised capitalist production and ensured the maintenance of traditional social relations for colonial needs (Lovett 1989: 323). Men used their patriarchal power 'to take up prestigious innovations like modern dress, ploughing, cash cropping, and largely monopolised them just as they had monopolised iron-work since long ago - leaving their goatskin-clad women with their handmade utensils of clay and stone, wood and grass, to get on with the daily business of subsistence in what must have been much more literally "the ways of their ancestresses" ' (Mayer cited in Rwezaura 1985: 133; Usman 1989: Ch 4). Ranger (1983: 258) makes the stronger assertion that 'throughout Africa, customs derived from male informants ensured that men's dominance over women was expressed even more clearly in colonial invented customs than it had ever been before'. The mutuality between the interests of the colonial state and those of traditional rulers even resulted in attempts at legal control of the migration of women (Lovett 1989: 29). The creation of customary law and particularly customary marriage and property relations encapsulated these changed social relations (Chanock 1985: 12; Lovett 1989: 25).

The post-colonial period has witnessed some attempt to ameliorate the position of women, particularly under the influence of socialism as in Tanzania, Zimbabwe, Mozambique and Eritrea. In part this was a consequence of the important role played by women in independence and national liberation struggles (Davies 1983). The Tanzanian *Law of Marriage Act* in its provisions on marriage, particularly the principle of individual consent, the possibility of marriage without brideprice, the requirement that polygamous marriage was only possible with the existing spouses' consent, and maintenance in the case of need seemed to be inspired by the then socialist concerns of the regime. But the motor for the changes was the 'modernising' Kenya *Commission on Marriage and Divorce*.[10]

Mozambique has been prepared to mount a fundamental challenge to traditionalist discriminatory practices (Sachs & Welch 1990), but the ravages of war have limited their effectiveness. An attempt was also made to develop a different strategy in the liberated zones of Eritrea, with the development of a family law based on fundamental equality for women and men for the EPLF cadres, but a more circumspect approach for the rest of society (Silkin 1988). In general however, even where changes have been attempted, their effect has been constrained (Rwezaura & Wanitzek 1988; WLSA: Zimbabwe 1992; WLSA: Mozambique 1991). Post-colonial regimes have generally continued the colonial practice of preserving traditional family systems which subordinate women. One reason is the continuation of colonial economic structures in the post-colonial period, another must be the overwhelmingly male cast of colonial and post-colonial regimes and elites which has marginalised and even demonised women's issues (Parpart & Staudt 1989; Dennis 1987). As Rwezaura (1985) and Snyder (1981) have demonstrated, the impact of capitalist relations on women has increased their subordination within traditional family systems, but contradictorily also provided avenues of escape. The role of law has been to attempt mediation between these two contradictory facets of colonial and post-colonial capitalism.

Contemporary African women may therefore face three burdens, each exacerbating the other. The patriarchal burden of traditional society, that of a modern society which privileges male power and the general international oppression of third world peoples. The crisis for many women with the misfortune or courage to obtain a divorce may be that they may lose their children. If exceptionally they retain their children, they may be unable to obtain adequate support from a crumbling extended family system, a reluctant husband or an impoverished state. In addition they face all the discriminatory impediments of multiple dependency and sexist attitudes in attempting to earn an independent living. Yet, as Stewart and Hellum suggest in this volume, the issue is not one of a uniform system of oppression of unresisting women. Social changes affect different groups of women in very different ways, therefore simple solutions such as Western custody and maintenance laws will not work.

In the face of these constraints women's liberation movements in Africa remain generally weak despite their significant record in national liberation struggles (Mohanty 1988; Davies 1987). The overwhelming dominance of men in politics in post-independence periods has operated to co-opt women's movements within oppressive party structures. Equally significantly, effective cooperation between Western and Third World women's movements is constrained by the ethnocentrism of Western feminism (Amos and Parmar 1984; Barrett and McKintosh 1985; Stewart this volume). Nonetheless, the need to address the issue of gender is increasingly obvious, not merely at the sites of public discrimination such as in employment but also in the totality of women's roles in productive and reproductive processes, both within the 'public' sphere and family (Rathberger 1989).

The Ideology of Mothering

An apparent agent of change in this respect is increasing consciousness of women's roles as mothers. The development of national and international initiatives on 'mothering' specifically address women's reproductive role. This focus on child care issues may tend however to ignore the wider nature of gender issues in society. Donzelot has described the way in which the ideology that children are best looked after by mothers contributed to legislative change in 18th and 19th Century France. Similar analyses have been carried out for the United Kingdom by

Smart (Smart 1989; Smart & Sevenhuijsen 1989). Concern for the welfare of children led to an alliance between the medical and social agencies and mothers. International organisations working in third world countries are similarly concerned with reinforcement of mothering in order to ensure child development. The World's Children Report by UNICEF for example states:

> Whether we are talking about breastfeeding or weaning, oral rehydration therapy or immunization, regular growth checking or frequent hand washing, it is obvious that the mother stands at the centre of the child survival revolution (UNICEF 1986 cited in Jokes 1990: 65, cf UNICEF 1990: 34, World Bank 1987).

It is not surprising that in the burgeoning urban areas of Africa, with their enormous social problems, mothering should be seen to be a factor for social stability. The first step in this equation is the attachment of children to mothers rather than fathers through changes in laws relating to child custody. The second step is the provision of adequate financial support for those mothers. Such provisions have two objectives. First, they apparently promote the upkeep of children by the most appropriate parent. Second, they are a deterrent to men seeking to escape too easily from their marriage and family responsibilities. The focus thus shifts from maintenance of spouses to maintenance of children; that is, the consideration is not whether a spouse will be supported on breakdown, but whether maintenance will be provided for the mother of the children. As some Zambian women say, '*Balya ku bana*' or 'you eat through children' (WLSA: Zambia 1992: 66). The question of who has charge of a child on the breakdown of a relationship therefore becomes crucial. It is here that African societies are currently facing issues of transition that affected Western societies in the late 19th and early 20th centuries. The dominant principle in most African societies has been that custody goes to the father. This may in practice even be applied in Islamic sub-Saharan societies such as in Nothern Nigeria in spite of the principle of *Sharia* under which custody of boys until puberty and of girls remains with the mother (Usman 1989: 239-57). Colonial regimes introduced 'welfare of the infant' as a principle which could override the dictates of customary law (Maboreke 1987: 140; Usman 1990: 213-57). These provisions were interpreted by the courts as ameliorative of the strict rule of traditional law under which custody belonged to the mother's husband even if the child was born of another man. Nonetheless, Nigeria may be typical of most African societies in that the welfare principle has been constrained by customary influences (Usman 1989: 213-57). In Zimbabwe, for example, the principle was interpreted to assume that father's right would prevail unless it was not in the interest of the children to go to the father (Maboreke 1987). It remains to be seen whether recent legislative changes, particularly the *Customary Law and African Courts Act* 1981 and the *Age of Majority Act* 1982 have affected this position. Significantly, if women feel more able to ask for custody than used to be the case, will this improve their chances of obtaining maintenance? (Maboreke 1987). In Tanzania, although the *Law of Marriage Act* has promoted a clear principle of equality in custody applications, Rwezaura and Wanitzek's research (1988) suggests that customary influences still appear to prevail particularly in the lower courts. While women are generally reluctant to apply for custody, an increasing number are doing so.

As asserted by feminist scholars (Smart 1984; Smart and Sevenhuijsen 1987), the welfare principle did not mean the substitution of father right by mother right, but the substitution of father right by judicial discretion or new forms of state social control. Mothers only became significant because of medical and psychological opinion that they were best able to provide for the welfare of the child resulting from an alliance forged between welfare professionals and mothers. Nevertheless, only 'good mothers' would pass this test. Furthermore, this mothering strategy promotes a culture of mother as child carer dependent on maintenance which is often not forthcoming from the father and may not be possible to obtain from the state in African societies.

The alliance between mothering and the child welfarists is currently under strain in Western societies with the resurgence of 'fathering' which has led to development of principles such as joint custody, or in the case of the United Kingdom the replacement of the concept of custody by that of continuing parental care by both parents (Smart & Sevenhuijsen 1987; *Children Act* 1989).

The advance of mothering at the behest of international agencies may therefore be tempered by changes in Western psychological perspectives on child care. It may also be affected by the resistance offered by the traditionalist African perspective that child custody belongs to the father. Further difficulties arise because of the existence of extended family structures. When custody was given to fathers, the child was often brought up by either a new wife or its paternal grandmother. When it is given to the mother, particularly if she is developing another relationship, the child may be brought up by its maternal grandmother (WLSA: Zimbabwe 1992).

The Non-Welfare State

Perhaps the most awkward question underlying the issue of financial consequences of breakdown is the role of the state. The most obvious way in which this arises is the role of the state as an alternative to private maintenance. In Western societies, welfare laws provide such alternative means for support. There is of course a continuing tussle both in the courts and in the legislature as to the respective roles of each form of support. It is not entirely surprising that legislatures, as in the case of the UK *Child Support Act* 1991, would attempt to shift the burden of support as much to private maintenance as possible in order to save the public purse.

However problematic state support may be in Western societies, it is generally assumed that such state welfare is not possible in poor societies such as those in Africa (Benda-Beckman *et al* 1988; Woodman 1988). The colonial state was constructed in order to maximise the extraction of surplus, a deliberate non-welfare edifice, with the expense of welfare transferred on to the shoulders of the extended family. Post-colonial states have succumbed to the same syndrome. Even where resources have existed, as in Nigeria, they have been funneled out to feed the international economic system. The non-welfare state is therefore as much an international as a national issue.

It is a mistake to assume that welfare edifices are not possible in poor societies. Sophisticated welfare systems have been developed in countries such as Cuba and the Chinese Peoples' Republic in spite of a general state of underdevelopment. Substantial welfare provisions in Eastern and Central Europe survived decades of economic decline only to be decimated by the shift to free market economic ideology. Recent events in the famine affected areas of Africa indicate that there is a grudging and limited acceptance of international responsibility for destitution.

Options for Change

There is therefore a dilemma for family law systems. The intensification of free market strategies in the prescriptions of organisations such as the IMF are likely to lead to a greater dissolution of extended family ties. This in turn is likely to lead to increasing destitution for women and family dependents involved in relationship breakdown. It is therefore necessary to consider a variety of options for change, including welfare provision, private law maintenance and improving the power and self-reliance of women. All three possibilities face considerable difficulties.

Improving Welfare

We have noted the difficulties in the way of achieving a comprehensive welfare system. There are, however, other forms of state intervention. Colonial policies towards extended family systems were premised on the absence of state welfare (Woodman 1988) and may have contributed to an increase in women's disabilities. Reforms such as constitutional provisions on equality have, with a few exceptions, carefully circumvented the question of customary law structures, in effect preserving inequality within the family. The state also intervenes in other aspects of welfare through matters such as taxation regimes which provide allowances for married women and children, but which are still premised on the male breadwinner concept. A married woman of independent means has to show that she is separated from her husband and has an independent income. This can place a significant obstacle in the path of women who are not being properly maintained by their husbands. Perhaps the more significant problem of 'negative welfare' are poll and cattle taxes. These hated colonial tax regimes, willingly continued by independent governments do not discriminate between those who can pay and the destitute (Usman 1989: 66). Usman (*Ibid*) cites the moving instance of Binta whose husband was in jail. A demand was made for her to pay poll tax for both herself and her husband, which she could not comply with because she was destitute. Fearing a sentence of imprisonment, and its consequences for her children, she went to the Social Welfare Office to see if they could persuade the Ward head to exempt her from the tax. The attempt was unsuccessful, but in the end the Welfare Officer paid the money out of his own pocket.

Zimbabwean legislation providing for separate taxation regimes for women and men shows the possibilities for change. A proper approach to welfare therefore requires examination of provisions such as taxation, education and housing firstly to remove aspects of 'negative welfare' and secondly to channel low cost welfare to the destitute and the needy in ways which are appropriate to local conditions. While there are some minimal state provisions for the destitute, these are often tokens (WLSA: Zambia 1992: 53-5). A more significant welfare role is generally played by the charitable sector, including the mosques and churches. Even though state based economic support provisions are generally inadequate, the growth in destitution, the relative decline of traditional social security systems and other social problems particularly in burgeoning urban areas has resulted in the development of state social welfare agencies in many countries. Women who are not being properly maintained by their husbands or who are separated or divorced increasingly turn to welfare officers for advice and assistance (Usman 1989; WLSA: Zimbabwe 1992: 24; WLSA: Zambia 1992: 117). It is clear that these agencies are preferred even when court based remedies are available, because they are informal and free. These agencies which do not always follow the technicalities of the law, and use techniques of mediation and persuasion, constitute a new and developing system of family law, an addition to the already plural legal orders in most societies. The responses of the welfare officers tend to vary greatly, but in essence their work is to promote interparty arrangements.

Private Law Maintenance

It is not surprising that the inadequacies of the welfare state would lead to a greater emphasis being placed on private law maintenance. However, this has never been an adequate remedy in any society, and faces even greater problems in Africa. Most customary societies recognise an obligation to maintain on the part of the husband during marriage, however there is no obligation on divorce either for customary or Islamic marriages. While colonial laws enacted provisions on financial support in the case of divorce, they were initially only applicable to expatriates. Subsequently they were extended to those married under statute law as well, but the evidence suggests that they were scarcely used (Usman 1989: 323).

There is contradictory evidence about the popularity and success of provisions extending post-divorce maintenance to all families, whatever the form of marriage, in Tanzania, Zimbabwe and Zambia. On the one hand, as Rwezaura and Wanitzek (1988) point out in the case of Tanzania, some women may use the maintenance law enforceable in state courts to escape from the power of traditional institutions. On the other, the extent of use depends very much on the overall economic context of marriage. In Zimbabwe, where spousal maintenance is limited to cases of need, the enforcement of maintenance laws encounters problems of access and court process, problems of enforcement and sexist attitudes. Even though maintenance is available in community courts, it is not a simple procedure. Many do not know about the law, particularly rural women, and some women fear provoking their husbands by claiming maintenance. Many parties did not know that they could claim maintenance in their own right and not just through children. There has been a serious backlog of cases and the amounts awarded have tended to be lower than those claimed. Enforcement is a major and frustrating problem, with government agencies being more lax in making payments from salaries than private firms (WLSA: Zimbabwe 1992: 106-10; WLSA:Zambia 1992: 82-4).

Perhaps the most difficult problem is one of attitudes. The Zimbabwe study does not include an analysis of the courts' attitudes. What indications there are suggest that the magistrates are primarily swayed by the principle of welfare of the child, but nevertheless do not award orders which are adequate for maintenance. (WLSA: Zimbabwe 1992: 101). Court based private maintenance therefore can at best provide solutions for a tiny if not insignificant minority. The rest have to depend for their fate on public acceptance of state derived divorce, property and maintenance law as establishing normative patterns of non-litigious behaviour. Neither men nor women in Usman's study in Northern Nigeria appeared to want to change the rule that women should go to their family home on divorce and, while some women were in favour of post divorce support, most men were opposed (Usman 1990). In the Zimbabwe study 101 of the 216 respondents said that the maintenance law was good and a further nineteen indicated that they had little or no knowledge of the law (1992: 61-2). Most of those who liked the law nevertheless thought its administration needed improvement. Men against whom maintenance awards were made were very resentful. There were various allegations, including by parliamentarians, of abuse of maintenance. Court officials also had mixed views about the law. One community magistrate asked: 'Do you know why these women claim for the custody of their children? It is because they can claim maintenance from the husband and some of that money can be used for themselves. Then the children suffer (Cutshall 1991 as cited in WLSA: Zimbabwe 1992: 56-62).

Lawyers may be reluctant to actively pursue maintenance on divorce for female clients because it is against custom. Such attitudes are not confined to men. Older women fear that maintenance provisions may lead to decline in morals and easy divorce. Second wives resent their new husbands being sued for maintenance. There was also resentment at the fact that some women obtain custody only to pass on their children to their own mothers. Men felt that custody to mothers was destructive of traditional genealogical systems. An underlying issue is that of male power against that of women, but this is intimately involved with the disruption of traditional family patterns.

Maintenance laws may be one of the few avenues of support for those affected by relationship breakdown, but attitudes towards them and the difficulties in their enforcement suggest that they will continue to be a weak vessel.

Power and Self-Reliance

The third alternative is the advancement of women's power and self-reliance. Maintenance laws are contingent on a dependency culture. The removal of such dependency must remain a more significant goal than that of the improvement in the laws themselves. Ann Stewart's chapter in this volume indicates how colonisation had contradictory impacts on women's dependency. It enabled some women to strike out for themselves, but this was limited by colonial collaboration with traditionalist forces to restrain women. The dependency culture reinforced by colonial and post-colonial practices is institutionalised in that it is reflected in the attitudes of both women and men. The issue is clearly not merely of legal change but general institutional change, with enormous obstacles in the way of such change.

Carolyne Dennis' (1987) study of the experience of Nigerian women shows how it is at the precise points where women's assertiveness needs to be recognised that they tend to be demonised. Three groups of women, petty traders, single women and working women with children, are categorised as 'indisciplined' in the 'War against Indiscipline' (*Ibid*: 17). Dennis suggests that this is a consequence of the psychological construction of a male military leadership which fails to recognise forms of energy and creativity which do not conform with their own disciplinary consciousness.

Change must therefore encompass relationships both within and outside the family. It must address the construction of marriage, succession and property relations within the family as well as women's position outside the family. While so-called traditional attitudes and customary laws affect the situation, these are not as strong as they might otherwise seem. Many customary societies have recognised women as independent economic operators, the conversion of men into the main money earners being a colonial legacy.

Conclusion: De-Centering and Refocussing the Law

The economic consequences of family breakdown are significant for two reasons. There is a growing concern with the effects of such breakdown in a significant minority of situations in which the 'extended family solution' does not operate. Such concern is resulting in ameliorative legal change in a few African societies such as Tanzania, Zimbabwe and Zambia. This is mainly directed at laws of maintenance and property redistribution on breakdown. Such changes are often accompanied by the growth of an alternative system of family law through the development of social welfare agencies. These agencies are, however, mediators rather than providers of resources. An underlying factor in change is support for the role of 'mothering', particularly at the behest of international agencies. New legal remedies are slow to emerge and beset by ignorance, lack of access, prejudice, male resistance and difficulty of implementation, but nevertheless provide limited avenues of escape for women.

The situation of women must be viewed within the overall context of dependency and the subordination of women within the extended family system. Dependency raises wider issues than the law relating to maintenance and property redistribution on breakdown. The most significant task for lawyers is how to unpick the overall legal framework within which dependency operates - the construction of marriage and brideprice, unequal property relationships in the allocation of land and succession rights, and the division of labour within the family. They also need to address questions such as the relationship between the sexes outside the family in education, work and politics. Nevertheless, simple Westernising solutions cannot be appropriate in societies where extended family systems, however changed, continue to exercise a strong hold. The Mozambican example suggests that non-sexist democratic approaches can be integrated by communities into their family systems (Sachs & Welch 1990). These issues all take place within a global developmental context in which Third World women are on the bottom rung of the ladder. While strategies and struggles cannot await the arrival of a new international millenium, they do need to take into account fully that national and international issues are intertwined even in the construction and maintenance of family relationships.

Although law plays a very significant role in constructing both family and external relationships, the issues go beyond the law into the realms of politics, economics and consciousness. In particular, there may be a need to de-centre the law in order to develop effective strategies for social change. I have avoided the presentation of a blueprint for change because a blueprint can't address the diversity of societies, economic conditions and laws (Hellum this volume). Nevertheless, as Ann Stewart (*infra*) and I suggest, there is need to consider the impact on a local situation of national and international state instrumentalities which often have conflicting aims. At the national state level, we should be concerned as much with welfare officers, community court judges, local administrators and party officials as with the national constitutions and laws.

A second concern must be to deconstruct the dichotomy between traditionalism and modernisation within the context of the economics of family breakdown because they lead to mythologised solutions (Fitzpatrick 1992). The conflation of modernisation, feminism and mothering ideologies might dictate private law maintenance from husbands as the remedy, whereas an alliance of traditionalism and patriarchy suggests the opposite. Yet, crude ideological posturing is counter-productive, so our concern must be with realities and the perspectives of participants. In order to do so we must examine the actual role of the extended family system: once it is recognised that there are problems, what are the perspectives of men and women on the best approach to resolving issues arising from family breakdown? I am suggesting trusting the people themselves, providing them with the range of choices, but taking due consideration of the balances of views and power. That this is possible is shown by the consultative approach adopted to family matters during the Eritrean liberation struggle (Silkin 1989).

Law's role may be limited but it is significant; what is required is an approach that does not ascribe too much power to law while accepting both the inevitability of law and its capacity to regulate social order. De-centering law means ensuring that our primary concern is with the analysis and solution of real problems, not legal ones. Refocusing implies changing our gaze away from exclusive concern with legislative and superior court based solutions. These remain legitimate avenues of concern, but much greater emphasis needs to be given to law's tendency to operate differently in different institutions, locations and situations. The concern is less with the pluralism of legal rules and more with the different relations of power in different law based environments. Re-focusing also involves an analysis of the law's role in the construction of family relationships, not merely the law relating to marriage and divorce, but areas such as education, taxation, employment and housing.

In the context of financial support for spouses and children on relationship breakdown, de-centering means starting not with the law of maintenance, but with general socio-economic issues such as the nature of extended family and gender relationships, the availability of land, employment, child care patterns and welfare provisions. Consideration of legal issues would, in addition to substantive issues, involve dispute settlement and enforcement. Only then can there be effective consideration of legal needs in different environments and an avoidance of crudely uniform solutions. For example, should we disrupt a well established and effective pattern in which women go back to their natal family on breakdown? Would it not be better to ensure the effectiveness of support within this context by improving women's rights to land, inheritance, business, employment, education and welfare?

Maintenance regimes modelled on Western systems may be an inevitable consequence of a global development climate characterised by modernisation. This is not merely through a desire on the part of the LDCs to imitate, but because of the extension of capitalist relations throughout the South. The extension of such regimes is contradictorily placed between the tendency of colonial capitalism to preserve or construct customary traditionalism and the general homogenising tendencies of modern capitalism under which little account is taken of historically specific social and cultural practices. An adequate consideration of the economic consequences of family breakdown requires a deconstruction of the remains of colonial traditionalism followed by a consideration of the specific practices in their local, national and international contexts.

Notes

1. I dedicate this chapter to the late Dr. Hamidu Usman who died in 1989 shortly after completing his PhD on *The economic consequences of family breakdown in Northern Nigeria: A case study of Borno State*. I gained much from supervising his work, and many of the ideas in this chapter are derived from our mutual discussions. I also thank my students in the LLM class on *Family, Gender and Law: A comparative perspective* and Sammy Adelman and Ann Stewart for their support and constructive comments.

2. This assumes a patrilineal and patrilocal family culture, which, while dominant in African societies ignores the considerable incidence of matrilineal cultures (See *eg* Hellum this volume).

3. *Coker v Coker* Suit No WD/19/1961, High Court, Lagos 7/1/1963 (unreported).

4. For Nigeria see Usman (1989); For Tanzania, Rwezaura (1985) & Rwezaura & Wanitzek (1987); For Zimbabwe, Ncube (1989), WLSA: Zimbabwe (1992); For Mozambique, Welch *et al* (1987), Sachs & Welch (1991), WLSA: Mozambique (1991). For other interesting studies in African family law, see Roberts (1977), Harrell-Bond (1975), Poulter (1976), Benda-Beckman *et al* (1988). I have for similar pragmatic reasons, and with the exception of Mozambique, concentrated on Anglophone rather than Francophone societies.

5. The principles of English Law were applied through a mixture of 'enabling' statutes which provided for the application of the principles of common law and equity and statutes of general application, and specific local ordinances such as the *Gold Coast Marriage Ordinance* of 1884 (for present day Ghana), the *Marriage Act* 1914 (for Nigeria) and the *Marriage Ordinance* Cap 109 and the *Matrimonial Causes Ordinance* Cap 364 for Tanzania.

6. The *Matrimonial Causes Act* 1857 provided for judicial divorce, the *Married Women's Property Act* 1882 provided for separate property for men and women; the *Divorce Reform Act* 1969 and the *Matrimonial Proceedings and Property Act* 1971 (now incorporated into the *Matrimonial Causes Act* 1973) provided for divorce on breakdown of marriage and a wide discretion on maintenance and reallocation of

property rights; The *Child Support Act* 1991 provides fixed formula based child maintenance which can be enforced by a state agency.

7   For example, the Nigerian enabling Act only provided for adoption of statutes of general application in force in 1900: *Law (Miscelaneous Provisions) Act* Cap 89 (Usman 1989). In contrast the Zambian law provided for statutes of general application in force for the time being: *English Law (Extent of Application) Act* Cap 50 (WLSA: Zambia 1992).

8   *Bi Hawa Mohamed v Ali Sefu* (unreported), Tanzania Court of Appeal Civil Appeal No 9 1983.

9   *S.M.Otieno Case* (1988) Unreported, Nairobi Law Monthly.

10 Historically, the difference between socialist perspectives and those of liberal reformers such as John Stuart Mill and Harriet Taylor have been about the significance of laws (Smart 1984: 15). The latter considered that legal disabilities regarding property ownership and divorce led to conditions of virtual slavery which could only be relieved by granting women equal rights. Engels on the other hand argued that legal inequalities were a reflection of social inequalities, and the law by itself could not be a solution to women's oppression.

References

(Note: Full references for edited works are given under editor's name)

Abel, R (ed) (1982) *The Politics of Informal Justice* Vol 2 (New York: Academic Press)

Ackroyd, K et al (1977) *The Technology of Political Control* (Harmondsworth: Pelican)

Adelman, S (1990), 'International Labour Standards and the Third World: The Need for a New Theoretical Approach' *9th Commonwealth Law Conference Papers* (Auckland: Commerce Clearing House)

Adelman, S (1993, forthcoming) *Law as Power: A Jurisprudence of Class, Race and Gender* (London: Pluto Press)

Afshar, H (1987) 'Women, Marriage and the State in Iran' in H Afshar (ed) q.v. 70-88

Afshar, H (ed) (1987) *Women, State and Ideology* (Basingstoke: MacMillan)

Agrawala, S K (1985) *Public Interest Litigation in India: A Critique* (Bombay: Tripathi for Indian Law Institute)

Akinsaya, A (1980) *The Expropriation of Multinational Property in the Third World* (New York: Praeger)

Akinsaya, A (1987) 'International Protection of Direct Foreign Investments in the Third World', *International and Comparative Law Quarterly* 36, 58-76

Alavi, H (1972) 'The State in Post-Colonial Societies: Pakistan and Bangladesh' in Y Ghai, R Luckham and F Snyder (eds) (1987) q.v.

Alston, P (1981) 'Commodity Agreements as Though People Don't Matter' *Journal of World Trade Law* 15, 455-460

Alston, P (1988) 'Making Space for New Human Rights: The Case of the Right to Development' *Harvard Human Rights Yearbook* 1 (Cambridge: Harvard University Press)

Alter, R G (1990) 'Export Processing Zones for Growth and Development: The Mauritian Example' *IMF Working Paper* WP/90/122, December 1990

Amin, S (1987) 'Approvers Testimony', Judicial Discourse: the Case of Chauri Chaura' in R Guha (1987) q.v.

Amos, V and P Parmar (1984) 'Challenging Imperialist Feminism' 17 *Feminist Review* 3

Anderson, B (1990) 'Murder and Progress in Modern Siam' 181 *New Left Review* 33

Apter, D (1987) *Rethinking Development: Modernisation, Dependency and Postmodern Politics* (Newbury Park: Sage)

Armstrong, A with W Ncube (eds) (1987) *Women and Law in Southern Africa* (Harare: Zimbabwe Publishing House)

Armstrong, A and J Stewart (eds) (1990) *The Legal Situation of Women in Southern Africa* (Harare: University of Zimbabwe Publications)

Armstrong, A (1992) *Struggling over Scarce Resources: Women and Maintenance in Southern Africa. Regional Report Phase One. Women and Law in Southern Africa Research Trust* (Harare: University of Zimbabwe Publications for WLSA)

Arnold, D (1985a) 'Crime and Crime Control in Madras, 1858-1947' in A Yang (1985) *q.v.*

Arnold, D (1985b) 'Bureaucratic Recruitment and Subordination in Colonial India: The Madras Constabulary' in R Guha (1987) *q.v.*

Arthurs, H (1985) *Without the Law: Administrative Justice and Legal Pluralism in Mid-19th Century England* (Toronto: University of Toronto Press)

Ascherson, N (1981) *The Polish August* (Harmondsworth: Penguin)

Aschwanden, H (1982) *Symbols of Life: An Analysis of the Consciousness of the Karanga* (Gweru: Mambo Press)

Austin, J (1861-3) *The Province of Jurisprudence Determined* 2nd edn and *Lectures on Jurisprudence* 3 vols (London: John Murray)

Axtell, J (1985) *The Invasion Within: The Contest of Cultures in Colonial North America* (New York: Oxford University Press)

Azicri, M (1980) 'Change and Institutionalisation in the Revolutionary Process: The Cuban Legal System in the 1970s' 6 *Review of Socialist Law* 164

Azicri, M (1988) *Cuba: Politics, Economics and Society* (London: Frances Pinter)

Baade, H (1980) 'The Legal Effects of Codes of Conduct for Multinational Enterprises' in N Horn (ed) *q.v.*

Bakari, A (1991) 'African Paradoxes of Legal Pluralism in Personal Laws: A Comparative Case Study of Tanzania and Kenya' *African Journal of International and Comparative Law* 3 (3) 545-557.

Ball, G (1967) 'Cosmocorp - The Importance of Being Stateless', *Columbia Journal of World Business* 2 (6) 25

Ball, G W (ed) (1975) *Global Companies: The Political Economy of World Business* (Englewood Cliffs: Prentice-Hall)

Bandarage, A (1984) 'Women in Development: Liberalism, Marxism and Marxist Feminism' *Development and Change* 15, 495-515

Barrett, M (1988) *Women's Oppression Today* (London: Verso)

Barrett, M and M McIntosh (1985) 'Ethnocentrism and Socialist Feminist Theory' *Feminist Review* 20, 23

Barron, R and G Norris (1976) 'Sexual Divisions and the Dual Labour Market' in D Barker and S Allen (eds) (1976) *Dependence and Exploitation in Work and Marriage* (New York: Longman)

Barse, S (1987) 'No Respect for Courts' *Lex et Justitia* May 1987, 38

Bartlett, C and S Ghoshal (1989) *Managing Across Borders* (London: Hutchinson)

Bates, R H (1981) *Markets and States in Tropical Africa* (Berkeley: University of California Press)

Baxi, U (1980) *Indian Supreme Court and Politics* (Lucknow: Eastern Book Co)

Baxi, U (1982) *The Crisis of the Indian Legal System* (New Delhi: Vikas)

Baxi, U (1985) 'Taking Suffering Seriously' in R Dhavan (ed) *Judges and the Judicial Power* (Bombay & London: Tripathi & Sweet & Maxwell)

Baxi, U (1988) 'Taking Suffering Seriously' in Baxi, U (ed) *Law and Poverty* (Bombay: Tripathi)

Beckman, B (1990) 'Empowerment or Repression? The World Bank and the Politics of African Adjustment' *Symposium on the Social and Political Context of Structural Adjustment in Sub-Saharan Africa* (Bergen, Norway, 17-19 October 1990)

Beechey, V (1987) *Waged Work: A Reader* (London: Virago)

Benda-Beckman, F and K Benda-Beckman (1991) 'Law in Society: From Blindman's Bluff to Multilocal Law' in *Living Law in the Low Countries: Special Issue of the Dutch and Belgian Law and Society Journal* (Recht der Werkelijkheid)

Benda-Beckman, F von *et al* (eds) (1988) *Between Kinship and the State: Social Security Law in Developing Countries* (Dordrecht: Foris)

Bennholdt-Thomson, V (1990) 'Why Do Housewives Continue to be Created in the Third World Too?' in M Mies (ed)(1990) *q.v.*

Bentzon A W (1990) 'Women and Courts in Developing Countries. The Application of Law at Courts with Lay Judges in Mozambique and Greenland', paper delivered at NORAD Diploma Course in Women's Law at the Faculty of Law, University of Zimbabwe

Bentzon A W (1992) 'Women's Identity and Resources: Between State Law and Customary Law' *Wellington Congress of the Commission on Folk Law and Legal Pluralism* (August 1992)

Berg N and A Gundersen (1991) 'Legal Reform in Mozambique: Equality and Emancipation for Women through Popular Justice?' in K A Stolen and M Vaa (eds) (1991) *q.v.*

Bergman, M S (1983) 'Bilateral Investment Protection Treaties', *New York University Journal of International Law and Politics* 16 (1) 1-45

Berman, J (1969) 'The Cuban Popular Tribunals' 69 *Columbia Law Review* 1317

Bhagwati, J (1983) 'Justice Limited' *Second Annual Conferecnce of the People's Union for Democratic Rights* (23 January 1983) reproduced in A R Desai (ed) (1986) *q.v.*

Bhagwati, J (1985) 'Judicial Activism and Public Interest Litigation' *Columbia Journal of Transnational Law* 23, 561

Bhanumurthy, K V (1986) 'How Much Can The Judiciary Do?' in A Desai (ed) (1986) *q.v.*

Bjorkman, M, L Lauridsen and H Marussen (1988) 'Types of Industrialization and the Capital-Labour Relation in the Third World' in R Southall (ed) (1988) *q.v.*

Blackstone, W (1825) *Commentaries on the Laws of England*, 16th edn (London: T Cadell and J Butterworth & Son)

Blanpain, R (1979) *The OECD Guidelines for Multinational Enterprises and Labour Relations 1976-1979 Experience and Review* (Deventer: Kluwer)

Bloch, M and J Bloch (1980) 'Women and the Dialectics of Nature in Eighteenth-Century French Thought' in C P MacCormack and M Strathern (eds) (1980) *q.v.*

Boddewyn, J J and R Torneden (1973) US Foreign Divestment: a Preliminary Survey, *Columbia Journal of World Business* 8, 25-29

Bolton, D (1985) *Nationalization- A Road to Socialism? The Lessons of Tanzania* (London: Zed Books)

Bordua, D (ed) (1967) *The Police: Six Sociological Essays* (New York: John Wiley)

Boserup, E (1970) *Women's Role in Economic Development* (London: Earthscan)

Botchie, G (1984) *Employment and Multinational Enterprises in Export Processing Zones: The Cases of Liberia and Ghana*, Multinational Enterprises Working Paper No 30 (Geneva: ILO)

Bouin, O, & C-A Michalet (1991) *Rebalancing the Public and Private Sectors: Developing Country Experience* (Paris: OECD)

Bourdillon, M (1987) *The Shona Peoples* (Gweru, Mambo Press)

Boyd, R, R Cohen and P Gutkind (eds) (1987) *International Labour and the Third World: The Making of a New Working Class* (Aldershot: Avebury)

Brady, J (1981) 'A Season of Startling Alliance: Chinese Law and Justice in the New Order' 9 *International Journal of Sociology of Law* 41

Brady, J (1982) 'The Revolution Comes of Age: Justice and Social Change in Contemporary Cuba' in C Sumner (1982) *q.v.*

Brandstadter, E (1985) 'Dangerous Castes and Tribes' in A Yang (1985) *q.v.*

Brookfield, H (1975) *Interdependent Development* (London: Methuen)

Brophy, J and C Smart (1981) 'From Disregard to Disrepute: The Position of Women in Family Law' *Feminist Review* 9, 3-16

Brownlie, I (1979) 'Legal Status of Natural Resources', *International Law* (1) 245-318

Bujra, J (1982) 'Women 'Entrepreneurs' of Early Nairobi' in C Sumner (ed) (1982) *q.v.*

Bullock, C (1913) *Mashona Laws and Customs* (Salisbury, Argus Co)

Bullock, C (1928) *The Mashona (The Indigenous Natives of S Rhodesia)* (Cape Town & Johannesburg: Juta)

Calathes, W (1990) 'Jamaican Firearm Legislation: Crime Control, Politicisation and Social Control in a Developing Nation' 18 *International Journal of Sociology of Law* 259

Campbell, H and H Stein (1991) *The IMF and Tanzania* (Harare: SAPES)

Cassirer, E (1955) *The Philosophy of the Enlightenment* (Boston: Beacon Press)

Chan, L, M Young and K Salih (1983) 'Women Workers in Malaysia: TNCs and Social Conditions', in I Norlund, P Wad and V Brun (eds) *Industrialization and the Labour Process in Southeast Asia* (Copenhagen: Institute of Cultural Sociology, University of Copenhagen, Repro-serie 1984, No 6)

Chanock, M (1982) 'Making Customary Law: Men, Women and Courts in Colonial Northern Rhodesia' in Hay, M J and M Wright (eds) *African Women & the Law: Historical Perspectives* (Boston University Papers on Africa VII 53-67)

Chanock, M (1985) *Law Custom and Social Order: The Colonial Experience in Malawi and Zambia* (Cambridge: Cambridge University Press)

Charnovitz, S (1986) 'Fair Labour Standards and International Trade' *Journal of World Trade Law* 20, 61-78

Charnowitz, S (1987) 'The Influence of International Labour Standards on the World Trade Regime' *International Labour Review* 565

Chetley, A (1986) *The Politics of Baby Foods: Successful Challenges to an International Marketing Strategy* (London: Pinter)

Child, H (1965) *The History and Extent of Recognition of Tribal Law in Rhodesia* (Salisbury: Ministry of Internal Affairs)

CHRI (1991) *Put Our World to Rights* Commonwealth Human Rights Initiative, Report of Advisory Group (London: Commonwealth Secretariat)

Clark, D (1985) 'Concepts of Law in the Chinese Anti-Crime Campaign' *Harvard Law Review* 98, 1890

Cleaver, H (1989) 'Close the IMF, Abolish Debt and End Development: A Class Analysis of the International Debt Crisis' *Capital & Class* 39, 17-50

Cohen, J (1978) 'China's Changing Constitution' *China Quarterly* 76, 794-841

Cohen, R (1986) *Endgame Apartheid?* (Paris: Unesco)

Cohen, R (1987) 'Theorising International Labour' in R Boyd, R Cohen and P Gutkind (eds) (1987) *q.v.*

Colson, E (1958) *Marriage and the Family among the Plateau Tonga of Northern Rhodesia* (Manchester: Manchester University Press)

Colson, E (1980) 'The Resilience of Matrilineality: Gwembe and Plateau Tonga Adaptations' in L S Cordell and S Beckerman (eds) *The Versatility of Kinship* (New York: Academic Press)

Commonwealth Secretariat (1990) *International Economic Issues* (London: Commonwealth Secretariat)

Conrad, J (1990) *Heart of Darkness* (Oxford: Oxford University Press)

Cooper, F (ed) (1983) *Struggle for the City: Migrant Labour and Capitalism in Urban Africa* (Beverley Hills: Sage)

Copans, J (1991) 'Some Debates on the Debates' in Hartman, J (ed) (1991) *q.v.*

Corrigan, P and D Sayer (1981) 'How The Law Rules: Variations on Some Themes in Karl Marx' in R H Fryer *et al* (eds) *q.v.*

Corrigan, P and D Sayer (1986) *The Great Arch* (Oxford: Blackwell)

Cory, H & H M Hartnoll (1945) *Customary Law of the Haya Tribe. Tanganyika Territory* (London: Frank Cass)

Cory, H (1953) *Sukuma Law & Custom* (London: Oxford University Press)

Cottrell, J (1990) 'Courts and Accountability: Public Interest Litigation in the Indian High Courts' *Proceedings of INTWORLSA Conference* (June 1990)

Craig, P P and S L Deshpande (1989) 'Rights, Autonomy and Process: Public Interest Litigation in India' *Oxford Journal of Legal Studies* 9, 356

Crawford, J (1988) *The Rights of Peoples* (Oxford: Clarendon Press)

Cross, R (1978) 'The Reports of the Criminal Law Commissioners (1833-1849) and the Abortive Bills of 1853' in P Glazebrook *q.v.*

CSE (Centre for Science and Environment) (1984-5) *The State of India's Environment: A Citizens' Report* 1984-85 (New Delhi: CSE)

Curtin, P P (1971) *Imperialism* (London and Basingstoke: Macmillan)

Cutshall, C R (1991) *Justice for the People: Community Courts and Legal Transformations in Zimbabwe* (Harare: University of Zimbabwe Publications)

Dahl, T S (1987) *Women's Law: An Introduction to Feminist Jurisprudence* (Oslo: Norwegian University Press)

Das, G (1987) *Supreme Court in Quest of Identity* (Lucknow: Eastern Book Co)

Davis, M (ed) (1987) *Third World Second Sex* Vol 2 (London: Zed Press)

Davis, M and S Ruddock (1990) 'Los Angeles: Civil Liberties between the Hammer and the Rock' *New Left Review* 170, 37

De Waart, P, P Peters and E Denters (eds) (1988) *International Law and Development* (Dordrecht: Martinus Nijhoff)

Delaney, C (1986) 'The Meaning of Paternity and the Virgin Birth Debate', *Man (N.S.)* 21, 494-511

Dennis, C (1987) 'Women and the State in Nigeria: The Case of the Federal Military Government 1984-5' in Afshar H. (ed) *q.v.* 13-27.

Desai, A R (1986) *Violation of Democratic Rights in India* Vol I (Bombay: Popular Prakashan)

Deutscher, I (1963) *The Prophet Outcast* (Oxford: Oxford University Press)

Deutscher, I (1967) *The Unfinished Revolution* (Oxford: Oxford University Press)

Dhavan, R (1992) 'Law as Concern: Reflecting on 'Law and Development', *International Seminar on Law and Development*, Nakuru, Kenya, 21-25 April 1992 (mimeo)

Dias, C J and J C N Paul (1981) 'Observations on Lawyers in Development and Underdevelopment' and 'Lawyers, Legal Resources and Alternative Approaches to Development' in C J Dias et al (eds) *q.v.*

Dias, C J et al (eds) (1981) *Lawyers in the Third World: Comparative and Developmental Perspectives* (Uppsala: Scandinavian Institute for African Studies and International Center for Law in Development)

Dicken, P (1992) *Global Shift: The Internationalization of Economic Activity* 2nd edn (London: Paul Chapman Publishing)

Diderot, D (1950) *Le Neveu de Rameau* (Geneve: Droz)

Dixon, C, D Drakikis-Smith and L Watts (eds) (1986) *Multinational Corporations and the Third World* (Sydney: Croom Helm)

Dolzer, R (1981) 'New Foundations of the Law of Expropriation of Alien Property' *American Journal of International Law* 75, 553-590

Dornbusch, R (1989) 'Debt Problems and the World Macroeconomy' in J Sachs (ed) (1989) *q.v.*

Dror, D M (1984) 'Aspects of Labour Law and Relations in Selected Export Processing Zones', *International Labour Review* 123 (6) 705-22

Dunning, J H (1988) *Explaining International Production* (London: Unwin Hyman)

Earth (1992) (*The Guardian*, London, June 1992)

Eekelaar, J (1991) *Regulating Divorce* (Oxford: Clarendon)

Egan, S (ed) (1987) *SM Otieno: Kenya's Unique Burial Saga* (Nairobi: Nation Newspapers)

Egero, B (1987) *Mozambique: a Dream Undone* (Uppsala: SIAS)

Eichengreen, B and P H Lindert (eds) (1989) *The International Debt Crisis in Historical Perspective* (Cambridge: MIT Press)

Eliade, M (1965) *The Myth of Eternal Return or, Cosmos and History* (Princeton: Princeton University Press)

Elson D and R Pearson (1981) 'Nimble Fingers Make Cheap Workers: An Analysis of Womens' Employment in Third World Export Manufacturing' *Feminist Review* 71

Emmerij, L (1988) 'Peace and Poverty: Europe's Responsibility' in Hettne, B *q.v.*

Farrell, T (1985) 'Incentives and Foreign Investment Decisions: An Opposing View', *CTC Reporter* 20, 39-42

Fatton, R (1989) 'Gender, Class and State in Africa' in J L Parpart and K Staudt (eds) (1989) *q.v.*

Faundez, J and S Picciotto (1978) *The Nationalisation of Multinationals in Peripheral Economies* (Basingstoke: Macmillan)

Feilchenfeld, E H (1931) *Public Debts and State Succession* (New York: MacMillan)

Ferguson, A (1966) *An Essay on the History of Civil Society 1767* (Edinburgh: Edinburgh University Press)

Fimbo, G M (1992) 'The Nyalali Commission and the Role of the Judiciary in Tanzania', *Tanganyika Law Society Seminar on Democracy and the Rule of Law*, Dar es Salaam, 22-3 April 1992 (mimeo)

Findlay, M (1989) 'Show Trials in China: After Tiananmen Square' *Journal of Law and Society* 16, 251

Findlay, M and T Wing (1989) 'Sugar Coated Bullets: Corruption and the New Economic Order in China' *Contemporary Crises* 13, 145

Fisch, J (1983) *Cheap Lives and Dear Limbs* (Wiesbaden: Franz Steiner)

Fitzpatrick, P (1980) *Law and State in Papua New Guinea* (London: Academic Press)

Fitzpatrick, P (1982) 'The Political Economy of Dispute Settlement in Papua New Guinea' in C Sumner (1982) *q.v.*

Fitzpatrick, P (1983) 'Law, Plurality and Underdevelopment' in D Sugarman (ed) *q.v.*

Fitzpatrick, P (ed) (1991) *Dangerous Supplements: Resistance and Renewal in Jurisprudence* (London: Pluto Press)

Fitzpatrick, P (1992) *The Mythology of Modern Law* (London: Pluto Press)

Foster, J (1974) *Class Struggle and Industrial Revolution* (London: Weidenfeld and Nicolson)

Foucault, M (1973) *The Order of Things: An Archeology of the Human Sciences* (New York: Vintage)

Foucault, M (1977) *Discipline and Punish* (Harmondsworth: Peregrine)

Franck, T (1972) 'The New Development: Can American Law and Legal Institutions Help Developing Countries?' *Wisconsin Law Review* (3) 768-801

Frank, A G (1981) 'Superexploitation in the Third World' in A G Frank (ed) (1981) *Crisis in the Third World* (New York: Holmes and Meiers)
Frank, A G (1989) 'Debt Where Credit is Due' in H W Singer and S Sharma (eds) (1989) *q.v.*
Frankenberg, G and Knieper, R (1984) 'Legal Problems of the Overindebtedness of Developing Countries: The Current Relevance of the Doctrine of Odious Debts' *International Journal of the Sociology of Law* 12 (4) 415-38
Freitag, S (1985) 'Collective Crime and Authority in North India' in A Yang (1985) *q.v.*
Froebel, F, J Heinrichs and O Kreye (1980) *The New International Division of Labour: Structural Unemployment in Industrialized Countries and Industrialization in Developing Countries* (Cambridge: Cambridge University Press)
Fryer, R (ed) (1981) *Law, State and Society* (London: Croom Helm)
Fuentes, A and B Ehrenreich (1983) *Women in the Global Factory* (Boston: South End Press)
Fukuyama, F (1992) *The End of History and the Last Man* (London: Hamish Hamilton)
Garland, D (1985) *Punishment and Welfare* (Aldershot: Gower)
Garland, D (1990) *Punishment and Modern Society* (Oxford: Oxford University Press)
Geertz, C (1983) *Local Knowledge: Further Essays in Interpretative Anthropology* (New York: Basic Books)
George, S (1988) *A Fate Worse Than Debt* (London: Penguin)
Ghai, Y and P McAuslan (1970) *Public Law and Political Change in Kenya* (Nairobi: Oxford University Press)
Ghai, Y (1986) 'The Rule of Law, Legitimacy and Governance' *International Journal of Sociology of Law* 14, 179-208
Ghai, Y (1987) 'Law, Development and African Scholarship', *Modern Law Review* 50, 750-76
Ghai, Y, R Luckham and F Snyder (eds) (1987) *Political Economy of Law: A Third World Reader* (New Delhi: Oxford University Press)
Ghai, Y (1991) 'The Role of Law in the Transition of Societies: The African Experience' *Journal of African Law* 35 (1-2) 8-20
Gittings, J (1991) *China Changes Face* (Oxford: Oxford University Press)
Glazebrook, P (1978) *Reshaping the Criminal Law* (London: Stevens)
Glazewski, J (1991) 'The Environment, Human Rights and a New South African Constitution' *South African Journal on Human Rights* 7, 167
Goel, R L (1989) 'International Trade, Protectionism and Third World Debt' in H W Singer and S Sharma (eds) (1989) *q.v.*
Goldberg, D T (1993, forthcoming) *Racist Culture* (New York: Blackwell Publishers)

Goldin, B and M Gelfand (1975) *African Law and Custom in Rhodesia* (Cape Town: Juta)

Gomez de Estada, O and R Reddock (1987) 'New Trends in the Internationalisation of Production: Implications for Female Workers' in R Boyd, R Cohen and P Gutkind (eds) (1987) *q.v.*

Gonsalves, C (1988) 'Sliding Backwards' *Lex et Justitia* June 1988, 37

Goode, W (1963) *World Revolution and Family Patterns* (Glencoe: Free Press)

Goodrich, P (1990) *Languages of Law: From Logics of Memory to Nomadic Masks* (London: Weidenfeld and Nicolson)

Goodrich, P and Y Hachamovitch (1991) 'Time Out of Mind: An Introduction to the Semiotics of Common Law' in P Fitzpatrick (ed) (1991) *q.v.*

Gordon, S (1985) 'Bhils and the Idea of a Criminal Tribe in Nineteenth Century India' in A Yang (ed) (1985) *q.v.*

Green R H (1978) 'A Guide to Acquisition and Initial Operation: Reflections from Tanzanian Experience 1967-74' in J Faundez and S Picciotto (eds) (1978) *q.v.*

Griffiths, J (1986) What is Legal Pluralism? *Journal of Legal Pluralism* 24, 1

Guha, R (1987) 'Chandra's Death' in R Guha (1987) *q.v.*

Guha, R (ed) (1983) *Subaltern Studies: Writings on South Asian History and Society* Vol 2 (Delhi and Oxford: Oxford University Press)

Guha, R (ed) (1985) *Subaltern Studies: Writings on South Asian History and Society* Vol 4 (Delhi and Oxford: Oxford University Press)

Guha, R (ed) (1987) *Subaltern Studies: Writings on South Asian History and Society* Vol 5 (Delhi and Oxford: Oxford University Press)

Guisinger, S E et al (1985) *Investment Incentives and Performance Requirements: Patterns of International Trade, Production and Investment* (New York: Praeger)

Gundersen, A (1992) 'Popular Justice in Mozambique: Between State Law and Folk Law' *Social & Legal Studies* 1 (2) 257-282

Gupta, U (1988) *Supreme Court and Civil Liberties* (Delhi: Mittal)

Habel, J (1991) *Cuba: The Revolution in Peril* (London: Verso)

Hadfield, G K (1990) 'Problematic Relations: Franchising and the Law of Incomplete Contracts' *Stanford Law Review* 42, 917-92

Haeri, S (1989) *The Law of Desire: Temporary Marriage in Iran* (London: I B Tauris)

Haeri, S (1990) 'Divorce in Contemporary Iran: A Male Prerogative in Self Will' in C Mallat and J Connors (eds) (1990) *q.v.*

Hale, M (1677) *The Primitive Origination of Mankind, Considered and Examined According to the Light of Nature* (London: W Godbid)

Hall, M (1988) 'The International Debt Crisis: Recent Developments', *Capital & Class* 35, 7-18

Hall, S et al (1977) *Policing the Crisis* (London: MacMillan)

Hanlon, J (1984) *Mozambique: the Revolution Under Fire* (London: Zed Press)

Hansen, P and V Aranda (1991) 'An Emerging International Framework for Transnational Corporations' *Fordham International Law Journal* 14, 881-891

Hansson, G (1983) *Social Clauses and International Trade: An Economic Analysis of Labour Standards in Trade Policy* (New York: Croom Helm)

Harding, S (ed) (1987) *Feminism and Methodology: Social Science Issues* (Bloomington: Indiana University Press)

Harrell-Bond, B & U Rijnsdorf (1977) 'The Emergence of Stranger-Permit Marriage and Other Forms of Conjugal Union in Rural Sierra-Leone' In S. Roberts (ed) (1977) *q.v.*

Harris, N (1986) *The End of the Third World: Newly Industrialised Countries and the Decline of an Ideology* (Harmondsworth: Penguin)

Hartman, J (ed) (1991) *Rethinking the Arusha Declaration* (Copenhagen: Centre for Development Research, Copenhagen)

Hay D (ed) (1975) *Albion's Fatal Tree* (Harmondsworth: Peregrine)

Hay, D (1975a) 'Property, Authority and the Criminal Law' in D Hay (ed) (1975) *q.v.*

Hay, D (1975b) 'Poaching and the Game Laws on Cannock Chase' in D Hay (ed) (1975) *q.v.*

Held, D et al (eds) (1983) *States and Societies* (Oxford: Martin Robertson)

Hellum, A (1990a) 'Legal Advice as a Research Method: The Case of Women's Law in Norway and Its Relevance for the Women and Law in Southern Africa Research Project' in WLSA (1990) *q.v.*

Hellum, A (1990b) 'Building Comparative North-South Perspectives of Women, Law and Development' in Hellum, A (ed) *Women, Law and Development. Report from a Seminar* (Oslo, Third World Seminar Series No 49)

Henderson, J W (1986) 'The New International Division of Labour and American Semiconductor Production in Southeast Asia' in C Dixon, D Drakikis-Smith and L Watts (eds) (1986) *q.v. Multinational Corporations and the Third World* (Sydney: Croom Helm)

Hettne, B (1988) *Europe, Dimension of Peace* (London: Zed Books)

Hettne, B (1990) *Development Theory and the Three Worlds* (Harlow: Longman)

Higgins, R (1982) 'The Taking of Property by the State: Recent Developments in International Law', *Receuil des Cours de l'Academie de Droit International* III 259-392

Higgott, R (1984) 'Export-Oriented Industrialisation, the New International Division of Labour and the Corporate State in the Third World: An Exploratory Essay on Linkages', *Australian Geographical Studies* 22, 58-71

Hill, D (1991) *Development Assistance and Human Rights: Principles, Criteria and Procedures* (London: Commonwealth Secretariat)

Himonga, C (1985) *Family Property Disputes: The Predicament of Women and Children in a Zambian Urban Community* PhD thesis, University of London

Himonga, C N, M Munachonga and A Chanda (1988) *Women Access to Agricultural Land in Zambia* A study carried out and prepared for the Department of Lands funded by CIDA cited in WLSA Zambia (1992) *q.v.*

Hirschon, R (ed) (1984) *Women and Property-Women as Property* (London: Croom Helm)

Hobbes T (1952) *Leviathan* (Chicago: Encyclopaedia Britannica)

Hobsbawm, E & T Ranger (eds) (1983) *The Invention of Tradition* (Cambridge: Cambridge University Press)

Hodgen, M T (1964) *Early Anthropology in the Sixteenth and Seventeenth Centuries* (Philadelphia: University of Pennsylvania Press)

Holleman, J F (1952) *Shona Customary Law, With Reference to Kinship, Marriage, the Family and the Estate* (Cape Town: Oxford University Press)

Holleman, J F (1979) 'Law and Anthropology: A Necessary Partnership for the Study of Legal Change in Plural Systems', *Journal of African Law* 23 (2) 117-130

Holloway, J, and S Picciotto (1977) 'Capital, Crisis and the State' *Capital & Class* 2, 76-101

Hooker, M B (1975) *Legal Pluralism: An Introduction to Colonial and Neo-Colonial Laws* (Oxford: Clarendon Press)

Horkheimer M and T W Adorno (1979) *Dialectic of Enlightenment* (London: Verso)

Horn, N (ed) (1980) *Legal Problems of Codes of Conduct for Multinational Enterprises* (Deventer: Kluwer)

Hu, H T C (1980) 'Compensation in Expropriations: a Preliminary Economic Analysis', *Virginia Journal of International Law* 20

Hume, D (1988) *A Treatise of Human Nature* (Oxford: Clarendon Press)

IDS (Institute of Development Studies) (1983) *Proceedings of the Symposium on Marxism* (University of Dar es Salaam: IDS)

ILO (1972) *Report on Freedom of Association of Workers' and Employers' Organisations and Their Role in Social and Economic Development in Asia* Labour Management Series No 41 (Geneva: ILO)

ILO/ARPLA (1982) *Developing Countries and International Labour Standards: Proceedings of the Regional Seminar on Practice and Procedures in Formulating Labour Standards* (Geneva: ILO)
ILO (1985) *Women Workers in Multinational Enterprises in Developing Countries* (Geneva: ILO)
ILO (1988) *Economic and Social Effects of Multinational Enterprises in Export Processing Zones* (Geneva: ILO)
ILO/UNCTC (1988) *Economic and Social Effects of Multinational Enterprises in Export Processing Zones* (Geneva: ILO)
Institute Of Race Relations (1978) *Police Against Black People* (London: Institute of Race Relations)
Isaacman, A and B Isaacman (1982) 'A Socialist Legal System in the Making: Mozambique' in R Abel (ed) (1982) *q.v.*
Jacobs, S and T Howard (1987) 'Women in Zimbabwe: Stated Policy and State Action' in H Afshar (ed) (1987) *q.v.*
Jagger, A (1988) *Feminist Politics and Human Nature* (Rowman and Littlefield)
Joerges, C (ed) (1992) *Franchising and the Law: Theoretical and Comparative Approaches in Europe and the United States* (Baden-Baden: Nomos)
Jokes, S (1990) 'Women's Work and Social Support for Child Care in the Third World' in J Leslie and M Paolisso (eds) (1990) *q.v.*
Jones, L (1990) 'Murder in Guatemala' *New Left Review* 182, 53
Joshi, K C (1988) 'Compensation Through Writs: Rudul Shah to Mehta', *Journal of Indian Law Institute* 30, 69
Kabeberi, J (1991) 'Hvor Kvinnerett er Propaganda' *Hefte for Kritisk Juss (Critical Legal Studies)* Oslo (2) 57-64
Kagarlitsky, B (1989) 'The Importance of Being Marxist' *New Left Review* 178, 29
Kagzi M C Jain (1987) *The Present Constitutional Issues and Views* (New Delhi: Metropolitan)
Kaletsky, A (1984) 'Seizing Assets Is Not So Easy' (*The Financial Times*, London, 25 June 1984)
Kaletsky, A (1985) *The Cost of Default* (New York: A Twentieth Century Fund Paper, Priority Press Publications)
Kanywanyi, J L (1989) 'The Struggle to Decolonise and Demystify University Education: Dar's 25 years Experience Focused on Faculty of Law (October 1961-October 1986)' *Eastern Africa Law Review* 16 (1) 1-70
Kapstein, E B (1989) 'Resolving the Regulators' Dilemma of International Coordination of Banking Regulations', *International Organisation* 43, 323-47
Kazembe, J (1990) 'Maintenance Law Research in Zimbabwe: Methodological Issues' in A Armstrong and J Stewart (eds) (1990) *q.v.*

Kelley, D R (1984) *History, Law and the Human Sciences: Medieval and Renaissance Perspectives* (London: Variorum Reprints)

Khan R (1988) 'The Right of a State to Choose Its Social and Economic System: Some Reflections on the Interface of International and National Legal Orders' in P de Waart, P Peters and E Denters (eds) (1988) *q.v.*

Kindleberger, C P (1980) *A GATT for Foreign Investment; Further Reflections* (New York: Carnegie Center for Transnational Studies)

Kitching, G (ed) (1989) *Development and Underdevelopment in Historical Perspective: Populism, Nationalism and Industrialization* 2nd edn (London: Routledge)

Krugman, P and M Obstfeld (1991) *International Economics: Theory and Policy* 2nd edn (New York: Harper Collins)

Kuan, H (1984) New Departures in China's Constitution' *Studies in Comparative Communism* 17, 53-68

Kuan, H (1983) 'Socialist Constitutions in Comparative Perspective' *Chinese Law and Government* Summer-Fall 1983, 12-44

Lafitau, J F (1724) *Moeurs des Sauvages Ameriquains Comparées aux Moeurs des Prémiers Temps* (Paris: Saugrain l'ainé et Charles Estienne Hochereu)

Lange, D and G Born (1987) *The Extraterritorial Application of National Laws* (Paris: International Chamber of Commerce)

Leslie, J and M Paolisso (eds) (1990) *Women, Work and Child Welfare in the Third World* (Boulder: Westview)

Lever, A (1988) 'Capital, Gender and Skill: Women Homeworkers in Rural Spain' *Feminist Review* 30

Lieberman, D (1989) *The Province of Legislation Determined: Legal Theory in Eighteenth-century Britain* (Cambridge: Cambridge University Press)

Lillich, R B and B H Weston (1975) *International Claims: Their Settlement by Lump-Sum Agreements* (Charlottesville: University Press of Virginia)

Lillich, R B, and B H Weston (1988) 'Lump-Sum Agreements: Their Continuing Contribution to the Law of International Claims' *American Journal of International Law* 82

Lim, L (1978) *Women Workers in Multinational Corporations: The Case of the Electronics Industry in Malaysia and Singapore* Michigan Occasional Papers No IX, University of Michigan

Lim, L (1983) 'Capitalism, Imperialism and Patriarchy: The Dilemma of Third World Women Workers in Multinational Factories' in J Nash and M Fernandez-Kelly (eds) (1983) *q.v.*

Lindert, P H (1989) 'Response to Debt Crisis: What is Different About the 1980s?' in B Eichengreen and P Lindert (eds) (1989) *q.v.*

Lindert, P H and P J Morton (1989) 'How Sovereign Debt Has Worked' in J Sachs (ed) (1989) *q.v.*
Locke, J (1960) 'The Second Treatise of Government', in *Two Treatises of Government* (New York, Cambridge University Press)
Long, E (1774) *The History of Jamaica*, 3 vols (London: T Lowndes)
Lovett, M (1989) 'Gender Relations, Class Formation and the Colonial State in Africa' in J L Parpart and K Staudt (eds) (1989) *q.v.* 23
Lugakingira, K S K (1990) 'Personal Liberty and Judicial Attitude: The Tanzanian Case' *Eastern Africa Law Review* 17 (1) 107-33
Mabirizi, D (1986) 'Some Aspects of Makerere's Education in Development' *Third World Legal Studies* 63-78
Maboreke, M (1987) *The Legal Status of Women in Zimbabwe: The Laws Relating to Violence Against Women and Child Custody as Illustrations* MPhil thesis, Department of Law, University of Zimbabwe
Maboreke, M (1988) 'Women under Zimbabwean Law' *The Zimbabwe Law Review* 6, 64.
Maboreke, M (1990) 'Introducing Women's Law' in A Armstrong and J Stewart (eds) (1990) *q.v.*
MacCormack, C P and M Strathern (eds) (1980) *Nature, Culture and Gender* (Cambridge: Cambridge University Press)
MacCormick, N and Z Bankowski (eds) (1989) *Enlightenment, Rights and Revolution* (Aberdeen: Aberdeen University Press)
MacPherson, C B (1962) *The Political Theory of Possessive Individualism* (Oxford: Oxford University Press)
Maex, R (1983) *Employment and Multinationals in Asian Export Processing Zones* Multinational Enterprises Working Paper No 26 (Geneva: ILO)
Mahalu, C R (1986) 'Three Decades of Law in Context Approach' in I G Shivji (ed) (1986a) *q.v.*
Mahjoub, A (1990) *Adjustment or De-linking?: The African Experience* (London: Zed Books)
Mallat C and J Connors (eds) (1990) *Muslim Family Law* (London: Graham and Trotman)
Mann, F A (1981) 'British Treaties for the Promotion and Protection of Foreign Investment' *British Yearbook of International Law* 52, 241-54
Marshall, P (1987) *Cuba Libre* (London: Unwin Hyman)
Marx, K (1968) 'Critique of the Gotha Programme' in *Selected Works in One Volume* (London: Lawrence and Wishart)
Massell, G (1968) 'Law as an Instrument of Change in a Traditional Milieu' *Law and Society Review* 2, 82
Massey, I M (1985) *Administrative Law* 2nd edn (Lucknow, Eastern Book Co)

May, J (1983) *Zimbabwean Women in Customary and Colonial Law* (Gweru: Mambo Press)

May, J (1987) *Changing People Changing Laws* (Gweru: Mambo Press)

Mayo, E (1992) 'A Crisis of Dollars and Sense' (*The Guardian*, London, 24 August 1992)

Mbilinyi, M (1988) 'Runaway Wives in Colonial Tanganyika' *International Journal of Sociology of Law* 16, 1

Mbunda, L X (1980) 'Limitation Clauses and the Bill of Rights in Tanzania' *Lesotho Law Review* 4, 153-70

McBarnet, D (1981) *Conviction* (London: MacMillan)

McBarnet, D (1984) 'Law and Capital: The Role of Legal Form and Legal Actors' *International Journal of the Sociology of Law* 3, 231-38

McConville, M and C Mirsky (1988) 'The State, the Legal Profession and the Defence of the Poor' *Journal of Law and Society* 15, 342

McLane, J (1985) 'Bengal's Bandits, Police and Landlords after the Permanent Settlement' in A Yang (ed) (1985) *q.v.*

McLennan, J F (1986) *Macmillan Dictionary of Anthropology* (Hong Kong: Macmillan Press)

Meek, R L (1976) *Social Science and the Ignoble Savage* (Cambridge: Cambridge University Press)

Mehdi, R (1990) 'The Offence of Rape in the Islamic Law of Pakistan' *International Journal of Sociology of Law* 18, 19

Merry, S (1988) 'Legal Pluralism' *Law & Society Review* 22 (5) 869

Messick B (1992) *The Calligraphic State: Textual Domination and History in a Muslim Society* (Berkeley: University of California Press)

Mies, M (1986) *Patriarchy and Accumulation on a World Scale: Women in the International Division of Labour* (London: Zed Books)

Mies, M (1982) *The Lace Makers of Narsapur: Indian Housewives Produce for the World Market* (London: Zed Books)

Miliband, R (1969) *The State in Capitalist Society* (London: Quartet Books)

Milsom, S F C (1981) 'The Nature of Blackstone's Achievement' *Oxford Journal of Legal Studies* 1 (1) 1-12

Mitchell, T (1988) *Colonising Egypt* (Cambridge: Cambridge University Press)

Mohanty, C (1988) 'Under Western Eyes: Feminist Scholarship and Colonial Discourses' *Feminist Review* 30, 61-88

Mohanty, C, A Russo and L Torres (eds) (1991) *Third World Women and the Politics of Feminism* (Bloomington: Indiana University Press)

Molokomme, A (1991) *Children of the Fence: Maintenance of Extra-marital Children Under Law and Practice in Botswana* (Leiden: African Studies Centre Research Reports 1991/46)

Montaigne, M (1978) 'Des Cannibales' in *Essais* chapitre XXXI (Paris: Presses Universitaires de France)

Montesquieu, Baron de (1949) *The Spirit of the Laws* (New York: Hafner Press)

Moore, S F (1973) 'Law and Social Change: The Semi-Autonomous Social Field as an Appropriate Subject of Study' *Law and Society Review* 7, 719-46

Moore, S F (1986) *Social Facts and Fabrications: 'Customary law' on Kilimanjaro 1880-1980* (Cambridge: Cambridge University Press)

Morris, H & J Read (1972) *Indirect Rule and the Search for Justice: Essays on East African Legal History* (Oxford: Clarendon Press)

Morris, H (1979) 'The Development of Statutory Marriage Law in 20th Century British Colonial Africa' *Journal of African Law* 23 (1) 37-64.

Mridul, M (1986) *Public Interest Litigation: A Profile* (Jaipur: Bharat Law House)

Mueller, S (1981) 'The Historical Origins of Tanzania's Ruling Class' *Canadian Journal of African Studies* 15, 459

Munck, R (1988) *The New International Labour Studies: An Introduction* (London: Zed Books)

Mwaikusa, J T (1990) 'Government Powers and Human Rights in Africa: Some Observations from the Tanzanian Experience' *Lesotho Law Journal* 6 (1) 75-105

Mwaikusa, J T (1991) 'Genesis of the Bill of Rights in Tanzania' *RAIDC (Journal of the African Society of International and Comparative Law* 3, 680-98

Naffine, N (1990) *Law and the Sexes* (Sydney: Allen & Unwin)

Nash, J and M Fernandez-Kelly (eds) (1983) *Women, Men and the International Division of Labour* (Albany: State University of New York Press)

National Lawyers Guild (1988) 'Criminal Justice in Cuba' (New York: NLG)

Ncube, W (1986) *The Matrimonial Rights of Women During and After Marriage in Zimbabwe: A Study of Property Relations, Domestic Labour and Power Relations Within the Family* (MPhil thesis, Department of Law, University of Zimbabwe)

Ncube, W (1989) *Family Law in Zimbabwe* (Harare: Legal Resources Foundation)

Neumann, F (1986) *The Rule of Law: Political Theory and the Legal System in Modern Society* (Leamington Spa: Berg)

Nigram, A (1990) Disciplining and Policing the 'Criminals by Birth' *Indian Economic and Social History Review* 131

Nijjar, G S (1991) 'Public Interest Law: The Third World Experience' *NELA/LAWASIA Conference on Environmental Law* Bangkok, August 1991

Norrie, A (1990) 'Locating the Socialist Rechtsstaat: Underdevelopment and Criminal Justice in the Soviet Union' *International Journal of Sociology of Law* 18, 343

Norrie, A (1991) *Law, Ideology and Punishment* (Dordrecht: Kluwer)

Norrie, A (1992) 'Subjectivism, Objectivism and the Limits of Criminal Recklessness' *Oxford Journal of Legal Studies* 12, 45

Norrie, A (1993) *Crime, Reason and History* (London: Weidenfeld and Nicolson)

Norrie, A and S Adelman (1989) 'Consensual Authoritarianism' and Criminal Justice in Thatcher's Britain' *Journal of Law and Society* 16, 112

Norton, P M (1991) 'A Law of the Future or a Law of the Past' *American Journal of International Law* 85 (3) 474-505

Nyalali Commission (1991) (3 Vols) *Jamhuri ya Muungano wa Tanzania, Tume ya Rais ya Mfumo wa Chama Kimoja au Vyama Vingi vya Siasa* (Tanzania: Gov't Printer)

Nyongo, P A (1988) (ed) *Popular Struggles in Africa* (London: Zed Books)

O'Donnell, G (1980), 'Forms of State and Socio-Economic Change', *International Social Science Journal* XXXII, 4

ODI (1990) *Briefing Paper on Debt* April 1990 (London: Overseas Development Institute, London)

OECD (1987) *Minimizing Conflicting Requirements* (Paris: OECD)

OEF (1990) *Women, Law and Development in Africa* (WILDAF: Origins and Issues, Series on Women, Law and Development: Issues and Strategies for Change No 4 - Africa)

Oloka-Onyango, J (1989) 'Law, 'Grassroots Democracy' and the National Resistance Movement in Uganda' *International Journal of Sociology of Law* 17, 465

Ong, A (1983) 'Global Factories and Malay Peasants in Peninsular Malaysia' in J Nash and M Fernandez-Kelly (eds) (1983) *q.v.*

Owori, M (1982) *The Hegemonic Function of Ideology and Law in the Postcolonial State: Tanzania* LL M dissertation, University of Dar es Salaam

Paley, W (1828) *Moral and Political Philosophy in The Works of William Paley D.D.* Vol I (London: J F Dove)

Paliwala, A (1982) 'Law and Order in the Village: Papua New Guinea's Village Courts' in C Sumner (1982) *q.v.*

Pande, B (1986) 'Vagrancy, Beggary and Status Crimes in India' in N Saraf, *Social Policy, Law and Protection of the Weaker Sections of Society* (Delhi: Eastern Books)

Parpart, J L (1988) 'Sexuality and Power on the Zambian Copperbelt 1926-1964' in S Stichter and J Parpart (eds) (1988) *q.v.*

Parpart, J and K Staudt (eds) (1989) *Women and the State in Africa* (London & Boulder: Lynne Rienner)

Pashukanis, E (1978) *General Theory of Law and Marxism* (London: Ink Links)

Pateman, C (1988) *The Social Contract* (Cambridge: Polity Press)

Pearce D, E Barbier and A Markandya (1990) *Sustainable Development: Economics and Environment in the Third World* (London: Earthscan Publications)

Pecchioli, C M (1983) *The Internationalisation of Banking The Policy Issues* (Paris: OECD)

Pecchioli, R M (1987) *Prudential Supervision in Banking* (Paris: OECD)

Peet, R (1991) *Global Capitalism: Theories of Social Development* (London: Routledge)

Peter, C M (1983) 'The Economic Sabotage (Special Provisions) Act, 1983: Some Notes', Lecture delivered at the Tanzania School of Journalism, Kurasini, Dar es Salaam on 4 August 1983 (mimeo)

Peter, C M (1990a) *Human Rights in Africa: A Comparative Study of the African Charter and the New Tanzanian Bill of Rights* (Connecticut: Greenwood Press)

Peter, C M (1990b) *Promotion and Protection of Foreign Investments in Tanzania A Comment on the New Foreign Investment Code* (Dar es Salaam: Friedrich Ebert Stiftung)

Peter, C M (1991) 'Five Years of Bill of Rights in Tanzania: Drawing a Balance-Sheet', *Conference on Constitutionalism and Human Rights*, Arusha 2-5 April, 1991 (mimeo)

Peters P (1988) 'Investment Risk and Trust: The Role of International Law' in P de Waart, P Peters and E Denters (eds) (1988) *q.v.*

Petras J and D Engbarth (1988) 'Third World Industrialization and Trade Union Struggles' in R Southall (ed) (1988) *q.v.*

Picciotto, S (1984) 'Political Economy and International Law' in S Strange (ed) (1984) *q.v.*

Picciotto, S (1986) 'Law, Life and Politics' in I G Shivji (ed) (1986a) *q.v.*

Picciotto, S (1989) 'Slicing a Shadow: Business Taxation in an International Framework' in L Hancher and M Moran (eds) *Capitalism, Culture and Economic Regulation* (Oxford: Clarendon Press)

Picciotto, S (1991) 'The Internationalisation of the State' *Capital & Class* 43, 43-63

Picciotto, S (1992) *International Business Taxation* (London: Weidenfeld & Nicolson)

Pieterse, J (1990) *Empire and Emancipation* (London: Pluto)

Pietila, H and J Vickers (1990) *Making Women Matter: The Role of the United Nations* (London: Zed Books)

A Podgerecki, C Whelan, D Khosla (eds) (1985) *Legal Systems and Social Systems* (London: Croom Helm)

Poggi, G (1978) *The Development of the Modern State* (Stanford: Stanford University Press)

Poulantzas, N (1973) *Political Power and Social Classes* (London: New Left Books)

Poulter, S (1976) *Family Law and Litigation in Basotho Society* (Oxford: Clarendon Press)

Preston, J (1989) 'The Trial that Shook Cuba', *New York Review of Books* (7 December 1989)

Pursey S (1980) 'The Trade Union View on the Implementation of Codes of Conduct' in N Horn (ed) (1980) *q.v.*

Radzinowicz, L (1948) *A History of the English Criminal Law* Vol 1 (London: Stevens)

Radzinowicz, L and R Hood (1986) *A History of the English Criminal Law* Vol 5 (London: Stevens)

Raffer, K (1989) 'International Debts: A Crisis for Whom?' in H W Singer and S Sharma (eds) (1989) *q.v.*

Raghavan, C (1990) *Recolonization: GATT, the Uruguay Round and the Third World* (London: Zed Books, Third World Network)

Ranger, T (1983) 'The Invention of Traditionalism in Colonial Africa' in E Hobsbawm & T Ranger (eds) (1983) *q.v.*

Rao, M (1991) 'Tanners Try to Skin Through Law' *Sunday Mail* October 6 1991 reproduced in *Green File* 46, 87

Rathberger, E (1989) 'WID, WAD, GAD' *Pearsonnotes* (Summer) 4

Rawls, J (1973) *A Theory of Justice* (Oxford: Oxford University Press)

Read, J (1979) 'Studies in the Making of Colonial Laws: An Introduction' *Journal of African Law* 23 (1) 1-9.

Redclift, M (1987) *Sustainable Development: Exploring the Contradictions* (London: Methuen)

Reddy, C J (1983) 'Inaugural Address to Seminar on "Socialism, Constitution and the Country Today"' *AIR* 1983 Jour 33

Repetto, R (1986) *World Enough and Time* (New Haven: Yale University Press)

Reynolds, P (1991) *Dance Civet Cat: Child Labour in the Zambezi Valley* (London: Zed Books)

Riley, P (1986) *The General Will Before Rousseau: The Transformation of the Divine into the Civic* (Princeton: Princeton University Press)

Roberts, S ed (1977) *Law and the Family in Africa* (The Hague Mouton)

Rosa K (1991) 'Working Conditions in EPZs Create the Need for Women Workers to Organise Themselves' *International Workshp on Women Organising in the Process of Industrialisation*, Institute of Social Studies, The Hague, April 15-26, 1991 (mimeo)

Rostow, W (1960) *The Stages of Economic Growth* (Cambridge: Cambridge University Press)
Roxborough, I (1979) *Theories of Underdevelopment* (Basingstoke: MacMillan)
Rwezaura, B (1985) *Traditional Family Law and Social Change in Tanzania* (Baden-Baden: Institut fur Internationale Angelengenheiten der Universitat Hamburg)
Rwezaura, B & U Wanitzek (1988) 'Family Law Reform in Tanzania: A Socio-legal Report' *International Journal of Law and the Family* 2, 1-26.
Rwezaura, B (1990) 'Researching on the Law of the Family in Tanzania: Some Reflections on Method, Theory and the Limits of Law as a Tool for Social Change' in A Armstrong and J Stewart (eds) (1990) *q.v.*
Sachs, A (1985) 'The Two Dimensions of Socialist Legality' *International Journal of Sociology of Law* 13, 133
Sachs, A and G Welch (1990) *Liberating the Law* (London: Zed Press)
Sachs, J (ed) (1989) 'Introduction' to *Developing Country Debt and the World Economy* (Chicago: University of Chicago Press)
Sack, A H (1927) *Les Effets des Transformations des États sur leur Dettes Publiques et Autres Obligations Financièrs* (Paris: Recueil Sirey)
Safa, H (1981) 'Runaway Shops and Female Employment: The Search for Cheap Labour' *Signs: Journal of Women in Culture and Society* 7 (2) 418-33
Sahlins, M (1976) *Culture and Practical Reason* (Chicago: University of Chicago Press)
Saith, A (ed) (1988) *The Re-Emergence of the Chinese Peasantry* (London: Croom Helm)
Salacuse (1990) 'BIT by BIT: The Growth of Bilateral Investment Treaties and Their Impact on Foreign Investment in Developing Countries' *International Lawyer* 24
Salas, L (1979) *Social Control and Deviance in Cuba* (New York: Praegar)
Salas, L (1985) 'The Judicial System in Post Revolutionary Process in A Podgerecki, C Whelan, D Khosla (eds) (1985) *q.v.*
Sangari, K and S Vaid (eds) (1990) *Recasting Women: Essays in Indian Colonial History* (Rutgers University Press)
Sanyee, G (ed) (1989) *Narrowing the Gender Gap* (Basingstoke: MacMillan)
Saul, J (1974) 'The State in Post-Colonial Societies: Tanzania' in R Miliband and J Saville, *The Socialist Register 1974* in Y Ghai, R Luckham and F Snyder (eds) (1987) *q.v.*
Saxena, D R (1986) *Ombudsman (Lokpal): Redress of Citizens' Grievances in India* (New Delhi: Deep & Deep)
Schachter, O (1984) 'Compensation for Expropriation' *American Journal of International Law* 78, 121-30

Schregle, J (1982) *Negotiating Development: Labour Relations in Southern Asia* (Geneva: ILO)

Schuler, M (1986) *Empowerment and the Law: Strategies of Third World Women* (Washington D C: OEF International)

Scott, J (1986) *Capitalist Property and Financial Power: A Comparative Study of Britain, the US, and Japan* (Sussex: Wheatsheaf)

Seidman, R B (1972) 'Law and Development: A General Model' *Law and Society Review* 1972 325

Semmel, B (1960) *Imperialism and Social Reform* (London: Allen and Unwin)

Shafer, M (1983) 'Capturing the Mineral Multinationals: Advantage or Disadvantage?' *International Organisation* 37 (1) 93-120

Shaidi, L (1989) 'Crime, Justice and Politics in Contemporary Tanzania: State Power in an Underdeveloped Social Formation' *International Journal of Sociology of Law* 17, 247

Sheriff, A (1990) 'Incentive Schemes, Scopo and the Need for a Living Wage' *UDASA Newsletter* No 10, February 1990 (Dar es Salaam)

Shewring, W (1980) *Homer: The Odyssey* (Oxford: Oxford University Press)

Shils, E (1991) 'The Virtue of Civil Society', *Government and Opposition* 26 (1) 3-20

Shivji, I G (1972) 'From Analysis of Form to the Exposition of Substance: The Tasks of a Lawyer-Intellectual' *Eastern Africa Law Review* 5, 1-7

Shivji, I (1982) 'Semi-Proletarian Labour and the Use of Penal Sanctions in the Labour Law of Colonial Tanganyika (1920-1938)' in C Sumner (ed) (1982) *q.v.*

Shivji, I G (ed) (1986a) *Limits of Legal Radicalism: Reflections on Teaching Law at the University of Dar es Salaam* (Dar es Salaam: Faculty of Law, University of Dar es Salaam)

Shivji, I G (1986b) *Law, State & the Working Class in Tanzania* (London: James Currey)

Shivji, I G (1989a) 'Equality, Rights and Authoritarianism in Africa' in N MacCormick and Z Bankowski (eds) (1989) *q.v.*

Shivji, I G (1989b) *The Concept of Human Rights in Africa* (Dakar: CODESRIA)

Shivji, I G (1990a) 'Tanzania: The Debate on De-linking' in Mahjoub, A (ed) (1990) *q.v.*

Shivji, I G (1990b) *Tanzania: The Legal Foundations of the Union* (Dar es Salaam: Dar es Salaam University Press)

Shivji, I G (1990c) 'The Politics of Liberalisation in Tanzania: Notes on the Crisis of Ideological Hegemony' in H Campbell and H Stein (eds) (1991) *q.v.*

Shivji, I G (1990d) 'State and Constitutionalism in Africa: A New Democratic Perspective' *International Journal of the Sociology of Law* 18, 381-408

Shivji, I G (1990e) *State Coercion and Freedom in Tanzania* (Lesotho: ISAS)

Shivji, I G (1991a) 'Law, Democracy and the Rights-struggle: Preliminary Reflections on Experiences at the University of Dar es Salaam' *UDASA Forum*, No 11, June 1991 (Dar es Salaam)

Shivji, I G (1991b) 'Contradictory Developments in the Teaching and Practice of Human Rights in Tanzania' *Journal of African Law* 35 (1-2) 116-27

Shivji, I G (1991c) 'The Jurisprudence of the Dar es Salaam Declaration on Academic Freedom' *Journal of African Law* 35 (1-2) 128-41

Shivji, I G (1991d) (ed) *State and Constitutionalism: An African Debate on Democracy* (Harare: SAPES)

Shivji, I G (1991e) 'Minimum Legal Conditions for a Popular Debate on Democracy' *Eastern Africa Law Review* 17 (2) 134-82

Shivji, I G (1991f) 'The Democracy Debate in Africa: Tanzania', *Review of African Political Economy* 50, 79-91

Shivji, I G (1992a) 'Shivji on Nyalali Report', *Family Mirror*, Dar es Salaam, 1 June 1992 *et seq*

Shivji, I G (1992b) 'Fiasco at Law: Comments on Bills for the Eighth Constitutional Amendment 1992 and the Political Parties Act 1992' *Tangyanika Law Society Seminar on Democracy and the Rule of Law*, Dar es Salaam, 22-3 April 1992 (mimeo)

Silkin, T 1989 'Women Can Only Be Free when the Power of Kin Groups is Smashed: New Marriage Laws and Social Change in the Liberated Zones of Eritrea' *International Journal of Sociology of Law* 17 (2) 147

Silver, A (1967) 'The Demand for Order in Civil Society' in D Bordua (ed) (1967) *q.v.*

Singer, H W and S Sharma (eds) (1989) *Economic Development and World Debt* (London: MacMillan)

Singh, P (1985 et seq) 'Public Interest Litigation' *Annual Survey of Indian Law* (Delhi: Indian Law Institute)

Sivanandan, A (1982) *A Different Hunger* (London: Pluto)

Smart, C (1984) *The Ties That Bind* (London: Routledge)

Smart, C & S Sevenhuijsen eds (1987) *Child Custody and the Politics of Gender* (London: Routledge)

Smart, C (1989) *Feminism and the Power of Law* (London: Routledge)

Smart, C (1991a) 'Feminist Jurisprudence' in P Fitzpatrick (ed) *q.v.*

Smart, C (1991b) 'The Woman of Legal Discourse', unpublished inaugural lecture, University of Utrecht

Smith, A (1978) *Lectures on Jurisprudence* (Oxford: Clarendon Press)

Snowden, P N (1985) *Emerging Risk in International Banking: Origins of Financial Vulnerability in the 1980s* (London: Allen & Unwin)

Snyder, F G (1980) 'Law and Development in the Light of Dependency Theory' *Law & Society Review* 14, 723

Snyder, F G (1981) 'Capitalism and Legal Change: An African Transformation' (New York: Academic Press)

Snyder, F G (1981a) 'Colonialism and Legal Form: The Creation of 'Customary Law' in Senegal' *Journal of Legal Pluralism* 19, 49

Snyder, F and D Hay (eds) (1987) *Labour, Law and Crime* (Oxford: Oxford University Press)

Sokoine, E (1983) 'The Role of the Intellectual in Socialist Transformation' *TAAMULI* (13) 1-8

Soliman, H D (1990) 'The Practice, Problems and Prospects of Alternative Lawyering in the Philippines' *Alternative Law Forum* VI (2) 1-7

Southall, R (ed) (1988) *Trade Unions and the New Industrialization of the Third World* (London: Zed Books)

Spear, P (1965) *A History of India* Vol 2 (Harmondsworth: Penguin)

Spitzer, S (1981) 'The Dialectics of Formal and Informal Control' in R Abel (1981) *q.v.*

Standing, G (1989) 'Global Feminism through Flexible Labor' *World Development* 17 (7) 1077-1095

Stansbury, P R (1990) 'Planning against Expropriation' *International Lawyer* 24

Staudt, K (1986) 'Women, Development and the State: On the Theoretical Impulse' *Development and Change* 17, 325-333

Stein, P (1980) *Legal Evolution: The Story of an Idea* (Cambridge: Cambridge University Press)

Stichter, S and J Parpart (eds) (1988) *Patriarchy and Class: African Women in the Home and the Workforce* (Boulder & London: Westview)

Steiner, H J (1991) *Diverse Partners: Non-Governmental Organizations in the Human Rights Movement* (Cambridge: Harvard Law School & Human Rights Internet)

Stokes, E (1959) *The English Utilitarians and India* (Oxford: Oxford University Press)

Stolen, K A and M Vaa (eds) (1991) *Gender and Change in Developing Countries* (Oslo: Norwegian University Press)

Stolen, K A (1991) 'Chastity, Sexuality and Gender Perceptions in Rural Argentina' in K A Stolen and M Vaa (eds) (1991) *q.v.*

Storch, R (1975) 'The Plague of Blue Locusts' *International Review of Social History* 61

Strange, S (ed) (1984) *Paths to International Political Economy* (London: Allen & Unwin)

Strathern, M (1985) 'Discovering "Social Control"' *Journal of Law and Society* 12 (2) 111-134

Strauss, L and J Cropsey (1972) *History of Political Philosophy*, 2nd edn (Chicago: Rand McNally)

Stubbs, J (1989) *Cuba: The Test of Time* (London: LAB)

Sturgess, G and P Chubb (eds) (1988) *Judging the World: Law and Politics in the World's Leading Courts* (London: Butterworths)

Sumner, C (ed) (1982) *Crime, Justice and Underdevelopment* (London: Heinemann)

Sugarman, D (ed) (1983) *Legality, Ideology and the State* (London: Academic Press)

Suryawanshi, N (1987) 'Social Action Litigation under s 91 Civil Procedure Code' *The Lawyers* January 1987 20

Sweet, L (1982) 'Inventing Crime: British Colonial Land Policy in Tanganyika' in C Sumner (1982) *q.v.*

Tandon, Y (1982) *Debate on Class, State and Imperialism* (Dar es Salaam: Tanzania Publishing House)

Tegambwage, N (1990) *Who Tells the Truth in Tanzania?* (Dar es Salaam: Tausi)

Tenga, R W (1986) 'The Historical and Socio-economic Approaches in Learning the Law: Dar es Salaam and 3rd World Perspectives in Jurisprudence' in I G Shivji (ed) (1986a) *q.v.*

Thomas, C Y (1984) *The Rise of the Authoritarian State in Peripheral Societies* (New York: Monthly Review)

Thompson, E P (1975) *Whigs and Hunters: The Origin of the Black Act* (Harmondsworth: Penguin)

Thompson, E P (1987) 'Capitalism and the Rule of Law' in Y Ghai, R Luckham and F Snyder(eds) (1987) *q.v.*

Todaro, M P (1989) *Economic Development in the Third World* 4th edn (New York: Longman)

Triggs, G (1988) 'The Rights of "Peoples" and Individual Rights: Conflict or Harmony?' in J Crawford (ed) (1988) *q.v.*

Trubek, D and M Galanter (1974) 'Scholars in Self-Estrangement: Some Reflections on the Crisis in Law and Development Studies in the United States', *Law and Society Review* 1974 (4) 1062-1102

Tsanga, A (1990) 'Action Research in Zimbabwe: Two Case Studies' in WLSA (1990) *q.v.*

Twining, W (1963) 'The Restatement of African Customary Law: A Comment' *Journal of Modern African Studies* 1, 221-8

UNCTAD (1990a) *Draft International Code of Conduct on the Transfer of Technology* (E/1990/94) (United Nations Conference on Trade and Development)

UNCTAD (1990b) *Technology, Trade Policy and the Uruguay Round* (UNCTAD/ITP/23) (United Nations Conference on Trade and Development)

UNCTC (1988) *Bilateral Investment Treaties* (ST/CTC/65) (United Nations Center on Transnational Corporations)

UNCTC (1988a) *Bilateral Investment Treaties* (ST/CTC/65) (United Nations Center on Transnational Corporations)

UNCTC (1988b) *Transnational Corporations in World Development: Trends and Prospects* (ST/CTC/89) (United Nations Center on Transnational Corporations)

UNDP (1990) *Human Development Report 1990* (Oxford: Oxford University Press)

UNGA (1980) *UGA UNCTAD RBP Code: Set of Mutually Agreed Equitable Principles and Rules for the Control of Restrictive Business Practices*

UNICEF (1986) *The State of the World's Children* (New York: UNICEF)

UNICEF (1990) *Development Goals and Strategies for Children in the 1990's* (New York: UNICEF)

UNIDO (1980) Export Processing Zones in Developing Countries, *UNIDO Working Paper on Structural Changes* No 19 (Vienna: UNIDO)

Unterhalter,E (1987) *Forced Removal* (London: IDAF)

Urdang, S (1979) *Fighting Two Colonialisms: Women in Guinea-Bissau* (New York: Monthly Review)

Usman, H (1989) *The Consequences of Family Breakdown in Post-Independence Nigeria: A Case Study of Borno State.* (PhD Thesis: Warwick University).

Van Der Plas, A (1983) *Revolution and Criminal Justice: The Cuban Experiment 1959-1983* (Dordrecht: Foris)

Van Doren, J (1989) Death African Style: The Case of S.M. Otieno. *American Journal of Comparative Law* 35, 329-50

Van Onselen, C (1976) *Chibaro* (London: Pluto)

Wachtel, H (1986) *The Money Mandarins: The Making of a Supranational Economic Order* (New York: Pantheon)

Wamba-dia-Wamba, E (1990) 'It is Not the Number of Parties: People's Agitation for Democracy is a Search for a New Historical Mode of Politics in Africa' *History Seminar*, 12 April 1990, University of Dar es Salaam (mimeo)

Wamba-dia-Wamba, E (1991) 'Some Remarks on Culture, Development and Revolution in Africa' *Journal of Historical Sociology* 4 (3) 249-55

Wangel, A (1988) 'The ILO and Protection of Trade Union Rights: The Electronics Industry in Malaysia' in Southall, R (ed) (1988) *q.v.*

Weinrich, A K H (1982) *African Marriage in Zimbabwe* (Gweru: Mambo Press)

References

Weiss, E B (1989) *In Fairness to Future Generations: International Law, Common Patrimony and Intergenerational Equity* (Tokyo: UN University)

Weitzman, L and M Maclean (1992) *Economic Consequences and Divorce: The International Perspective*, (Oxford: Clarendon)

Welch, G H, F Dagnino and A Sachs (1987) 'Transforming Family Law: New Directions in Mozambique' in A Armstrong and W Ncube (eds) (1987) *q. v.*

Weston, A (1981) 'Women and Handicraft Productions' in H Afshar (ed) (1987) *q.v.*

Weston, B H, R A Falk and A D'Amato (1990) *International Law and World Order* 2nd edn (West Publishing, St Paul)

White H (1978) *Tropics of Discourse: Essays in Cultural Criticism* (Baltimore: John Hopkins)

White, G (1983) *Revolutionary Socialist Development in the Third World* (Brighton: Harvester)

White, G (1988) 'Riding the Tiger' in A Saith (ed) (1988) *q.v.*

White, L 1983 'A Colonial State and the African Petit-Bourgeoisie: Prostitution, Property and Class Struggle in Nairobi' in F Cooper (ed) (1983) *q.v.*

White, L (1987) 'Vice, and Vagrants: Prostitution, Housing and Casual Labour in Nairobi in the mid 1930s' in F Snyder and D Hay (eds) (1987) *q.v.*

WHO (1990) *The International Code of Marketing Breast-Milk Substitutes: Synthesis of Reports on Action Taken 1981-1990* (WHO/MCH/NUT/901) (Rome: World Health Organisation)

Williams, D (1981) 'The Authoritarianism of African Legal Orders' *Contemporary Crises* 5, 247

Williams, D (1982) 'State Coercion Against Peasant Farmers: The Tanzanian Case' *Journal of Legal Pluralism* 20, 95

Williamson, J (1988) 'The Logic of Economic Organisation' *Journal of Law, Economics and Organisation* 4, 65

WLSA (1990) *Perspectives on Research Methodology* (Harare: WLSA Working Paper No 2)

WLSA Botswana (1992) *Maintenance in Botswana: Women and Law in Southern Africa Research Project Report* (Harare: WLSA)

WLSA Lesotho (1992) *Maintenance in Lesotho: Women and Law in Southern Africa Research Project Report* (Harare: WLSA)

WLSA Mozambique (1991) *Maintenance in Mozambique: Women and Law in Southern Africa Research Project Report* (Harare: WLSA)

WLSA Zambia (1992) *Maintenance in Zambia: Women and Law in Southern Africa Research Project Report* (Harare: WLSA)

WLSA Zimbabwe (1992) *Maintenance in Zimbabwe: Women and Law in Southern Africa Research Project Report* (Harare: WLSA)

Wong, Y L (1983) *Ghettoisation of Women Workers in the Electronics Industry*, M Phil Dissertation, Institute of Development Studies, University of Sussex

Woodman, G (1985) 'Customary Law, State Courts and the Notion of Institutionalisation of Norms in Ghana and Nigeria' in *People's Law and State Law: The Bellagio Papers* (Dordrecht: Foris)

Woodman, G (1988) 'The Decline of Folk-law Social Security in Africa' in F von Benda-Beckman et al (eds) (1988) *Between Kinship and the State: Social Security Law in Developing Countries* (Dordrecht: Foris)

World Bank (1985) *World Development Report* (Washington DC: World Bank)

World Bank (1980) *World Development Report 1980* (Washington DC: World Bank)

World Bank (1988) *World Development Report 1988* (Washington D C: World Bank)

World Bank (1989) *World Development Report 1989* (Washington D C: World Bank)

World Bank (1990) *World Development Report* (Washington DC World Bank)

World Bank (1991) *Managing Development: The Governance Dimension* (Washington DC: World Bank)

World Bank (1992) *Summary, World Debt Tables 1991-1992* (Washington DC: World Bank)

Yang, A (ed) (1985) *Crime and Criminality in British India* (Tucson: University of Arizona Press)

Zeytinoglu, I U (1986) 'The Impact of the ILO's Freedom of Association Standards on African Labor Laws' *Comparative Labour Law Journal* 8 (1) 48-88

Index

academic freedom 134
Africa 243-244
    and family breakdown 270-300
    low-income countries 181
    sub-Saharan 176, 177, 184
Albania 156
aleatory contracts 184
Argentina 172
    and debt 180, 181, 193
Asia, South-East 5-6, 163
Asian-Africa Legal Consultative Committee 167
Austin, John 36-40, 43, 44
authoritarianism 6, 13-14, 16-17, 25, 30, 71, 77-78, 88, 90, 95, 97, 143
Bail
    in India 107
Baker Plan 178, 181
Ball, G 157, 161
Bandhua Mukti Marcha 115-116, 118 *ff*
Baraza 133 *ff*
Barse, Sheela 105, 110-111
basic needs 8, 28
Basle Committee of Bank Supervisors 164
BCCI 164
Bhagwati, Justice 104, 105, 116, 126
Bhopal 161
Bihar State 107-109
BITs 153, 161, 169
Blackstone, W 41, 42
Boer War 101
Brady Plan 179-180, 181
Brandt Commission 5
Brazil 172, 199
    and debt 178, 191, 193
brideprice 272
bridewealth 232-233, 248-249, 252, 255
bureaucracy 3, 64, 90, 91, 92, 94, 96, 97 139
Burma 156
Calvo doctrine 166
capital 38
capitalism 54-56, 68-72, 76, 79-81, 95-97, 282-283, 285, 298
Caribbean 196
CCM (Tanzania) 131, 133, 141, 146
Charter of Economic Rights and Duties of States (CERDS) 152, 165
child care and custody 271, 288-291
Chile 180
China 90, 96
CIDL 197
CIIME 160, 170

civil society 41-42
class 5-6, 18, 70, 81-2, 90, 94, 127, 143-144, 223, 229
    and peasants 82
Claus rebus sic stantibus 194
Cold War 171, 174, 273-276, 280, 285
colonialism 30, 40-41
    and criminal justice 76, 81-85, 87
    and law 253-258
    and women 231-235
Colson, E 246, 247
compensation 167
Conrad, Joseph 76, 77
Constitution, of India 103, 106-107, 116-118
Constitution, of Kenya 61-68, 73
constitutions 51-75, 280
    Africa 51, 60-63
    liberal 53-56, 59-63
    socialist 56-60
constitutionalism 16-17, 72-73
corruption 69, 130, 139
Costa Rica 180
courts 294
    colonial 232-233
    community 258, 262-266
    native 233
    village 259-262
Craxi, Bettino 183
criminal justice 16, 76-101
critical legal scholars 78
Cuba 77, 78, 90-93
custom 50
customary law 15-16, 272-285
    and women 243-267
Dahl, T S 227-229
Daruso 134
DUSO 129
De Beers 155
debt 87, 172-194
    crisis 2, 19-20, 155, 172-194
Debt Crisis Network (DCN) 180
deconstruction 9-10, 22
democracy 18, 24-25, 53-54, 219
    and Tanzania 134 *ff*
dependency theory 5-10, 128
development
    meaning of 7-10, 22-23
    theory 1-10
Dhavan, R 12
Dias, C 28
dispute settlement 78, 273
divorce 233-237, 249-250, 252-253, 254-266, 270-271, 273-275
Dominican Republic 182, 199

Doon Valley 109-110, 115
economic liberalisation 132
EIWU 206, 217
Enlightenment 30, 35
environment 7-9, 24-25, 161
EPZs 6, 195-218
European Convention on Human Rights 167
Export-oriented industrialisation (EOI) 6, 195, 200
export-processing zones (see EPZs)
Faculty of Law (University of Dar es Salaam) 127, 128, 130, 131, 132
family 22, 226-227
   breakdown 270-300
   extended 281-285
FIDA (Malaysia) 201, 204
female infanticide 227
feminism 21-22, 219-241
   liberal 220-222
   Marxist 220-223
   radical 220
   socialist 221
   Western 288
feminist legal theory 224-226
Fitzpatrick, P 284-285, 297
foreign aid 74-75
Foucault, Michel 49
Four Little Dragons 195
Frank A G 3
Frankenberg, G 186*ff*
freedom 78
   of education 134-135
Galanter, M 12
Gandhi, Mahatma 126
GATT 1, 7, 24, 157, 163, 165, 196, 212
   and Social Clause 209 *ff*
General Agreement on Multinational Enterprise (GAME) 157
Germany 153
good governance 52, 72, 189, 219
Goodrich, P 28-29
Great Britain 154
Great Depression 174
Guha, R 229-230
Haeri, S 236-239
Harding, S 220-222, 228
Hingorani, Kapila 107-108
Hobbes, Thomas 32-36
Holleman, J 246, 247
Hong Kong 195, 200, 215
Hull Formula 166
human needs 8, 28
human rights 17-19, 23-24, 52, 72-75, 219
Iceland 194

ILO 169, 196, 202, 203, 208*ff*
IMF 2, 24, 132, 141, 145, 172, 173, 176, 179, 180, 182, 184, 191, 193, 195, 215, 285
Import substitution industrialisation (ISI) 5, 200
India 41, 81-85, 102-126, 161
indigenous peoples 28-29, 34, 47
indirect rule 275
individualism 79
Institute of Development Studies (Tanzania) 130, 146
International Development Strategy for the Second UN Decade 188
international economy 68, 71
International Labour Code 208 *ff*
international regulation (see TNCs)
IPRs 162, 163
   and Paris Convention of 1883 167
Iran 235-239
Islamic Law 83, 84, 235-239, 272, 275-276, 289-290
Jamaica 86-87
Japan 149
judiciary 17-18, 52, 72-73, 79, 278, 294-295
jurisdiction, national 152, 163
justice 78
Kagarlitsky, B 77
Kenya 196, 198, 215, 284
Khatoon, Husainara 107 *ff*, 113
Kindleberger, C 157, 158, 161
Kneiper, R 186*ff*
land 29, 82-83, 90, 96, 231-232, 280, 283
Latin America 196
   and debt 173
law
   colonial 77
   as command 33, 36-38
   in context 271
   decentering of 271, 296-298
   and development 4, 10-25, 27-28, 127-129, 226-231
   form of 143
   as myth 30-36, 45-47, 49-50
   as infamy 27
   and instrumentalism 51, 59, 72
   and order 39, 82
   positive 35, 42-43, 50
   power of 241
   refocussing 271, 296-298
   and savagery 30-45, 49-50
   reform 77-78, 88, 90, 95, 97
   role of 72-73, 224-226
Law Society (Tanzania) 130
legal aid 108, 109, 111, 129, 130, 132

Index

legal education 18-19
legal form 80
legal formalism 78
legal pluralism 15-16, 228, 243-246, 271-281
legal profession 72-73
legal scholarship 11-14, 22-23
legitimation 59-60
Lenin, V I 129
liberal legality 3-4, 11-14, 79
LIBOR 192
Locke, John 40-43
Lome II Convention 167
Macau 199
maintenance 270-300
  enforcement of 279- 289
Malaysia 125, 199*ff*
  laws of 200 *ff*
market 6, 11, 59, 219, 285
marriage 231-239, 270-276
  temporary 236-239
Marx, Karl 15, 76, 78, 99, 210
Marxism 56-59, 64, 67, 128, 174, 220-223, 228-229
matrilineality 247, 252-254
Mauritius 199
Mexico 172 (and debt) 180, 191
modernisation 27, 30, 45-50, 51, 87, 127-128, 226-227 272, 274-275, 281-282
  paradigm 2-5, 10-12
Montesquieu, Baron de 36, 45-46
Moore, S F 271
Most Favoured Nations Status 166
Mozambique 77, 78, 90, 93-95, 280-281
Mrema, Augustine 139
multi-party
  politics 11, 61-63, 133, 141-143
  systems 52
Naffine, N 224-225
Namibia 125
national liberation 288
nationalisation (and National ownership) 151*ff*
nationalism 5, 87
natural law 50
neo-colonialism 61
  and criminal justice 76, 85-89
New International Division of Labour (NIDL) 197
New International Economic Order (NIEO) 5, 8, 24, 214
New World Order 1
newly industrial countries (NICs) 5-6
NGOs 18, 103, 124, 219
Nicaragua 77, 78

Nigeria 125, 276-277, 293
Nyalali Commission (Tanzania) 141
OAS 184
odious debts 186-187
OECD 158, 159, 160, 161, 162, 169, 170, 181
Ombudsman 103
OPEC 174
Pacta Sunt Servanda 186*ff*
Pakistan 153
Papua New Guinea 28, 125
Paris Club 181, 193
Paris Convention (see IPRs)
patriarchy 205-206, 222, 223, 286-288
patrilineality 248-252
patrimonialism 63-68, 73-75
Paul, J 28
Peru 192
Philippines 125
PIL procedure 113-116
Poland 90-91
police 81, 83
popular justice 16, 78, 92, 93-95, 97-100
post-colonialism 76, 278-281, 287-288
  and law 258-266
postmodernism 4, 9-10, 226-227
power 77, 295-298
privatisation 155, 168
property 35, 38, 41-42, 47, 79, 233
  redistribution 271
prostitution 234-235, 238-239, 241
public interest litigation (PIL) (see social action litigation)
public-private dichotomy 226, 239-240
Rechtsstaat 78-79, 81, 88
rectification
  and criminal justice 92
reformism 94
relationship, family 270-300
relocation
  and TNCs 197
reproduction 227-231, 243-269
revolution 90, 94, 99, 100, 130
Bill of Rights (Tanzania) 131
rights 40, 53, 56
  children 107, 110, 111
  environmental 102, 109-110, 122
  fundamental 106, 117-118
  group 102-126
  struggle 127, 134*ff*, 145
  third generation 102-126
Rostow, W 3
Royal Dutch Shell 156
rule of law 3, 5, 10, 42-44, 50, 53-56, 73-74, 76-101, 189, 219

Rwezaura, B 285-287
SAPs (see structural adjustment)
Seidman, R 11
self-determination
  right to 130
self-reliance 295-298
semi-autonomous social fields 271
Senegal 282-283
separation of powers 3, 5, 53, 57, 59
sexuality 236-239
Shona 245, 248-252, 254-257, 259-261
Singapore 195, 199
Smart, C 224-225
Smith, Adam 43, 47-48
Snyder, F 282-283
social action litigation 17-18, 102-126
Social Clause (see GATT)
social justice 56
social welfare 273, 277, 285, 291-293
socialism 16, 87, 88, 91-93, 95
solidarity rights (see rights, third generation)
South Africa 196, 215
South Korea 195, 199
sovereignty (and debt) 186-8
sovereignty 33, 36, 43-44, 151 *ff*
Soviet Union (see USSR)
Sri Lanka 199
Stalin, Josef 89, 90
Stalinism (market) 77
state 6, 11-13, 17, 23, 67-72, 228-229
state socialism 76, 77, 78, 89-97
state, one-party
state, post-colonial 61-63
structural adjustment 6-7, 14, 17, 25, 52-53, 77, 89, 94-95, 141, 145, 172, 182, 189, 190, 191, 219, 285
student struggle 127-148
Sungusungu 88
Supreme Court, of India 102
Switzerland 153
Taiwan 195, 199
Tanzania 88-89, 127-148, 155, 156, 168, 277-278, 283, 293-294
taxation
  and TNCs 162
taxation 292-293
Taylorization 198
Tellis, Olga 114, 115
Thatcherism 189
Tianamen 132 *ff*
TNCs 55, 68, 197-198, 104-205, 149-71, 207
  and international regulation 156*ff*
  and market forces 157

Tonga 245, 247, 252-254, 261-262
Toronto terms, for debt 182, 193
trade unions 199, 201
traditional law 228
traditionalism 271, 281-292
Trinidad terms 182, 193
Trubek, D 12
Ujamaa 89
UK 154
UN General Assembly
UN General Assembly Resolution 1803 152
UNCTAD 158, 183
UNCTC 158, 180
UNICEF 169
Union Carbide 161
United Nations (UN) 4
Universal Declaration of Human Rights 214
University of Dar es Salaam 2127-148
urbanisation 233-235
US Bankruptcy Code 183
USSR 2, 89-90, 171
  and Bolshevik Party 89
  and NKVD 90
Uttar Pradesh State 109-110, 122
Venezuela 180
Vienna Convention on the Law of Treaties
Weber, Max 16, 56, 63-68
West Germany 153, 194
WHO 159
WILDAF 268
Williamson Group 155
WLSA 268, 273, 285
women
  and criminal justice) 100
  and customary law 243-267
  and dependency 271, 285-288, 295-296
  and development 20-22, 219-241
  and law courses 243
  and law in development 226-231, 243-244
  and rights 219-220
  as mothers 271, 283, 286-291
  childless 244-267
  workers 20
  in Malaysia 204*ff*
World Bank 2, 24, 169, 173, 176, 179, 180, 182, 184, 189, 190, 191, 195, 285
Zaire 154
Zambia 154, 231-235, 283
Zanzibar 130-131, 147
Zimbabwe 243-269, 278-280, 283-284, 294-295